THE WRITINGS OF ANNA FREUD
Volume III

INFANTS WITHOUT FAMILIES
REPORTS ON THE
HAMPSTEAD NURSERIES
1939–1945

THE WRITINGS OF ANNA FREUD
VOLUME III

INFANTS WITHOUT FAMILIES
REPORTS ON THE HAMPSTEAD NURSERIES
1939-1945

Written in collaboration with
Dorothy Burlingham

INTERNATIONAL UNIVERSITIES PRESS, INC.
NEW YORK

Copyright © 1973, by International Universities Press, Inc.

All rights reserved. No part of this book may be reproduced by any means, nor transmitted, nor translated into a machine language, without the written permission of the publisher.

Library of Congress Cataloging in Publication Data

Freud, Anna, date
   Infants without families.

   (The writings of Anna Freud, v. 3)
   Bibliography: p.
   1. Hampstead Nurseries. 2. Child study.
3. World War, 1939-1945—Children.   I. Title.
BF721.F692, vol. 3 [HQ784.W3]   618.9'28'9008s
ISBN 0-8236-6872-X   [362.7'3'0942142]
                                               72-8788

First Printing, 1973

Manufactured in the United States of America

Contents

Foreword   xvii

Acknowledgments   xxiii

Publishing History   xxvii

Part I
Monthly Reports (February, 1941–December, 1945)

1. MONTHLY REPORT (FEBRUARY, 1941)   3
   - Our Setting   3
   - Reasons for Admission   5
   - Conditions of Life   7
   - Relation to Parents   9
   - Future Decisions   10

2. MONTHLY REPORT (MARCH, 1941)   11
   - Health Report   14
   - Food Report   16
   - Nursery Problems   18
   - Staff Meetings   22

3. MONTHLY REPORT (APRIL, 1941)   24
   - Statistics   29
   - Discussion of the Newly Admitted Children   29
   - Health Report   33
   - Food Report   35
   - Nursery Problems   35

CONTENTS

4. MONTHLY REPORT (MAY, 1941) — 42
   - Statistics — 47
   - Food Report — 48
   - Problems — 49

5. MONTHLY REPORT (JUNE, 1941) — 54
   - Statistics — 55
   - Health Report — 56
   - Problems: Parents and Children — 58

6. MONTHLY REPORT (JULY, 1941) — 67
   - Statistics — 67
   - Remarks on Organization — 68
   - Remarks on Admission — 68
   - Problems of a Wartime Nursery — 71
   - 5 Netherhall Gardens, N.W.3 — 74

7. MONTHLY REPORT (AUGUST, 1941) — 79
   - The Country House — 79
   - Statistics — 81
   - Problems of Separation — 81

8. MONTHLY REPORT (SEPTEMBER, 1941) — 87
   - Statistics — 87
   - Food Report — 88
   - Kitchen Department — 89
   - Disturbances — 89
   - Remarks about the Country House — 90
   - Problems — 94

9. MONTHLY REPORT (OCTOBER, 1941) — 103
   - Statistics — 103
   - External Disturbances — 103
   - Food Report — 107
   - Problems — 108

10. MONTHLY REPORT (NOVEMBER, 1941) — 117
    - Statistics — 117
    - Troubles — 119

CONTENTS vii

New Ventures 122
Problems 125
The Need of the Small Child to Be Mothered 125

11. MONTHLY REPORT (DECEMBER, 1941) 132
   Statistics 132
   Health Report 132
   Christmas 136
   Problems 136

12. ANNUAL REPORT (JANUARY, 1942):
    SUMMARY OF FIRST YEAR'S WORK 142
    Statistics 142
       AGE OF RESIDENT CHILDREN ON ADMISSION 142
       FAMILY SITUATION OF RESIDENT CHILDREN 143
       WAR EXPERIENCES 144
       DISCHARGED CHILDREN 147
    Survey of the Food Situation 148
       GRADUAL DEVELOPMENT OF FOOD RESTRICTIONS 148
       PREFERENTIAL TREATMENT FOR CHILDREN UNDER 5 149
       CONSEQUENCES FOR THE NURSERY DIET 149
       FOODS WHICH HAVE DISAPPEARED 150
       SPECIMEN MENUS 150
       AMERICAN PARCELS 151
    Medical Report 152
       SLEEP 152
       WEIGHT 153
       RESPIRATORY DISEASES 154
       INFECTION 154
       SPREAD OF INFECTION 155
       VERMIN 155
       MEDICAL TREATMENT 156
    Survey of Psychological Reactions 156
       THE CHILD'S UNDERSTANDING OF THE SITUATION 157
       REACTION TO DESTRUCTION 160
       FIVE TYPES OF AIR RAID ANXIETY 163
       REACTION TO EVACUATION 172
       NORMAL AND ABNORMAL METHODS OF OUTLET 193
    Practical Conclusions 208
       ARTIFICIAL WAR ORPHANS 211

CONTENTS

13. MONTHLY REPORT (FEBRUARY, 1942)   212
- Statistics   212
- Health Report   212
- Soap Rationing   213
- Country House   213
- Financial Report   215

14. MONTHLY REPORT (MARCH, 1942)   217
- Statistics   217
- Applications, Visitors, Etc.   217
- Health Report   218
- Finances   218
- Children's Problems   219

15. MONTHLY REPORT (APRIL, 1942)   223
- Statistics   223
- Finances   224
- Health Report   225
- Problems   225

16. MONTHLY REPORT (MAY, 1942)   237
- Statistics   237
- Holiday Scheme   239
- Finances   240
- Health Report   240
- Problems   240

17. MONTHLY REPORT (JUNE, 1942)   247
- Statistics   247
- Finances   248
- Health Report   248
- Problems   250

18. MONTHLY REPORT (JULY, 1942)   258
- Statistics   258
- Food Production   258
- Medical Report   260
- Problems   264

CONTENTS

19. MONTHLY REPORT (AUGUST, 1942) — 270
- Statistics — 270
- Air Raid Warnings — 270
- Country House — 271
- Food Report — 271
- Clothes Report — 272
- Medical Report — 273
- Problems — 273

20. MONTHLY REPORT (SEPTEMBER, 1942) — 276
- Statistics — 276
- Air Raid Warnings — 276
- Food Report — 277
- Medical Report — 277
- Problems — 277

21. MONTHLY REPORT (OCTOBER, 1942) — 284
- Statistics — 284
- War Events — 284
- Medical Report — 285
- Workshop — 285
- Problems — 286

22. MONTHLY REPORT (NOVEMBER, 1942) — 295
- Statistics — 295
- War Happenings — 295
- Finances — 295
- Food Report — 296
- Medical Report — 296
- Problems — 296

23. MONTHLY REPORT (DECEMBER, 1942) — 306
- Statistics — 306
- Problems — 306

24. MONTHLY REPORT (JANUARY, 1943) — 310
- Statistics — 310
- Medical Report — 310
- Problems — 311

CONTENTS

25. MONTHLY REPORT (FEBRUARY, 1943)   324
    Statistics   324
    Medical Report   324
    Problems   325

26. MONTHLY REPORT (MARCH, 1943)   326
    Statistics   326
    Air Raids   326
    Medical Report   327
    Remarks on Training   328

27. MONTHLY REPORT (APRIL, 1943)   329
    Statistics   329
    Air Raids   329
    Medical Report   330
    Problems   330

28. MONTHLY REPORT (MAY, 1943)   336
    Statistics   336
    Air Raids   336
    Medical Report   337

29. MONTHLY REPORT (JUNE, 1943)   338
    Statistics   338
    Finances   338
    Air Raids   339
    Medical Report   339

30. MONTHLY REPORT (JULY, 1943)   340
    Statistics   340
    Air Raids   340
    Medical Report   340
    Workshop   341

31. MONTHLY REPORT (AUGUST, 1943)   342
    Statistics   342
    Medical Report   342
    Transport   342

32. MONTHLY REPORT (SEPTEMBER, 1943)   344
    Statistics   344
    Medical Report   344
    Harvest   344

33. MONTHLY REPORT (OCTOBER, 1943)   346
    Statistics   346
    Medical Report   346
    Air Raids   346
    Shoe Repair Shop   347

34. MONTHLY REPORT (NOVEMBER, 1943)   348
    Statistics   348
    Medical Report   349
    Air Raids   349
    Problems   349

35. MONTHLY REPORT (DECEMBER, 1943)   351
    Statistics   351
    Medical Report   351
    Air Raids   352
    Problems   352

36. MONTHLY REPORT (JANUARY, 1944)   367
    Statistics   367
    Medical Report   367
    Air Raids   367
    Problems   368

37. MONTHLY REPORT (FEBRUARY, 1944)   374
    Statistics   374
    Medical Report   374
    Air Raids   374
    Problems of Admission   375

38. MONTHLY REPORT (MARCH, 1944)   384
    Statistics   384
    Medical Report   384

Air Raids	385
Problems	385

39. MONTHLY REPORT (APRIL, 1944) — 392
- Statistics — 392
- Medical Report — 392
- Air Raids — 393
- Parents' Problems — 393

40. MONTHLY REPORT (MAY, 1944) — 396
- Statistics — 396
- Medical Report — 396
- Air Raids — 397
- Problems: Regression as a Disturbing Factor in Child Development — 397

41. MONTHLY REPORT (JUNE, 1944) — 406
- Statistics — 406
- Medical Report — 406
- Air Raids — 406
- Problems — 407

42. MONTHLY REPORT (JULY, 1944) — 418
- Statistics — 418
- Medical Report — 418
- Air Raids — 418
- External Problems — 419
- Children's Problems — 423

43. MONTHLY REPORT (AUGUST, 1944) — 436
- Statistics — 436
- Medical Report — 436
- Air Raid Problems — 437
- Children's Problems — 437

44. MONTHLY REPORT (SEPTEMBER, 1944) — 452
- Statistics — 452
- Medical Report — 452
- Air Raid Statistics — 452
- Children's Problems — 454

45. MONTHLY REPORT (OCTOBER, 1944) — 457
   Statistics — 457
   Medical Report — 457
   Air Raid Problems — 458
   Children's Problems — 458

46. MONTHLY REPORT (NOVEMBER, 1944) — 461
   Statistics — 461
   Medical Report — 461
   Air Raids — 461

47. MONTHLY REPORT (DECEMBER, 1944) — 463
   Statistics — 463
   Medical Report — 463
   Air Raids — 463

48. MONTHLY REPORT (JANUARY, 1945) — 465
   Statistics — 465
   Medical Report — 466
   Air Raids — 466

49. MONTHLY REPORT (FEBRUARY, 1945) — 469
   Statistics — 469
   Air Raids — 469
   Medical Report — 472
   Children's Problems — 472

50. MONTHLY REPORT (MARCH, 1945) — 481
   Statistics — 481
   Medical Report — 481
   Air Raids — 481
   Children's Problems — 482

51. MONTHLY REPORT (APRIL, 1945) — 495
   Statistics — 495
   Air Raids — 495
   Sickroom Report — 496

52. MONTHLY REPORT (MAY, 1945) — 504
   Statistics — 504

Medical Report	504
VE Day	504
Problems of Resettling the Children	505
Correspondence	509
53. MONTHLY REPORT (JUNE, 1945)	511
Statistics	511
Medical Report	512
Social Work	512
Children's Problems	512
54. MONTHLY REPORT (JULY, 1945)	519
Statistics	519
Medical Report	519
Social Work	519
Children's Problems	520
55. MONTHLY REPORT (AUGUST, 1945)	527
Statistics	527
Medical Report	528
Correspondence	528
Children's Problems	528
56. FINAL REPORT (SEPTEMBER TO DECEMBER, 1945)	530
Resident Children	532
Resident Mothers	535
Training Activities in the Nurseries	537
War Happenings	539

Part II
Infants Without Families:
The Case For and Against Residential Nurseries

1. SOME COMPARISONS BETWEEN THE EARLY DEVELOPMENT OF INSTITUTIONAL AND FAMILY CHILDREN	543
Birth to Five Months	544
Five to Twelve Months	545

CONTENTS xv

    One to Two Years of Age   547
        MUSCULAR CONTROL   547
        SPEECH DEVELOPMENT   549
        TOILET TRAINING   553
        FEEDING   554
        SUMMARY   558

2. EARLY RELATIONS BETWEEN RESIDENTIAL INFANTS   559
    Other Children Treated Like Toys or Lifeless Objects: Indifference Toward Their Feelings   562
    Other Children Treated Merely As a Disturbance: Aggressive Acts Against Them   564
    Other Children Treated As a Menace: Methods of Defense Adopted Against Them   570
    Other Children Consoled, Comforted, Soothed   572
    Infants Helping Each Other   574
    Direct Educational Influence of Infants on Each Other   576
        RESTRICTION OF AGGRESSION, GREED, DIRTY HABITS   576
    Friendship Between Infants   581
    Instances of Love Play, Tenderness, Affection   583

3. INTRODUCTION OF THE MOTHER RELATIONSHIP INTO NURSERY LIFE   586
    Formation of Artificial Families   586
    Specific Nature and Consequences of the Mother Relationship   590
    Further Consequences of the Substitute Mother Relationship in the Nursery   595
    Spontaneous Attachment to an Adult   596

4. SOME ASPECTS OF INSTINCTUAL SATISFACTION AND FRUSTRATION IN FAMILY AND NURSERY LIFE   599
    Bodily Intimacy Between Infant and Mother   600
    Autoerotic Habits in a Residential Institution   605
        THUMB SUCKING   606
        ROCKING   607
        HEAD KNOCKING   608
        MASTURBATION   611
        SUMMARY   611

xvi CONTENTS

  The Small Child's Wish to Be Appreciated and Admired: Infantile Exhibitionism   612
   INDISCRIMINATE EXHIBITION   615
   EXHIBITION WITH ARTICLES OF CLOTHING   616
   EXHIBITIONISM WITHIN THE SUBSTITUTE-MOTHER RELATIONSHIP   617
   SHOWING OFF TO PLAYMATES   619
   TRANSITION FROM INFANTILE EXHIBITIONISM TO SHYNESS   620
  Infantile Curiosity   621
   CHILDISH CURIOSITY UNDER INSTITUTIONAL CONDITIONS   624
    Curiosity Directed Toward Toys and Learning   624
    The Child's Pleasure in Adventure and Discovery   625
    Curiosity Directed Toward Sex and Family Matters   626
  Summary   633

5. THE ROLE OF THE FATHER IN THE RESIDENTIAL NURSERY   635
  Relationship to Dead Fathers   641
  Relationship to an Absent Father   643
  History of a Fantasy Father   645

6. THE GROWTH OF THE CHILD'S PERSONALITY UNDER NURSERY CONDITIONS   650
  Imitation in the Nursery   650
   IMITATION OF ADULTS   650
   IMITATION OF CONTRASTING BEHAVIOR PATTERNS   653
   OTHER MODELS FOR IMITATION IN THE NURSERY   654
   SUMMARY   655
  Family Behavior Patterns in the Nursery   655
  Development Through Identification: Character Formation   658

7. CONCLUSIONS   663

Bibliography   665

Index   667

List of Some Individual Children   681

Foreword

Since World War II, when these reports were written and the conclusions drawn from them, they have been followed by a long line of studies of young children who have to pass through their infancy deprived of family care. Some of these publications contain material which is more impressive in its tragic impact than the observations recorded by us; or which has had a much wider impact on the public mind; or which surpasses us by far in scientific accuracy. Nevertheless, we can claim the merit to have been first on the scene, and thereby to have initiated the series.

Owing to the date and circumstances of their appearance, our publications have occasionally been designated as war books, i.e., publications the topical interest of which is tied to a particular period of history and is apt to fall into oblivion with the passing of the relevant events. As the authors, we feel this classification to be misapplied. It is true that the opportunity to carry out the study was afforded us by a war charity, the Foster Parents' Plan for War Children, Inc., New York, and that the observed conditions were accompaniments of the war of 1939-1945. But the part played in them by the war itself was no more than that of a precipitating and aggravating agent. Infants are orphaned or torn away from their families for a variety of reasons such as death, illness, accident, divorce, financial disaster, i.e., through circumstances which occur at all times and in all strata of society. Wars merely favor and multiply the dissolution of family units and thereby bring into greater prominence the harmful effect of such breakdowns on the individual child.

So far as physical medicine is concerned, valuable lessons applicable to peacetime conditions are attributed to all wars and comprise many areas such as surgery, antiseptics, and nutrition. The experiences described by us merely extended these advances of knowledge to the mental side by stressing that an infant's deprivation of parental care can be as disastrous to his personality development as the lack of proteins, fats or vitamins has been proved disastrous for the growth of his body.

As regards development under institutional versus family conditions, most of the conclusions reached by us have retained their worth over the years, even in the face of the mass of additional data that have been collected in the last three decades. We still maintain that of the personality achievements of the infant's first two years it is muscular control and independent motility which are predominantly maturational advances and therefore comparatively independent of external circumstances, while speech, food intake, and bladder and bowel control are more dependent on an intimate mother-child relationship and on the constant interaction of maturational forces with external stimulation.

As regards the social relationships of infants and young children to each other, much has been learned in the interval, especially from the unrivaled opportunity to observe the development of young concentration camp victims after their liberation. These children, who grew up oblivious of the existence of parents and without permanent ties to adult figures, demonstrated in pure culture what our separated war children had displayed to us in approximation, namely, the deviations in personality formation that arise if family ties are replaced by ties to a group of peers, and the greater or lesser extent to which these latter can be utilized for satisfying an infant's need for emotional closeness to other human beings.

As regards parental and especially maternal influence on the growth of the child's personality, this topic has assumed overriding importance in the developmental literature of the last 30 years, and new data have been added to it from many aspects. Here, the impact of this vital factor has been studied by way of the personality distortions which arise in its absence; that is, the war displacement of our children has been viewed as if it were an experimental situation provided by fate for our investigation. That this method of examining a specific environmental or innate agent via its elimination from the situation is a fruitful one is borne out by the many subsequent studies of deprived or handicapped infants in which the same procedure has been adopted.

But, apart from detail, when we consider the case for or against residential upbringing as a whole, our verdict today is less favorable even than that pronounced 30 years ago. Our advances in knowledge of child development, whether gained in the field of education, of child care, or of child analysis, all point toward three needs of the growing child which override all others: the need for intimate interchange of affection with a maternal figure; the need for ample and constant external stimulation of innate potentialities; and the need for unbroken continuity of care. Experience shows that even the most strenuous efforts of the organizers of residential institutions inevitably fail in providing even for any one of these needs in full measure, let alone for all three of them.

We hope that readers will not find it too presumptuous on our part if in this volume we try to engage their interest not only in the conclusions drawn from our work, but also in the day-to-day happenings as they occurred in the Hampstead War Nurseries and were laid down in the Monthly Reports. The latter were the only condition imposed on us by the Foster Parents' Plan for War Children in New York, a demand justified from their side by the need to collect financial contributions from well-wishers. Although this additional task of writing on top of much practical work was often experienced as burdensome, it proved beneficial in the long run since it served a more systematic collection and preservation of data. In any case, the long sleepless nights imposed on all Londoners by the incidence of air raids provided sufficient time for thinking, formulating, and conceptualizing.

The authors are glad to note that during the last 30 years many of the findings presented here as new have become familiar tenets on which a much more critical view of residential upbringing and its consequences for personality development are based. It is to be regretted that not the same can be said for those institutions which serve young children's daytime needs. It is true that for the ages between 2 to 5 nursery school education has proved its inestimable value as an addition to the opportunities for stimulation and growth which are only too often lacking in individual families. But nursery school education never claims more than a comparatively small portion of the child's day and does not include the basic care of his body. There is no justification to extend what we recognize as the benefits of the nursery school for the older child to the care of infants, especially not for those between birth and year 2. What is needed at that time is not impersonal and professional hygiene, care, and supervision, but personal and intimate interchange with *one* or at most two familiar figures in contact with whom a step can be taken that will be decisive for the individual's whole emotional life in later years: the transition from the demand for physical gratification to firm emotional attachment to its providers.

Acknowledgments

In October, 1940, some English friends presented us with a sum of money to be used toward relieving the need of London children who were made homeless by air raids, and who were either still unevacuated or unevacuable. Together with the loan of a very suitable house and a great deal of equipment offered by a Swedish Committee, this proved sufficient to build a fairly safe half-basement shelter and to open our first Children's Rest Center at 13 Wedderburn Road, Hampstead.

The sum given was slowly spent during the next 3 or 4 months and was enlarged once more by a similar gift in March, 1941. By that time four regular contributors had appeared who were willing to carry the monthly expenses for one child each. Gifts and some money arrived from America, sent with difficulty through the few permitted channels, e.g., the British War Relief Society, which also added a donation of its own. But none of these gifts, welcome as they were, would have assured the continued existence of the Children's Center for any length of time. It became necessary to envisage the need for restricting the number of children and even of closing down altogether after helping the children over the worst period of emergency in London.

At this moment the American Foster Parents' Plan for War Children, through its representative, Eric G. Muggeridge, came to the rescue. They had already contributed subsidies for a small number of children in December and January. In February, 1941 they multiplied their contribution by five; they also undertook to collect in America whatever money might still be waiting there to be sent over. In March, they took over complete responsibility for the financial situation. They gave us the opportunity to improve and stabilize the situation in Wedderburn Road, to engage further staff, to raise the number of children to 30, and generally to promise the parents cooperation in taking care of their children for the duration of their need. They further suggested that we might open two new houses, a Babies' Rest Center in London for small children who should not be sent to the country without their mothers, and a country house in Essex, for purposes of evacuation. Again they undertook full responsibility for the upkeep of these two new ventures.

From then onward the Foster Parents' Plan supplied almost the total budget of the Hampstead War Nursery; additional small contributions were made voluntarily by the parents of the children (approximately 3% of the total). Our faithful British friend, Mr. W. Gilchrist, never ceased to help the Nursery in material ways.

Thus the Hampstead War Nursery was a colony of the Foster Parents' Plan for War Children, Inc., New York, and as such owed its whole existence to American generosity. Like the other colonies of the Foster Parents' Plan it provided wartime homes for children whose family life had been broken up temporarily or permanently owing to war conditions. Like the other colonies of the Foster Parents' Plan, although residential, it was not run on institutional lines. It tried to re-establish for the children what they have lost: the security of a stable home with its opportunities for individual development. The only characteristic of "institutional" life which it was powerless to avoid was the absence of the family itself.

Publishing History

PART I
MONTHLY REPORTS
February, 1941–December, 1945

Of the 56 Monthly Reports included in this volume, only one has been published previously, namely, Report 12, the first Annual Report, January, 1942:

English

1942   (Dorothy Burlingham and Anna Freud) *Young Children in War-Time: A Year's Work in a Residential War Nursery*. London: George Allen & Unwin Ltd. for The New Era

1943   (Anna Freud and Dorothy Burlingham) *War and Children*. New York: Medical War Books [selections from the above]

1944   New York: International Universities Press [selections from above]

Spanish

1944 *La Guerra y los Niños.* Buenos Aires: Ediciones Iman
1964 Buenos Aires: Editorial Hormé

German

1949 *Kriegskinder: Jahresbericht des Kriegskinderheims Hampstead Nurseries.* London: Imago Publishing Co.
1971 In: *Heimatlose Kinder: Zur Anwendung psychoanalytischen Wissens auf die Kindererziehung.* Frankfurt: Fischer Verlag, pp. 1–61

Japanese

1972 Tokyo: Seishin Shobo

PART II

INFANTS WITHOUT FAMILIES

The Case For and Against Residential Nurseries

English

1944 (Anna Freud and Dorothy Burlingham) *Infants Without Families: The Case For and Against Residential Nurseries.* London: Allen & Unwin

1944 New York: Medical War Books
New York: International Universities Press
1965 London: Allen & Unwin

Spanish

1947 *Niños sin Hogar*. Buenos Aires: Ediciones Iman
1961 *Niños sin Familia*. Barcelona: Editorial Luis Miracle
1964 Barcelona: Paideia Biblioteca Practica de Pedagogi, Psicologia y Psicopatologia de la Infancia

Czech

1948 *Deti bez rodin*. Prague: Obris

Swedish

1948 *Barn utan familj*. Stockholm: Kooperativa Förbundets bokförlag
1973 Stockholm: Raben & Sjögren Bokförlag

French

1949 *Enfants sans Famille*. Paris: Presses Universitaires de France

Dutch

1949 *Kinderen zonder eigen thuis*. Amsterdam: Scheltama & Holkema's Boekhandel

German

1950 *Anstaltskinder: Argumente für und gegen die Anstaltserziehung von Kleinkindern.* London: Imago Publishing Co.

1971 In: *Heimatlose Kinder: Zur Anwendung psychoanalytischen Wissens auf die Kindererziehung.* Frankfurt: Fischer Verlag, pp. 65–161

Portuguese

1957 Rio de Janeiro: Editora Fundo de Cultura

Danish

1965 *Smaborn uden Familie.* Arhus: Forlaget Sirius

Italian

1972 *Bambini senza Famiglia.* Roma: Casa Editrice Astrolabio (Ubaldini Editore)

Japanese

1972 Tokyo: Seishin Shobo

Part I
MONTHLY REPORTS
February, 1941—December, 1945

1

Monthly Report
February, 1941

OUR SETTING

In February, the second month of its existence, our organization was busy mainly in three directions. (1) The house which had been fixed up as a Rest Center for bombed families had to be rearranged to suit the new purpose of being a Children's Rest Center with only an occasional mother added. Equipment had to be increased for the larger number of children. (2) The staff had to be partly changed and also greatly increased in numbers. (3) Out of the numerous applications that came in, 25 children were chosen. The result of our endeavors is the following:

1. We now have a house containing one large nursery equipped as a complete Montessori nursery school; one toddlers' room with plenty of space to run around in; one very large room with straw matting equipped as dressing

room and as a room for afternoon naps; one babies room fitted out with cribs; one doctor's office with a sunray lamp; one hospital room for children who are ill with noninfectious diseases; one parents' clubroom which is used especially on Saturdays and Sundays; one work and staff room for meetings, sewing purposes, unpacking of gifts, etc.; four staff bedrooms. In addition, the basement of the house contains kitchen and dining room and, last but not least, two shelters, one with 18 beds, the other with 6 beds and 3 baby cribs. This shelter belongs to the type of indoor, half-basement shelter which is strengthened with heavy wooden beams, calculated to carry the weight of the whole upper house in case it collapses. Shelters of this kind are no protection against direct hits by a high explosive bomb, but they are supposed to withstand blast and all other emergencies, even if the high explosive bomb should drop only a few yards away. The beds are not the usual type of shelter bed but the ordinary type of bed with spring mattresses used in peacetime, built in tiers of twos or threes. They are so big that one child can be placed at each end without their feet touching in the middle. (The house further contains three bathrooms and four toilets.)

2. Our staff at the moment consists of: a pediatrician, Josephine Stross, M.D., who is in attendance two or three hours every day; a head nursery school teacher, Miss Hedy Schwarz, with two assistants and two trainees; a baby nurse; a cook, Miss Sofie Wutsch; a social worker, Mr. James Robertson; a bookkeeper, Miss Jula Weiss; various help for laundry, cleaning, etc. This seems a large number, but they are all kept busy owing to the helplessness of the infants we are dealing with. Four members of the staff

are British; the rest are refugees from Austria, Germany, Czechoslovakia, and Holland. Four important members of the staff are volunteer workers.[1]

3. At this date we have admitted:
   - 3 babies, 6-7 months
   - 7 toddlers, 13 months-2 years
   - 11 children, 2-5 years
   - 2 sisters, 6 and 9 years, for whom we have procured admission in an excellent Hampstead school
   - 2 children for day attendance only
   - 2 mothers; one is the mother of one of the babies, the other of a boy, 3 years old, who had to join her child for reasons that we shall explain in a subsequent report (see the example of Billie in Monthly Report 2).

REASONS FOR ADMISSION

The children are sent to us by the Hampstead Billetting Authorities, by hospitals from the poorer parts of London, by psychiatric social workers from the East End Rest Centers, by the Women's Voluntary Service, and by all kinds of charitable organizations. Among the children we received are the following:

Children from Bombed Houses, (a) which have been declared uninhabitable by the authorities, so that the whole family is forced to leave until new lodgings are found for them by the local Council; (b) from bombed houses where one or two rooms still remain habitable so that the

---

[1] One of these workers, Mrs. Martha Herzberg, was head of household of all homes throughout the existence of the Hampstead War Nurseries.

parents continue to live there. Children from these houses usually develop bronchial colds or other illnesses owing to draught caused by broken doors and windows and by dampness of the walls due to bursting of the pipes. Of all the children we have admitted there were only two who did not come with bronchitis or some feverish illness.

Tube Sleepers, i.e., children who have been taken by their mothers to the deep Tube shelters at night since the *blitzkrieg* in September. They slept on the platform with the trains running in and out until 1 A.M. Some of them in this way lost their ability to sleep, cried out continually, and had to be hushed and quieted by their mothers with various methods so as not to disturb the adult population around them, a state of affairs not favorable either to mother or to child.

Children Sent Back from Evacuation, (a) because they could not stand the sudden separation from their mothers and developed conditions that their foster parents were unable to deal with; (b) because the mothers were dissatisfied with the billets or wanted the children where they could at least keep an eye on them; (c) infants who had been evacuated with their mothers now come back because their mothers had to return home to look after an ill husband.

Children with Shelter Bronchitis, the effect of sleeping in damp Anderson shelters.

Children Who Leave the Hospital after an infectious disease (measles) whose parents do not dare to take them home to the unhealthy conditions in houses which have suffered from blast.

Children Whose Families Have Been Dissolved, the father joining the armed services, the mother taking a job (for instance, post office or munitions factory).

CONDITIONS OF LIFE

In daytime the life of the children does not differ in any way from that in an institution under peacetime conditions. The children play, paint, draw, sing, dance in the nurseries, go for walks in the street, or play in our garden where they learn to climb on a jungle gym (which was lent to us by a school for the duration). We disregard daylight raids, except for calling the children in from the garden or the street when the sirens give the alarm. Adults in London ignore daylight raids, except when a plane is heard directly overhead. But it is thought best to keep children home during raids as much as possible, to avoid the chance of their being hit by odd pieces of shrapnel.

Every evening, whether there is an air raid or not, the children are settled down in their shelter beds, the communal shelter taking the place of an ordinary bedroom. This is much wiser than putting the children to bed upstairs and taking them to the shelter only when the sirens go on. In this way the routine of their waking and sleeping remains independent of air raids and lulls. They go to bed at their usual time, and there is no need to disturb them when hostilities begin outside.

It is surprising how little interest children show in sirens, bombs, guns, or all clears; and this is true even of those children whom their mothers describe as being very frightened of raids. We get an occasional question from a 5-year-old whether our shelter is really safe; an inquiry from a 4-year-old girl, after admittance, whether there is an air raid shelter in the house. Another 4-year-old suggested to the nursery school teacher, who was trying to quiet a noisy boy in his shelter bed, that if he would not promise to be good, she should "take him upstairs to a danger-room." A little girl of 3½, asked whether she was pleased to see a visiting uncle, said crossly: "No, I want him bombed." Our big girls, 6 and 9 years old, when we take them for a walk and pass by damaged houses, make expert casual remarks: "Incendiary bomb" (this is where the roof is burned out); "high explosive" (where the walls are badly shaken). The same two girls spoke about the time when they still lived with their parents in a badly bombed area: "Every evening when the first bombs came down, Daddy would grab his coat and run out to help and Mummy would always call after him: 'Don't forget that we have two spare beds and bring in people if you find them homeless.' " Children whose parents behave in this way naturally show no sign of fear themselves. The father of the 6-year-old girl said: "You would have to drop a bomb down her back before she would take notice!"

The situation is different with two of our children who were brought in by excessively nervous mothers, women who had developed states of severe anxiety after having been bombed, one at home and one in a shelter. These mothers used to pull their children out of bed and stand around trembling; one child stood near his mother all night, unable to leave her. These women naturally imparted their own fears to their children. But even these children, after the separation from their mothers, quickly lose their state of tension and settle down to ordinary life.

We have installed a voluntary fire service in contact with the local air raid wardens' post (one man every night, among them fathers of the children). The fire watcher sleeps, fully dressed, on a divan in the entrance hall. He is responsible that night for the proper distribution in the house of buckets of sand and water and the stirrup-pump arrangements to fight incendiary bombs. He is allowed to sleep during the all clear and is awakened by an alarm worked by the fire patrols in the street when danger becomes imminent. Gas masks for the bigger children and gas boxes for the babies are ready in the shelters.

RELATION TO PARENTS

We were warned in the beginning that we would find the London parents of the poorer classes to be rather unappreciative, critical, and only too glad to dump their children on us and forget all about them and their further obligations. What we experienced is exactly the opposite. With the exception of three mothers whom one can hardly regard as responsible personalities, one can only admire the efforts which the parents make for their children under the worst possible conditions, their attempts to cooperate with us, and their real delight about every opportunity which is offered to their children. They appreciate every progress in health, weight, and happiness of the child. Although we do not demand payment, several of the parents insist on paying at least 3-5 shillings weekly toward the upkeep of their child, which is an appreciable sum for them. These payments come regularly without our ever reminding them.

Parents of this class are used to obeying hospital rules regarding visiting. They are surprised and delighted when they hear that we are glad to have them come at any time. If their occupation allows, they can come freely to take their children out for walks, bathe them and put them to bed in the evening, share their meals without any undue insistence on our household routine. In practice this only happens during weekends when our home sometimes takes on the character of a coffee house, club or restaurant.

It is true that in this way children take a longer time to get over the separation from their parents, and the repeated "separations" after visiting days are often followed by outbursts of crying and violent emotions. We shall try to explain in later reports why we consider this slower method of overcoming the shock of separation much less harmful to the child than the traumatic one usual in evacuation, when many little children who have never been away from their mothers for a single night are suddenly taken from them, not to see them again for weeks or even months.

FUTURE DECISIONS

At the present time none of our children has been with us for more than 8 weeks; some of them have arrived only during the last fortnight. Our plan is to keep them with us until they have overcome the illnesses, symptoms or difficulties with which they arrived; and then to send them on to safe places in the country and admit others who are in great need of similar help. It proves less easy than we thought to find billets or homes in the country that satisfy our requirements.

2

Monthly Report
March, 1941

INTRODUCTORY REMARKS

Since the date of our last report life in London has been greatly influenced by the fact that bombing was less regular and that there was even a long succession of quiet nights. The very few bad air raids that occurred did no damage in the immediate neighborhood of the Children's Rest Center. Since darkness now comes later, the children are usually asleep before any noise is to be heard.

The exception was one evening raid when noise of terrific antiaircraft fire struck the children at the time of settling down to sleep. There was only one child, Bobbie (4¾), who showed genuine signs of anxiety. Phyllis (4½), who usually adopts a motherly attitude toward him as a playmate, advised him to cover himself right over, as she always did in such cases. All the other children did not seem to pay overmuch attention either to the danger or to Bobbie's state of anxiety. It may be interesting to note in this respect that Bobbie, who is the child most easily worried about war dangers, is one of the few children in the house who has not been through the experience of actually being bombed. Phyllis, on the other hand, is one of the "bombed-out" children. A landmine which fell in the street next to the one on which she lived with her mother and grandmother took off part of the roof of her house and destroyed the attic room from which the family had escaped downstairs just a few seconds before.

Altogether it is our experience that oversensitiveness to danger has nothing to do with the actual experience of bombing which has gone before. Rather, the children's fears are to a large extent dependent on their parents' anxiety. After separation from these parents, fears either vanish or at least decrease. The anxiety of playmates does not seem to be infectious in the same sense.

Although most of the Rest Centers in all parts of London were empty during the month of March, we received a great number of applications for admission. Most of these requests were so urgent in nature that it was very difficult to refuse them. It seems all wrong to let one child live in comparative safety and comfort and to explain to the next mother that her child cannot be given the same advantages. Our task was made especially difficult by a certain amount of publicity that the Nursery was given in the daily press. Mothers who read the article about the safety of our shelter, the good food, the general care, and the freedom of visiting took the chance of bringing their children unannounced in the hope that we would be persuaded that their need was no less urgent than that of the children we had already admitted.

Although the house was full to its capacity we actually let ourselves be persuaded in a few cases. We admitted Dell, a little girl of 2½, who only had the choice of sleeping with her grandmother, ill with active tuberculosis, in an attic room or in an unsanitary basement shelter crowded together with a number of old people from the neighborhood. We also admitted Rodney, in a state of great neglect from various causes (2 years, 8 months); Martin (16 months), from an unsatisfactory babies' home outside London where his mother could not visit him and where the only space allowed to him was his crib so that he was unable to learn crawling or walking; and Paul, almost 4 years, an extremely delicate and nervous boy, a tube sleeper, whom various doctors had tried to evacuate, but who was torn between his fear of air raids and his extreme fear of being separated from his mother. (Paul's mother also had to be admitted.) Lastly, we admitted Hilda who had been with us for several weeks as a day child in preparation for her mother's confinement.

To make room for those five children only one child left us: a little girl of 3, who had entered the Center two months ago to wait for her expected evacuation. Her mother now was lucky enough to secure a billet for herself and the child in the same village to which her older schoolchildren had already been sent a long time ago. The child left us quite happy and contented, pleased with the new American clothes which we were able to give her as a parting gift.

A closer examination of the applications received shows that the children physically most endangered by the present state of affairs are those up to 2 years of age. It is easy to understand that infants simpy cannot live in a state of emergency. The same conditions which to the fully developed individual mean only a passing state of discomfort of body or mind are capable of completely arresting or seriously damaging the development of the immature human being. The younger and more undeveloped the individual is, the more serious are the consequences. We have, after all, always known that healthy development requires its own conditions, irrespective of war and peace or all other happenings in the outer world.

A great deal has recently been written on the bad effects of overindulgence and pampering of young children. The war in Europe is certainly an excellent opportunity to study the opposite, i.e., the effects of traumatic shock and excessive privations in childhood life. These and similar considerations started a strong desire in us to open a second house for even younger children and with wider possibilities for admittance. With the very generous help and understanding of the American Foster Parents' Organization it seems as if this wish fantasy will very soon be turned into reality.

HEALTH REPORT

Our last report stressed the fact that most of our children were admitted with some kind of feverish illness, mostly shelter bronchitis. We also had to get accustomed to another fact, namely, that those who arrived apparently healthy had in reality a latent illness which usually made its appearance during the first week of their stay with us. In most cases these initial illnesses did not take very long to clear up. On the basis of our three-months' experience we can say that the bigger children do not need more than four weeks to regain a normal standard of health; children under one year will take one or two months at least to attain the same. It is true, of course, that of the 29 children admitted there was only one who had been declared to be in a state of undernourishment that was bad enough to threaten his life. It is interesting to speculate, though, how long the time needed for recuperation would have been if help had come to these children six or twelve months later. Whoever has had the opportunity to observe the damage suffered by European children during the First World War knows that the generation born between 1914 and 1918 showed outstanding signs of having undergone physical hardships which never were fully eradicated.

The current bill of health during the month of March was surprisingly good. The hospital room of the Center was empty for nearly two weeks. A wave of influenza which had gone through London reached the Center only in its mildest form. Communal sleeping in the two shelters did not increase the danger of infection as much as we had feared. Regular treatment with the sunray lamp has evidently done a lot to increase resistance against illnesses.

Most children have gained weight very satisfactorily, and this is specially satisfying to the parents and does a great deal toward increasing their good relationship with the Center. It is surely no coincidence that one of these mothers suddenly presented the Nursery with a big bunch of flowers.

Medical treatment in the Nursery has no horrors for the children. It usually takes a week or two until they know our doctor well. Some of the bigger ones behave more affectionately toward her than usual when they feel ill or disturbed in some way. They show their good relationship to her by trying to be first in the daily medical inspection, by assisting the doctor in various ways, calling the other children to take their turn to open their mouths or even thinking up all sorts of imaginary little symptoms which they then bring to the doctor half in fun but with special pride. There is another group of children who feel friendly to the doctor when they feel well, but who completely withdraw their affection when they fall ill. A third and most interesting form of behavior can be observed in those children who get attached to the doctor only after an illness, even though, or perhaps because, medical treatment has been rather painful. Attachments of this kind usually last for quite a while.

FOOD REPORT

The children's gain in weight is due largely to the careful planning and excellent cooking of the kitchen department. Although by now most private households are feeling the restriction of food supply, the children in the Center get more and better food than they have ever had. The kitchen department tries its best not to spend too much money, to plan every meal according to food value, and nevertheless to keep an eye on whatever is still obtainable of rationed and unrationed food. The work of catering is, of course, infinitely more difficult than under peacetime conditions. We manage to supply three meals a day for at least 40 people. On Sundays when parents come visiting, the number easily rises to 60.

Rationed Food

Meat: very short; the meat ration is used up on weekends so that parents and children get a proper Sunday dinner.

Bacon: rather plentiful, changed partly into gammon to fill up meat ration, partly used as a separate dish with Yorkshire pudding.

Sugar: very short; the weekly ration for the whole house is used for the children and for cooking purposes only. All the adults get only saccharine with their drinks. The local food office has done its utmost to help, but the kitchen must still be very careful with this article.

Tea: plenty, ration not used up.

Margarine: rather short; we use unrationed nut oil for cooking purposes.

Butter: fairly sufficient, together with the margarine ration, for baking purposes and for spreading on sandwiches.

Unrationed Food

Milk: The Center is now registered under the Government Free Milk Scheme, which means for every child under 5 years one pint of free milk daily. With the milk price thus reduced we use a great deal of milk for cooking (milk puddings, custards, blancmanges) and drinking. We take the best sort of pasteurized milk so that the children can drink it unboiled.

Chocolate: rather short at the moment, though we still have some for eating and drinking. Gifts of chocolate are always received with great joy.

Fresh fruit and vegetables: As all the local tradesmen are very much interested in the work of the Center we get a fairly good supply whenever needed. We try to keep their interest alive by showing them through the house and maintaining personal contact in every way. They like to hear how much the children have gained every week and are somehow proud that they feel happy in our house. The storekeepers have developed a feeling that it is very much more important to supply our place, i.e., the children, than any other customer. When onions, lemons, oranges, and bananas were scarce but still available, we could rely on our greengrocer saving for us whatever he could get. These articles have now entirely disappeared from the market, so our babies get tinned tomato juice instead of orange juice. The older children are given plenty of apples, partly stewed with custard, in apple pies or raw. Apples are the only fresh fruit available at the moment. Besides we use plenty of raw carrots, lettuce, and beetroot for vegetable salads.

Sweets: apart from those prepared in the kitchen, the children get cakes, buns, biscuits, chocolate biscuits, and Swiss rolls.

Bread: we use white bread, but also try to encourage the use of brown bread and find that the children like it very much.

NURSERY PROBLEMS

Although, as we stressed in our last report, life in our nursery does not differ from the daily routine of peacetime institutions, the outstanding problems that the children present are certainly those caused by wartime conditions.

We hope in time to be able to contribute toward the current discussion of evacuation problems of children. At the moment the best we can do in this respect is to collect examples which demonstrate the psychic effects of sudden separations of young children from their mothers.

Example 1, Billie

Billie, a boy of 3 years and 2 months, of pleasing appearance, well built and rather big for his age, was sent to us after one unsuccessful attempt at evacuation to the country. In the billet where he had been placed, he had, as the report stated, "fretted" so much for his mother that he was sent back to her after a very few days. Unluckily, their reunion was of short duration. He contracted measles and had to suffer another enforced separation from his mother. After dismissal from the hospital she brought him directly to us since she had been warned not to take him after illness to the Tube station where she herself was sleeping regularly with her husband. She admonished him to be "a good boy," and promised to visit him if he would promise not to cry for her.

The state of affairs that developed after she left was a most unhappy one. Billie tried to keep his promise and was not seen crying. Instead, he would nod his head whenever anyone looked at him, and assured himself and anybody who cared to listen with the greatest show of confidence that his mother would come for him, she would put on his overcoat and would take him home with her again. Whenever a listener seemed to believe him, he was satisfied; whenever anybody contradicted him, his self-control left him and he would burst into violent tears.

This same state of affairs continued through the next two or three days with several additions. The nodding took on a more compulsive and automatic character and to the sentence "My mother will put on my overcoat and take me home again" was added an ever-growing list of clothes that his mother was supposed to put on him. "She will put on my overcoat and my leggings, she will zip up the zipper, she will put on my pixie hat." When the repetitions of this formula became montonous and endless, somebody asked him whether he could not stop saying it all over again.

Again Billie tried to be the good boy his mother wanted him to be. He stopped repeating the formula aloud, but his moving lips showed that he was saying it over and over to himself. At the same time he substituted for the spoken words gestures that showed the position of his pixie hat, the putting on of an imaginary coat, the zipping of the zipper, etc. What showed as an expressive movement one day was reduced to a more abortive flicker of his fingers the next day. While the other children were mostly busy with their toys, playing games, making music, etc., Billie, totally uninterested, would stand somewhere in a corner, moving his hands and lips with an absolutely tragic expression on his face. These movements did not stop even when he was dressing or eating, going up or downstairs. He refused most kinds of food, but he faithfully drank milk.

We were shocked to see an apparently healthy child develop a compulsive tic under our very eyes. All attempts to get in contact with him were unsatisfactory. Not that it was impossible to break in on his compulsive behavior with understanding words, affection, and sympathy. But in such moments, instead of reiterating his false assurances, he would break through to the truth, burst into tears, and develop an excess of grief that one felt at a loss how to meet.

From the second day on we had made attempts to reach his mother and induce her to visit him regularly. Unluckily again, she had fallen ill with a bad influenza and was lying in a hospital. A Sunday afternoon visit from his father did not bring the slightest comfort. It took more than a week before his mother was dismissed from the hospital. Then she came immediately to us. We discussed the situation with her and persuaded her to stay in our house for a while.

Billie's state changed immediately. He dropped his symptom and instead clung to his mother with the utmost tenacity. For several days and nights he hardly left her side. Whenever she went upstairs or downstairs, Billie was trailing after her. Whenever she disappeared for a minute, we could hear his anxious questioning through the house or see him open the door of every room and look searchingly into every corner. No one was allowed to touch him; his mother bathed him, put him to sleep, and had her shelter bed next to his.

A few days were sufficient to do away with this abnormal state of affairs. Slowly Billie lost his excessive clinging and turned at times to the other children to join in their play. His mother was first allowed to go home for an hour to cook a meal for his father. Billie waited anxiously for her reappearance and signs of his former anxiety appeared in his expression. But after a further week or two these symptoms too disappeared. Billie's mother was allowed to come and go freely and Billie became a member of the nursery like any other child. At the present time he is one of the most active children in the playroom, his former rather girlish appearance has changed to definitely boyish behavior, he jumps and climbs, he is very good at building and keeps himself busy from morning till night. He is a very good eater, satisfied only after repeated helpings.

After some consideration we offered the mother, who is a specially nice woman and had previously been employed as charwoman in a day nursery, the post of emergency night nurse in our two shelters. That means that she still spends five nights weekly in the same house with Billie, the other two at home or in the Tube station with her husband. But it does not seem to affect Billie now whether she sleeps in or out.

The interesting point about this story is that it does not seem to be the fact of separation from the mother to which the child reacts in this abnormal manner; rather, he seems to react primarily to the traumatic way in which this separation took place. Billie can dissociate himself from his mother when he is given three or four weeks to accomplish this task. If he has to do it all in one day, it is a shock to which he responds with the production of symptoms. This means that even children with neurotic potentialities such as Billie's could be spared much unnecessary suffering and symptom formation by more careful handling.

We shall try to show in our next report what conclusions can be drawn from Billie's case for the handling of others.

STAFF MEETINGS

Practical problems of daily organization and the wish of the Center staff to exchange experiences and observations have prompted us to start the habit of a short, nearly daily, staff meeting in the middle of the day. Among the subjects discussed were the following:

> Parents of our children, their war experiences and attitudes,
> Observations of war games among the children,
> Observation of war conversations among the children; and since we cannot help being interested in the psychological problems of all times:
> Thumb sucking and toilet training,
> Toddlers' games and toys,
> Toddlers' aggression and the ways to deal with it,
> Discussions about individual children and their difficulties.

3

Monthly Report
April, 1941

INTRODUCTORY REMARKS

A Big Air Attack

An outstanding event during this month was the big air attack on London in the night of Wednesday, April 16th. Even for people who had gone through the period of the so-called blitz in September and October, the events of this night were rather surprising and alarming. There was more gunfire than ever before, the sound of falling bombs was continuous, the crackling of fires which had been started could be heard in the distance, and again all these sounds were drowned by the incessant droning of airplanes which flew over London, not in successive waves as in former raids, but in one uninterrupted stream from 9 o'clock in the evening until 5 in the morning.

The neighborhood of the Children's Center was lucky enough to escape all damage since the raid was concentrated on various other parts of London. Not even incendiaries were dropped on our district, and the nearest landmine fell at the safe distance of half a mile from Wedderburn Road.

The elder members of the staff were, of course, awake and patrolled the house; the younger members went down from their attic bedrooms and joined the children in the shelter. The children themselves, to our astonishment, slept peacefully as usual and never noticed what was going on above them. Whether it was due to the fact that the heavy wooden beams of the shelter ceiling lessen all noise or whether the quiet atmosphere in which they had fallen asleep carried them through the restlessness of the night outside, the facts are that no one took notice except Billie, who sat up suddenly and said, "Gunfire." His mother, who was on shelter duty, answered: "Yes, but gunfire does not hurt anybody," whereupon Billie lay down and slept again.

Janet woke as usual and asked to be put on the pot, but remained completely oblivious of the bombing. The two babies, Jeffrey and Ralph, woke once and cried for a while, but since that happens nearly every night, it is difficult to determine whether it had any connection with the outside noises.

Everybody slept in the shelter after the all clear at 5 A.M. The morning, of course, was different from usual. Whoever came in from outside brought tales of damage and destruction. Our old odd-job man, who lives in a more exposed district, can on such occasions hardly be stopped from counting corpses and reveling in lurid details to which the children like to listen eagerly.

The most exciting moment was when Mrs. R., baby

Ray's mother, rushed in, disheveled but still more painted up than usual, full of things that had happened to her and her friends during the night. The roof had been taken off the top of their house, several people had been killed or injured, and they had sat huddled together in a small shelter for the rest of the raid. Her excitement was also heightened by the fact that the factory where she was working had been damaged to some extent and had been closed down for the day.

In the state of shock in which she found herself, her first instinct was to snatch her baby and take him off to the country somewhere. We did not discourage her, of course, only told her that we had good hopes to have ourselves a place in the country soon and promised that certainly Ray would be one of the first to go there. After she had told everybody about her experiences, her excitement soon spent itself. She resolutely declined the offer to spend the next night in our shelter near her child, said she did not dream of leaving her husband and friends, and, after a few hours, returned to her bombed district to take up work again. Three days later, when she appeared for her usual Sunday visit, she was her normal self again, laughed and joked at tea with the other mothers, sang music hall tunes while she helped washing up dishes, and boasted loudly how many shells she could turn out in an hour in her factory.

After Mrs. R.'s visit on Thursday morning, eight of the other parents called up to inquire about the safety of their children. Otherwise the usual routine was followed. Two new children duly arrived according to arrangements made before the raid. The grownups in the house, like all Londoners, naturally showed some signs of stress and strain after their worries of the night.

In the garden in the later morning the children had occasion to watch an airplane in the sky. Some adult said: "Look, it is writing!" a statement which Janet corrected by saying: "Only scribbling." None of the children seemed to connect the sight of an airplane with the idea of possible danger.

Still, the children seemed rather more restless and excitable than usual as a result of the tales which they had overheard. They were observed playing a new kind of game. Some of them climbed up on the jungle gym and, regardless of danger to those standing underneath, tried to drop on them a heavy iron shoe scraper which they had removed from the doorstep and carried up to the heights. When warned not to do this, they proudly asserted that this was a bomb which they were about to drop. Little Bella, who had not been big or strong enough to join in the game, suddenly brought a handful of sand, threw it at the others, and declared it was a "gas bomb." Since the sand got into the children's faces and eyes, this game was not found to be enjoyable.

Nothing further of an unusual kind happened during the rest of the day. The children showed no anxiety when they were put to bed in the evening.

Only three days later, on Saturday night, when again a bigger raid seemed to develop, little Dell suddenly asked whether "the Germans were coming again." But she did not pursue the subject, nor did fear develop.

The events of Wednesday night, followed by several alarms during the next few days, had the general effect of disturbing the false sense of security in which Londoners had accustomed themselves to live during the period of lull in the last few weeks. In the atmosphere of uncertainty and alertness that resulted, we rather expected several of the parents to urge the evacuation of their children or to look for billets in the country for them on their own. Nothing of the kind happened; on the contrary, the mere chance which had spared our colony all damage or inconvenience during that night seemed to have heightened the trust of the parents in the security of our shelter.

Still, the greater difficulties in the outside world during that time induced us to accept rather more new children during the next days than we should have done otherwise. Applications that came flowing in also turned all our thoughts once more to the plans for the new house for infants that we hope to open in 5 Netherhall Gardens, Hampstead, in the beginning of June and, even more, to the possibilities of a country center to which we can send children continually and which offers us the chance to receive all our children in case our London base should ever be destroyed or badly damaged.

A New House

On April 29th, we were at last able to finish negotiations for the new house in Netherhall Gardens, that is, to sign a tenancy lease which had been delayed through legal formalities and to receive the keys which give access to the upper house. The shelter in the basement has in the meantime been as good as completed.

Staff Accommodations

Accommodation for the staff in 13 Wedderburn Road has become inadequate for our purposes. The generosity of the Foster Parents' Plan has made it possible to rent a furnished apartment in 25 Belsize Park Gardens, Hampstead, and open it as a hostel for our staff.

STATISTICS

Date	Arrival	Dismissal	Total
April 1			31 children
3	3		34
17	2		36
21	1	1	36
23	1		37
25	1		38
27		1	37
28		1	36

The average number of visiting parents on Sundays is 16. This number is greatly enlarged by the fact that most parents bring visitors of their own, brothers, sisters, uncles, aunts, grandmothers, friends, sometimes even lodgers or sisters-in-law to whom they show off the house. Although they are invited for the midday meal, they are too afraid of inconveniencing us or upsetting our rationing system to act on the invitation. They usually accept only high tea. The largest number of high teas served out on a Sunday (for children, staff, and guests) was 71.

DISCUSSION OF THE NEWLY ADMITTED CHILDREN

During the month of April, 3 permanent and 5 temporary children were admitted.

Permanent Children

1. Paul, of unknown age, probably between 18 months and 2 years, the son of a refugee from the continent, now interned in Holloway Prison, where she has given birth to a second illegitimate child. Paul has spent his life so far in institutions, children's homes, and hospitals, and was brought to us under the auspices of the Refugee Committee (Bloomsbury House). He is a delicate and intelligent-looking boy with a ready smile and a rather impartial greeting for everybody.

2. Albert, 20 months, the cousin of two of our children, came straight from a hospital, where he had recovered from double pneumonia. The hospital dismissed him earlier than they would have done otherwise because half their premises were bombed. We accepted him, though we had not expected the addition and found it rather difficult to make room for him.

3. Bertie, aged 4 years, 4 months, had been referred to us actually before the opening of our house. He is an especially tragic case. His father was killed by a bomb while working during an air raid. Soon thereafter the child was taken to the hospital with scarlet fever. The mother's psychic health broke down under the double shock of separation first from her husband, then from her child. She developed an acute psychotic state and is at the moment waiting for recovery in a mental hospital. In the meantime Bertie spent five months in his hospital with one contagious illness after the other. He was at last free from infection on April 23rd and came to us, where we hope to keep him. He is a thin, delicate, good-looking

boy, friendly, a little excitable. Since his hospital too was bombed, he was dismissed suddenly and came straight out of bed to our sickroom. He seemed restless and overtalkative while confined there, but adapted quickly when allowed to join the other children in the nursery. We do not yet know whether he has been informed of his father's death and his mother's illness.

Transitory Children

Since most of the charitable institutions dealing with children in distress have moved out of London, we are asked at times to give shelter to a homeless child for a few days or weeks for various purposes connected with or independent of the war.

1. Daniel D., 18 months, was bombed out with his mother for the second time; his father had deserted them, not for the first time. Mrs. D. insisted that she needed shelter for the child only for three days until she had moved into a new apartment. So Daniel came for three days and remained for three weeks. Then his mother, giving way to pressure, took him home resignedly.

2. Carol, 17 months, a charming girl of serious appearance, is the seventh child of a mother who is going to the hospital to be delivered of her eighth baby. A charitable organization gave shelter to her mother to await confinement and would have liked to take the baby, but, as they wrote us, "Our house is most unsuitable for it and can just house some destitute grownups." Carol's father is on a stretcher party and therefore out of the house most of the time. Carol is meant to stay with us for three weeks until her mother can take her home again.

3. Jeffrey, 5 months, was placed with a foster mother while his father was in the army and his mother working on munitions. He developed fits of unknown origin, was taken to the hospital, and sent to us for an observation period. He is doing well with us, has had no fits so far, and is so well liked that we shall probably try to keep him permanently.

4. Mabel, aged 6 months, is the child of a former manager of an ironmonger's shop who is now in the air force. The mother was taken ill soon after the father had joined up and went to the hospital for observation. While there she contracted pneumonia, the hospital was bombed on the night of April 16th, and she was evacuated with other patients to the country. Some girlfriends who had promised to take care of the baby for a day or two found themselves unable to do so for a longer period because they themselves were working. The child was turned over to the Women's Voluntary Service who brought her to us. Mabel is a lovely baby, evidently well cared for, with a beautiful baby carriage and other possessions of her own which were delivered to us. She is doing well with us and by now her father has been notified of her whereabouts. We have been told by the hospital that the mother is on the way to recovery. She will collect the child when she returns home.

5. William, 1 year, 10 months, suddenly found himself without anybody to take care of him because his mother had a serious miscarriage with hemorrhages. She cannot be moved and is being looked after by the district nurse. His father is an ambulance driver with alternate 24 hours on and off duty, who therefore cannot properly look after the house or child. He brought the child to us and visits him

every morning. William will return home in about a month's time.

Although our Center is not meant for such emergency cases except where the emergency has been caused by bombing, it is very satisfying to be able to extend the hospitality of the house beyond the number of the children who are the real guests of our community. On the other hand, we are of course aware of the difficulties any temporary placement may mean to a child.

HEALTH REPORT

The sickroom was never empty during the month of April; for some days as many as 6 or 7 children had to be put to bed. Illnesses fortunately were slight, mostly bronchial colds accompanied by a rise in temperature.

An exception from this was Isabel, who had originally been sent to us partly because her family had been bombed out, partly because of a nervous cough which she had started soon after her father died as the result of lung trouble. While she lived with us, her nervous symptom came and went. Lately she has been free from it for some time. During April she fell ill with tonsillitis. While she was in bed with a temperature, her nervous cough returned and developed into a regular attack of bronchial asthma with all the usual somatic accompaniments. Her tonsillitis, together with her asthma, disappeared within a few days. She was well for a while and then again returned to the sickroom with a slight cold aggravated by her usual nervous cough.

So far we understand little about the origin and development of Isabel's symptom; there is the suspicion, of course, that her cough had started in imitation of her father's cough. The mother herself reports that a neighbor suddenly said to her: "Don't you notice that Isabel coughs exactly the way her father did." A tendency to hysterical identification is very evident in Isabel's case. She picks up habits from the other children, adopts them as her own, drops them again after a while, and picks up new ones. In the beginning, when she had formed a friendship with Bertha, a little girl of her own age, she suddenly started the same temper tantrums that had made Bertha conspicuous in the house. Although Isabel is no thumb sucker herself, she suddenly started sucking her thumb in a way that is peculiar to Calvin, a boy more than a year her junior. Her latest habit is a sort of grimacing, the origin of which we are at the moment attempting to find among the other members of the house. It is interesting to note that during every illness her always noticeable affection for the doctor is greatly increased. This was especially marked during the periods of asthma, when the presence of the doctor helped to lessen her anxiety during attacks.

Carol (17 months) was the only other child whose bronchitis developed into a slight touch of pneumonia. She was apathetic and listless in her bed for days, showed no interest in anybody, did not play with toys, and disliked the doctor to whom she had shown great friendliness during the first few days after her arrival. It is difficult to determine in this case how far the psychic behavior of the child is the result of the illness and how far her resistance to infection was lowered by the very definite state of mourning in which she found herself after the sudden separation from her mother.

We are still puzzled by the fact that many of the children develop a slight illness shortly after their admittance to the house. This is especially true of those between 12 and 30 months.

FOOD REPORT

On the whole the rationing system has worked out all right for us, although we are rather hard hit where the freshly rationed foodstuffs (cheese, jam) are concerned. We used to consume about 7-10 lbs. of jam weekly. From now on our monthly supply will be 10½ lbs. Tinned fish and tinned fruit are still obtainable, although these supplies are getting shorter every week. This is especially sad since fresh fish is much more expensive than it used to be, and fresh fruit and vegetables are practically unobtainable. We still get some apples, though every time our order comes in the grocer says: "Sorry, Madam, you cannot have as much as that, but I will do my best for the kiddies." Thus we expect to hear in the near future, "Sorry, Madam, but there are no apples at all."

NURSERY PROBLEMS

While daily all over England more and more children are separated from their mothers and evacuated for the sake of safety, we are still concerned with the various possible effects of such separations. Billie, the boy described in Report 2, is still doing excellently. In his present life, where he is at times with his mother, and on other days and nights without her, he is completely undisturbed. He has made a remarkable development toward manliness. He has shed all remaining soft girlish ways, which were apparent when we first saw him; he likes only boyish pursuits, is respected in the nursery as the leader of games, and is extremely active in the garden. It remains to be seen whether he is also able to stand a more complete separation from his mother. An opportunity to make that experiment may occur when we ourselves open a country house for our children.

We had another opportunity of observing the worst effects of sudden separation in Dell, a little girl of 2½ years, whose admittance was mentioned in Report 2. In accepting Dell we gave in to the urging of her mother, who was frightened that the child would be infected either with tuberculosis by the grandmother with whom she shared the room or with some kind of shelter disease in the very primitive place where they all spent the nights. The mother seemed rather desperate and worn out with anxiety. She begged us to let Dell benefit from the favorable conditions in our house, at least for the few weeks which she would need to find a billet in the country for herself and the child. Dell was a beautiful little girl, marvelously developed, sparkling with life and gaiety, and seemed extremely independent for her age. It was this very independence of the child, together with her evident interest in the toys, the other children, and the new surroundings which induced us to fall in with the mother's wishes. Dell was taken to the nursery where she was deep in play after a few minutes. She said good-bye to her mother in a friendly way, but hardly noticed when her mother left her. Only half an hour after her mother had left the house, Dell suddenly realized what had happened. She interrupted her play, rushed out of the nursery, and opened every single door in the house to look for her mother in the room behind it. In her running around she behaved exactly like a stray dog who has lost his master. This lasted a few minutes and then she rejoined the play group.

These attacks of frantic search repeated themselves with ever greater frequency. Dell's expression changed, her brightness disappeared, her smiles gave way to an unusually sullen frown which changed the whole aspect of the child. It is difficult to say, of course, whether this sullenness of Dell's was completely new or whether this was the way in which she had previously reacted to difficulties in her life.

The hope that Dell, with her outgoing manner, would soon attach herself exclusively to some adult person in the house was not fulfilled. Her interest seemed to turn first to one of the workers in the nursery itself, but before a real attachment was formed she suddenly developed a great liking for our nurse and clung to her with unexpected affection. But this attachment too had no time to ripen. Dell suddenly showed a decided preference for men, turned to all male visitors, claimed other children's daddies loudly as her own, and would on evenings or Sunday afternoons sit for hours on a visitor's or fire watcher's lap, much to the men's embarrassment. Her attitude was little influenced by visits from her mother, who came at times and took her out for walks. Her preference for men would indicate that her affection had turned from her mother to her father; but when during her stay with us her father suddenly appeared on army leave, she did not appear to treat him differently from other visitors.

Something had evidently gone completely wrong in her relations with the adult world. Her outstanding symptom was the continual abandoning of people she was attached to at the moment for the sake of others who were new to her. Whereas in Billie's case separation from the mother had brought on a compulsive clinging to her memory, in Dell's case the result was outwardly the opposite. She lost the stable relationship to her parents which had so far governed her life, was unable to form lasting attachments, and lived continually in search and expectation accompanied by feelings of deep discontent. We know this symptom of flight from one object to the other in adult neurotics as one of the results of early disturbances in their mother relationship.

Although Dell's symptoms quieted down and were less apparent after a few weeks, especially after a prolonged stay in the sickroom where she was surrounded by a quiet homelike atsmosphere, she never regained the high spirits and bright appearance which had been her main characteristics when she came.

Dell's mother found a billet in the country and took her off according to arrangement after she had been with us for eight weeks. In her case, the physical advantages of being saved from shelter life were outweighed by the shock the separation from her mother meant for her. She was given no time for psychic preparation: on the one hand, separation was too complete; on the other hand, her stay under the new conditions was too short to make up for all the misery of adaptation.

The next two examples are meant to show two children who found themselves in essentially identical situations but who reacted completely differently.

Hilda (2 years, 1 month) and Carol (17 months) were both brought to us while their mothers went to the hospital to be delivered of another baby. In Hilda's case, this was done with foresight and intelligent planning by the mother. She brought her as a day child more than two months before the expected birth of the new baby. She helped the child through a period of adaptation to daily life shared with other children, which was by no means easy. Hilda was shy, at times aggressive, withdrawn, and often unresponsive. She slowly accustomed herself to the nursery. A week before the expected confinement she entered the house as a boarder, slept in the shelter with the other children whom she already knew well, and was rewarded in daytime by frequent visits from her mother. When her mother at last disappeared into the maternity hospital, Hilda was used to her new surroundings, felt at home, and showed no ill effects of any kind.

Carol, on the other hand, was brought two or three days prior to her mother's confinement and left at once and completely, though she had never before left her mother's side and had evidently been taken care of very well by her mother. She found herself unexpectedly in completely strange surroundings to which she reacted in a most bewildered way. For days she sat or stood around quietly or crying and at intervals would only say "Mum, Mum" in a surprisingly deep voice. Similar to Dell but again in a completely different manner, she would sometimes stretch out her arms to visitors. She was at times content when she could sit on somebody's lap with her face averted. Probably, she imagined herself in this position to be sitting on her mother's lap without being disturbed by the sight of a strange face. As described in the health report, she fell ill about a week after her arrival and during her illness reacted with apathy and listlessness.

In the last week, when she was gradually getting better in the sickroom, she was at last reported to have smiled and even joined in play with other children.

Again, these descriptions show that it is not the task of separation from the mother itself which is impossible to accomplish for the small child. The decisive factor for the normal or abnormal outcome seems to be the manner in which the separation is handled, the time given to preparation and gradual adaptation which after all means the presence or absence of traumatic shock.

We tried to utilize the experiences gained from Billie's case when we admitted Paul, a very delicate and nervous boy aged 3 years and 8 months. His young mother had previously been evacuated with him, but had returned from the country after some unhappy experiences. She now refused to leave her husband, a full-time war worker. She slept with Paul in Baker Street Tube Station, where two shelter doctors had objected to the presence of the child owing to his delicate appearance. We invited Paul's mother to stay in the house with him and wait until he felt less strange in his new surroundings.

Paul was frightened of the other children, turned away from everybody, and for three days at least sat in the nursery on his mother's lap with one arm thrown around her neck. At night she had to stand near his shelter bed for an hour or two until he fell asleep. At resttime in the afternoon she would be found, to everybody's horror, arched with her whole body over his when he was lying on his mattress as if she were protecting him against the world. It was not easy to convince the staff that even though this behavior of the mother was certainly excessive and not favorable for the child, still, a week's patience with it would bring greater benefit than sudden separation,

The following week saw Paul slowly enter the nursery life. He played with the others, would at times forget about his mother, looked less anxious and more interested. He suddenly discovered a tricycle and claimed it as his own. From that moment onward Paul was seldom seen on his two feet. Whether it was in the garden or in the playroom, Paul would suddenly dash by on wheels at high speed and with remarkable skill and cleverness. He evidently had decided to be more independent and pursue some pleasures of his own.

His mother also tired of the situation, looked for work outside, and found it in a machine sewing factory. She now comes to sleep at night whenever her husband is on duty, but stays with him whenever he comes home. Differently from Billie, Paul is reported to be more nervous in his mother's presence and to fall asleep quite easily and quickly when she is not around.

In this case of a nervously unstable mother and child, it was certainly only the ample time given for adaptation which prevented serious outbreaks of neurotic symptoms and behavior.

4

Monthly Report
May, 1941

INTRODUCTORY REMARKS

During May, life in the Center did not run as smoothly as it had in the preceding months. As the detailed reports will show, difficulties of all sorts began to crop up everywhere.

At the beginning of the month we still fought against the plague of head lice which somebody, either a child or a Sunday visitor, had brought into the house. We hated to see the children go around with lice caps on their heads, but with repeated treatments and constant combing we were lucky enough to wipe out the last remnants of this invasion without having to resort to drastic measures like cutting the children's hair. After final victory had been achieved in this respect, the menace of threadworms appeared on the horizon. This danger past, a well-founded suspicion of scabies arose in connection with one mother and her child. This in turn was followed by a wave of impetigo.

The beautiful country house on which we had centered all our hopes for the evacuation and a summer holiday for our children threatened to disappear from sight.

In addition to all this, we had to suffer the presence of an unexploded bomb on the other side of our garden fence for more than a fortnight.

It would be mere repetition to describe the situation in the Center during the night of the last big air attack on London of Saturday, May 10. We are by now used to the contrast between the undisturbed sleep of the children in the shelter and the noise and destruction going on outside. There was again very little sleep for the staff that night. The fire watcher stayed up on the roof most of the time and his unceasing watchfulness gave everybody a certain sense of security.

There were many people who felt that the events of this night were even worse than those of April 16th. Curiously enough, there was not the same state of excitement and restlessness on the day after. When our old gardener again appeared with the story of a big bomb which had fallen next to us, nobody believed him. Whether it was the feeling that we again had had a lucky escape, or whether it was that this time no one among our parents had suffered personally, the facts are that the Sunday following the raid developed into the most peaceful day we had experienced in the Center. It was the first sunny springlike Sunday, parents came and went from morning till evening, fetched their children for a walk on the Heath, sat down to meals, or strolled around our garden watching their children at play.

In this atmosphere of peace it slowly transpired that our old gardener had after all been right in his report: a big bomb had actually fallen near us and lay unexploded in the garden below ours. It had buried itself in the soft ground and spattered the streets around with clods of black earth. We went to visit the bomb, looked at it over the fence, and found it rather imposing but perfectly at rest in its good-sized crater.

Next morning we noticed that the neighboring house and the street leading to it were roped off. When we questioned the police, we were told the following: there was a possibility that the bomb might still explode; in that case it would bring down the next house; ours was considered to be just outside the danger zone, but on no account should we let the children go into the garden. We were grateful to escape the great discomfort of being evacuated on the spot because it would have been none too easy to find good accommodation for 34 children at short notice.

We kept the children in the house for one whole day; after that, through the great friendliness of the Women's Voluntary Service, we were offered the loan of a garden just across the street. A procession of our children was continually on the way either to or from that other garden, the older children making a weak attempt to walk in orderly fashion, the toddlers escaping in all directions, and the babies being wheeled over in their baby carriages. Although it caused a great number of inconveniences for the staff, the loan of that garden was a real blessing to us during that time.

While a discussion of bombs and our relations to them has become a stale topic here in England, our American friends may still be interested in the way in which such a situation develops. A bomb at a great distance may be an object of horror; a bomb which settles down so near to one's own household, on the other hand, is somehow included in it and soon becomes a familiar object. It is true that on the first day an unexploded bomb is contemplated with respect and suspicion. When it delays exploding, the reaction in the people around is not, as one should expect, one of thankfulness and relief. The reaction is rather one of annoyance with it, which develops into contempt for the bomb as the days go by. The bomb is treated more like an impostor who has forced us into an attitude of submission under false pretenses. In the end, when no one believes in its explosiveness anymore, it sinks down to the position of being a bore.

Since the children knew of course about this situation, we watched them closely for signs of anxiety. But in spite of the fact that most of them had been driven out of their own homes by bomb explosions, they did not seem to connect the idea of the bomb with the idea of possible danger. Even Marion (over 9 years old) was heard to say in an angry tone: "I wish the bomb would explode so that we can use the garden again." The nursery children were most impressed by the fact that our garden was closed to them. They were resigned during the first week, but on the tenth day a group of them, after mealtime downstairs, suddenly made a dash for the garden entrance. When caught and brought back, Janet (4 years 2 months) insisted: "There is no bomb." When this was turned down, they all screamed in chorus: "There is no bomb! We are going out in the garden." Janet then came in again and said firmly: "It has exploded."

This attitude of denying what is unpleasant and disturbing in reality is natural enough to children. It is more surprising that our adult staff too was not inclined to act otherwise. Our social worker, James Robertson, decided that this was the appropriate time to give the garden a really good overhaul. Whatever grass had survived on the children's playground was cut, a new sandpit dug, and the jungle gym repainted. Whenever anyone tried to send a member of the staff out of the garden, he was met with the indignant remark that, after all, "the bomb would not go off just at this moment." Although all our windows would certainly have been smashed if the explosion had occurred, no one in the house was ever seen to keep away from windows.

Our bomb became impressive once more when after much hard labor a bomb disposal detachment of soldiers had dug it out of its crater and loaded it on a truck to remove it. Its presence in the street, which by now had been reopened, excited much comment among the passers-by. We saw mothers lift up small babies to admire it and everybody watched while the soldiers tied red silk ribbons to the rear of the car as a sign of danger in case of collision. They explained that they had defused it, sat all around it, and drove off joking and singing.

When the good news that the bomb was gone spread through the house, we again watched for reactions of relief. All we could find was an immediate desire on the part of the children to regain possession of the garden. Bobbie (4 years, 10 months) asked with great interest whether the soldiers had driven the bomb off "in a lorry." To him the ever-fascinating question of transport was more outstanding than the danger element implied. The complete reversal of all values was most distinctly shown in the way our social worker met the good news. He said: "I wish they had left it two days longer so that the jungle gym would have had time to dry."

When the soldiers returned to fill up the empty crater, they were invited to have tea in our dining room where the children met them. It was on this occasion that some of the children showed definite signs of fear or anxiousness. "Fear of the bomb" was outside the range of their infantile emotions. "Fear of the big men" is a recognized and typical childhood fear. That the bomb meant real danger to them and the "big men" protection against it did not play a part in the situation. Some of the children were perfectly natural, played with the soldiers, made friends with them, and tried on their caps. Billie put on an overboisterous and joking manner, which he does only when he is afraid of something. Phyllis and Isabel, on the other hand, covered their eyes with their hands and could not be induced to look at the soldiers.

This ended the incident of the bomb, which might easily have been an unlucky one for our house. But even in the event of explosion we feel confident that the shelter itself would have withstood the blast. The bomb was found to weigh 1,000 lbs. Its distance from our doorstep was approximately 30 yards.

STATISTICS

During May only 3 children could be admitted. Sally and Julia Black (2 years and 3 years, 4 months), who are supposed to stay with us during their mother's confinement; further, a baby girl, aged 6 months, who was in bad physical condition and had conjunctivitis from shelter sleeping. She is expected to stay with us for the duration of the war.

The 2 children who had been admitted as emergency cases during severe illnesses of their mothers were fetched home. Hilda, who had already left once, returned to our sickroom because of sudden illness.

A list of visits paid by parents, relatives, and friends of the children shows that we had at least 126 single visits during May. Apart from that, a constant stream of interested visitors goes through the house, among them members of the Women's Voluntary Service, almoners from hospitals, psychiatric social workers, welfare inspectors from various districts, teachers and matrons from infants' schools, members of the Society of Friends, etc.

We receive constant applications to join our staff, mostly from refugee workers trained in child welfare.

FOOD REPORT

In keeping with the other troubles which pursued us, the food situation also was less satisfactory than it had been the months before. Several most necessary items have now definitely disappeared: there is very little sugar, no Quaker Oats, and scarcely any corn flakes; above all, fresh fruit has been off the menu for the last two weeks and will probably not return until the end of June. There is rhubarb which unfortunately requires a lot of sugar for cooking; there are a few oranges, but they are kept strictly for the babies' department. Tinned fruit has disappeared from the market.

To make up for the lack of fruit we give raw vegetables in the form of salads of all descriptions (cucumber, occasional tomatoes, lettuce, cabbage, and carrots). Young carrots are eaten after dinner once or twice a week instead of apples.

After June 2nd the situation will get worse since we have to expect a general cut in the sugar, jam and meat rations. With honey unobtainable and chocolate rather difficult to get, it will be none too easy to think up enticing menus.

PROBLEMS

When we questioned the parents about a possible evacuation of their children to a country place, we found that the same mothers who three months earlier had absolutely refused to separate from their children would now be perfectly ready to let them go. Much has been said in the newspapers, by various authorities, and in the reception areas about the unreliability of mothers who will send their children to the country one day and drag them back to the bombed areas a week later. We so far have not had a single experience of this kind. No child whom we were ready to keep has ever been taken back to more dangerous surroundings. The few children who left did so according to plan either for evacuation or because the emergency state at home which had been the cause of their admittance had been removed. One mother who wanted to take her little girl home to the East End for the Whitsun holidays was easily persuaded to drop that plan and spend her two free days in our house instead. If we succeed in finding a country house, we now feel perfectly certain that none of the mothers who make up their mind to send their children will go back on their decision afterward.

As far as occupation goes, the mothers have now all

settled down to work either in munitions or in machine sewing or in offices. They have also settled down emotionally. Those who have husbands in the services in London (A.R.P., Fire Service, Ambulance Driving) are glad to stay and look after them. Their weekly visits to the children mean a great deal to them, but it is possible to foresee that, when the distance is greater, they will also settle down to the idea of rare visits and that it will not be too difficult for them to retain their emotional relationship with their children so long as they are informed in detail about the children's new surroundings, behavior and development. Their position will be more or less like that of mothers who after careful consideration of all the factors involved have voluntarily sent their children to boarding school. This means that if evacuation is carried out in slow stages and in full cooperation with the parents, the psychological problem of the war mother does not seem insoluble.

The psychic problem of the infant who has been evacuated is less easy to solve. For a child under 3 years of age, it is extremely difficult to maintain a normal emotional relationship with an absent love object. We say in ordinary language that the small child forgets quickly. It really means that the material and emotional needs of the child cannot be satisfied at a distance. The love of the infant for his mother is closely bound up with the fulfillment of these needs. If the mother is absent, the child forms, after a short period of longing, a new relationship to a substitute mother. The relation to the real mother has become unsatisfactory and is driven from consciousness. We can only surmise from later behavior what changes it has undergone inside and what has become of it. Normally this period of "mourning" lasts only a very few days. After that, if the mother does not show herself again, the child settles down "quite happily."

When the psychic makeup of the child is more advanced or more complicated, adaptation takes a longer time. Some children will cling to the memory of their mother in a compulsive manner. We have given an example of this type of behavior in the case of Billie. Others will build up a constant fantasy of family life, put it in the place of the lost reality, and work it off in play. An example of this kind is Beryl, a girl of 3, who will continually play with a baby doll, take care of her regardless of what happens around her, invite everybody to admire her baby or, at other times, be the baby herself in play.

In Report 3 we gave the example of Dell, whose whole relationship to the adult world was spoiled: consciously she was continually on the lookout for substitute parents; in reality she was only searching for the parents of her lost past. We further gave the example of Carol, a girl of 17 months, who had an excessive period of mourning unrelieved by visits, since her mother was in the maternity hospital and therefore unable to see her. When after barely four weeks the mother at last came to fetch her, Carol remained unmoved and gave no sign of recognition. Every outward evidence seemed to show that she had forgotten all about her mother. But the parents report that after her return home when she felt once more united with them, she showed the most exact remembrance of every single object and had complete familiarity with her surroundings.

This seems to prove that "forgetting her mother" is not an intellectual process at all but an emotional one.

Through lack of satisfaction, disappointment and longing, her affection, which had until then been closely tied to her mother, was shaken, changed, and cut off from expression. When the real object returns, her relationship to the person has in the meantime undergone a complete reversal. That looks outwardly as if she does not "recognize" the formerly loved person anymore.

The most serious objection to the wartime evacuation of young children without their mothers is therefore that it produces artificial orphans. It is common knowledge that after the death of father or mother small children behave as if their parents had just gone away. We can certainly say that when the parents have only "gone away," the children behave as if they had died. This only means to say that the important factor for the small child is physical absence or presence of the mother. The question of existence or nonexistence in the real world seems to be beyond the child's emotional comprehension.

But even though in that sense all these little children who are separated from their parents are war orphans, the attitude of the world around disregards the identity of the inner psychic situation of the two kinds of children and clings to the importance of the outer reality. The child whose parents have been killed in an air raid is an object of pity, and all the difficulties that he shows seem somehow natural and are met with tolerance. The child who is merely billeted in the country while his parents continue to live in London is considered only to "fret" and expected to get over it "in no time." Therefore, it is precisely the study of the real war orphan and his reactions which may be of help to create a better understanding of the "evacuated" child.

We have at the moment one child in the house who has lost both parents, one permanently through death, the other temporarily through mental illness as a result of bombing. We shall give his story in greater detail in the next report. We also expect to receive four little orphans who have lost their father in the air raid of April 16th.

5

Monthly Report
June, 1941

INTRODUCTORY REMARKS

There was little or no bombing activity during June. A very few alarms were given at night, just enough to prevent us from altering the sleeping arrangements of the children. Several times we allowed sick children to sleep upstairs since there are always enough helpers ready to carry them down in case an alarm should be sounded. We tried to use this unexpected spell of peace to consolidate and also to enlarge our activities.

The extension in 5 Netherhall Gardens, N.W.3: A great deal of time and energy was spent this month on completing the furnishing and general equipment of this new house, which we intend to open on July 1st. In the meantime we have received applications for 20 to 30 children under 2 years of age, some of them cases of extreme urgency. To ensure the smooth working of this extension, the heads of the various new departments (Babies, Sophie Dann; Toddlers, Gertrude Dann; Sickroom, Sister Mary; and Milk Kitchen, Fini Hyndman) were invited for the last weeks before opening to join in the work and staff meetings at Wedderburn Road and in this way to profit from the experiences which we have gained so far. The kitchen department of Wedderburn Road also took over the catering for the whole new staff of Netherhall Gardens while they were engaged in putting the finishing touches on the house. Many new applications from trained workers for the new house had to be considered.

The Country House which we had lost reappeared on the scene. It transpired that it had been bought as an investment only and that the new owner was willing to rent it to us. We expect this time really to sign the lease during the coming week.

Hostel: The enlargement of staff made it necessary to look for further living quarters. In addition to the furnished flat in 25 Belsize Park Gardens, we rented a small attic flat above it and took over a small flat from a member of the staff; 5 Netherhall Gardens itself has an independent attic staff flat for 5 people.

STATISTICS

There were 31 children resident in Wedderburn Road at the beginning of the month. Three children were admitted out of the great number of those waiting for the opening of the new house, one of them a baby of 10 days, together with the nursing mother. One child left for evacuation with his mother. This brings the numbers up to 33 children and 1 mother.

Two further additions to the house are a very gentle and well-behaved cocker spaniel and a black rabbit which was given as a present to the nursery children.

HEALTH REPORT

The state of health during this month was good. Only three items are of interest from the medical point of view.

1. The number of children who were infected with impetigo last month has been reduced to 6 and even these show only the last remnants of the trouble. They are kept strictly separated from the others in daytime, and at night the smaller of the two shelters is reserved for their use. They are also kept separate in the garden and the continual exposure to sun and air has done a great deal to quicken their recovery.

2. There was considerable trouble about one child, Albert (21 months). As mentioned in Report 3, he was dismissed by the hospital before he had fully recovered from double pneumonia because the hospital had been bombed. He went straight into the sickroom because of bronchitis, which cleared up in the course of a few days. He was in good spirits for a short while. After that free interval, he suddenly felt extremely miserable and developed an otitis with discharge but without temperature. He was again in good spirits after the pain had stopped; then suddenly he came down with high fever, swollen glands back of his ear. With M & B 693 the symptoms disappeared after 24 hours, but 48 hours later a rash appeared which had every appearance of scarlet fever. If the Schick-Carlton test had not proved negative and if the fact that the rash had appeared only after the middle-ear disease and not before

had not invalidated the diagnosis, he would have been sent to a hospital for infectious diseases. As it was, we decided to isolate him in the house and to keep him in this way until he had completely recovered. The step proved correct; no scarlet fever developed and we were glad to have prevented his exposure to the infections of the fever hospital. He is a delicate child who has not yet fully overcome the effects of his double pneumonia. Since he is an only child and little used to the company of others, he did not suffer from his complete isolation but rather enjoyed the sole attention of his nurse.

It may be interesting to note that it was very difficult to make Albert's mother understand the seriousness of the situation. When the child was in danger of a mastoid operation and she was asked to give her written consent so that there would be no delay in case of need, she did so willingly and with no special sign of worry. When she was informed of the probability of his having to go to a fever ward and asked whether she wanted to stay and take him herself, she said it was not necessary and she was sure that we would attend to it all right. She did not show any special sign of relief when told that all the various dangers were past. But when on the night before leaving he slightly bumped his forehead on the bars of his crib and developed a black and blue spot, she was greatly upset and quite indignant about it.

3. In the six months of our existence for the first time the doctor had to be called for at an unusual hour to attend to an accident. Rosette had had a fall in the hall of the house and had cut her forehead. Luckily, the wound was small so that she only had to have one clip. Since Rosette suffers from a form of Little's disease and has ac-

cordingly difficulties in walking, we were afraid that the shock might seriously damage her newly acquired confidence in her bodily powers. But she showed no special disturbance and after a few days of a more subdued mood and restricted activity she was as gay and courageous as before. When her bandage finally came off, she said: "My mother will be glad to see my real head again."

PROBLEMS: PARENTS AND CHILDREN

A. Billie, whose abnormal behavior after separation from home was described in the Report 2, was now exposed to the same situation once more. Since his recovery he had seen his mother almost daily or at least four or five times a week while she worked on night duty in our shelter. She had to stop her duties because of her pregnancy with a new baby and in the eighth month of pregnancy went to the hospital with varicose veins. She was immediately evacuated to the country. Billie, on our insistence, was permitted to see her once before she went, but he was, of course, unable to visit her again during the last three weeks.

To our astonishment he remained normal this time. Slight signs of anxiousness and disturbance disappeared after his one visit to the hospital. Since then he has remained perfectly normal, has not changed his behavior or his activities in the nursery, and has not shown compulsive symptoms of any kind. The only faint traces of his former trouble are an occasional overinsistence in asking whether "Daddy is sure to come and take me out on Sunday," and a certain withdrawal of interest when his mother is mentioned by outsiders. On the other hand, he quite normally questions his father about his mother's whereabouts, is perfectly aware of the whole situation, and even passes on to us reports about his mother's state of health. He can now sensibly manage the same situation that previously made him ill.

This would be easy to understand if in the meantime he had undergone psychological treatment. Since this has not been the case, the factor responsible for the change is evidently the time factor: as stated in our earlier report, he was able to digest in the course of several months the same experience which had acted on him as a traumatic shock when he had been given only a few hours to adapt to the situation.

B. Under the conditions in our house where children see the parents from whom they are separated fortnightly, weekly, and in some cases even two or three times a week, it is instructive to follow the changes which the parent-child relationship undergoes. The first three or four visits by the mother usually only have the effect of reproducing the shock of the original separation. The children long for the coming of the parents, greet them with all signs of pleasure, cling to them during their visit, and usually burst into tears at the renewed parting.

After this experience has been repeated several times, the parting loses its dramatic significance and the children seem to feel certain that the mother who disappears will reappear again. During the week there is a great deal of talk about the parents who in conversations are compared with each other. When Beryl, for instance, spoke with great pride about her father, who had joined the air force, Isabel clearly searched for details about her own father to compete with her. She could not find any and said in the end: "My daddy is just an ordinary daddy." In reality, her father is dead. When other children asked Bobbie at a time when his mother was forbidden to visit because of illness when his "Mummy was coming," he answered shortly: "Soon." He evidently felt that it was a point against him and his mother that he received no visits. Presents and sweets brought by the parents are valued highly, treated as something special, and usually secured in the individual "lockers."

This period of *overvaluation* of the parents lasted approximately three months (with the older children, 3 and 4 years of age). During the past month we have entered into a new phase of the parent-child relationship. The children were still very pleased to see their parents, but the time spent with them was not as much valued as before. Beryl's parents, for instance, say: "She hardly talks to us when we take her out for a walk; and whenever she sees another child, she wants to run away and play with her; she is evidently more used to children than to grownups now." On her visiting days Rosette's mother will sit for hours on end and never say a word. Rosette dutifully stands next to her and remains as silent as her mother. As soon as her mother is gone, she revives and returns to her usual activity and endless talking. Dan, who gets visits from his mother very often, runs back to the other children afterward as if he were afraid of having missed too much. All this is, of course, the natural process of shifting affection and interest which is so well known in children of boarding school age.

An unusual case in this respect is Phyllis. Like all the other children, she used to look forward to her mother's visit and make great scenes after her mother left her. Lately she refuses to open the door when she sees her mother coming, does not want to join her and her grandmother in the mothers' room, and hardly allows them to handle her or to help her with her clothes, etc. She will ask the nursery worker to tie a ribbon for her even in the mother's presence.

In Phyllis's case it would be wrong to conclude that what has taken place is simply a shifting of loyalties, that she now loves and trusts the people in the nursery as she previously loved her mother. The real explanation is that Phyllis is reacting to a tragic conflict that has taken place in her parents' married life. She has overheard her mother talk against her father. The split in her loyalties is due to the deeper conflict between the now incompatible affection for her two parents. This is best proved by the fact that, as before, Phyllis still bursts into bitter tears when her mother leaves; the other night she woke out of a deep sleep and said to the night nurse: "Put my mother in my locker." For her, the locker is the place where her most cherished possessions are kept safely. The mother shows no understanding of this inner conflict. She can only see that Phyllis has turned away from her and toward us. Her reaction to it was an offer to "stay away for a few weeks since Phyllis does not want me anyway."

C. The child for whom the loss of his parents has had the most serious consequences is Bertie, now 4½ years.

Bertie's father was killed while working during an air raid in the course of the autumn raids on London. We were already asked to receive him and his mother in Wedderburn Road before the house was ready for use. We had to refuse at the time, and when, three weeks later, we sent word for them to come, we learned that Bertie had gone to a hospital for infectious diseases and his mother had had a complete breakdown and had been certified and committed to a mental hospital. From that time onward we were notified of Bertie's arrival more or less regularly every few weeks, but unluckily he contracted one infectious disease after another and altogether had to stay in the hospital for more than five months. He arrived at last in April, and even then was in and out of our sickroom with bronchitis, tonsillitis, and various other troubles for several weeks.

Bertie is a slim, good-looking boy, very clean with a clear skin and delicate features. He is extremely friendly, rather gay, and, in the manner of children who have spent a long time in hospitals, he does not differentiate overmuch between the various adult figures but greets everybody with an impartial smile. Confined to bed, he was always deep in play and kept himself busy with a few tiny toy cars, a set of paper houses, and similar playthings. He never mentioned his parents and seemed so unconcerned about everything that we doubted whether any knowledge of the family tragedy had ever reached him.

After a while we had the opportunity to question a cousin of his mother's who visited. We learned that Bertie not only knew of his father's death but had actually shared all his mother's grief and anxiety. His parents had been devoted to each other, his mother had never let Bertie out of her sight. One day during the period of the big raids the father had not returned from work for his midday meal, and after waiting for him for hours the mother had started the usual search. She took Bertie along wherever she went, to all the people she questioned, to the police, and even in the end to the morgue. There he was denied admission, but he waited outside while his mother found and identified his father's body. He was taken to the funeral and to first visits to his father's grave. It was after this that he fell ill with tonsillitis and was taken to the hospital where he came down with scarlet fever.

For his mother the separation from the child renewed the shock which she had received from the father's death. She believed that Bertie too was dead and began to search for him in the same frantic manner. A psychotic attack with hallucinations followed soon thereafter. The mother's cousin repeatedly said how good Bertie had been to his mother and how he had tried to comfort her in every way.

Once we knew the story, we tried carefully to lead Bertie's mind back to his past experiences. He now began to admit that his mother was in hospital. Certain things reappeared which he had probably been told during his stay in the hospital. "He should always eat his midday meal like his father, then he would soon be a big boy and would be taken to visit his mother." Whenever anybody asked what he wanted to be, he would say automatically and quickly: "Big boy." When questioned about his father, he said that he was "a workman who tidies away the bricks from the houses which Hitler threw down."

When the unexploded bomb was lying near the house, Bertie's mind was filled with ideas of soldiers, Hitler and bombing. He would bomb his paper houses by the hour, throw them down, and carefully put them up again. When he was near a window, he would vaguely point in some direction and say: "Look what Hitler has done."

One morning he suddenly woke in a state of great excitement. He first talked to himself loudly for a while, then called a young nurse to his bed and told her to listen to him. From then on during the day he repeated his story to whoever wanted to hear it. He told how his father and other men had been at work when the bombs started to fall. They had all crowded into the Underground station, which was enormously strong, so strong that no bombs could hit it. Then a "puff-puff train" had come and taken them all in and taken them to a place in the country where workmen were needed. They were still working there. When the war was over, his father would get another "puff-puff train" and come back.

Another version of the story said: in the morning his father had taken his hat and stick and his mackintosh, because it was raining. And when he did not come back, he, Bertie, had also taken his hat and his overcoat and put on his shoes and had gone out and had caught him and had brought him home. An addition to the story said: his mother was not in the hospital anymore. She was all well and living in the country, and after the war was over, she would also get into a train and come back. Bertie had evidently found a happy solution for the insoluble problem of his parents' fate.

It is possible that all this talking represented the contents of a dream which he had had at night. But it is also possible that this story had slowly prepared itself in him in the foregoing weeks and that he had shifted and reshifted all the facts and with the help of wish fantasies had altered the events to his own satisfaction. We realize that the fact of his father's death is denied from the beginning; his mother's illness, which at first he had accepted as a fact, has also been denied. The fantasy of himself as the hero who finds his father and triumphantly returns him to the mother probably originated at the time of his mother's search when he tried his best to comfort her. Whenever an anxious situation arises, reassurance is immediately given by stress on the opposite fact: he tightly clenches his hands in the effort to show the strength and safety of the underground station. The fulfillment of all wishes, i.e., the reunion of the family, is promised for a vague future.

Talk about these matters disappeared completely after two days. What remained was a great pleasure in playing bombing, killing, and war in general, a game in which several other boys joined with delight.

When Bertie was promised that he would be taken on a shopping expedition, he again woke in the morning in great excitement and declared to several people: "My daddy is by now ready to come back." In his thoughts, or maybe again in a dream, he had mixed up the event of the shopping expedition with the expected event of his father's return. In the street he showed great fear of and interest in motor cars; he refused to cross the street whenever one was anywhere in sight. In the same way he showed a great fear of catching cold and falling ill. When on a stifling day his cardigan was taken off, he immediately ran for his overcoat so as not to "fall ill and go to the hospital." In the shop he was very friendly with the shop assistant and told her: "I used to live in London before. But London is bombed to pieces, all the houses have fallen down and all the people are gone." London, in his mind, evidently stands for his past with the parents.

Lately he has had many visits from his mother's cousin who, during a fortnight's holiday from work, has taken him several times to her small flat. There he saw pieces of furniture which used to belong to his parents. He returns from these visits greatly agitated. He shows not the least outward sign of mourning or longing for his parents, but he will sometimes during play suddenly jump up and rush aimlessly to the far corners of the nursery in a curious rabbitlike manner. Such spells of unaccountable behavior are usually of very short duration; he will stop them just as suddenly and continue whatever occupation he was following before.

It seems certain that Bertie finds it difficult to distinguish between the manner of disappearance of his father and his mother. He probably believes that his mother is as dead as his father. This is indicated in his fantasy by their both being in the country and by their both returning in the same manner after the war. It is interesting to note, though, that in his fantasy father and mother are not together: they are kept in different places.

We are anxiously waiting for the time when the hospital authorities will declare his mother well enough to see Bertie. Once he can feel sure that at least his mother is alive, it seems to us the right time to go further in assisting him to face reality and to disentangle the unhappy facts from his fantasy products.

6

Monthly Report
July, 1941

STATISTICS

The event of this month was the opening of the Babies' Center in 5 Netherhall Gardens on July 3rd. Between this date and today 29 children were admitted there. Three children were admitted in the same period to 13 Wedderburn Road, which will from now on be referred to as the old house. The youngest babies from the old house were transferred to the new one. This brings the numbers at the present date to 32 children for the old house and 29 for the new house, which makes a total of 61 children.

The new house can accommodate more than 29 children; yet, in spite of pressure from outside, we attempt to admit new children slowly and gradually, so that each new child who comes in as a stranger is received by a group of children who are in some degree settled in their new surroundings.

The intended age limit for the new house is 2½ years. A few older children had to be received to avoid unnecessary splitting up of families. When their younger brothers and sisters feel more at home, these older ones will be evacuated to the country, together with the nursery school children of the old house.

REMARKS ON ORGANIZATION

In spite of many outward differences between the old and new houses, they are in no way separate ventures but rather two halves of one unit. Medical supervision is, of course, the same for both houses. Catering, social work, bookkeeping, and secretarial work are done by the same members of the staff for both. Staff meetings are held alternately in each house, with workers from the other house attending as guests. The older children of the new house will attend nursery school in the old house. The larger hospital department of the new house will be ready to receive patients from the old house if the number of beds in the sickroom there should at any time prove insufficient. Staff members from each house will be able to substitute for one another; there is naturally a great deal of visiting from one house to the other. The staff hostels are used indiscriminately by both houses. In the same way our garage serves as a storeroom and workshop for the needs of both.

REMARKS ON ADMISSION

Welfare work for children in wartime naturally varies in accordance with the different aspects of the external situation. In September-October, when the plan of opening the house in Wedderburn Road was first conceived, the need of the moment was accommodation for whole families who had lost their homes through bombing. The house was therefore equipped in the beginning to receive adults as well as children. Since the permit for the shelter material delayed the opening until January 1st, the needs had changed before the house began to function. Damaged houses had by that time been repaired sufficiently for adults to return to them or new accommodation had been provided in some manner by the Borough Councils. In most cases the sanitary conditions were not good enough for small children to remain there. Parents therefore sought admission only for their small children, and the arrangement and equipment of 13 Wedderburn Road had to be changed from that of a Family Rest Center to a Children's Rest Center.

In the following months of comparative lull, the cases admitted were mostly those who had drifted back from the country after unsuccessful billeting. An equal number of children were received because it proved impossible to evacuate them to the country without their mothers; their mothers on the other hand had to stay in London either for family reasons or for reasons of work. The single raids in March, April, and May brought a number of applications which we tried to answer favorably to the best of our capacity. But on the whole the reasons for admission during this second period were less acute ones (damage done by bombing) and more of a chronic kind (states of ill health or maladaptation during a longer term of living under emergency conditions).

The absence of raids in June and July brought no decrease in applications. On the contrary, the ever-increasing number of mothers who are doing war work greatly heightened the demand for admission of small children into nurseries. Homes which had already been split up owing to the husbands being called up were in many cases now completely dissolved.

Of the 32 children admitted during this month to our two houses, war work of the mothers was the reason of admission in 15 cases. Seven children were admitted as war orphans: one family of 4, whose father was killed while fire watching in an air raid; one family of 2, whose father was killed in an air raid while on duty as a stretcher bearer; and one child whose father was killed in a civilian accident. The mothers of these 7 children also gave up their homes to take up work. Four children were sent by nurses of big East End shelters where they had slept since the beginning of the war; one little child had slept in Oxford Street Tube Station for 12 months without showing too many ill effects. Three newborn babies were admitted with their nursing mothers; one of these mothers who had left the hospital in a state of agitation after giving birth and who had been sent to us from her East End shelter could not be quietened down enough to stay and left again with her babies after 24 hours. Three children were received as guests because no accommodation could be found for them while their mothers were giving birth to new babies in maternity hospitals; experience shows that these temporary visitors usually adapt so well that they become permanent children of the Nursery.

The state of health of most of the new children was incomparably better than during the winter months. Even in shelters or in blasted houses, bronchitis and pneumonia are very much rarer in good weather. On the other hand, several children had to be refused admittance after the medical examination because they showed early signs of whooping cough. Most of the babies between 12 and 24 months had had measles, bronchitis or pneumonia during the winter. Many of them had been in and out of hospitals for several months. A certain amount of undernourishment in some of the new children was shown not only by looks and weight but also by an excessive appetite during the first three weeks.

PROBLEMS OF A WARTIME NURSERY

The seven months of work spent in 13 Wedderburn Road are not long enough to make any definite statements about the effects of war conditions on children, their reaction to bombing, and the consequences of the various shocks for their later development. All we have been able to do so far is to collect observations and impressions which we expect to enlarge upon in constant contact with the material which presents itself.

This period of work is, on the other hand, long enough to give us a definite idea of the place residential nurseries can take in wartime education; of the demands they have to meet, and the task they can fulfill if the work is done under favorable conditions.

1. The primary reason for separating children from their parents at an age when such separations are avoided under peace conditions is of course the *safeguarding* of the child's life and health.

Though in general the argument that small children should not be exposed to war dangers is agreed upon by everybody, it is surprising to find that in very many individual cases the safety of the child is not the first concern of the parents. Parents will bring back children from evacuation places where they are not welcome, not properly washed, clothed or looked after even if these defects in care are in no way seriously endangering the child. That means that though the idea of "safety for the child" attracts parents in theory, in practice a residential nursery has to offer very much more than just safety if it does not want to see its population diminish and drift back to the danger of the badly bombed areas.

2. As indicated in our earlier reports, children have to pay a very high price for this removal from danger: they have to sustain the shock of being *separated* from their mothers whom many of them had never before left for even one night. According to some observers, this shock is much greater than the one a child receives when the house in which he lives together with his parents is destroyed by bombing. The bad effect of such separations could have been avoided by evacuating children under 5 together with their mothers, but the government plan had no such provisions. Residential nurseries were opened only when many mothers refused to leave either their husbands or their work in the danger zones.

Since children at this age need more than group life alone can provide, it is clearly the task of such nurseries to provide not only substitutes for the bodily care and supervision given by the individual mother but also a substitute for the emotional tie to the mother. The healthy development of children at this age is largely dependent on the fulfillment of the child's emotional needs. This task for the nursery is made all the more difficult by the fact that the children are expected to rejoin their own parents after the war and therefore not only should have substitute mothers but should at the same time be at all costs kept in some kind of contact with their real parents.

3. Since very few mothers make up their mind to part from infants before events have convinced them that the child is in real danger, most children enter the war nursery after something has upset their bodily *health*. Many children have slept in the Tube stations or East End shelters for months or even more than a year. The mothers usually decide to make a change only after serious sleep disturbances have set in. Children are kept home in Anderson shelters until a shelter bronchitis convinces the mother that something has to be done about it. In the same way infants live with their parents in blasted houses until pneumonia, bronchitis, or ear trouble brings the child to the hospital, where the mother then receives a serious warning not to expose the patient once more to similar dangers. This state of affairs almost invariably presents the war nursery with tasks which in peacetime were reserved for convalescent homes: underfed children have to be brought back to a normal state of nourishment; children, delicate after serious illnesses, have to be slowly nursed back to strength; lack of light and air in boarded-up rooms has to be made up for by exposure to sun or to sunlight treatment.

4. The child who enters a war nursery usually presents *psychological problems* as well as physical ones. The picture of the "bomb-shocked" child is in theory a very dramatic one and sure of engaging everybody's sympathy. In reality, we have little knowledge of such states in children. On the other hand and in a less dramatic way, the children received in nurseries show all the bad effects of having lived with mothers who were nervous and anxious during raids, of having been restricted in darkened houses, of having been exposed to the lack of privacy in big shelters,

etc. It is only natural that all the difficult conditions of family life in wartime have a lasting effect on the child's mental state: there are the financial worries of mothers who try to live on the army allowance; there is the separation of parents and in some cases the loss of fathers. Thus, the war nursery also has the task of being a "convalescent home" for problems of adaptation and neurotic disturbances.

5. Besides these war demands, the war nursery has its own positive and constructive educational task which it must fulfill. As adults we get used to the idea that many good things of life have to be discontinued "for the duration" and will be taken up again when peace has returned. The same point of view cannot be upheld where the life of children is concerned. Training, education, exercise, occupation, and above all the formation of the proper emotional relationships to the outer world cannot be postponed. What the child misses at the age of 1, 2, or 3 cannot be made up for when the child is 5 or 6. The appropriate period for certain experiences will by then be past and the child will have missed something that cannot be replaced in later life. This simply means that education cannot be interrupted or put off. The war nursery has to fulfill its peacetime tasks alongside with the special demands made on it by the war conditions.

5 NETHERHALL GARDENS, N.W.3

It is on the basis of these considerations that the Hampstead Nursery has been given the opportunity to build up a residential war nursery for small children in a beautiful and spacious house lent by the owner for the purpose and generously financed by the Foster Parents Organization.

The size of the house makes it possible to find room for 40 to 50 small children. Sun and daylight are guaranteed by an unusual number of enormous windows. A brick garden terrace provides room for a great number of baskets and baby carriages, and a lawn encircled by trees makes an ideal playground for the toddlers.

1. *Safety.* Hampstead is of course no safe area, but, compared with the real danger zones in the East End, it is comparatively safe. So far very little has happened in the immediate neighborhood. Whereas nearly all the houses in Wedderburn Road are slightly blasted and therefore empty of inhabitants, the environment of 5 Netherhall Gardens has all its glass windows and does not show signs of destruction. Nearly the whole basement of the house has been converted into an indoor shelter. Wooden beams slipped between iron girders and held up by brick pillars secure the ceiling. Openings are either bricked up or shuttered with enough space left to ensure a cross-current of air. In one part of the shelter a half circle of shelves provides room for 20 to 25 babies in baskets and carry-cots. Another part of the shelter is divided by partitions into bays, each bay containing three tiers of beds for toddlers; in addition, there are 9 beds for adults, nursing mothers, staff, etc. The children's beds are secured with nets, and each bed is easily accessible to the nurse on duty. The partitions between the bays are thick enough to prevent one crying child from disturbing all the others. A separate sick bay in another part of the basement contains 9 beds for the children from the hospital department. The equipment of every bed as far as mattress, sheets, blankets, pillow cases are concerned is not of the shelter type but of the kind used in every private household or good school.

2. *Separation from Parents.* The comparative nearness

to the children's own homes provides the Hampstead Nursery with the possibility of working out solutions for the double task of fulfilling the needs of the children while keeping them in contact with their own parents. We are conscious of the fact that no nurse can give proper attention to the individual child when the number of children she has to supervise is unduly large. Since nearly all the children under 2½ not only have to be fed, washed, bathed, dressed, but also need to be carried upstairs and downstairs, we consider that one nurse can usually handle at the most 3 or 4 children. A strict limiting of these numbers insures not only proper care for the child but also real interest being taken and time provided for unhurried attention to the various needs of each individual child.

In addition, the parents are free to come and go at will. Some who live nearer look in on their children sometimes after working hours. They bathe and feed their children on such occasions; they can also take them out for walks. Parents who live at a greater distance visit freely on Saturdays and Sundays. This arrangement of course leaves the child with the task of keeping up a relationship with the parents on the one hand and with the nurses on the other hand. Seven months of experience in 13 Wedderburn Road have convinced us that this situation, though it is a difficult one, is not in itself insoluble. It only requires a staff of workers who are capable of patience, tact, and an intelligent interest in the problems involved.

3. *Bodily Health.* It was due to the continual medical supervision in the old house that the nursery there was considered a convalescent home by the outside world. The new house adds to this reputation many facilities usually found only in hospitals. There are two large baby wards

on the ground floor, with a room added for three nursing mothers with their newborn babies. Bathtubs with hot and cold water are fitted in the rooms. The ward for the babies between 9 and 15 months also contains a playpen and small tables and chairs where the children can take meals. A separate milk kitchen prepares the bottles, fruit juices, and vegetable diet for the children of this floor. Apart from these three wards for the well or convalescent babies, there is a separate hospital department consisting of the doctor's surgery and two sickrooms with 4 and 3 beds respectively. This hospital department is situated in a separate wing of the house and can, if necessary, be reached by a separate staircase. It is used for current illnesses and, whenever necessary, as a quarantine station for new arrivals.

4. *Psychological Health.* The Hampstead Nursery is prepared to admit children with all sorts of difficulties of behavior and adaptation and to serve as a convalescent home in this respect as well. All the workers who handle the children are trained in their profession and most of them have joined the Hampstead Nursery because they feel a special interest in the psychological side of the children's problems. The difficulties which the children show are therefore not considered a nuisance or merely a disturbance of routine but a starting point for thought and effort. They give rise to theoretical discussions and exchange of opinions. Attempts are made all the time to use and apply theoretical knowledge to solve the practical problems presented by each child.

5. *Education.* Whereas the baby wards, the milk kitchen, and the hospital department are equipped to fulfill the war tasks outlined above, the toddlers' department serves

the purpose of nursery school education. There is sufficient room for those who have to learn crawling and walking as well as for occupation with educational and other toys. There is all the equipment needed to give the children the opportunity to learn how to sit at table, how to feed themselves, to wash their own hands at low washstands, and to find their own washing and dressing utensils. Toilet training is started in the baby room and continued with the toddlers. The whole toddlers' nursery consists of playroom, restroom, dressing room, wash and bathroom, and a separate lavatory. The parents have free access to this part of the Nursery as well and can join in the life of their children whenever possible.

7

Monthly Report
August, 1941

THE COUNTRY HOUSE

The month of August was an exceptionally busy one so that less time than usual was left for thought and observation. Exactly four weeks after the opening of the Babies' Rest Center we were able at last to take possession of the Country House. Since we were eager to send our children out to catch the last remnants of summer and also to have them in safety before a possible new period of air attacks in autumn, all preparations were hurried as much as possible. This meant buying the necessary equipment (furniture, beds, bunks, mattresses, linen, etc.), seeing to the children's teeth, sorting out the necessary country clothes for each individual child for winter as well as summer, buying shoes (all this made more complicated since clothes rationing also had been introduced for children under 4). Several new staff members had to be engaged. The local authorities in the country (police, labor office, medical officer, billeting officer) had to be consulted. The rationing of fuel and food had to be provided for.

We succeeded in completing these preparations in three weeks and set the date for sending out the first children on August 23rd. The children's excitement to see the Country House had by then reached its highest pitch. Innumerable questions and remarks cropped up continually. Though no one had ever promised them cows or horses, these two animals seemed to be inseparably bound up with their idea of country life. Bobbie said whenever he felt angry that he would "hit all the cows and horses in the Country House." Phyllis said she would "jump on the cows." Janet asked whether "the cows were ready now." Whenever the children felt angry with somebody, they would say: "You cannot come to our Country House."

On Saturday, August 23, 18 children were taken out in the American ambulance and two further cars, accompanied by 4 adults, one dog, and one canary. Only slight mishaps occurred on the journey. Janet was sick and another child had an "accident." On arrival the children were overjoyed to see their new home, a charming, friendly modern building with all the necessary conveniences, an immense ground floor studio serving as the big nursery, two huge south rooms with bay windows for the toddlers' bedroom and playroom, a covered porch leading down to terraced lawns for perfect playgrounds, outhouses, a vegetable and a berry garden, and a huge orchard with three little chicken houses. The absence of horses and cows was not commented on. The children found their bedrooms faultlessly set up and ready to be slept in, the first meal set out on their small tables, and the nursery prepared with material for play and work. Beryl said with great satisfaction after a visit to the dormitories: "I am going to sleep upstairs tonight and not downstairs." This meant: I am going to sleep in a proper bedroom again after eight months of shelter sleeping in a basement.

Since the Country House has been occupied for only one day at the time of this report, a fuller description of life and activities there will be postponed until the next report in September. A group of 10 or 12 toddlers will follow the bigger children to the Country House next Saturday.

STATISTICS

In August, 17 new children were admitted to the Hampstead Nursery: 5 to the old house to join in evacuation to the country, 12 for permanent stay in the new house. Two children who had been received temporarily during the confinement of their mothers returned home again. This brings the number for the new house to 49, and the number of children either evacuated or in the state of evacuation to 28, which makes a total of 77.

PROBLEMS OF SEPARATION

Among the 22 toddlers there are only 2 who hardly showed any signs of distress, both of them children of extremely nice, young, sensible and energetic mothers. The other children reacted to the shock of separation in varying degrees. Some outstanding examples are the following:

There was Maggie, 2 years, 8 months, whose mother

had never left her before and now brought the child to the Nursery so that she could take up munitions work. Maggie, who is a gay and beautiful girl, well-developed for her age, seemed at first delighted with the new experience. But when, after several hours, she understood that this meant separation from her mother, she broke down completely, cried incessantly, and was hard to quiet. Frequent visits from the mother only seemed to aggravate her state. She formed apparently violent attachments, first to one teacher, then to another, but changed her attachments with surprising quickness. She had to hold somebody's hand continually. Since this completely put one teacher out of commission for work with other children, a substitute was invented, half in earnest and half in play or joke. A skipping rope was tied around the waist of her last favorite and Maggie held on to it and followed her around. This unsatisfactory state of affairs lasted for two weeks. After that time her clinging became less insistent. She allowed even her favorite teacher to leave the room at times and she began definitely to enjoy her mother's visits without bursting into tears at every new parting. Now, six weeks after her arrival, she is definitely well settled in the house.

There was Derrick, 2½, a boy of charming, delicate appearance who in states of fright would roll his eyes until only the whites were seen. His mother reported that he as well as his older brother were frightened and nervous and inclined to have temper tantrums. The older brother had for this reason been removed from several billets. (He has now been admitted to the old house and sent to the country with our children.) She herself was in a highly nervous state.

Derrick seemed quiet and comparatively happy during the first two days. He was inseparable from a toy dog, Pat, whom he had brought from home. Pat slept with him, ate with him, was in his arms even when Derrick was being bathed and dressed, and Derrick insisted that Pat should be taken care of as if he were another child in the Nursery.

When his mother visited him after two days, Derrick had his first temper tantrum, a kind of hysterical attack, in which he alternately embraced his mother, clung to her, kissed her, scolded her, and hit out at her. He insistently demanded that she should kiss Pat on the mouth and hug him as if he were her baby. From then on for quite a while he reacted with temper to every imaginary insult done to Pat. He would cry whenever another child knocked against the toy and would throw himself on the floor with despair whenever the dog inadvertently fell out of his arms. Pat is evidently a symbol of Derrick himself and has to be treated as he himself wants to be treated. His mother has to make up in affection to the dog for the wrong she had done to Derrick by sending him away from home.

In Derrick's case the difficulties caused by separation from his mother are hard to disentangle from the neurotic troubles he had certainly already shown in his life with her. At present he is well adapted to nursery life in spite of many peculiar habits and is beginning to tolerate brief periods of separation from his dog. His difficulties present material for further observation.

The case of Susan, 3 years, 4 months, provides a very different kind of example. She entered the Nursery with a very charming little brother of 2 years. Susan is a rather plain little girl who has suffered from eczema since her babyhood. She lost her father in an air raid and seems definitely unloved by her mother, who resents the trouble and expense occasioned by the eczema and greatly prefers the little brother to the girl. Susan, who is used to looking after her brother and generally seems to have led the life of a miniature charwoman, continued this existence in the Nursery. She would scrub the floor, wipe the tables, feed little children, and report all matters of importance to the teachers. In the middle of all these activities she suddenly discovered the joy of being a loved child herself. She developed a tender affection for Dr. Ilse Hellman, the Nursery Superintendent, and, in the middle of doing something else, would suddenly run to her, throw herself into her arms, and hug her. She definitely lost very little through separation from her mother, and everything she meets in the Nursery is a gain for her.

There are four children of one family, aged from 1 to 6 years, who had also lost their father in an air raid and were admitted to the Nursery with their mother. In the beginning they showed their feeling of strangeness by sticking closely together and defending their rights as a family against all outsiders. The older sisters tore toys away from the other children to present them to their little brother, and they saw to it that each member of the family was fed before any other children were allowed to eat in peace. Their adaptation to the community announced itself by the outbreak of quarrels within the family circle. The children are now forming friendships in spite of, or in addition to, their family ties. Now, that the period of adaptation is past, it is also possible to form ideas about all the other difficulties presented by them; these are mostly due to the tragic death of their father and their mother's intense mourning.

The most troubled child of all was Evelyn, aged 3¼, a good-looking girl with a curious hard look in her eyes, the pupils of which are narrowed down to pinpoints. Evelyn is the eighth child of an engine driver and his wife who is now doing munitions work. She had been evacuated at the beginning of the war and changed her billets six times for varying reasons. She was removed from one because of maltreatment and from other places because her various foster mothers had to undergo operations, confinements, etc. She was so bewildered in the end, or so cross with her own mother, that she did not recognize her anymore when she visited her, although she recognized her father without difficulty.

During her first day in the Nursery she behaved normally but refused to be undressed, washed, and put to bed in the evening. She first cried for a long time and then suddenly burst into uncontrollable laughter. This condition dragged on for several hours. She played in the shelter dormitory with her teddy while the other children slept. At times she longingly looked at the beds, yawned, put her teddy to sleep, but would sit up with a jerk whenever her own head began to droop in sleepiness. It was not far from midnight when at last she put a finger in her mouth, sucked audibly, and fell asleep in the Superintendent's arms. After she was carried to bed she never woke up until morning. Even then she refused to be undressed; but after all the other children had gone to breakfast, she was taken to the wardrobe and given her choice of dresses. She fell in love with a pink dress and from then on let herself be washed, changed, and dressed without further difficulties. She behaved normally at bedtime the next evening.

She now behaves normally in the Nursery, though she

is easily tearful and feels quickly insulted by the other children. She knew her mother when she came to take her out on Sunday. But she is certanily a child whose development has been harmed by the variety of experiences she has gone through, i.e., a child whose further behavior will bear watching.

8

Monthly Report
September, 1941

STATISTICS

Since the evacuation of the oldest children to the country the Hampstead Nursery has again run with only two houses: 13 Wedderburn Road has been closed for cleaning and repair. A large list of applications still awaits consideration.

The number of children at the end of September is 80, 50 in Netherhall Gardens and 30 in the Country House. Twenty-seven of these country children are our own from Wedderburn Road; 2 are just now being admitted on the urgent request of the Essex Medical Authorities, who seem eager to cooperate with us. The 30th child, whose arrival is expected, is a little West African girl of 6 who, because of her color, had difficulties in being accepted either in a private billet or in a boarding school.

Requests for further admittances to Netherhall Gardens

become more and more pressing. There is an ever-growing need for mothers to find accommodation for their babies since there are ever more opportunities for them to find well-paid war work. For the moment we have made up our minds not to go beyond the number of 50 children.

Three of the mothers who have children in the toddlers' department and have found work in a war factory in North West London have taken rooms together near the Nursery. In this way they form a private little hostel, lead their lives attached to the Nursery, and come in every evening after working hours to attend to their children. This is a very satisfactory arrangement, especially for Keith's mother. He had previously been evacuated to a nursery where he never had a chance to see her and had gotten completely out of touch with her.

FOOD REPORT

As expected in early summer, fresh fruit and vegetables were plentiful, but prices soared. As soon as this was realized, the expenses were cut again so that by now the weekly average of the last four months has almost been re-established. Whatever difference still exists is due to the fact that we cannot make up our minds to cut out fresh fruit completely.

We were able to make 84 lbs. of red and black currant jam with the sugar saved by Wedderburn Road, the fruit from the country house, and many voluntary helpers who turned up in their off time from Netherhall Gardens.

With milk being rationed in the very near future and nearly every other commodity either rationed or government controlled, we look confidently forward to the next month.

KITCHEN DEPARTMENT

The kitchen of Netherhall Gardens has provided excellent meals for the children. It is in ideal working order. Although it is equipped with only a small gas stove and a small electric stove, a continual stream of meals for 50 to 80 people is turned out daily. The food is cooked so well that the children never want to stop eating; there never is any difficulty about punctuality of meals for the departments on the one hand and about meals at odd times for visiting parents, latecomers and early goers among the staff on the other. The last meal in the house is served late in the evening for the nightly fire watcher.

We are now debating the question whether the kitchen should also be turned into a training department so that our assistants and trainees could have the opportunity to learn about nursery diets and about running the kitchen of an institution of this kind.

DISTURBANCES

For the first time during the existence of the Hampstead Nursery our relations with the outer world have not been entirely friendly ones. With 13 Wedderburn Road we had been lucky enough to be surrounded nearly entirely by empty houses. The only neighbors who existed were extremely friendly and followed the activities of the Nursery with interest. The Country House in Lindsell is situated in its own grounds, and these grounds again are very much at the end of the world with no neighbors within easy reach.

The garden of the Babies' Center, on the other hand, is

overlooked by a small block of modern flats, the tenants of which find their former peace disturbed by the crying of the babies. Numerous complaints have been addressed partly to us, partly to the Hampstead Borough Council, and partly even to the National Society for the Prevention of Cruelty to Children. The neighbors find it hard to believe that even healthy and well-cared-for babies will cry at times, or rather that with 50 children in one house there is seldom complete peace and quiet. We are trying at the moment to pacify the neighbors and the babies simultaneously, but the result is still uncertain.

REMARKS ABOUT THE COUNTRY HOUSE

Since the children we sent to the country remained within their own groups and were accompanied by the staff who had looked after them for several months, evacuation for them was no shock of any kind. It took them only a very few hours to feel acquainted with the rooms of the new house. They arrived at lunchtime and already at tea, their second meal in the new surroundings, no child had the slightest difficulty in finding his place at the table. The toddlers were delighted to have "real beds" again. No child seemed to miss or question the absence of a shelter. (A few weeks later a fonder memory of the shelter in Wedderburn Road seemed to wake up in them. An empty bookcase in the nursery was suddenly declared to be a dolls' shelter with all the individual dolls sleeping peacefully in tiers above each other. The workers were asked by the children to crochet nets to safeguard the dolls against falling out of their beds and in this way to make the resemblance to former shelter life complete.)

It took the children less than one day to get accustomed to outdoor life. They took possession of the playgrounds immediately and already on the day after arrival showed their familiarity with the lawns by standing on their heads on them and by using the space for all sorts of acrobatic stunts. The same children who in London had been tired after walking once around the block now take walks of more than two hours and are untiring in meeting adventures of all kinds. They pick berries and have great pleasure in smearing their faces with them until they are hardly recognizable. They get acquainted with the flowers of the countryside and they make frequent visits to a friendly farmyard where they meet cows and pigs. The Nursery itself owns 50 chickens which the children visit for feeding and collecting eggs. Two beautiful black and white rabbits have been given to them by a friend in the village. The dog from Wedderburn Road has been joined by a Labrador puppy and by a foxterrier who came as a stray, did some damage to the chickens, but then repented and refused to leave again. Some children, for instance Billie, still show signs of anxiety when surrounded by the chickens. Some of the smaller children get disturbed when walking on the country road. They had been warned so often against the danger of walking in the London streets that the fear of being run over is still with them.

On days when the lawns are wet, the children can play on a short drive connecting the staff cottage and the house entrance. At such times the drive is densely populated by every kind and make of tricycle, children's motor car, cart or wagon that we could lay our hands on. There are never enough tricycles to go round, and here for the first time the boys assert their superior rights over the girls by claiming possession. The latest addition is a small and low children's bicycle which the biggest boys (4 to 5) are already using fearlessly and expertly.

The greatest pleasure for the smallest toddlers is to walk off by themselves. Teddy (2 years, 2 months) especially has developed the habit of going for walks in the garden all alone. He seems to love solitude and while all the other children always return very soon, he has to be searched for and is usually found sitting in the grass with a picture book open on his knees. He cries bitterly when is "fetched home," but the members of the staff are always worried that some day he might vanish completely and they keep an anxious eye on him. He seems to have no intention of hiding himself; he just wanders off in a state of dreamy contentment, and a feeling for the passing of time and the idea of returning never enter his mind.

The spaciousness of the Country House makes it possible to give the children a freedom of movement which was denied to them in the more narrow confines of Wedderburn Road. Mary (8), Beryl, and Marion (6) spend quite a lot of time helping in the kitchen. Sofie Wutsch, the cook, confirms that their help is quite real and that they show great interest and perseverance when they are at work. The bigger boys like to follow the gardeners around, and all the children like to look for apples in the orchard.

It is not quite easy to teach the smaller children proper respect for the flowers, shrubs, and trees, and to prevent them from stepping on borders, etc. Children who have grown up in the East End of London do not have a natural feeling for plant and animal life.

All the children like to take turns in waiting at table, clearing the table after meals, and in helping to tidy up the bathrooms. Duties of this kind are discussed and assigned once a week at a "meeting" of the older children. (The word meeting has a special meaning for them from the regular staff meetings at Wedderburn Road, which, since "entrance was forbidden" to the children, used to make them very jealous.)

All the children in the Country House now consider themselves too big for an afternoon nap. Since it seems wise anyway to make the best use of sunlight hours, no one is urged to rest and everybody falls asleep all the more easily after the evening bath. Nearly all the children sleep very well. There are one or two exceptions as, for instance, Bobbie, who usually calls out repeatedly, and little Gladys, who for a week or two developed one of the typical sleep disturbances of childhood. Since the troubles which prevented her from falling asleep were discussed with her, the symptom has nearly disappeared.

Little more than a week after their arrival in the country the children were disturbed at night by a solitary stick of bombs which was dropped several miles distant. Since the noise of bombing makes itself heard in the open country even more than in a city, all these Londoners—grownups and children alike—in spite of having lived through the whole period of blitz, jumped out of their beds and had quite a fright. Many of the very little children were untouched by the event. The older children and the staff met in the hall and the corridors and some of the children needed quite a lot of quieting. Bertie especially was excited and disturbed and wanted somebody to stay near his bed and protect him. The children talked for quite a while about the bombing before they fell asleep again. Some of them, like Janet, quickly regained their good humor and were ready to joke.[1] One of them said that they should write to Jimmy in London that he could come to the country now, that there were bombs there also, and that he could do fire watching.

PROBLEMS

Both in the Country House and in Netherhall Gardens the various departments have settled down to the task of solving the problems presented by the children.

Baby Department

The baby room with its 12 occupants is this month especially proud of its dealings with two individual children.

Rose came to the Hampstead Nursery, sent by a hospital. She was 10 weeks old and weighed 7 lbs. and was altogether in a very bad state of health. The child had been delicate from birth; the birth weight was 4 lbs., 13 oz. She was breast-fed for one month until her mother fell ill and lost her milk. The child got artificial food, lost half a pound within a few days, was constipated, vomited after each bottle, and cried incessantly. The mother took her to the hospital in despair and was advised after a few days to bring her to us.

Rose looked shockingly miserable when she was admitted. Her face was pale with deep shadows under her eyes, her skin hung in folds, the fontanelle sunken. Her body was so thin that one could see the peristalsis. She did not shut her eyes properly during sleep and never

[1] See Report 20 for an account of how Janet remembered this event one year later.

stopped crying when awake. Though her voice was weak, it was penetrating and gave the impression of actual suffering. She did not move her hands or her head and screamed when she was bathed.

During the first days, in spite of all efforts, her weight went down to 6 lbs. 11 oz., but her crying diminished and her hands began to show some activity. There were moments when she slept peacefully with her hands lifted to both sides of her head, in a position that one sees in normal infants.

It took a fortnight until she could be bathed without crying. She was at that time able to sleep nearly from one meal to the next, that is, two hours, without interruption. At that time her first faint smiles could be observed. Distressingly enough, she mostly smiled after vomiting. She seemed to be relieved when she got rid of food. Her food at that time consisted of half milk, half rice water with sugar and glucose added. The sugar and glucose were slowly raised from 4 to 9 percent. She was greatly helped by some few ounces of breast milk which the mother of one of our country children who was feeding her new baby brought us daily. We were extremely grateful to this mother who did not mind half an hour's walk on hot days to have her milk pumped for Rose.

Rose gained weight very slowly, She showed no keenness to take her bottle; after 1 oz. she would have liked to stop altogether. It would take 20 to 40 minutes for her to drink 4 to 5 ounces. Vomiting and constipation had by that time disappeared.

When Rose was 3 months old, the breast milk stopped because the mother had only just enough milk for her own baby. Five days later our glucose also came to an end and none seemed obtainable anywhere. Orange juice was started, which she took nicely, but then, a week later, oranges disappeared. Things looked black for Rose for a few days, but then suddenly glucose reappeared and a promise for further supply was made to us. Billie's mother returned from the maternity hospital with a newborn baby and plenty of breast milk. Besides feeding her own child, she supplies 8 to 12 oz. daily for Rose.

Rose is still fed every three hours. Semolina and a tiny bit of tomato juice have been added to her diet. She still drinks very slowly, but she never vomits. Her weight has gone up to 9 lbs. 5 oz. She still looks tiny and delicate but not ill or suffering anymore. She has a charming smile and sometimes laughs and makes noises. She pays attention to her surroundings, especially so at the times when she ought to drink her bottle. When she is awake, she mostly looks at her hands which are well formed and which she moves about slowly and gracefully. Her face is tanned from lying almost continuously in the open air. Her cheeks are beginning to be red. She has very beautiful deep blue eyes and very soft, fair hair.

Her mother is a friendly, shy woman whose first child, a boy of 5, though rather tall looks nearly as delicate as Rose. Rose's father came on Army leave when she was 3 months old and then saw her for the first time. His leave lasted 10 days and the parents visited Rose every second day.

Rose was at one time the greatest worry of the baby nursery. Now she gives every hope of progressing steadily and satisfactorily.

The baby room was confronted by a problem of the opposite kind by Julius. His parents brought him when he was 6 months old and they showed great pride in the enormous size of their baby. When he was born, he weighed only 5 lbs., but by the time he was 6 months he weighed 18 lbs. 2 oz., the weight of a normal child of 10 months. He had been brought up exclusively on a dried milk specially rich in fats. Though he had been given cod-liver oil from birth, he was suffering from rickets in the highest degree. He had an enormous head with the bones soft to the touch like parchment. He took no interest in anything and lay in his bed immobile and hardly ever cried or smiled. His parents thought that he was not only a very beautiful but also a very "good" child.

He was started immediately on a diet of fruit juice and vegetables. He got two vegetable meals, juice and two bottles of ⅔ milk, ⅓ water, and 5 percent sugar. Besides being in the open air continuously and having a natural sunbath whenever possible, he was given a series of twenty artificial sunlight treatments.

The result was exactly what we wanted it to be. He never lost more than 2 oz. and then only gained a very little, so that now, after 10 weeks, his weight is changed only by 4 oz. The child, at the same time, has changed completely. The bones of his skull have hardened, he has become lively, interested in his surroundings, moves his arms and legs playfully, and has lost his flabbiness. He has developed four teeth without difficulties. When given some help he can sit up and then looks around with astonishment and pleasure.

The problem which has been successfully solved in this case was keeping his weight down in spite of his healthy appetite. The reduction of fattening nourishment never for one day caused him distress or spoiled his good relationship to the world around him. I think we can safely say that during all this time he never felt unhappy or deprived. He is still an outstandingly pleasant child. He greets his parents and the people he knows with a laugh, he enjoys his bath and his meals, and he is hardly ever heard crying.

Nursery Problems

While the baby department is in this way wrestling with the task of undoing the bodily harm which has been done to these infants, the nursery departments are faced with similar worries on the psychological side. There are at the moment several children who express their memory of the unhappy experiences which they have gone through in all sorts of behavior problems.

The violent temper tantrums of two little brothers, one in the country and one in the London house, have been revealed to be repetitions of scenes which they had witnessed at home between their parents. Their father, home on army leave, suddenly discovered that their mother had been unfaithful to him and attacked her violently while on a visit to the Nursery. His violence, which very soon turned into intense love-making, was, as the mother confirmed later, only one of a long series of similar rows. It was the prototype of the attacks of both children; or rather, they communicated their knowledge of what went on at home with the help of their symptom.

We have not yet succeeded in translating Evelyn's behavior problems (see Report 7) into the story of her wanderings during the war. She presents a different problem nearly every day. Her fear of going to bed disappears and instead she starts being afraid of being undressed. This again gives way to anxiety of going downstairs or coming out into the garden. She gets used to the garden and becomes frightened of entering the front door after an outing. She still shows her scared expression at times, but she can overcome most of her inhibitions when gently forced. If she is left alone with them, she tends to restrict all her activities and to retreat to the safety of one single chair. There is a curious contrast between this mode of behavior without speech and a very glib way of talking in which she refers to herself as a third person. "Isn't she a charming girl!" When asked who this charming girl is, she answers quite astonished: "This little girl here, Evelyn." At other times she says: "Silly fool!" and she will repeat the word "silly" many times. Both may be ways in which other people have addressed her. But these at the moment remain disconnected and vague bits of information.

One of last month's newcomers to the Country House, Georgie (3 years, 9 months) is at varying times distressed, shy, cross, affectionate, and violent. He had never been separated from his mother during the first 2½ years of his life, and then was taken from her very suddenly when she had to go to the hospital in the last stages of a tuberculous illness. His father, who knows that the mother's death is expected shortly and who is in the Merchant Navy, brought Georgie and his older sister to the Hampstead Nursery just before his leave expired.

Georgie at the beginning spoke very little and never made any references to his past. Instead of that he would get into short fits of temper and defend himself against all sorts of harmless routine happenings with the utmost vigor but without any consistency in his behavior. He would refuse, for instance, to be put to bed or to be washed or to have his throat inspected at one moment and then willingly allow to have it done the next. He would sit endlessly at table apparently finishing his lunch. The most difficult time for him was the evening, when he was supposed to go to bed.

On one such occasion he had one of his outbursts of anger against the Nursery Superintendent and assured her that he did not like her. She said simply that she was very sorry because she did like him. He said: "I don't like you and I don't like nobody. I only like myself." Immediately afterward he told her for the first time how his mother had gone away in a big car and had never come back again. The evening after this conversation he did not make his usual fuss but called her to his bed and said: "Stay with me. You are my mother now." He is now very closely attached to her, very affectionate, and much easier to handle.

He has succeeded in expressing the most important event in his past life in words and conscious thought and this relieves him of the necessity of expressing his memory of it in abnormal behavior. Day after day he now adds new pieces of information about his past. Whenever he is at cross-purposes with one of the grownups, he says threateningly: "I will put you to bed" or "You will get no pudding." In this way he remembers and relates the educational measures taken in the little school where he had lived with his sister before they came to us. This also explains why his behavior was always most cranky when he was supposed to be either eating or sleeping.

The same outlet into conscious thought and speech with consequent relief in their behavior is unluckily denied to some of our children who are most in need of it. As reported before, we have quite a number of war orphans in our groups. Among them are two families where the children have not been informed about their fathers' death. Both men were killed in air raids, the body of one has not even been recovered. Though both mothers are competent women who immediately faced the task of going out to work to support their families, they are too much hit themselves to be able to face their children knowing and possibly talking about their fathers' death. They built up a legend of the father being "in the North of England," being "ill in hospital," and they force the children to believe in it.

There is not the slightest doubt that all these children (except, of course, the baby) must know all about their fathers' death. They have seen their mother cry and for weeks and even months lived in close contact with her mourning before they came to us. The mothers even take them to church at the annniversary of their fathers' death, to visit neighbors who condole with them; they even had to accompany the mother to the officials to debate the question of pensions, guardianship, and proving of death.

In spite of their emotional life being completely under the impact of their deprivation, they are denied the relief given by talking about the matter. One of these children (5 years) the other day suddenly in the presence of her mother made the triumphant statement: "I know all about my father. He has been killed and he will never come back." The mother answered with a fit of anger, closely questioning the child who had told her "such a lie." The child only repeated: "You have told me yourself. You have told me yourself." She evidently meant: You have told me yourself through your behavior. But in the end the mother won. She made the child repeat: Father is in Scotland and will certainly return. The little girl repeated the words after her with a sullen expression and had to promise never to say or think it otherwise. Such children show the effects of this discrepancy between the truth they know and feel and the legend they are forced to adopt in wild and unruly behavior and general contempt for the grownup world.

The other little girl, Susan, the little charwoman of 3½ described in the last report, reacts to every outing with her mother, especially when it takes her back to the father's world, with a new excess of washing, scrubbing, and looking after the other children, far beyond her years.

There is no doubt that all these children can be helped by an open discussion of their misfortunes. But at the moment it cannot be done against the mothers' wishes and it will take some patient and careful work to influence the mothers to adopt this point of view.

9

Monthly Report
October, 1941

STATISTICS

The number of children in both houses has remained stationary (80). Two children left us and two others were admitted in their place.

EXTERNAL DISTURBANCES

The quarrel with our neighbors about the noise caused by our children has subsided for the moment. This is due less to an interchange of letters than to the interference of the autumn and winter weather. The garden is less used and it is easier to shut windows when one child or another creates more disturbance. We expect the unpleasantness to revive with the return of spring and summer.

GENERAL REMARKS

During the month of October a larger number of children had to be refused than ever before. There was the usual demand for short-term admittance in cases of sudden illness of mothers, of confinements, deaths, and of court decisions. There was an unsually great number of applications for newborn illegitimate children whose mothers are anxious to return to their various forms of war work as soon as they can leave the hospital. There is a new type of application from mothers whose husbands have been discharged from the army as unfit and who now take it upon themselves to support the family.

There was another new and unusual element this month: fathers who are home on short army leave either find their children in unsatisfactory billets or discover that their wives are estranged as a result of new contacts and neglectful of their children. Before returning to their regiments or to their ships they try very actively and sensibly to find a place where they can leave their children well taken care of. It now happens more frequently than before that a father or mother with a child on their arm will appear without previous inquiry, sent either by some welfare organization or recommended by friends whose children are under our care.

As reported above, we were able to take only two of all these cases. The children chosen were one of the illegitimate babies, 3 weeks old, and Minna, a little girl of 4½, the daughter of a soldier discharged for mental illness. The father had developed the delusion that he could foresee the future and predicted, among other things, that his little girl would be killed in a London air raid. On his first visit he brought evidence of a widespread correspondence which he had started in his attempt to evacuate the child to the country where an older child, a boy of school age, already lived. He showed us all the letters of regretful refusal which he had received. To relieve the tension of his state and eventually also to relieve the intolerable pressure on the mother, who had to cope with her husband's anxiety, we accepted Minna for the Country House.

To make her acquaintance we visited her in the late evening on the platform of Regent's Park Tube Station, which had served as her sleeping quarters for the last 12 months. We found her sleeping peacefully on the stone floor, covered with a few rags and undisturbed by the incredible noise of the trains in this very narrow station. She is a typical shelter child, pale, peaked, restless when awake and alert to everything that is going on around her, evidently fully conscious of the tragedy her father's illness has brought into the family. But in spite of these conditions we found her clean, free of infections, and well looked after medically by the shelter nurse, who had taken a special interest in this case.

This pressure for admittances naturally made us wish to create more empty places. Nothing can be done in this respect in Netherhall Gardens. It is completely filled with 50 children. On the contrary, all sorts of difficulties about space are arising. Some of the babies have grown out of their baskets and had to go into cribs. Some babies in cribs have become so active that they need the playpens in the junior toddlers' room. The junior toddlers on the other hand, who last month still spent more than half the day in their cots, are now crawling and even walking continually and their room is overfilled. But even if some more beds could be put in odd places, it does not seem advisable to have more than 50 children of that age in one shelter in case of air raids.

The natural step seems of course the reopening of Wedderburn Road, which could again provide a home for 25 to 30 children. Plans have been delayed so far because we had decided to inquire from various authorities, the local Borough Council, the London County Council, and the Ministry of Health, whether there was any possibility to run the houses in connection with one of the current schemes for the welfare of London children. The idea was that all the facilities existed to run it either as a feeding center, a day nursery, a residential nursery, or even a convalescent home. So far all answers have been negative. These attempts were made as an effort to relieve our American friends, at least to a certain degree, of the great expense of a third house. To have three houses running, fully staffed for night and day service, with health service, laundry, feeding, and full clothing of the children is certainly a heavy responsibility. Since we try to attain hospital standards as far as cleanliness, hygiene, medical supervision, and diet are concerned, and try to combine with that the freedom and the educational possibilities of nursery life, a child in our house naturally costs more than in an ordinary nursery school, though, of course, still very much less than in the ordinary children's hospital. Welfare organizations that knew about us have used the opportunity to send us on the one hand children with behavior problems and on the other hand children in need of very special bodily care. The effort to fulfill the functions of a nursery school, a place for problem children, and a convalescent home rolled into one naturally also shows up in our budget. We are, therefore, still trying to find ways and means to reduce or to share expenses before we take the step to reopen Wedderburn Road.

It has struck us that the enlargement of existing accommodations in the country house might be a cheaper solution. We are at the moment converting a garden shed into a row of small rooms for the staff. There is the chance that we may acquire a large type of army hut, formerly in use in a boys' camp. Re-erected near our house, it might become an excellent little hospital and convalescent pavilion for our children. This would release one staff room and one sickroom in the house itself and thus create room for another group of 15 children. We are still negotiating about the hut. In the meantime, we have converted one third of the large greenhouse into a sun lounge where children can take their afternoon rest in deck chairs or where patients after illness can have all the sun available in wintertime. To enlarge the Country House would, of course, be more economical than to refill Wedderburn Road.

FOOD REPORT

Our food situation has been improved by three new regulations which appeared this month.

1. Of the oranges now on the market preference is given to hospitals and nurseries for children under 5.

2. The same preference to children has been given in regard to eggs. That means that our babies now get one egg weekly instead of one egg fortnightly. In addition, the hens in the Country House supply about 2 dozen eggs weekly for the Babies' Center.

3. The third regulation concerns dried fruit, which is

now rationed. The monthly ration for Netherhall Gardens amounts to 25 lbs. and goes mostly in the form of sultanas and raisins into milk puddings and cakes.

Although prices are rising, the food budget has remained stationary.

PROBLEMS

This last month seemed specially filled with conversations, correspondence, and interviews with parents.

We have at the moment five mothers living with us: three of these are nursing their own babies and working at the same time as paid workers in our kitchen and household; one works in our laundry; one works outside the house in a post office. Besides, as reported last month, three mothers are living as a small community in close contact with us and are engaged in war factory work at the same time.

Altogether 95 percent of our mothers are full-time workers, mostly in some form of war work. The remaining 5 percent are either ill in hospitals or tied down with the care of still another baby whom we have been unable to admit so far. There are only three mothers with whom we have lost contact altogether and are at the moment trying to regain it with the help of the social worker or the probation officer who had originally sent them to us.

Though our relations with the mothers are on the whole excellent, difficulties do arise in certain cases. The stories of the departure of the two children who left us in October are an excellent demonstration of difficulties of this kind. The motives behind the action of the mothers are, of course, far from reasonable.

1. Max's mother entered Wedderburn Road in January, 1941, together with her baby who was then 5 months old and suffering from shelter bronchitis. She immediately became greatly attached to the nursery and at her own request stayed and worked for us for several weeks before she began to look for war work outside the house. She visited regularly, took Max out for walks, bought his own clothes, and became very proud of his beauty, his good health, and his general appearance. Her friendly relations with us seemed the one stable point in her otherwise unstable life. She changed jobs nearly fortnightly, complained about conditions and treatment nearly everywhere, and had upsets and difficulties wherever she worked.

It was evidently too much to hope that her stormy nature could really tolerate a peaceful continuance of Max's life with us; a transference of her difficulties onto her relations with the Nursery was to be expected. During autumn she became less open and friendly when she was visiting and we had the feeling that Max's father, an equally unstable man with whom she was then living, rather turned her against us. She then used the opportunity, when Max got an attack of eczema on his feet, to declare herself dissatisfied with the care given to him and took him away without letting us know her further plans about him.

2. The second departure, Nathan's, was determined by factors of a similar kind. Nathan had also arrived in Wedderburn Road last January. His mother had brought him under the pressure of the National Society for the Prevention of Cruelty to Children. She had been charged in court with neglect of her two children and described as a danger to them because she herself and the man she

was living with at the time were both infected with venereal disease and took no proper precautions against passing on the infection to the children.

Since separation from the child had been more or less enforced upon her, in her case relations were rather strained from the beginning. Because of her illness she could not be encouraged to visit as freely as the other mothers. (She would kiss the children, drink out of the same cup with them, etc.) Whenever she wanted to take Nathan home for a night or for a weekend, we had to refuse permission. She realized, of course, that a difference was made between her and the other parents in that respect, but she could only see the injustice of it and failed to understand the underlying reasons. She would say that her illness "had nothing to do with the child." He would be "beautifully looked after" when she took him home.

After adventures of various kinds she finally left the man in whose house she had been living and who declared that she had absolutely ruined him. She appeared on her visits with a succession of friends whom she invariably introduced to Nathan as his future daddy. Now, in October, she has finally found somebody to marry her and after that she immediately claimed Nathan for a week's holiday "at home." Again we had to refuse permission since we had no evidence whether she had finished her hospital treatment or whether contact with her would still be dangerous to the child. She refused to understand and took him "for good."

Since Nathan is a court case, we expect that he will be brought back sooner or later by an order of the court. He is an affectionate child and deeply attached to his mother for whose visits he has always longed. It can only have the worst effect on him to be first snatched away from the life in which he had settled down (he had also just started to go to the village school in Lindsell), to be taken home with hopes to stay with his mother forever, and then to be snatched away from her once more, probably after witnessing all sorts of violent scenes about the matter. His little stepbrother (Teddy, 2 years) is still with us, and his father, the mother's discarded friend, implores us to "hang on to him" and not to hand him over to his mother if she should come and claim him. This is more easily said than done without an explicit court order.

To offset these rather hopeless situations, we are pleased to find that our efforts not to break the contact between parents and children in Wedderburn Road have really been successful. Now that their children are in Essex, the parents make all efforts to pay their bus fares and visit regularly. They write letters to the children whenever they are unable to come, and send small packages and messages through other parents or the office.

Transport from the last bus station in Dunmow to our Country House (8 miles) is becoming quite a problem. We had previously arranged for private transport for 6 to 8 people every Sunday. The last Sundays in October 15 to 16 parents managed to come. For the present the following solutions have been found: we received a petrol permit from the Ministry of Transport for one bus direct from Wedderburn Road to the Country House monthly, For this bus the Nursery will pay the fares so that the parents get one free visit monthly. On other Sundays the parents pay their own fares as far as Dunmow and a private bus has been secured to cover the distance to and from the Country House. This bus is also paid for by the Nursery. Besides, several money gifts from individual foster parents for individual children have been handed over to the parents to help with the bus fares. A Sunday visit from a member of the family means more to the child than any kind of material present. Blackout conditions in the coming months will, of course, make the winter visits much shorter and therefore less satisfactory. Some children always need some time before they get accustomed to and can enjoy the visit of their parents.

From rash and inconsiderate actions of some mothers, like Max's and Nathan's, it would be very wrong to generalize and suppose that these untaught mothers have little understanding of their children's needs or do not appreciate the more subtle and complicated methods of dealing with their children. We find that the mother's own diagnosis of the child's state is very often correct. Isabel's mother, for instance, suggested from the beginning that the child's attacks of nervous coughing might have something to do with her father's incessant coughing in the year before his death. Jim's mother always knew that his bed wetting and general state of restlessness were due to her own attacks of anxiety during air raids. Billie's mother, who showed great concern and understanding about his abnormal state whenever he was separated from her, asked us later to take her older girl, who had developed an overtimid and frightened manner in her billet where she was excellently cared for in all material ways. She said it could not be good for a child to lose all confidence in her own actions in that way; she had noticed that whatever the girl did, she would stop afterward and wonder whether she had done right.

Several mothers who were rather doubtful of our methods in the beginning admitted after a while that our ways of handling the children seemed more successful than theirs. Little Dan's mother, for instance, begins to see the part she used to play in his temper tantrums and says, "It is lovely now to put him to bed without excitements." Maggie's mother, on the other hand, still insists that her spankings are more sensible than our indulgence when Maggie is upset.

All mothers relate how much they mind when they see their children continually restricted in their activities in billets or in institutions. They are upset about the fact that in some places children are not allowed to handle freely the presents which the parents bring to them. Georgie's and Marion's father, for instance, reported as one of the instances which completely turned him against their former nursery that a doll which he had given to his little daughter on one visit was still in the same perfect condition when he returned for a next visit after several months at sea. This, he said, could only mean that the toy had been withheld from the child and that the people in charge did not understand what a toy of this kind could mean in comforting a child separated from both parents. (The children's mother is in the hospital with tuberculosis.) In the beginning insight of this kind came as a surprise to us. We would rather have expected the parents to wish that their presents should be respected and preserved.

Understanding of this type is shown with special clearness in a letter received last week from Tony's mother. Tony (3) was admitted to the Country House in September, at the special request of the Assistant Medical

Officer in Dunmow. As a bed wetter he had been handed on from one billet to another (five or six changes in all) and no further place could be found for him. He is a delicate little boy of graceful, charming appearance, friendly but noncommittal, rather frightened and lost, and without emotional contact with anybody. All we could learn about him was that his father was a private in the army and that his mother was in a sanitarium with tuberculosis. When an aunt from London visited him after a short time, we asked for particulars of his past history. She told us only that she was the mother's sister, that she belonged to a family of thirteen, and that she knew hardly anything about the child, But she would write and ask the mother to let us know as much as possible of the experiences the child has had all by himself during the mother's illness. We quote the following from the mother's letter:

. . . Tony hasn't had any complaints, only measles which he had last December, they lasted a week, but nothing else whatever; he has always eaten well and slept well. When Tony was 8 months old his daddy was called up for the Army; up till he was 2 years of age there was just Tony and I on our own, so of course he had his freedom, was allowed to play in the garden, etc., and was a happy, carefree little boy, but last year we decided to go to Yorkshire to his daddy for a while. I was only there quite a short time when I had a hemorrhage; of course, it came as quite a shock to me when I learned what was wrong as I had felt so well; I never had the slightest suspicion of it or I should not have gone all those miles from home to leave my baby at the mercy of strangers. However, I went into the sanitarium in December, 1940 and the woman who we were staying with said she would take care of Tony. During the time she had him his daddy used to go to see him and he said it got on his nerves to hear her keep saying to the child, "Don't do this and don't do that." As time wore on he noticed Tony was being cowed down and when his daddy took him sweets, he would give them to his lady and sit there and wait for her to give him one. He was never allowed to play out in the garden and when his father went on Sunday mornings to take him out, she always made the excuse that he was not bathed, and then on evenings she would put him to bed just before his dad arrived. This went on for six months—this was the period I was in the sanitarium. I was up all day and had been for quite a while and I was feeling very well, so I decided to come back to London and let someone in my own family take care of Tony, and I would finish my treatment in a sanitarium down here, but I was disappointed. When I got home, I found my sisters had all got government jobs and could not leave them; so I said unless I found somebody suitable I would never leave him again. It was during this time I had him that I noticed he was not the happy carefree little boy that I had left; he had altered completely, seemed to be frightened of every little thing he did, he would say, "Can I do this, can I do that?" He would never do anything of his own free will in case it was wrong. I would say "yes" to everything he wanted just to get him back to his old ways, and it made me realize how very much he must have been kept down. . . .

I then got the chance to come to this sanitarium and as we know someone in the country, we thought it would be a good idea to ask her if she would like to have Tony, thinking he would have a good home and the freedom of the fields to play in. She seemed to jump at the idea of having him and she asked me to pay her 15 shillings a week, but I was so pleased to think that she was going to have him that I asked her to accept 18 shillings as the cost of living was so dear and [there] would not be much money in it for her labour, This she accepted, so I came away to settle down and get better, thinking that little Tony was now settled and I would not have the same worry as I had before of him being tied down and watched about. But she was very particular, in the home, and I guessed that she turned out to be the same as the other one. However, she wrote me a letter after a month and told me what a good little soul Tony was and what clean ways he had, but at the same time referring to not wanting him any longer. I never took no notice and a fortnight after I got a letter from her saying she had turned him over to a nursery with the feeble excuse that he wetted the bed.

But now when I sit and think of the different places he has been to and the way he has been treated, Mrs. B. has done me a good turn in the long run by getting Tony into your Nursery; now he can play with other children and do just as he pleases without somebody continually saying, "Don't do this and that." So I hope he will soon get back to his jolly carefree ways, as I am sure he will do by the description my sister gave me of the Nursery. Well, Matron, I hope I have not bored you stiff with this long letter, but I have described to you as best I can as to where Tony has been since my illness. . . .

10

Monthly Report
November, 1941

STATISTICS

The number of children under our care has been raised to 90. Among the new admittances are 3 newborn babies, one of them, Iris, accompanied by her mother, who will stay with us and nurse her. The other two mothers were, to our great regret, unable to come. One of them, Violet's mother, is a bad case of tuberculosis who had to be separated from her child and sent to a sanitarium as quickly as possible. The other one, Glen's mother, could not be persuaded to stay, but wanted to return to her work as bus conductress at the earliest possible moment. She planned to come at least once a day after her working shift and give one breast feeding to the baby. We warned her that she would be unable to carry the double load of feeding and that kind of work in winter weather. She was full of confidence and optimism when she left the baby with us. We began to worry when she did not reappear for several days. We then learned that she had collapsed in a friend's house with a severe hemorrhage from which she is now recovering.

Another newcomer is Ben, 2 months old, one of a pair of twins, whose sister died soon after birth in the hospital. He had a birth weight of 4 lbs., weighed 6 lbs. 7 oz. at the time of admittance, and still looks smaller, thinner, and more delicate than the newborn babies with whom he shares a room.

Another newcomer is Ruth, aged 16 months. Her admission is a good example of the almost insurmountable difficulties which crop up in some cases. Ruth's mother had applied and received our promise for the admission of her child before the Babies' Center had ever been opened. But we were unable to fulfill our promise and take the child because the institution for the poor, where she then lived, was under quarantine for infectious diseases. This quarantine seemed unending so that, after a long period of waiting, we found a lady in Hampstead who was willing to take care of the child for a few weeks in her own home until our doctor was satisfied that the danger of infection was past. The child was taken there, but within a day she showed all symptoms of whooping cough so far advanced that they really should have been apparent to the institution authorities. Ruth was removed to a local fever hospital with great inconvenience to the foster mother. When at last she was pronounced fit to be released from the hospital again, we were once more faced with the task of finding a temporary foster home to avoid infection to be brought from the fever hospital to our babies. The former foster mother was unable to receive the child again.

We now tried the following: (1) Invalid Children's Aid Association, Hampstead Branch, who put us on to (2) Invalid Children's Aid Association, Head Office, Westminster; they had no foster mothers and their homes, like ours, do not take children who might bring infection; they put us on to (3) Office of the Hampstead Medical Officer of Health; they were unable to help because the child's mother did not live in Hampstead; they suggested it would be useless to try the Department of the Medical Officer in Westminster, where the mother lives, as in that district foster mothers are not encouraged since it is a danger area. They referred us to (4) District Rescue Workers, Willesden, who had no free foster parents; they passed us on to (5) Infant Protection Officer, Willesden Health Center, who also was unable to help. That exhausted official sources, short of the Relieving Officer, who could only have sent the child to an institution of the type from which it had originally been so difficult to get free of quarantine.

In the end, when everything seemed quite hopeless, friends who had heard about our efforts suddenly offered privately to receive the child. Ruth stayed with them for a few weeks, got the most wonderful care and attention, and has now safely arrived in our house. Her waiting period before admittance extended over 5 months.

TROUBLES

Our troubles and worries during this month were purely concerned with illnesses.

In the Babies' Center we had an influenza infection

which on the whole was slight but took on a more disagreeable form in one or two children from each department.

Shirley (3 years) woke suddenly one night with bad coughing attacks, gasping for air and quite hoarse. She had a typical attack of pseudo croup. She was kept in a steam tent all day and night and regained her normal health after a few days.

Maurice (16 months) developed pneumonia with evening temperatures as high as 105. He was treated in the usual ways, with the addition of Prontosil and Coramine drops. He is now well on the way to recovery and kept out in his pram in the garden whenever there is the slightest chance of the sun appearing.

Edith (6 months) also developed slight symptoms of pneumonia, but improved very quickly and has completely recovered.

Earl (6 months) was the child about whom we worried most. Usually a serene and happy baby who always liked his food and gained steadily, he suddenly started projectile vomiting. In two days he presented the typical appearance of a slight parenteral intoxication, dehydration, sunk fontanel, dry mouth; as a further symptom he started to shake his head in an automatic manner. In spite of this state he never stopped to react to outward stimuli; he followed the light with his eyes, but when at his worst was too weak to turn his head toward the light. We had an anxious time with him. He had his stomach washed out, as well as rectal feedings, tube feedings, and at other times was fed once or twice hourly. He was given all the extra breast milk available in the house, enriched with glucose. He slowly improved after two weeks.

The Country House in the meantime went in for infectious diseases. Teddy (2½ years) developed mumps, and Isabel (4½) followed after Teddy had recovered. The isolation of these two children was still in the center of our interest when suddenly three others came down with scarlet fever. They in their turn were isolated when two members of the staff (one in the kitchen and a boy helper of 17 years) also came down with it. Since then one more child has followed suit.

Since our facilities for isolation are satisfactory, we sent only the 17-year-old boy to the hospital and established two isolation rooms at one end of the house. Luckily, the cases are extremely light ones and so far no complications have appeared.

Life in the Country House has of course been completely changed by these events. The house is under quarantine, which means that our bigger children cannot go to school (which rather pleases them), the parents' visits are forbidden (which is a source of great regret to everybody), and the members of the staff cannot spend their free days in London as usual, but really live the life of prisoners of war. Two extra nurses have been sent out for reinforcement from the Babies' Center, and since the local charwoman and the kitchen help from the village are forbidden to come, everybody has a double share of work. Our doctor now visits the Country House three times weekly and endless numbers of packages and messages go out to comfort the patients and those who are forced to share their isolation. Everybody is reported to be very cheerful.

This influx of illness has only strengthened our desire to erect an extra hospital hut in the garden of the Country House.

NEW VENTURES

Outside Children

The generosity of the Foster Parents has now made it possible to extend some help to children who are not resident with us but whose parents are in some way closely connected with our houses. These children can receive help according to their needs, as, for instance, extra clothing, meals, or help for schooling. Some of them will spend part of the day in our house as day children.

Training Scheme

We have at the moment about twenty young girls ranging in age from 16 to 21 years working for us in our houses. Apart from the very youngest, they have all had some training as nurses, baby nurses, or nursery school teachers, partly on the continent and partly in England. To give a sounder foundation of some common knowledge to our work with the children, we have now decided to start out on a purely private and unofficial training scheme of our own. This training scheme is strictly limited in several directions.

(a) We can give no certificate at the end, apart from a private letter of recommendation in cases where the young worker has been found satisfactory.

(b) We spend no money on our training scheme, just as we demand no fees for our tuition.

(c) We are not able to teach everything that the curriculum of a children's nurse or nursery school teacher should include; we simply utilize whatever knowledge and experience we find among the older members of the staff to teach the younger ones. Our task is very much facilitated by the fact that nearly all our heads of departments have in their former professional life taught either at a university, a training college, or welfare institutions.

(d) The hours used for theoretical instruction were formerly rest hours for the staff which the girls were glad to give up for the purpose of learning. The practical instructions form part of the regular working day. Each girl is supposed to spend a fixed time (at least 3 months) in each department (babies, junior toddlers, nursery, sickroom). Milk kitchen, shelter duty, kitchen, and household come in for slightly shorter periods of duty. The whole training is supposed to last for the duration of the war.

(e) The following is the timetable of this training scheme which already has begun to function during November:

PRELIMINARY NOTICE OF THE ARRANGEMENTS FOR THE LECTURES FOR ASSISTANTS AND TRAINEES

1. The Body of the Child in Health and in Sickness
   A course of 30 lectures, to be held on Mondays, 2:15-3:15 P.M.
   a. Anatomy
   b. First aid
   c. Nutrition
   d. Hygiene
   e. Children's diseases

   Commencing November 17, 1941

2. Mental Development
   A course of 16 lectures, to be held on Wednesdays, 2:15-3:15 P.M.
   a. Development of the senses
   b. Intellectual development
   c. First toys
   d. An idea of testing

   Commencing November 19, 1941
3. Emotional and Instinctual Development
   a. An introductory course
   b. Reading seminar

   Commencing October 27, 1941
4. General Management
   A course of 4 lectures, to be given on Fridays, 2:15-3:15 P.M.
   a. Budget
   b. Finance
   c. The building up of an institution

   Commencing November 21, 1941
5. Cooking
6. Sewing
   Two courses of 2-hour periods to alternate on Fridays after Course 4 at 2 P.M.
   a. Diet
   b. Practical cooking (at Wedderburn Road)
   c. Practical sewing
7. Gymnastics
   Practical demonstrations for the trainees of the respective departments.
   a. Baby gymnastics (Mondays and Thursdays, 4:30-5:00 P.M.)
   b. Gymnastics with the senior toddlers (Tuesdays and Saturdays, 11 A.M.)

c. Gymnastics with the junior toddlers (Thursdays, 11 A.M.)

Commencing November 17, 1941

8. Practical Tuition in the Montessori Method
Daily work with the biggest toddlers (9-11 A.M.)

PROBLEMS

On October 29th a Conference on the question of War-Time Nurseries was arranged for London and the Home Counties by The Nursery School Association of Great Britain and the National Society of Day Nurseries under the chairmanship of Lord Horder. On the basis of her work in the Hampstead Nursery Anna Freud was asked to speak in the discussion on the subject of "The Need of the Small Child to Be Mothered." Since the problem discussed in this 10 minutes' contribution is one of the main questions around which our nursery work is centered, we insert this contribution in its original form. The same subject was afterward discussed in two staff meetings and illustrated by various examples from our daily work.

THE NEED OF THE SMALL CHILD TO BE MOTHERED

Miss Marriott in her plea for the nursery school as it ought to be has used one definition which explains why wartime nurseries are so difficult to run, why so much more thought, energy, and money have to be spent on them than seemed necessary in former times.[1] Nursery

[1] Miss T. Marriott, Organizing Secretary of the Nursery School Association, read a paper on "The Child (2-5) in the Nursery Group."

schools, as Miss Marriott explains, have always been planned as extensions of the home. They provide space where the home is overcrowded, safety where the kitchens or streets are dangerous to play in, toys to be handled where family possessions have to be respected, and attention and interest from the nursery school teacher where mothers are overworked and harassed. This was true for the proletarian nurseries in Central Europe and Russia. In America, on the other hand, where nurseries for the middle classes are no less frequent than elementary schools, they provide the community life for which the child is ready and which the small American middle-class family is unable to give.

In none of these cases were nursery schools meant to substitute for the home, any more than a free milk scheme in school is meant as a substitute for home-cooked meals, than welfare clinics do away with the need for the mother's care or child guidance clinics with the need for educational efforts on the part of parents. All these services were simply extensions of the home, and they worked best when allowed to function each as one link in a chain of public services for child welfare.

We are all conscious of the fact that our present situation is widely different. Families are dissolved, homes hardly recognizable as such, many children scattered in billets, many clinics closed. The nursery schools, where they exist, find themselves suddenly confronted with the task of filling all these gaps; this really means: fulfilling all the functions of child welfare rolled into one. In wartime the nursery, even if not residential, becomes a foster home. Since most children have gone through long waiting periods before admittance to a nursery, they are harmed in some way by the war conditions. This means that the nurseries have to admit children in weakened bodily condition (for instance, shelter sleepers of 12 months' standing); they admit children shocked, not so much by bombing as by shelter life and war conditions in the family. This means that besides their program of ordinary education they have to fulfill the functions of convalescent home and school for problem children. As has been pointed out by several speakers, such tasks can be taken over wherever doctor, psychologist, teacher, and nurse combine forces. It is perhaps not widely enough recognized that the most difficult of these various tasks is to lessen the shock of the breaking up of family life and to find—during absence from the mother—a really good substitute for the mother relationship.

In this respect, too, many nursery schools have tried to do their best. Attempts have been made in many places to break up larger groups into smaller ones; to assign not more children to one worker than would be natural in an ordinary family; to let, as far as possible, the same workers always handle the same children.

I do not think that these attempts, necessary as they are, have been completely successful. In residential nurseries especially, no planning of this kind does away with the fact that workers need off hours during the day, off hours during the week, and have to have the night to themselves. The mother relationship in these early stages, on the other hand, is based on a 24-hour attendance to the child's needs. (Many children of 2 when entering the nursery have never been separated from their mothers for even one day or night.) Moreover workers are not tied to their jobs as mothers are tied to their children. Wherever we base nursery work purely on the personal tie between the individual child and the individual worker, we prepare the way for possible new shocks of separation, i.e., for repeated disappointment.

I have seen other nursery schools despair of these attempts. Instead of creating mother substitutes, they try to lay greater stress on the new and positive elements of nursery life itself. After all, the child gets more companionship and social life than he would at home. And what is lacking in mother's love might be given in a general atmosphere of friendliness and affection, in intelligent care and better educational efforts than the untaught mother would have been capable of.

I have seen astonishingly few attempts made to include the real mothers themselves in the life of the nursery. There are very few nurseries where mothers' visits are welcome, where efforts are made to bring home routine and nursery routine into one line. The danger evidently is not realized that the child who goes back and forth between home and nursery may in the end feel a stranger in both places. Even in residential nurseries no material help is given to make mothers' visits more frequent; or to provide facilities to lengthen the duration of such visits.

I once tried to explain to an official visitor why the nurseries I am connected with spend a good deal of time and planning on parents' visits and gladly suffer every disturbance of routine to make the parents take their share in the life of the nursery. My visitor said that, after all, the children could not have everything. "You can't have it all nice in a war." This evidently means that when the other needs of the child are provided for, love from the parents is a luxury. It is certainly nice for the child to have it. Only wartime has temporarily done away with that luxury as it has with others.

I heard this same remark applied in the last war, referring to material things like sugar, fresh fruit, and butter, of which continental children were deprived. At that time these things were considered luxuries. Since then they have been recognized as body-building materials. Today all efforts are made to provide children with sugar and vitamins; everybody is afraid of the consequences caused by deficiencies in this respect.

At some later date when knowledge about the psychic needs of the child is more widespread, we shall be just as scared at the thought of the deficiencies in the child's psychic development whenever necessary elements like the mother relationship are insufficiently existent in his early childhood. Today an important piece of knowledge is still restricted to a few psychiatrists and psychologists: namely, that certain types of mental maladjustment always coincide with the lack of an ordinary home life in the first five years.

The mother relationship of the small baby is still comparatively simple. The child needs care, i.e., food, warmth, cleanliness, if possible given with affection. The relationship is one-sided: the mother gives and the child receives. The only return made is contentment when the gift is satisfactory. At that time it seems comparatively easy to exchange the person of the mother for another one if this person takes over completely.

But this primitive form of love relationship begins to change before the end of the first year. On the basis of this "stomach love" the child develops a real attachment to the person of the mother. This new love of the child is personal, exclusive, violent, is accompanied by jealousies and disappointments, can turn into hate, and is capable of sacrifice. It is directed first toward the person of the mother, slowly includes the father, takes notice of brothers and sisters in various ways, and leads the child into all the complications of early emotional life.

If at the height of this development the child is suddenly removed from all the people significant for him, he goes through a short period of mourning. All his personal ties are broken. But since he is helpless and absolutely dependent on the strangers who now take care of him, he is thrown back once more into the former primitive stage of stomach love. He reacts once more like a baby; this means: at best to material comforts with material contentment.

The emotional relations of the small child with his parents are important for his development in two main respects:

One is that this childish love is the pattern for all later love relationships. The ability to love—like other human faculties—has to be learned and practiced. Whenever through the absence or the interuption of personal ties this opportunity is missing in childhood, all later relationships will develop weakly, will remain shallow. The opposite of this ability to love is not hate but egoism. The feelings which should go to outside objects remain inside the individual and are used up in self-love—which is not what we want to produce.

The second aspect is equally important. It is this first love of the child which education makes use of. Education demands from the child continual sacrifices. The child has to give up his primitive habits, to become clean, to lessen his aggression, to restrict his greed, to renounce his first sexual wishes. He is ready to pay this price if he gets his parents' love in return. If such love is not available, education either has to threaten or to drill or to bribe—all methods unsatisfactory in their results.

Our educational success in the war nurseries, therefore, will largely depend on the fact whether we can succeed in creating or in conserving for the children their proper emotional relationships with the outside world.

11

Monthly Report
December, 1941

STATISTICS

The number of children under our care has been raised to 100; of these 80 are resident children and 20 are non-resident children who receive regular help from us.

New admissions to the Country House were impossible because of the quarantine. We still have some empty places there which will be filled as soon as conditions permit.

HEALTH REPORT

We are conscious of the fact that during the eleven months of our existence we have been extremely lucky as far as illnesses are concerned. Up to November, 1941 we did not have a single infectious disease in the house. We avoided whooping cough, though at the opening of Netherhall Gardens three children were sent for admission who had typical attacks of coughing immediately after they entered our surgery. We miraculously escaped measles being brought in, though at one time there were many cases in the districts from which our children came. Our skin diseases were restricted to the very disagreeable but comparatively harmless one of impetigo. Scabies once did appear on the horizon. We always knew that this kind of luck was too good to last. As described in Report 10, it ended with the outbreak of scarlet fever in the Country House.

Scarlet Fever

The 4 children's and 2 adult cases last month were followed by 4 more children and 1 more adult case in December. Each case followed the last one after an interval of four to five days. Luckily, all the cases have remained extremely light ones. Most of the children only had temperatures for one day and then felt very well and comfortable in the isolation rooms. They look at the sickroom as a smaller and more intimate nursery where play can go on even more undisturbed and where close friendships are formed from one bed to another. So far no complications of any kind have arisen and those who were the first victims have by now returned to the nursery downstairs after their six weeks of separation. We shall be content if this epidemic finishes soon or at least continues only as it has started: with very little harm to the children and only a great deal of trouble and inconvenience for the staff and the management.

Colds and Influenza

While the scarlet fever we had dreaded remained comparatively harmless in the Country House, Netherhall Gardens was struck by a wave of flu which gave us the most worrying weeks we had ever experienced in the existence of the Hampstead Nursery. Whether it was due to the particular damp November and December days or to the fact that we had lately received some particularly delicate children, the flu spread quickly through the baby departments and affected nearly all the younger babies. Several developed acute pneumonia and two of them were so badly affected in the course of 24 hours that after consultation with the Medical Officer of Hampstead we had to send both to the hospital, where they were kept in an oxygen tent. They were the two small babies admitted last month: Ben, the survivor of a very weak pair of twins, and Glen, a small newborn whose mother could not stay for nursing in spite of our entreaties. Glen died in the hospital to our great sorrow. Ben is still in the hospital and the reports say that he is improving.

In our house both baby rooms took on the aspect of hospital rooms where the children slept in steam tents day and night. Big kettles were continually heated in the milk kitchen and exchanged under the tents every ten minutes. The babies had the usual treatment for pneumonia; Coramine drops were given and some had Prontosil. At the moment nearly all of them are well on the way to recovery, though it is not impossible that there still will be some setbacks.

Accident

Quite unrelated to these events, a tragic accident occurred in one of the families which have been in closest contact with the Hampstead Nursery from the beginning. Billie's father fell from a scaffolding while working and severely injured his spine. He was taken to the hospital where he will have to lie for many months in a plaster cast. We felt this accident to be all the more tragic since Billie's family was one of the very few where the parents had not yet been torn apart by the events of the war. Since we had united all their three children in the Hampstead Nursery (Billie and his sister Mary in the Country House, baby Agnes in Netherhall Garden), the parents had given up shelter sleeping and returned to their little flat. The mother worked in daytime in our milk kitchen, nursed her own baby, and gave as much breast milk as she could spare to others in need of it. The father spent regular nights as a volunteer fire watcher in the nursery. Their family life was intact in this way, a great rarity in wartime, but closely intermixed with the life of the Nursery. Now that the father has been incapacitated, the mother lives and works with us altogether and we try to take care of the children more than ever.

But even in the animal department this last month has not passed without disasters. Of the 50 chickens kept in the Country House, 40 died suddenly one morning. The examination proved that they were poisoned by food which had been transported in sacks formerly used for artificial fertilizer. We are in contact with the firm responsible for the damage and hope to be refunded for the loss. But it is not at all certain that it will be possible to buy good laying hens again at this time of the year. It is particularly unfortunate since this was the permitted way to have more eggs for the children than the rationing scheme allows for.

CHRISTMAS

In Netherhall Gardens the enjoyment of Christmas was greatly dampened by these sad events. Steam tents and Christmas trees stood side by side in the baby rooms. The toddlers, who had nearly all escaped the flu, enjoyed the stockings on their shelter beds and their Christmas party in the nursery.

The Country House, on the other hand, had a most exciting Christmas in spite of the quarantine. There were small parcels from the parents, big parcels from American Foster Parents, and all sorts of toys saved up for this occasion from the toy cupboard of the Foster Parents' office in London. The bigger children got quite confused between their fantasies about Father Christmas and the reality of the American parcel post. They enjoyed all their new things in the best spirits.

PROBLEMS

The Christmas holidays created special opportunities to observe certain facts about the parent-child relationship. Apart from short Sundays and occasional hours during the week, there is very little chance for the parents of the Babies' Center to feel that the children really are still their own. Many of them had therefore planned a long time beforehand to take their children "home" at least for one whole day, some of them for several days at Christmas. In many cases these hopes were disappointed through the illness of the children; in others, the reunion was not as happy as the parents had expected.

Baby Julius's (11 months) parents, for instance, had started planning three months ago to take him home to their room on Christmas day. The father's army leave and the mother's free day from factory work coincided, which was a rare occasion. They had prepared a temporary crib for him and in all ways set the stage for one whole day of family life. When they came to fetch him, they had to be told that he had run a high temperature the day before and though the fever was now down, it would be highly dangerous to take him out of his surroundings, to interrupt his routine, and to subject him to a day's festivities. The father got very angry about it, insisted that no baby could be harmed by being taken home in a pram, and that after all a cold was just a cold. The mother just stood by the crib and cried with disappointment. But when the father, a very young boy soldier, finally stormed out of the house to get a drink, she settled down quite happily and said: "Men never understand such things," and spent the whole day in the Nursery sitting with her baby. The plans for family life were immediately renewed for February 1st, when Julius will have his first birthday. We only hope that nothing will intervene at that time.

The toddlers, on the other hand, went on extensive Christmas leave. Bridget (17 months) was carried home in triumph in a new pink coat and leggings by her parents, both munitions workers in the East End. Though she is the brightest and sunniest child in the nursery, she did not behave very graciously at home. She would not eat, and this disturbed the mother, who had often seen her eat enormous quantities at our place. She even took her to the doctor of the nearest welfare clinic to find out what was the matter. But the doctor said with great insight: "Nothing is the matter. She is only fretting for her nurses and the other children." The mother, who is a specially kindhearted and good-natured woman, said when she brought her back: "I understand Bridget. It is so dull for her at home. There is nothing she can do."

Other mothers reacted to the same experience with less friendliness. When Bill (23 months) went home, he just lay down on the floor quietly, was not interested, and would not play with anything. His mother was greatly worried; but when she brought him back to the Nursery, he rushed around after the toys and was as lively as ever. She looked at him and said: "He just cheated us."

Martin (2 years, 1 month), who is the greatest eater in the toddler's room, would not take any food at home.

Nick's (2½ years) mother reported that she had to get up at 4 o'clock in the morning to make toast for him because he said continuously and montonously, "I want my toast, I want my toast, I want my toast."

Keith (3 years) was quite content with his mother for one day. He got restless the next morning, seemed more and more disturbed in the course of the day, and then, toward evening, said very decidedly: "And now I want to go home again to my Nelsa [Ilse, the Nursery Superintendent] and my nice bath" (the kitchen sinks, which we had put in as children's bathtubs and in which they love to sit and splash in safety).

It is naturally a bitter experience for the mothers that

already after half a year's absence these small children shift their affections and their loyalties, call the Nursery their home, and behave as strangers or as guests with their own parents. We try to help this situation to the best of our ability by putting no restrictions on the visits of the parents. Still, nothing can alter the fact that children of this age can feel fully at home in only one place and will turn their affection to the people who handle them day by day. It is easier for the mother to maintain her relationship to the child unbroken than it is for the child to do the same. But just because the mother's relationship remains more or less unaltered and what is half a lifetime to the baby is only half a year to her, the mothers cannot experience this situation without bitterness. They naturally think that it is the material comforts which the Nursery has to offer, the choice of toys, the good food, the "nice bath," which have stolen the affection of the children from them. In reality it is the extreme material and emotional dependence of the small child that forces him to form such strong ties with his immediate surroundings. For this very reason we may expect many difficult situations to arise at the end of the war when all these children are supposed to return home again.

The state of affairs with the bigger children in the Country House is quite different. Now that the quarantine has made the visits of parents impossible, we have the opportunity to see the children under conditions which more closely resemble those of other children in evacuation. There are still some differences, of course. It is astonishing that even the smaller children understand the reason why the parents have stopped coming. We encourage letters from both sides, small parcels are sent, and news is taken back and forth when the doctor makes her regular visits. We find that at this distance the relation to the absent parents is greatly idealized. Their letters are carried around and have to be read to the children innumerable times. Children who do not receive letters often get sulky and depressed.

It is interesting to note that the affection for the parents is transferred in many cases to material objects which have come as presents from the parents. Hilda (2 years, 10 months) had received a green knitted dress from her mother and went on wearing it with the greatest delight. When the dress was dirty and supposed to go to the laundry, she was upset and distressed and refused to be comforted. (In the same manner a little toddler in Netherhall Gardens had to go to bed in high black shoes which his mother had brought him that day as a present.) Toys enjoy an entirely different valuation according to whether they are given by the Nursery or by the parents. Rosette (5 years) possesses a collection of tiny toys from her mother which she carries about, shows to everybody, and calls "my very own." Dolls given by a parent are respected by everybody as private property; dolls given by the Nursery even to individual children are freely shared with everybody. Only sweets, even when sent by the parents, are shared out immediately as a matter of pride and principle. Katrina (7 years), who takes very little care of her clothes otherwise, looks at a little skirt made for her by her mother and says: "I won't wear it to school. Only for best."

This transference of affection from the parents to their presents can sometimes go quite beyond the limits of normal reactions. Georgie (4 years), for instance, who has never overcome the shock of separation from his mother, who is in a hospital with a bad case of tuberculosis, and from his father, who is a sailor on the ocean, has developed a craze for parcels since parcels are the one connecting link between him and his absent mother. He does not care about the contents, he just demands that all his old toys are wrapped up as parcels and given to him to open. As soon as he has opened them, he wants them wrapped up again. His continual and never satisfied wish to return to his mother cannot express itself in words. It has disappeared from consciousness and instead expresses itself in this compulsive wish to open parcels.

We are glad to report that Billie, who at one time could not be separated from his mother for one day without producing symptoms, is now behaving perfectly normally. He shows no bad effects of the separation, though it has by now lasted more than two months.

12

Annual Report January, 1942

Summary of First Year's Work

STATISTICS

To sum up our situation at the end of the first year of work, we can say the following:

Age of Resident Children on Admission

1–4 weeks	7
1–6 months	24
6–12 months	7
1–2 years	25
2–3 years	17
3–5 years	17
5–10 years	6
Total	103

This Report has previously been published in various forms (see Publishing History, pp. xxvii-xxviii).

Family Situation of Resident Children

OCCUPATION OF PARENTS

The fathers of 36 children and the mothers of 2 children are serving in the armed forces. The fathers of 25 children and the mothers of 27 are engaged in war work in munitions factories, etc.; 31 children still have fathers or mothers in civilian occupations, mostly laborers in the building and other trades, railway porters, lorry drivers, etc.; 6 mothers (of 11 children) are working in our own households; 4 of them at the same time nurse their own babies.

ILLNESS OF PARENTS

The mothers of 4 children are bad cases of tuberculosis and will have to remain in the hospital for many months; 1 father of 3 children is in a hospital after a bad accident at work; 1 father, a discharged soldier, is in a mental hospital with an anxiety state relating to the war; 1 mother suffers from an agoraphobia as a result of bombing; and 1 mother is in an asylum with an acute psychosis, following the double shock of being bombed and losing her husband in an air raid.

DEATHS OF PARENTS

The father of 1 child was killed in an accident; 1 father committed suicide during the war; 7 children (three families) lost their fathers as a direct result of bombing; 1 was killed while on duty as a fire watcher, 1 while on duty as a stretcher bearer, 1 while continuing work during an air raid. There are no children under our care who have lost both parents, though the one mentioned whose father was killed and whose mother is insane is for practical purposes in the position of an orphan.

War Experiences

BOMBING

All the children who were already alive during the period of the so-called blitz (that is, all those over 16 months of age) have gone through a long experience of air raids. The houses of 15 children were actually destroyed or badly damaged by bombing. Two little sisters were bombed three times in succession in houses to which they had been evacuated with their mother. During one of these experiences they were buried under the debris but remained unharmed. The blasting of houses, which was very widespread in the districts of London from which our children are drawn, is therefore not enumerated separately. One child (2½ years) had lived in perpetual blackout since the blasting.

With regard to the babies, the mothers' pregnancies were affected by bombing incidents in 14 cases. One mother was in a building which suffered a direct hit, and she lost one of her older children in consequence of it. Two mothers had bad falls during their pregnancies while running to the shelter in the blackout. One mother worked in a house where a bomb fell in the yard during a daylight raid; she lost consciousness and was taken to a hospital, where the baby was born immediately afterward 2 months premature. Two mothers were bombed out in the seventh month of their pregnancies; two in their ninth month. One mother was bombed out of a home three times during the later part of her pregnancy, and a fourth time immediately after the birth of a very miserable baby. One baby was bombed in the hospital two days after birth but remained unhurt. Several mothers lay in maternity hospitals which were partly bombed or blasted.

SHELTER SLEEPING

Thirty-five children were regular shelter sleepers before they came to us. The shelters used were the Tilbury shelter (Commercial Road, E.1, where as many as 8,000 people slept during the blitz), and some of the Tube stations, for instance, Oxford Circus, Piccadilly Circus, and Paddington Station. Some of the pregnant mothers slept in these shelters up to the last night before the birth and returned to the same places 10 days later with their newborn babies. All other children slept in their own homes, either in Anderson shelters, on ground floors, in basements, or under the stairs.

EVACUATION

Twenty-six children had been evacuated before they came to us—10 of them together with their mothers. These 8 mothers had felt certain in the beginning that it was their duty to leave London with their children. Afterward they found it impossible to adhere to their original decision.

1 mother was torn between the conflicting duties of looking after the child and after her husband. She left London with her boy of 2 when he fell ill with bronchitis in their blasted house; she returned to London with the child when the husband had a breakdown and the doctor urged her to return.

1 mother returned so as not to leave her husband alone in London where he did war work. She risked taking her delicate boy of 3 back to the shelters rather than breaking up her married life for an indefinite period of time.

1 mother with a newborn baby had gone into service in the country as a means of evacuation. She found herself underpaid and overworked, lost her milk as a result of the situation, and returned to London with the baby.

3 mothers with husbands in the army returned for war work to supplement the army allowance with their earnings.

1 mother of 2 children complained about an intolerable situation in the billet. Her children were considered a nuisance, had to be hushed and quieted continuously, and were not allowed in the garden even in the hottest summer weather. The atmosphere of strife and quarrel became equally impossible for householder and billeted mother.

1 mother proved to be completely unbilletable. She was ill with venereal disease, told everybody about it, but omitted to say that she had received hospital treatment and therefore was not as infectious as she led people to believe. She and her boy of 4 were turned out of one billet after the other.

The 16 unattended children returned home for a whole series of reasons:

5 billets were simply unsympathetic and either unwilling or unable to cope with the difficulties of the children.

4 billets had to be left because of outward circumstances such as illness, operation, confinement of the householder.
3 billets were unable to give the children proper conditions for healthy bodily development.
3 children were sent back because of temper tantrums, 1 of them because he became destructive in these states,
1 child changed hands several times because of bed wetting.
1 child was sent home because of an abnormal state of "fretting" for his mother.

In all these cases the permanent return of the children to their former homes proved impracticable, either because of the state of the buildings or because of the occupation of the mother. Return to London was therefore quickly followed by "re-evacuation" at least as far as Hampstead.

Discharged Children

A total of 108 children stayed permanently under our care as residents or nonresidents; 30 children left us during the year 1941 at various times and for the following reasons:

9 were temporary cases, taken as an emergency measure while their mothers were in the hospital either for childbirth or for operations; they returned home as soon as their mothers were able to do housework again.
7 were temporary cases, left with us while their mothers searched for private billets in the country; they were evacuated as soon as a billet was found.
2 were legally adopted and went to their new homes from us.

1 child was taken home after a week's trial because her mother was frightened about her abnormal state of homesickness. Her father had recently entered a mental hospital as a borderline case, so that her mother had added reason to be anxious about her.

3 children were taken to hospitals with severe infantile pneumonia. Two of them died subsequently.

8 cases (6 families) were failures in the sense that the relationship to the mothers did not continue on a smooth footing. After several months of friendly relations during which the children had done specially well, the mothers decided on the spur of the moment to "make a change." In one case this was due to the return of the father from the army; in another case to jealousy over the possession of the baby.

SURVEY OF THE FOOD SITUATION

Gradual Development of Food Restrictions

The 13 months of our existence are also the decisive months for changes in the food situation. During this period buying on the free market has given way almost completely to rationed supply and Government-controlled prices. This switchover from one method of catering to another did not turn out to be as difficult in practice as it sounds in theory. All the changes were gradual and there was always time to get fully used to one stage of development before the next one was reached.[1]

[1] *December, 1940* (opening): Food rationing already introduced but concerns only butter, margarine, cooking fats, sugar, tea, bacon, meat. It is still easy to obtain supplies to stock the larder.

Preferential Treatment for Children under 5

Compared with the more difficult food situation of single adults and of private households, a children's institution is distinctly favored. Under a scheme of the Ministry of Health, children under 2 receive cod-liver oil, fruit juice, and fruit purée (black currant) free of charge. They have priority for obtaining essential foods, and receive larger rations of others than adults. There even exists a priority scheme for supply of unrationed foods by which the Nursery benefits. This concerns articles like biscuits, cake, and flour confectionery, cocoa powder, and starch food powders.

Oranges: Whenever they are on the market, children under 6 have priority in obtaining them.
Milk: Children get 1 pint daily, compared with 2 pints weekly for adult people.
Eggs: Children get four times as many as adults; the actual number depends on the supplies. The usual ration at the moment is 2½ per child per week.

Consequences for the Nursery Diet

Cooking in a war nursery like ours has to adapt itself to certain unalterable facts. The diet will necessarily have to

---

Fresh and dried fruit, milk, cream, eggs, cereals, jams, honey, fish can be supplied whenever wanted.
 January, 1941: Cheese and jam are rationed.
 June, 1941: Eggs rationed. Chocolate disappears slowly.
 September, 1941: Milk rationing comes into operation. Cream and cream cheese have disappeared.
 December, 1941: Points rationing is introduced for tinned foods.
 January, 1942: Chocolate prices are officially controlled.

be restricted since certain kinds of foods are not available. Other foods have to be stretched or replaced by artificial substitutes which in peacetime were banned from children's diets. Further kinds of food are still to be had but, in comparison with peacetime, are restricted according to quantity and to variety. In spite of all these facts, it is perfectly possible to plan and to provide well-balanced, adequate, and attractive meals. The weight charts prove that there is certainly no scarcity in nourishing food. The children eat with pleasure, and there is so far no need to refuse them second, third, and even fourth helpings.

Foods Which Have Disappeared

Cream, creamy cheese, vegetable oil, vegetable fats, all early fresh vegetables, nuts, almonds, prunes, dates, figs, apricots (dried and fresh), bananas, grapefruit, lemons.

Specimen Menus

Breakfast: Porridge or corn flakes with milk and sugar; milk or cocoa. Buttered toast and bread. Honey or marmalade.

Lunch: Vegetables (spinach or carrots or tomato sauce or peas) and potatoes. Twice weekly meat, sometimes fish. Sweet (either stewed apples or rhubarb with custard, sometimes tinned fruit with custard, blancmange, jelly with sponge cake or trifle).

High Tea: Milk pudding (rice or semolina) with chocolate or fruit juice. Or vegetable soup or scrambled eggs (once weekly). Buttered toast and bread. Some milk or cocoa. Some apples or cake.

American Parcels

Certain foods which are either very difficult or impossible to obtain in England are still sent to the Nursery in parcels from America which arrive either through the Foster Parents' Plan or sometimes through the Red Cross. These parcels mostly contain chocolate, sweets, dried fruit, marmalade, and jam. These foods are so precious that we rarely use them in the ordinary diet. They are kept for children in the sickrooms, the only ones whose appetites need special tempting. And they are further given out to our nonresident children who lack the balanced diet of the Nursery and are, for the most part, badly undernourished.

Conclusions

There is, of course, a certain fallacy contained in the attempt to offset peace and war conditions in the feeding of our children against each other. Most of the children who live in our Nursery have never known a proper diet in peacetime. A large proportion of our cases come from families where the budget did not allow much money for food, where full meals were rare, and where fish and chips, bread and margarine played a large part in the feeding. In some instances this economic situation was complicated by neglect or inefficiency of the mother; for example, one child had never tasted solid, cooked food when he entered the Nursery at the age of nearly 2. His mother had found it simpler to give him nothing but a bottle several times a day.

For all children of this type war and peace conditions

are reversed as far as their food situation is concerned. They have lived under serious food restrictions at a time when there was plenty to be had, and they have entered into a world full of food for them at a time when the world around them had less than it has had before.

MEDICAL REPORT

It is still too early for official surveys to show whether the health of London children has been affected by the war conditions or whether the provisions made for them (preferential treatment in rationing, medical supervision in shelters, evacuation to the country) have proved sufficient to safeguard them against the worst dangers. Observations on a small scale like ours tend to lead to most conflicting impressions.

Sleep

Certain shelter sleepers whom we admitted showed all the typical signs of restlessness at night, disturbed sleep, and pallor as a consequence of lack of fresh air, many hours spent underground, and continual interruption of sleep by the noise of trains. In contrast to those cases, we admitted shelter sleepers who looked rosy, healthy, well rounded, and showed no disturbance of sleep, though they had spent all the nights of their short lives (several weeks to 10 months) underground. From the observations made on our children we would conclude that the big East End shelters, in spite of their mass population, are less harmful in their effects on sleep itself than the Tube stations, with their noise of trains. Added to this is the fact that in the former children can be settled down to sleep at earlier hours.

Moreover, all the inhabitants there now sleep in bunks, whereas in the Tubes the bunks provided are so narrow that mothers with small children invariably sleep on the stone floor of the platform.

Weight

The weight chart attached to this medical report shows that the state of nourishment of the children is not a direct result of food scarcity or food rationing. Their considerable gain in weight in their first month of Nursery life proves that they arrived in a state of undernourishment.[2] Their

[2] Examples of gain in weight during the first month in the Hampstead Nursery:

	Entrance	End of the first Month	Gain
TODDLERS (1-2 years)			
Robert	22 lb. 4 oz.	28 lb. 5 oz.	1 lb. 1 oz.
Julia	19 " 12 "	20 " 14 "	1 " 2 "
Katie	18 " 15 "	20 " 7 "	1 " 8 "
Paul	19 " 12 "	21 " 4 "	1 " 8 "
Pauline	23 " 4 "	25 " 1 "	1 " 13 "
Susie	20 " 11 "	22 " 11 "	2 " 0 "
Jane	31 " 0 "	33 " 11 "	2 " 11 "
CHILDREN (2-5 years)			
Janet	33 lb. 14 oz.	35 lb. 3 oz.	1 lb. 5 oz.
Jim	38 " 8 "	40 " 2 "	1 " 10 "
Sally	27 " 13 "	29 " 11 "	1 " 14 "
Mary	24 " 10 "	26 " 10 "	2 " 0 "
Phyllis	40 " 11 "	42 " 11 "	2 " 0 "
Bobbie	38 " 4 "	40 " 8 "	2 " 4 "
Rodney	31 " 14 "	34 " 2 "	2 " 4 "
Billie	30 " 6 "	33 " 7 "	3 " 1 "
Peggie (6 yrs. 4 mths.)	45 " 9 "	47 " 1 "	1 " 8 "
Marion (9 yrs. 8 mths.)	65 " 12 "	69 " 3 "	3 " 7 "

rations were the same at home as they are with us. But while the Nursery, as one part of its duties, plans proper meals on the basis of these rations, it seems impossible to do the same at home. Mothers who stay at home and live on the army allowance have time for cooking but little money to spend on food, while mothers who go out to war work earn enough money but have little time to spend on shopping and cooking.

Respiratory Diseases

Practically all the children of all age groups who arrived last January and February had recently overcome attacks of bronchial pneumonia, which we at the time ascribed to the unhygienic conditions in houses which had suffered from the blast, where pipes had burst, and where windowpanes were mostly absent. To our regret, a similar wave of influenzal pneumonias repeated itself this year, though the children certainly lived under hygienic conditions. This time, of course, the illness may have been rendered worse by the aggregation of a large number of children of young age, an age which is especially susceptible to this disease. That age played the largest part is shown by the fact that, while all the babies got bronchitis, and some developed pneumonias, the toddlers were affected in a much lesser degree, and the bigger children (2 to 4) mostly escaped with simple colds.

Infection

Children's diseases, which had been the dread of wartime residential nurseries from the beginning, certainly did not come up to expectations. Two cases of mumps and a mild epidemic of scarlet fever was all we had to deal with during the year. There was certainly no aggravation of disease through war conditions, with the only exception of impetigo, which ran its course through our houses as it did through nearly all the wartime nurseries. In spite of all precautions taken, two thirds of our bigger children were affected. This time it was the baby rooms which were exempt.

Spread of Infection

Again, the spreading of infection occurred in a manner which is difficult to account for. The house which seems most exposed to the danger of illness being brought in from outside is Netherhall Gardens, with its 50 children. There are no restrictions on visiting; fathers on leave come in from their army camps or billets; mothers, brothers, and sisters visit from the East End. Children are occasionally taken home for weekends (though not to shelters). Numbers of interested visitors wander in and out. In spite of all these factors the only epidemics in Netherhall Gardens were impetigo during the summer and the wave of flu around Christmas. The country house, on the other hand, which is most isolated and through difficulties of transport receives visitors only on given days, had mumps and scarlet fever which we were unable to trace to their sources. The strictness of visiting rules seems to bear little relation to the occurrence of illness.

Vermin

There is some fight against lice going on continuously. They are brought in partly by day children and partly by visiting mothers. This is hardly due to war conditions, though it may be slightly aggravated by communal shelter sleeping.

Medical Treatment

A medical inspection of the children is carried out daily; weights are taken weekly, with the bigger children monthly. Visiting and day children are inspected by the doctor or the sick nurse before mixing with the others.

All medical treatment is given in the house. The cases of mumps and scarlet fever were not sent to the hospital but nursed in a ward of the Country House which lent itself to isolation. Only the three worst cases of baby pneumonia had to be sent to hospitals.

All children (except babies) are inoculated against diptheria.

Sunray treatment is given to children with rickets, with skin trouble, and to all those otherwise in need of it.

SURVEY OF PSYCHOLOGICAL REACTIONS

The figures given in the previous surveys show that all our bigger children have had their fair share of war experiences. All of them have witnessed the air raids either in London or in the provinces. A large percentage of them has seen their houses destroyed or damaged. All of them have seen their family life dissolved, whether by separation from or by death of the father. All of them are separated from their mothers and have entered community life at an age which is not usually considered ripe for it. The following questions arise:

Which part do these experiences play in the psychological life of the individual child?

How far does the child acquire understanding of what is going on around him?

How does he react emotionally?

How far is his anxiety aroused?

What normal or abnormal outlets will he find to deal with these experiences which are thrust on him?

The Child's Understanding of the Situation

It can be safely said that all the children who were over 2 years at the time of the London blitz have acquired knowledge of the significance of air raids. They all recognize the noise of flying airplanes; they distinguish vaguely between the sounds of falling bombs and antiaircraft guns. They realize that the house will fall down when bombed and that people are often killed or hurt in falling houses. They know that fires can be started by incendiaries and that roads are often blocked as a result of bombing. They fully understand the significance of taking shelter. Some children who have lived in deep shelters will even judge the safety of a shelter according to its depth under the earth. The necessity to make them familiar with their gas masks may give them some ideas about a gas attack, though we have never met a child for whom this particular danger had any real meaning.

The children seem to have no difficulty in understanding what is meant when their fathers join the Forces. We often overhear conversations between children in which they compare their fathers' military ranks and duties. A child whose father is in the navy or air force, for instance, will be offended if somebody by mistake refers to the father as being "in the army." As far as the reasoning processes of the child are concerned, the absence of the father seems to be accounted for in this manner.

Children are similarly ready to take in knowledge about the various occupations of their mothers, though the constant change of occupation makes this slightly more difficult. Mothers of 3-year-olds will change back and forth between the occupations of railway porter, factory worker, bus conductor, milk-cart driver, etc. They will visit their children in their varying uniforms and will proudly tell them about their new war work until the children are completely confused. Though the children seem proud of their fathers' uniforms, they often seem to resent it and feel very much estranged by their mothers' appearing in such unexpected disguises.

It is still more difficult for all children to get any understanding of the reason why they are being evacuated and cannot stay in the place where their mothers are. In the case of our children, as in the case of many others, this is further aggravated by the fact that they actually did live in London with their mothers during the worst dangers and were sent to the country afterward when London seemed quite peaceful. They reason with some justification that they can live wherever their mothers do and that, if "home" is as much in danger as all that, their mothers should not be there either. (This, of course, concerns the bigger children of 5 or more.)

The understanding of catastrophes like the death of father has little to do with reasoning. In these cases children meet the usual psychological difficulties of grasping the significance of death at such an early age. Their attitude to the happening is completely a matter of emotion.

We may, of course, be often wrong in assuming that

children "understand" the happenings around them. In talking they only use the proper words for them but without the meaning attached. Words like "army," "navy," "air force," may mean to them strange countries to which their fathers have gone. America (for the children the place where all the good things, specially all the parcels, come from) was discovered the other day to mean, to one child at least, "a merry car." The word "bombing" is often used indiscriminately for all manners of destruction of unwanted objects. "London" is the word used for the children's former homes, irrespective of the fact whether the child now lives in Essex or still in Hampstead. Several of our children in Wedderburn Road used to say in talking: "When I was still in London...." And one boy of 4 once explained in a London shop, to the shop assistant's great astonishment: "I used to live in London, but London is all bombed and gone, and all the houses have fallen down." He was unable to realize the fact that the comparatively unbombed street in which he now lived with us was still the same city. "Home" is the place to which all children are determined to return, irrespective of the fact that in most cases they are aware of its destruction. "War" above everything else signifies the period of time for which children have to be separated from their parents.

A striking example of such "misunderstanding" was Janet, a girl of 4½, who, as we thought, had perfectly grasped the meaning of evacuation. She was a thrice-bombed child, lived in Wedderburn Road, and like all the others waited for the opening of our country house. We had carefully explained to all the children that they were being transferred to the country and why. But when at last, after weeks of expectation (because the lease of the country house did not materialize) she stood in our front hall, all dressed and ready, waiting for the American ambulance car to take her out, she exclaimed joyfully: "The war is over and we are going to the country. It has lasted a long time!" The longing for the Country House, which had been in the center of interest for the Nursery children for some weeks, had suddenly got confused in her mind with the more general longing for the end of the war, which would, as all the children firmly believed, take them all back into their former homes and to their parents.

Reaction to Destruction

In this war children are frequently to be found directly on the scenes of battle. Though here in England they are spared the actual horror of seeing people fight around them, they are not spared sights of destruction, death, and injury from air raids. Even when they are removed from the places of the worst danger, there is no certainty, as some of our cases show, that they will not encounter new bombing incidents at places to which they were sent for safety. General sympathy has been aroused by the idea that little children, all innocently, should thus come into close contact with the horrors of the war. It is this situation which led many people to expect that children would receive traumatic shocks from air raids and would develop abnormal reactions very similar to the traumatic or war neuroses of soldiers in the last war.

We can only describe our observations on the basis of our own case material, which excludes children who have received severe bodily injuries in air raids, though, as mentioned previously, it does not exclude children who have been bombed repeatedly and partly buried in debris. So far as we can notice there were no signs of traumatic shock to be observed in these children. If these bombing incidents occur when small children are in the care either of their own mothers or a familiar mother substitute, they do not seem to be particularly affected by them. Their experience remains an accident, in line with other accidents of childhood. This observation is borne out by the reports of nurses or social workers in London County Council Rest Centers where children used to arrive, usually in the middle of the night, straight from their bombed houses. They also found that children who arrived together with their own families showed little excitement and no undue disturbance. They slept and ate normally and played with whatever toys they had rescued or which might be provided. It is a widely different matter when children during an experience of this kind are separated from or even lose their parents.

It is a common misunderstanding of the child's nature which leads people to suppose that children will be saddened by the sight of destruction and aggression. When children between the age of 1 and 2 years are put together in a playpen, they will bite each other, pull each other's hair, and steal each other's toys without regard for the other child's unhappiness. They are passing through a stage of development where destruction and aggression play one of the leading parts. If we observe young children at play, we notice that they will destroy their toys, pull off the arms and legs of their dolls or soldiers, puncture their balls, smash whatever is breakable, and will mind only the result because complete destruction of the toy blocks further play. The more their strength and independence are growing, the more they will have to be watched so as not to create too much damage, not to hurt each other or those weaker than themselves. We often say, half-jokingly, that there is continual war raging in a nursery. We mean by this that at this time of life destructive and aggressive impulses are still at work in children in a manner in which they recur in adults only when they are let loose for the purposes of war.

It is one of the recognized aims of education to deal with the aggressiveness of the child's nature, i.e., in the course of the first 4 or 5 years to change the child's own attitude toward these impulses in himself. The wish to hurt people and later the wish to destroy objects undergo all sorts of changes. They are usually first restricted, then suppressed by commands and prohibitions; a little later they are repressed, which means that they disappear from the child's consciousness. The child does not dare anymore to have knowledge of these wishes. There is always the danger that they might return from the unconscious; therefore, all sorts of protections are built up against them: the cruel child develops pity, the destructive child will become hesitant and overcareful. If education is handled intelligently, the main part of these aggressive impulses will be directed away from their primitive aim of doing harm to somebody or something, and will be used to fight the difficulties of the outer world—to accomplish tasks of all kinds, to measure one's strength in competition, and to use it generally to "do good" instead of "being bad" as the original impulse demanded.

In the light of these considerations it is easier to determine what the present war conditions, with their incidents of wholesale destruction, may do to a child. Instead of turning away from them in instinctive horror, as people seem to expect, the child may turn toward them with primitive excitement. The real danger is not that the child, caught up all innocently in the whirlpool of the war, will be shocked into illness. The danger lies in the fact that the destruction raging in the outer world may meet the very real aggressiveness which rages in the inside of the child. At the age when education should start to deal with these impulses, confirmation should not be given from the outside world that the same impulses are uppermost in other people. Children will play joyfully on bombed sites and around bomb craters with blasted bits of furniture, and throw bricks from crumbled walls at each other. But it becomes impossible to educate them toward a repression of, or a reaction against, destruction while they are doing so. After their first years of life they fight against their own wishes to do away with people of whom they are jealous, who disturb or disappoint them, or who offend their childish feelings in some other way. It must be very difficult for them to accomplish this task of fighting their own death wishes when, at the same time, people are killed and hurt every day around them. Children have to be safeguarded against the primitive horrors of the war, not because horrors and atrocities are so strange to them, but because we want them at this decisive stage of their development to overcome and estrange themselves from the primitive and atrocious wishes of their own infantile nature.

Five Types of Air Raid Anxiety

What is true about the child's attitude to destruction applies in a certain measure to the subject of anxiety. Children are, of course, afraid of air raids, but their fear is neither as universal nor as overwhelming as has been expected. An explanation is required as to why it is present in some cases, absent in others, comparatively mild in most, and rather violent in certain types of children.

It will be easier to answer these practical questions if we draw on our theoretical knowledge about the motives for fear and anxiety reactions in human beings. We have learned that there are three main reasons for the development of fear reactions:

1. An individual is afraid quite naturally and sensibly when there is some real danger present in the outside world which threatens either his safety or his whole existence. His fear will be all the greater the more he knows about the seriousness of the danger. His fear will urge him to adopt precautionary measures. Under its influence he will either fight it or, if that is impossible, try to escape from it. Only when the danger is of overwhelming extent and suddenness will he be shocked and paralyzed into inaction.

This "real anxiety" plays its part in the way in which children are afraid of air raids. They fear them as far as they can understand what is happening. As described above, they have, in spite of their youth, acquired a certain degree of knowledge of this new danger. But it would be a mistake to overrate this understanding and, consequently, to overrate the amount or the permanency of this real fear of air raids. Knowledge and reason play only a limited part in a child's life. His interest quickly turns away from the real things in the outer world, especially when they are unpleasant, and reverts back to his own childish interests, to his toys, his games, and his fantasies. The danger in the outer world which he recognizes at one moment and to which he responds with fear is put aside in another moment. Precautions are not kept up, and the fear gives way to an attitude of utter disregard.

There was an incident observed by one of our colleagues during a daylight air raid in a surface shelter into which a mother had shepherded her little son of school age. For a while they both listened to the dropping of the bombs; then the boy lost interest and became engrossed in a story book which he had brought with him. The mother tried to interrupt his reading several times with anxious exclamations. He always returned to his book after a second, until she at last demanded in angry and scolding tones: "Now drop your book and attend to the air raid."

We observed exactly the same process in the Children's Center at the time of the December, March, and May raids. When our unexploded bomb lay in the neighboring garden, the children began by being mildly interested and afraid. They learned to keep away from glass windows and to avoid the entrance into the garden. By keeping up continual talk about the possible explosion we could have frightened them into continuation of that attitude. Whenever we let the subject alone, their interest flagged. They forgot about the menace from the glass whenever they returned to their accustomed games; when the threat from outside lasted more than a week, they began to get cross with it and denied its presence. In spite of the bomb still being unremoved they suddenly declared: "The bomb is gone and we shall go into the garden!"

There is nothing outstanding in this behavior of children toward the presence of real danger and real fear. It is only one example of the way in which, at this age, they deal with the facts of reality whenever they become unpleasant. They drop their contact with reality, they deny the facts, get rid of their fear in this manner, and return apparently undisturbed to the pursuits and interests of their own childish world.

2. The second reason for anxiety can best be understood by reverting to the child's attitude toward destruction and aggression which we have described above. After the first years of life the individual learns to criticize and overcome in himself certain instinctual wishes, or rather he learns to refuse them conscious expression. He learns that it is bad to kill, to hurt and to destroy, and would like to believe that he has no further wish to do any of these things. But he can keep up this attitude only when the people in the outer world do likewise. When he sees killing and destruction going on outside, this arouses his fear that the impulses which he has only a short while ago buried in himself will be awakened again. We have described above how the small child in whom these inhibitions against aggression have not yet been established is free of the abhorrence of air raids. The slightly older child who has just been through this fight with himself will, on the other hand, be specially sensitive to their menace. When he has only just learned to curb his own aggressive impulses, he will have real outbreaks of anxiety when enemy bombs come down and do damage around him. This type of anxiety we have seen only in our one girl of another age group (10 years), who ardently wished to leave England altogether and to return to Canada, where she had been born, where everything was peaceful and "no horrid things to see."

3. The third type of anxiety is of a completely different nature. There is no education without fear. Children are afraid of disobeying the commands and prohibitions of

their elders either because they fear punishments or because they fear to lose their parents' love whenever they are naughty. This fear of authority develops a little later into a fear of the child's own conscience. We regard it as progress in the child's education when commands and prohibitions from outside become more and more unnecessary, and the child knows what to do and what not to do under the direction of his own conscience. At the time when this nucleus of inner ideas which we call conscience is formed, he turns back continually to the figures of the outside world on the one hand, to the imaginations of his own fantasy on the other, and borrows strength from both to reinforce the inner commandments. The child of 4 or 5 who is afraid in the evening before sleep because he thinks he has done wrong or thought forbidden thoughts not only will have a "bad conscience" or be afraid of what father and mother would say if they knew about his wickedness. He also will be afraid of ghosts and bogeymen as reinforcements of the real parent figures and of the inner voice. Children have a large list of dangers which serve as convenient symbols for their conscience; they are afraid of policemen who will come and arrest them, gipsies and robbers who will steal them, chimney sweeps or coal carriers who will put them in their bags, dustmen who will put them in their bins, lions and tigers who will come and eat them, earthquakes which will shake their houses, and thunderstorms which threaten them.

When they receive religious teaching, they may leave all else aside and be afraid of the devil and of hell. There are many children who cannot go to sleep in the evening because they are afraid that God will look in on them and punish them for their sins. There are others who received no religious teaching who transfer the same fear to the moon. They cannot fall asleep if the moon looks at them through the window; there are even children who cannot fall asleep because their fears are busy with expectations of the end of the world. For children in this stage of development of their inner conscience air raids are simply a new symbol for old fears. They are afraid of sirens and of bombs as they are afraid of thunder and lightning. Hitler and German planes take the place of the devil, of the lions and the tigers.

In the Children's Center, for instance, Bobbie (4½) called from his bed in the evening that the shelter was not safe enough, and that the house would fall down on him. He would certainly have called out in the same way in peacetime to say that he had a fear of earthquakes or of thunderstorms. Paul (4) demanded that his mother should come every evening and stand arched over his bed until he fell asleep; it is well known that there are many children of that same age who at all times refuse to go to sleep unless their mothers stand by to hold their hands and safeguard them against forbidden actions. There is another boy of the same age whom the Nursery Superintendent has to assure with endless repetitions that if she leaves him at night, he will surely find her again in the morning. This fear also only disguises itself as a fear of air attack at night; when we inquire into it more closely, we realize that he is afraid that he has done wrong somehow, and that for punishment his teacher and protector will be spirited away at night. We can convince ourselves of the truth of this explanation when we have the chance to remove these children from danger and put them in surroundings where there is no talk of air raids. They will slowly revert to their former forms of anxiety. We shall know that peace has returned when nothing is left for the children to be afraid of except their own former ghosts and bogeymen.

4. This enumeration of the various types of air raid anxiety in children, long as it may seem, is still incomplete. Even superficial observation will show that children not only undergo and develop the fears which belong to their own age and stage of development, but that they also share the fear reactions of their mothers, and, more generally, of the grown-up world around them. No understanding of their own, no development of inhibitions against primitive aggression, and no guilty conscience are necessary for the development of this further type of anxiety. A child of school age, like the boy described above, may stick stubbornly to his own reactions. A child in the infant stage of 1, 2, 3, 4 years of age will shake and tremble with the anxiety of his mother, and this anxiety will impart itself the more thoroughly to the child the younger he is. The primitive emotional tie between mother and baby, which in some respects still makes one being out of the two, is the basis for the development of this type of air raid anxiety in children. The quiet manner in which the London population on the whole met the air raids is therefore responsible in one way for the extremely rare occurrence of "shocked" children.

An instance of this is the experience a medical colleague had a few days after the London fire in the St. Pancras Dispensary. A mother appeared as an outpatient with her little girl of 5. When asked what was the matter with the child, she simply said that she had brought her because she thought she had "a cough and a bit of a cold." When asked about its beginnings, she thought "being taken out from the warmth into the cold" might be responsible. When questioned further, she gave the information, bit by bit, that she and the little girl had been regular shelterers in a big basement shelter under a warehouse. The building above them, like so many others, had caught fire and been destroyed. The exits of the shelter were blocked, but a rescue party had come and dragged the shelterers out one by one. To use her own words, the mother had, "as a matter of fact, been quite worried about the little one because for a while they could not find her." It was the transition from this blazing furnace of the shelter to the cold December air which had given the child "the cough and a bit of a cold." We can be certain that this particular child, protected and fortified by her mother's lack of fear and excitement, will not develop air raid anxiety.

One of our own mothers, a comfortable and placid Irishwoman, the mother of eight children, when asked whether her rooms had been damaged by bombing, answered, with a beaming smile, "Oh, no, we were ever so lucky. We had only blast, and my husband fixed the window frames again." Blast, which removes the window frames, not to mention the windowpanes, can be a very uncomfortable experience; but again, we can be certain that for the children of this mother the occurrence of the blast was not a very alarming incident.

We had, on the other hand, the opportunity to observe very anxious mothers with very anxious children. There was Jim's mother, who developed agoraphobia during the air raids. She never went to bed while the alarm lasted, stood at the door trembling, and insisted on the child not sleeping either. He, a boy of 5, had to get dressed, to hold her hand and to stand next to her. He developed extreme nervousness and bed wetting. When separated from her in the Children's Center he did not show special alarm either in daylight or in night raids. Isabel, a girl of 3½, whose mother was "quite nervous" since their small flat had been bombed and they had been taken in by neighbors, would demand to be taken out of bed at night during raids and to sit all dressed on a chair. She never repeated this reaction while she was living with us.

We also had an opportunity to observe one mother with a newborn baby, who at a time before the shelter had been built slept in our house under the stairs. Whenever the whistling of a bomb was heard, she would snatch up the baby and could hardly be prevented from rushing outdoors. She must have known that the child was safer under the stairs than in the open with the continual rain of antiaircraft shrapnel. But this realization did not help matters; it was evidently abrogated by a more primitive fear of the baby being buried in the house. The baby, of course, remained unconscious of the danger, but, in watching the scene, we felt convinced that the mother's state of frenzy must have imparted itself to the baby in some harmful manner. Luckily, this particular mother was able to leave London soon for the comparative safety of the country.

5. The fear of air raids assumes completely different dimensions in those children who have lost their fathers as a result of bombing. In quiet times they turn away from their memories as much as possible and are gay and unconcerned in their play with the other children. We have four examples where their gaiety is of a specially uncontrolled and forced kind. The recurrence of an air raid forces

them to remember and repeat their former experience. Again, it is more the mother's emotion which they have to live through than their own. One little boy (4) then re-experiences in detail how they heard the bomb fall on the particular place where the father worked, the rising anxiety when he did not return home at the usual time, the mother's concern over the meal which she had prepared, and then, together with the mother, the search for the lost body, the endless inquiries at various official places, the waiting at the mortuary, and the mother's grief and sorrow when the loss was confirmed.[3] For these children every bomb which falls is like the one which killed the father, and is feared as such.

One of our war orphans is, quite in contrast to all other children, immensely excited when he sights any bomb damage, new or old. Another, a little girl of 6, transfers this fear and excitation from bombs to accidents of all kinds, to the sight of ambulances, talk of hospitals, of illnesses, of operations—in short, to every occurrence which brings the fact of death back to her mind. It is true, of course, that this latter fear is not a true type of air raid anxiety. It is, above everything else, a reaction to the death of her father.

Reaction to Evacuation

The war acquires comparatively little significance for children so long as it only threatens their lives, disturbs their material comfort, or cuts their food rations. It becomes enormously significant the moment it breaks up family life and uproots the first emotional attachments of

[3] For a more detailed account of Bertie's experiences, see Report 5.

the child within the family group. London children, therefore, were on the whole much less upset by bombing than by evacuation to the country as a protection against it.

The reasons for and against evacuation were widely discussed during the first year of the war in England. Interest in the psychological reactions of the children receded into the background when, in the second year, the air raids on London demonstrated against all possible objections the practical need for children's evacuation. In order to survey completely all the psychological problems involved, the subject would have to be studied from various angles.

SOCIAL PROBLEMS OF BILLETING

There is an interesting social problem involved in billeting. Children who are billeted on householders who are either above or below the social and financial status of their parents will be very conscious of the difference. If urged to adapt themselves to a higher level of cleanliness, speech, manners, social behavior, or moral ideals, they will resent these demands as criticism directed against their own parents and may oppose them as such. There are children who will refuse new clothes and hang on to torn and dirty things which they have brought from home. With young children this may be just an expression of love and a desire to cling to memories; with older children it is simultaneously an expression of their refusal to be unfaithful to the standard of their homes. Their reaction may, of course, also be of the opposite kind; the quickness with which they drop their own standards may be an expression of hostility against their own parents. When, on the other hand, children are billeted on families who are poorer than their own, they easily interpret the fact as punishment for former ungratefulness shown at home.

This situation of being billeted has a secret peacetime counterpart in the child's inner fantasy life. Most children of early school age (6 to 10) possess a secret daydream (the "family romance") which deals with their descent from royal or lordly parents who have only entrusted them to their real more humble families. Others have secret fears of being stolen from their families and then forced to live in poor and dingy surroundings. On the part of the child these fantasies are attempts to deal with the whole range of conflicting emotions toward the parents. Love, hate, admiration, criticism, and even contempt for the parents are worked out in them. When evacuation occurs at this time of life, the fact of being billeted with foster parents of a different social level may be upsetting to the child because it gives sudden and undesired reality to a situation which was meant to be lived out in the realms of fantasy.

PROBLEM OF THE FOSTER MOTHER

The psychological problem of the foster mother is evident even to those who otherwise refuse to take psychological complications too seriously. Possessiveness of the mother is, as we know, an important factor in the mother-child relationship. The child starts his life as one part of the mother's body; so far as the feelings of the mother are concerned, he remains just that for several years. Egoistic reactions of the mother normally include the child. Harm to the child is resented by the mother as if it were harm done to herself. Every human being normally overestimates his own importance, his own personality, and his own body; this overestimation on the part of the mother also includes the child. This explains why an infant who is neither good-looking nor clever may still seem to possess both qualities in the eyes of his own mother. It is this primitive possessiveness and overestimation at the bottom of motherly love which make it possible for mothers to stand the strain of work for their children without feeling abused. It is common knowledge that only love for children will prevent their continual demands, the continual noise caused by them, and the continual damage done by them from being considered a nuisance.

Foster mothers, i.e., householders, are expected to suffer children whom they neither love nor overestimate. There will only be two courses open to them: one is to retain the attitude of indifferent outsider, to complain about the imposition, and to try and get rid of the children as soon as possible. The other course taken is to adopt the mother's attitude, which means to feel toward the strange child as if he were her own. The foster mother will in these last cases not suffer from the children billeted on her, or rather she will take the trouble involved as a matter of course, as mothers do. But this second attitude, which is the cause of all billeting successes, contains another danger. The real mother of the child will suddenly turn up on Sundays or holidays and claim earlier right of possession. It has been said on many occasions, and once more after the failure of billeting mothers on householders, that it is impossible for two women to share one kitchen. This may be exaggerated. But it is certainly impossible for two mothers to share one child.

JEALOUSY OF FOSTER BROTHERS AND SISTERS

There is a third, minor, problem which so far has been less considered. It is the problem of jealousy and competition between brothers and sisters which is presented in evacuation in the new form of jealousy of foster brothers and sisters. Children never feel friendly toward newborn additions to their family. They sometimes pretend to do so; at other times they are mollified by the smallness and complete helplessness of the newcomer. The newly billeted foster brother, on the other hand, is very often neither small nor helpless. He usurps rights which the other child is unwilling to give up. The billeted newcomer for his part is deeply conscious of his second-rate position and is embittered by it. There are certainly all the elements for jealousy and discomfort given in the situation.

These reactions are interesting enough to be made the subject of surveys which are carried out by child guidance clinics set up in reception areas and by consulting psychologists attached to County Medical Offices. They keep an eye on trouble in the billets, smooth out difficulties, and remove the worst billeting misfits. They have in their positions a unique opportunity to study the situation (especially the situation of the school children).

EVACUATION OF YOUNG UNATTENDED CHILDREN

The Government scheme for evacuation of unattended children was never meant to include children under school age, with the exception of some little ones who were taken along with evacuation parties as younger brothers and sisters. Evacuation of unattended children under 5 was rightly considered a difficult undertaking. They were supposed to stay with their mothers and to be evacuated only with them whenever necessary. When the percentage of mothers who were unwilling to leave London and stay in billets was rather large, a scheme for under-fives was added to the other. These under-fives whose mothers had to have a good reason for staying behind were sent out unattended, either to nurseries or to selected billets. The difficulty remained that vacancies under this scheme were scarce compared with the onrush of mothers who were eager to send their small children to some place of safety.

In a London nursery like ours there is little opportunity for collecting evidence about the successful billeting of under-fives. Children who are happy in their billets, i.e., who find a foster mother ready to "adopt" them, stay in the country and little more is heard about them. "Billeting failures," on the other hand, wander back and forth between London and the country. Some of them may settle down in the end in residential nurseries like ours, which are created either by private initiative in England or by one of the American Relief Funds. As mentioned in our statistics, more than 20 percent of our cases are billeting failures of various types.

We should be more inclined to hold the billets responsible for the inability of such large numbers of children to adapt themselves to the new conditions if we did not possess firsthand evidence of the difficulties involved from our own observations of the children after their first separation from their families. The most impressive examples of this kind have been described in our monthly reports.

It is true that not many children present as frightening a picture as Billie (3½), who found himself reduced to a state in which compulsive formulas and symptomatic actions played the largest part; or Beryl (4), who sat for several days on the exact spot where her mother had left her, would not speak, eat or play, and had to be moved around like an automaton. Even apart from these unusual cases we have seen long-drawn-out states of homesickness, upset, and despair which are certainly more than the average inexperienced foster mother can be expected to cope with. We certainly see no similar states of distress in children when we make the round of London shelters, and find them sleeping on the platforms next to their mothers. Our own feeling revolts against the idea of infants living under the conditions of air raid danger and underground sleeping. For the children themselves during the days or weeks of homesickness this is the state of bliss to which they all desire to return.

There are so many obvious reasons why small children should not stay in London shelters that it is not easy to pay equal attention to the emotional reaction of the individual child to evacuation. A child who is removed from London to the country is certainly removed from a state of greater danger to a lesser one; he exchanges unhygienic conditions of life for more hygienic ones. He avoids possibilities of infection which multiply where thousands of individuals are massed together. If the child goes to a residential nursery, he will be better fed than before; he will be given proper occupation and companionship and will be spared the dreariness of an existence where at the worst periods he was dragged to and fro between home and shelter with long and empty hours of queuing-up at a Tube station. It is difficult to realize that all these improvements in the child's life may dwindle down to nothing when weighed against the fact that he has to leave his family to gain them.

This state of affairs is still more difficult to understand when we consider that many of the mothers concerned are not "good mothers" in the ordinary sense of the word. We deal with a large majority of mothers who are affectionate, intelligent, hardworking, and ready to make every possible sacrifice for their children; but there is a minority of mothers who are neither. They may be lazy and negligent, hard and embittered, and unable to give affection. There are others who are overstrict in their demands and make the life and upbringing of the child extremely difficult. It is a known fact that children will cling even to mothers who are continually cross and sometimes cruel to them. The attachment of the small child to his mother seems to a large degree independent of her personal qualities and certainly of her educational ability. This statement is not based on any sentimental conception of the sacredness of the tie between mother and child. It is the outcome of detailed knowledge of the growth and nature of the child's emotional life and of the structure of his mind in which the figure of the mother is for a certain time the sole important representative of the whole outer world.

DEVELOPMENT OF THE MOTHER RELATIONSHIP AND THE EFFECT OF SEPARATION FROM THE MOTHER DURING THE EARLY STAGES

In the relationship of the small child to his mother there are definite main phases to be distinguished from each other.

The first phase which comprises the first few months of life is characteristically selfish and material. The young baby's life is governed by sensations of need and satisfaction, pleasure and discomfort. The mother plays a part in it as far as she brings satisfaction and removes discomfort. When the baby is fed, warm, and comfortable, he withdraws his interest from the outer world and falls asleep. When he is hungry, cold, and wet or disturbed by sensations in his own intestines, he cries for attention.

It is certain that care and attention given by the mother, i.e., in a special atmosphere of affection which only the mother can supply, are more satisfactory to the baby than more indifferent and mechanical ministrations to his needs. But the fact is that a baby who at this time of life is separated from his mother will accept food and care from a mother substitute. His needs are overwhelming, his helplessness is extreme, and his distinction between one person and another is still in the beginning stage. Babies of this age who are left with us by their mothers will usually have a short time of upset, may cry a while, have more difficulty in falling asleep, and show some irregularity in their digestion for a day or two. We still have to learn exactly how much of this upset is due to the disturbance of routine and how much to the change away from the individual handling and from the particular atmosphere of intimacy created by the mother. The upset caused is, of course, of a more serious nature, and of far longer duration in cases where the mother has been breast feeding the baby and weaning has to occur simultaneously with the separation. Weaning in itself acts on the child as a loss of satisfaction and a separation from the mother in an important sense. When the mother who has left reappears after a few days, the baby at this stage will probably not show signs of recognition.

The second phase starts in, roughly, the second half of the first year of life. The material relationship to the mother still exists. The mother remains, as she will remain for several years, the instrument of satisfaction for the child. But out of this ignoble beginning of a human relationship something different begins to grow. The baby also begins to pay attention to the mother at times when there is no urgent necessity for him to be attended to. He likes his mother's company, enjoys her fondling, and dislikes to be left alone. So far the absence of the mother has only been a potential danger: some inner need might arise and there might be nobody outside to fulfill it. Now, in this later phase, the mother is already appreciated or missed for her own sake. The child is conscious of her presence, follows her around with his eyes, can answer her smile, and is, as described above, moved by her moods. His need for her affection becomes as urgent for his psychological satisfaction as the need to be fed and taken care of is for his bodily comfort.

Disturbances after parting from the mother will last somewhat longer at this stage. Babies of this age are sometimes off their feedings when left with us. Many show signs of restlessness during sleep, and often seem unfriendly or rather withdrawn from contact with the outer world. Smiles, friendliness, playfulness will reappear only after the bodily functions have returned to normality. This interruption of psychic contact with the outer world is *not* simply the consequence of the bodily discomfort which the baby experiences; once a baby is used to us, he will not cut off his contact with the nurse who handles him even in times of illness. But at this period of separation he repeats what he did in the beginning of his mother relationship—he establishes personal contact with the mother substitute only on the basis of the fulfillment and satisfaction provided for his bodily needs.

The personal attachment of the child to his mother, which starts in this manner in the first year of life, comes to its full development in the second one. It was said before that the child is attached to his mother; it can now be safely said that he loves her. The feelings for her which he is able to experience acquire the strength and variety of adult human love. This love makes demands and is possessive. All the child's instinctual wishes are now centered on the mother. While she is breast feeding him, he wants to "eat" her; later on he will bite her, handle her, and whatever impulse starts up in him will try to find satisfaction on her person.

This relationship between small child and mother might be a happy one except for two reasons. The child's demands are too great; he is virtually insatiable. However long the mother may have fed him at the breast, he will express by his resentment at weaning time that it was not long enough; however much time she spends near him, he will still bitterly resent being left alone at other times. Also, the child soon becomes aware of the fact that there are other people in the world besides him and his mother. He realizes the presence of brothers and sisters who claim equal rights and become his rivals. He becomes aware, sometimes at a very early age, of the presence of the father, and includes him in his world. He recognizes him as a dangerous rival (where family life is normal). He loves him at the same time. With this conflict of feelings he enters into the whole complicated entanglement of feelings which characterizes the emotional life of human beings.

Reactions to parting at this time of life are particularly violent. The child feels suddenly deserted by all the known persons in his world to whom he has learned to attach importance. His new ability to love finds itself deprived of the accustomed objects, and his greed for affection remains unsatisfied. His longing for his mother becomes intolerable and throws him into states of despair which are very similar to the despair and distress shown by babies who are hungry and whose food does not appear at the accustomed time. For several hours or even for a day or two this psychological craving of the child, the "hunger" for his mother, may override all bodily sensations. There are some children of this age who will refuse to eat or to sleep. Very many of them will refuse to be handled or comforted by strangers.

The children cling to some object or to some form of expression which means to them at that moment memory of the material presence of the mother. Some will cling to a toy which the mother has put into their hands at the moment of parting; others to some item of bedding or clothing which they have brought from home. Some will monotonously repeat the word by which they are used to call their mothers, as, for instance, Carol (17 months, described in Report 4), who said, "Mum, mum, mum, mum, mum . . . ," continually in a deep voice for a least three days.

Observers seldom appreciate the depth and seriousness of this grief of a small child. Their judgment of it is misled for one main reason. This childish grief is short-lived. Mourning of equal intensity in an adult person would have to run its course throughout a year; the same process in the child between 1 and 2 years will normally be over in 36 to 48 hours. It is a psychological error to conclude from this short duration that the reaction is only a superficial one and can be treated lightly. The difference in duration is due to certain psychological differences between the state of childhood and maturity. The child's life is still entirely governed by the principle which demands that he should seek pleasure and avoid pain and discomfort. He cannot wait for the arrival of pleasure and bear discomfort in the idea that in this way ultimate pleasure may again be reached.

An adult person may find himself in the same situation of being suddenly cut off from all the people he loves, and will also experience intense longing. But his memories of the past and his outlook into the future will help him to maintain an inner relationship to the loved objects and thus to bridge the period until reunion is possible. The psychological situation of the child is completely different. A love object who does not give him immediate satisfaction is no good to him. His memories of the past are spoiled by the disappointment which he feels at the present moment. He has no outlook into the future and it would be of no help to him if he had. His needs are so urgent that they require immediate gratification; promises of pleasure do not aid him.

The little child will, therefore, after a short while, turn away from the mother image in his mind and, though at first unwillingly, will accept the comfort which is offered. In some cases acceptance may come in slow stages. Carol, for instance, would at first let herself be fondled or held only by an unseen person. She would sit on somebody's lap, turn her head away, enjoy the familiar sensation of being held, and probably add to it in her own mind the imaginary picture of her own mother. Whenever she looked at the face of the person who held her, she began to cry. There are other children who are spared these violent reactions. They seem placid, dazed, and more or less indifferent. It takes a few days or even a week before this placidity is disturbed by a realization of the fact that they are among strangers; all sorts of slighter depressive reactions and problems of behavior will then result. All children of this age, those with the violent reactions as well as those where reaction is delayed, will show a tendency to fall ill under the new conditions; they will develop colds, sore throats, or slight intestinal troubles.

That the shock of parting at this stage is really serious is further proved by the observation that a number of these children fail to recognize their mothers when they visit after they have "settled down" in the new surroundings. The mothers themselves realize that this lack of recognition is not due to any limitation of the faculty of memory as such. The same child who looks at his mother's face with stony indifference, as if she were a complete stranger, will have no difficulty in recognizing lifeless objects which have belonged to his past. When taken home again he will recognize the rooms, the position of the beds, and will remember the contents of cupboards, etc.

Fathers also are treated better in this respect. The children were always more or less used to their coming and going and not dependent on them for their primitive gratifications. Consequently, parting from them is no real shock and their memory remains more undisturbed. Failure to recognize the mother occurs when something has happened to the image of the mother in the child's mind, i.e., to his inner relationship to her. The mother has disappointed the child and left his longing for her unsatisfied; so he turns against her with resentment and rejects the memory of her person from his consciousness.

THE MOTHER RELATIONSHIP OF THE CHILD BETWEEN 3 AND 5 YEARS

What is true about the small child remains true with certain modifications for the next 2 or 3 years of life. Changes are brought about slowly by development in various directions. Intelligence grows and enables the child to get some understanding of real situations, for instance, of the real reasons for being sent away; toward the age of 5 this mental understanding already acts as a real help in lessening the shock. More comfort can be derived from memories, and hopes for the future begin to play a part.

On the other hand, the relations between children and their parents are less simple and harmonious at this time of life. All sorts of complicating factors have been added to the home situation and confuse the picture when the family has to break up. The child of this age has ceased to live in partnership with his mother only; he has become a member of a larger family group, and this factor has a bearing on his emotions and affections.

So far the emotional development of boys and girls has appeared rather similar; at this age they begin to develop definitely along different lines. The boy begins to identify himself with his father and to imitate him in various ways. This changes his position toward the mother; he ceases to be a dependent baby and turns into a small demanding male who claims her attention, desires her admiration, and longs to possess her in more grown-up ways. The little girl, on the other hand, has grown away from her complete absorption in the mother. She begins to imitate her in her turn; she tries to play mother herself with dolls or with her younger brothers and sisters. She turns her affection and interest more toward the father and would like him to appreciate her in the mother's place.

Both sexes in this manner have their first experience of being in love. As a result of circumstances it is inevitable that this first love is disappointing. In comparison with the rival parent the child feels himself to be small, ineffective, and inferior. He experiences feelings of anger toward one parent, jealousy toward the other, and feels generally discontented that his fantastic wishes to be big can find no real fulfillment.

It acts as a second disturbing factor that the parents use the love which their children feel for them to educate the children. The early upbringing of children is not at all an easy undertaking. Children are born as little savages; when they enter school at the age of 5, they are expected to be more or less civilized human beings. This means that the first years of life are completely filled with the struggle between the demands of the parents and the instinctual wishes of the child. Already in the first 2 years weaning has been carried out against the desire of the child and toilet training has been enforced. The child's hunger and greed have had to adapt themselves to regular mealtimes. In this new period the parents criticize and restrict the child's aggression and his wishes to destroy things. They not only train him to cleanliness, they want him to dislike dirt as much as they do. When he is naturally cruel, they want him to feel pity. His first sexual impulses are interfered with when they try to satisfy themselves on the child's own body; they certainly find no satisfaction when they turn toward the parents'. The curiosity of the child is left largely unsatisfied, and his natural desire to be admired is criticized as a wish to "show off."

In this first education of the child, the parents do not usually apply compelling force; they simply make use of the dependence of the child and of his love for father and mother. The child is quite helpless in the hands of the parents; therefore, even a slight punishment will frighten him into obedience. The parent's love is all-important to the child; therefore it is used as a reward when the child is "good" and its withdrawal is threatened when the child is "naughty." In this unequal battle nothing is left to the child in the end but to give in and become civilized.

These two factors, disappointment in early love and the pressure of education, threaten to spoil the pleasantness of the relations between child and parent. Whenever the child is denied some pleasure, he becomes resentful; when he is too much restricted, he turns obstinate. When he is punished, he hates the parents; but he can never stand hating father or mother without feeling the strongest guilt about it. Children are quick in their anger and know only one main punishment for anybody who offends them, i.e., that this person should go away and not return, which in childish language means that he should die.

In everyday life at home these emotions are natural and necessary; they create small outbursts and settle down again. The father or mother who has been wished dead at one moment is reinstated in the child's affections in the next. On the other hand, it is probably these violent negative feelings of the child which determine his reaction to separation at this period. The negative feelings toward the parents are meant to be only transitory. Under the influence of daily contact they are held in check and neutralized by the affection for the parents which is constantly produced in response to all the satisfactions which the child receives. It does not seem so very dangerous to kill a parent in fantasy if at the same time outward evidence shows that this same parent is alive and well.

But separation seems to be an intolerable confirmation of all these negative feelings. Father and mother are now really gone. The child is frightened by their absence and suspects that their desertion may be another punishment or even the consequence of his own bad wishes. To overcome this guilt he overstresses all the love which he has ever felt for his parents. This turns the natural pain of separation into an intense longing which is hard to bear.

In these moods of homesickness children are usually particularly good. Commands and prohibitions which they formerly opposed at home are now religiously observed in the absence of the parents. Whatever might be interpreted as implied criticism of the parents is violently resented. They search their thoughts for past wrongs about which they might feel guilty. When Billie (3½) heard that his mother had gone to the hospital with a bad leg, he began to remember a time when he had kicked her and began to wonder whether her illness was his fault.

Visits or lack of them are understood as rewards and punishments. We had several little girls of 3 and 4 who would hang around the door for hours when their mothers were expected to come. But the visits at these times never brought the desired satisfaction. When the mothers were present, the children would be gloomy, shy, and hang on to them without talking; when the mothers left again, the affection broke through and violent scenes were produced. The children acted as if they could feel love only toward the absent mother; toward the present mother resentment was uppermost.

Again, the reactions toward the father do not develop on quite the same lines. There are two main attitudes which we were able to observe. The first is that many children will adopt every father who enters the nursery as if he were their own. They will demand to sit on his lap or wish to be carried around by him. (A visiting mother will never be claimed in this manner by strange children.) The second is that some little girls (2 to 4 years) will suddenly develop acute anxiety at the sight of any man, will turn their face away, cover their eyes with their hands, shriek with fear, and run to the nurses for protection. The first reaction may easily be due to the general scarcity of the male element in nursery life. The second is probably based on the inner rejection of the father due to the child's disappointment caused by separation.

FURTHER FATE OF THE CHILD-PARENT RELATIONSHIP

We began by describing how difficult it is at the start of nursery life to wean the child away from his mother. It is just as difficult in the later work to try and keep alive in the child at least remnants of his original relationship to the parents.

Most of the children under 3 will, because of the inner situation described, forget about their parents or at least become apparently indifferent toward them. They shift their affections to the new surroundings and, after some hesitation and some loss of valuable development to be described later, will restart normal life on a new basis.

After 3 years of age children will not normally forget their parents. Their memories are more stable; change of attitude takes the place of complete repression. It is already easier for the children to find active and conscious expression for their feelings. The image of the parents remains in their mind, especially when helped from the outside by frequent visits, receipt of parcels, and constant talk about the parents. Frequently these parental images undergo great changes and no longer resemble the real parent in the child's past. In fantasy life the absent parents seem better, bigger, richer, more generous, and more tolerant than they have ever been. It is the negative feelings, as shown above, which undergo repression and create all sorts of moods and problems of behavior, the origin of which remains unknown to child and teacher alike.

But even at this age, where the relationship with the parents persists in fantasy, the real affections of the children slowly leave the parents. Again, the child of this age lives mainly in the present. New ties are formed, favorites are found among the teachers and nurses, brother-sister jealousies are transferred to the small members of the Nursery community, friendships are established at a surprisingly early age. Pride in the home is changed to pride in the nursery, in the toys, and all the various possessions of the community.

In December, when many children were taken home for Christmas visits, we found some signs of this estrangement from the parents. In our houses, where every possible concession is made to visiting parents, it hardly ever occurs that a child will refuse to leave the Nursery with his mother. But there were several small children (about 2 years old) who showed little friendliness to their mothers when they were at home with them, and refused either to eat or to sleep or to play. They would cling to memories of the Nursery ("my bath," "my toast," "my Nelsa") as they had clung to their mother's name ("Mum, mum"), their pet animals, or some belonging of their mother's when they first came to the nursery.

The bigger children (3 to 4 years) know, of course, that this estranged woman who now showers affection on them is in reality their mother; but this rational conviction does not carry them far. The situation was most clearly expressed in the example of Jane (3¼ years). Jane was the child who took the longest time to adapt herself to nursery life. For at least 5 months every visit of her mother was accompanied by floods of tears. Her development was arrested through her concentration on her longing, her disappointments, and her varying moods of stubbornness and depression. She entered in July and began at last to settle down about Christmastime. She began to transfer her affections, to be gay, and to start all sorts of interests. In January, she paid a long visit to her mother and was very pleasant with her for two days. But when her mother asked her on the third afternoon whether she would rather stay another night or return to the Nursery, she said, politely and sensibly, "Don't you think, mummy, it would be better if we went home again"—home in that case, of course, meaning the Nursery.

Not every child expresses matters so clearly as Jane. But even if the parents are not overpossessive and nothing is done from the side of the Nursery to fan the mother's jealousy, this situation must be nearly unbearable for mothers with a real attachment to their children. Fears of losing the child completely in this way are often the reason why mothers make their sudden decision to give up work and take their children home.

More material of this nature will be available after a further year of evacuation and our work. At the present moment no one can quite define or even make a mental picture of the new shocks of separation and all the innumerable troubles which will arise when, at the end of the war, all these children are deprived of their present homes to which they have got accustomed and are expected to "go home" again.

It is especially difficult to predict the future reaction of those children who entered the Nursery in the first 6 months of life (25 in our Babies' Home) and who have never had any experience of a family situation.

Normal and Abnormal Methods of Outlet

It is impossible for children to go through upheavals of this kind without showing their effect in "difficult" behavior and in variations from normality. Infantile nature has certain means at its disposal to deal with shocks, deprivations, and upsets in outside life. Other psychological methods which are open to adults are not yet available in childhood. Children may therefore go apparently unharmed through experiences which would produce grave results in people of another age. On the other hand, they may break down completely under strain which to the ordinary adult person seems negligible. These peculiarities of the psychological makeup of the child may account on the one hand for the astonishing robustness of children, on the other hand for most of the problems of behavior and symptoms about which all the war nurseries complain.

OUTLET IN SPEECH

Whenever during the time of blitz mothers came to the Children's Center after a bad night's bombing, the best we could do for them would be to provide an interested audience for their tales. The kitchen in Wedderburn Road would reverberate with descriptions of neighbors who had been killed, possessions which had been destroyed, and miraculous rescues from burning shelters. We would even risk the children hearing more of the events than was strictly necessary rather than cut short mothers when they unloaded their minds of these horrors. If they repeated the description often enough, their excitement would visibly subside.

This most valuable outlet in speech and conscious thought, which acts as a drainage for anxiety and emotion, is denied to young children. It is possible that they would use this method at earlier ages if they were with their mothers. Under the conditions of nursery life the children do not talk about their frightening experiences immediately after they have happened. Among all the children received at Wedderburn Road after their houses had been bombed, there was not a single one who at that time related what had happened.

The only child who talked freely about bombing experiences was Bobbie, who had always lived in deep shelters, had heard a great deal of talk about bombing, but had never been himself in any bombing incident.

After a period of more than 6 months had elapsed,

several of these same children suddenly began to talk about the bombing as if it had happened yesterday.

Janet (4½) related how her ceiling fell down and how her little sister was all covered by it. Again, 4 months later, she drew the picture of a front door of a house and said, "The door is broken and there is a big hole in it." She knew that the door in the picture was the front door of her former home.

At the same time her friend, aged 5, began to describe her bombing experiences in the same way. She dictated letters to her American foster parents: "My house was bombed one time and my bath is broken and my windows. And my pussycat was hurt by a bomb and was hanging on the guard, and I picked him off and he jumped on again. And I was down in the shelter with my mammy and my granny." And in another letter: "My mammy and I were under the table and my poor little sister was in bed all by herself covered with stones, and my pussycat was thrown away." Georgie (3 years, 9 months) was in the Nursery several weeks before he could recount in words the event which had been a terrible shock for him, i.e., that his father had "taken away his mother in a big car."

The children who lost their fathers in air raids never mentioned anything of their experience for many months. Their mothers were convinced that they had forgotten all about it. Then, after a year, two of them at least told the complete story with no details left out. In all these instances speech does not serve as an outlet for the emotion which is attached to the happening. It is rather the other way round. The child begins to talk about the incident when the feelings which were aroused by it have been dealt with in some other manner.

OUTLET IN PLAY

While adults go over their experiences in conscious thought and speech, children do the same in their play. *War games* play a part in our Nursery as they do in others. Houses which are built are not simply thrown over as in former times; they are bombed from above, bricks being used as bombs. Playing train has given way to playing airplane; the noise of trains, to that of flying planes. Games like these will come more into the foreground after air attacks, and give way to peacetime games when things are again normal. After the raids in March and May the children (3 to 5 years) repeated in play what they had seen or heard. The climbing frame in the garden was used to provide a high point for the bomber. One child climbed to the highest bar and threw heavy objects on the children underneath. This was also the only time when one of our children was overheard to mention gas. A girl (3 years) filled both her hands with sand from the sandbox, threw the sand in the children's faces, and said, "This is a gas attack." This game was played without fear but with a great deal of unrestrained excitement.

A war game of a different kind was played by Bertie (4) at the time when he still refused to admit the truth of his father's death. He was ill in bed at the time of the spring raids, had a whole tray full of paper houses on his bed, and played indefatigably. He would build the houses up, cover them with their roofs, and then throw them down with small marbles which were his bombs. Whereas in the other children's game any number of people were "killed" and in the end everything was left in bits and pieces, the point in Bertie's play was that all his people were always saved in time and all his houses were invariably built up again.

The other children repeated incidents of a more impersonal kind in their games; they played active and embellished versions of events which had actually happened. This served the purpose of relief and abreaction. Bertie's play, on the other hand, had the opposite intention; he wanted to deny the reality of what had happened. Since the denial was never completely successful, the play had to be repeated incessantly—it became compulsive. The games of the other children remained transitory. Bertie stopped playing in his way when, half a year later, he at last gave up his denial and was able to tell his story. "My father has been killed and my mother has gone to the hospital. She will come back at the end of the war, but he will not return."

No war games are played in the Babies' Center where the oldest children are now about 3 years, which means that they experienced bombing when they were less than 2.

Dolls and teddy bears are used in play as substitutes for missing families. Children of 4 or 5 still go to bed with their pets, which they probably would not do at that age under normal family conditions. There are several children who will not be separated from some toy animal which they have brought from home and compulsively hold it in one hand, if possible even during washing, dressing, or eating. Lessening of that clinging is usually the first sign that the child has overcome the shock of separation and has found new living objects for his affection. Lending of a toy of this kind to another child is the sign of greatest love between two children. "Mother and child" is played with dolls continually. In observing the little girls one often feels that the doll does not represent the baby which the child can mother, but rather that the doll represents the absent mother herself. It is a sign of the greatest enmity between two children when they hurt each other's dolls or pet animals.

Shelters are, of course, built out of everything and take the place of what children formerly used to call "playing house."

OUTLET IN BEHAVIOR

Some children are unable to express what has happened to them either in speech or in play. Instead they develop behavior which seems cranky to the outside world until it can be recognized as their special way of bringing up memories.

With Bertie, for instance, it seemed for a time as if he really was going crazy. He would suddenly interrupt whatever he was doing, run to the other end of the room, look aimlessly into the corners, and return quietly as if nothing had happened. He would distort his face in the most horrible manner. He was restless and excitable, quick to pick quarrels, and very worried about his own health (see Report 5); he would not go out without warm clothes even in the summer heat, and so on.

It showed in time that this was his way of relating how his mother had behaved after his father was killed and before she went insane. She had aimlessly searched for the father, had expressed her grief in an unrestrained manner, had been excitable and quarrelsome and very worried about the health of the boy. In the end it had been Bertie's falling ill with scarlet fever which had completed her breakdown. In his behavior, Bertie combined the expression of her emotion, her attitude toward the people around, her attitude to himself, and possibly even some imitation of his father who is said to have been specially protective and affectionate toward his family. Curiously enough, these reactions reached their highest point at the time of the anniversary of the father's death.

One of the other boys has a very definite way of demonstrating the scenes which used to take place in his parents' home. He flies into violent tempers, turns against the people he loves most, attempts to destroy furniture, toys, etc. At the end of the scene he suddenly becomes gentle and affectionate, demands to sit on the teacher's lap, and sucks his thumb. His father is known to act in a similar manner toward the mother; he also ends up their violent quarrels with a love scene with his young wife.

With little Georgie (3¼) fragments of odd behavior are the only means to convey some idea of his past experiences. He will sit at table endlessly, apparently without eating; this means that he had conflicts about eating at the nursery where he lived before coming to ours. He threatens adults that they will "get no pudding"; this means that now he does to others what he experienced in a passive way. At bedtime he "acts up" in a curious way; this was found to be his remembrance of the times when he had been sent to bed for punishment, etc. (see Report 8).

Examples of this kind could be continued endlessly. They are instructive as far as they show that past experiences of all kinds appear on the surface in the form of the usual behavior problems.

OUTLET IN FANTASY

As already said, conscious fantasies are used largely to embellish and maintain the positive side of the child-parent relationship. In early childhood conscious fantasies are not restricted to the realm of thought. They go over into action and fill a large part of the child's life in the form of fantasy games. Conscious fantasy in its pure form (daydreams) finds its fullest expression only at a later stage of development.

There is one child who firmly refuses to join in any games where fantasy is used, where impersonations play a part, etc. Bertie gets frightened and anxious when he is urged by the other children to be a rabbit, a dog, a wolf, to play the role of another child, of one of the teachers, or whatever the game demands. His fantasy is exclusively reserved for dealing with the tragic story of his parents; it is inhibited in all other ways.

RETURN TO INFANTILE MODES OF BEHAVIOR (REGRESSION)

Every step in early education is closely connected with one of the phases of the child's attachment to some living object in the outer world. During the first years of life every child should make steady and uninterrupted progress toward social adaptation. He is egoistic and narcissistic at the beginning of life. In the same measure as his feelings turn away from himself and go out toward mother and father, the extended family, and the world beyond them, the child becomes increasingly able to restrict and gain control over his own instincts and to become "social." When something happens to shake his confidence in his parents or to rob him altogether of his loved objects, he withdraws into himself once more and regresses in social adaptation instead of progressing.

The advances he has made in becoming clean, in being less destructive, in modesty, pity, and unselfishness, i.e., the first setting up of moral ideals within himself, has on the child's part not only been a sacrifice. He has felt pleasure in these achievements because they were made for the sake of the parents and thus brought their own reward. When the attachment to the parents is destroyed, all these new achievements lose their value for the child. There is no sense anymore in being good, clean, or unselfish. When the child rejects his attachment to the parents who have deserted him, he rejects at the same time much of the moral and social standards which he has already reached. Most of the difficulties shown by children who now fill the residential war nurseries are due to such regressions in development.

Bed Wetting. Whenever training in cleanliness is achieved in the first few months of life, it is based completely on reflex action and has nothing to do with the child's psychological reactions. Experience has shown that this early control has a tendency to break down between the age of 10 and 13 months, when psychological factors of various kinds enter and complicate the situation. A second and more lasting control is then achieved by education proper, that is, by the usual methods of criticism or praise, reward or punishment within the framework of the mother-child relationship. It takes time before this bladder and sphincter control is purely automatic. During this time the child will be clean or dirty according to the steadiness of his relations with the person who brought him up from dirtiness to cleanliness. A small child will normally have a setback in his habits when he changes hands. When the break in attachments is as sudden and complete as it has been under the influence of evacuation, even older children may revert to wetting and dirtying themselves. The breakdown in toilet training is one of the expressions of a breakdown of the mother relationship.

This history of bed wetting is only one of the many possible reasons for the appearance of this symptom. Bed wetting can be simply caused by neglect; it can, on the other hand, be a complicated neurotic expression and as such only one symptom in the syndrome of a neurosis. But the wetting and dirtying which became one of the main stumbling blocks of billeting are usually not of the more complicated type. Their beginning coincided mostly with the break in the child's attachment, and they often disappeared after a few months when the child had succeeded in forming adequate new relationships.

Autoerotic Forms of Gratification. In the early phase of infancy when the child is still "all selfish," he turns to his own body as a source of pleasure. Whenever comfort from the outside world is slow in coming or seems inadequate, he provides extra pleasure for himself by sucking his thumb. As he grows older, other parts of the body, his skin, the body openings, rhythmic muscular movements, the sex parts themselves are used for the same purpose. Under normal conditions of development these autoerotic gratifications play a certain limited role in his life. As the child learns to send his feelings out toward loved objects, he also tries to derive his pleasures from them. When his attachments are interrupted, he regresses in this respect as well to his former methods of finding pleasure. Thumb sucking especially is very much in evidence in all the residential nurseries. We can observe big children of 4 or 5 eagerly and intently sucking their thumbs as if they were infants lying in their cribs. There is so far not enough evidence to show whether the same really applies to the other forms of autoerotic pleasures, such as rocking, masturbation, etc.

Greed. Under the influence of denial and regression the child's natural love for food, for sweets, for presents, is often turned to insatiable greed. Demand for affection is transformed back into a demand for material gifts. Parcels from the absent mother or sweets brought by the visiting mother seem for the child as important as the mother herself. This does not signify only that the present can be used as a symbol for the mother; it means that the mother relationship has regressed to the stage when the value of the mother was still measured in terms of the material comfort derived from her person.

Aggression. Under the present war conditions two factors combine to make children at the nursery stage more aggressive and destructive than they were found to be in normal times. One factor is the loosening of early repression and inhibition of aggression due to the example of destruction in the outside world. The other is the return to earlier modes of expression for aggressive tendencies. The bigger child then becomes as unrestrained in this respect as he has been in his earliest years. Like a small toddler he will again be loving and affectionate at one moment, enraged, full of hate, and ready to bite and scratch in the next. His destructive tendencies will turn equally toward living people and toward lifeless objects.

Temper Tantrums. Return to infantile behavior also concerns the nature of the child's wishes and tendencies and the manner in which the child strives to get satisfaction for them. Babies can announce their needs only by crying, screaming, and kicking; they have no other means at their disposal to enforce the arrival of the desired pleasure. Bigger children can understand the situation with their reason; they can speak, ask, demand; they can alter their position by their own volition, can go and get what they want; i.e., they can actively bring about all sorts of changes in the outward situation. Normally their wishes should also be felt with less urgency and despair. When a child of 3 or 4 sets up a howl because the sweets he wants are not forthcoming or because a meal is later than his appetite demands, we have a right to feel that he is "childish." The temper tantrums which are so frequent in all the residential war nurseries seem to be the combined expression of the regressive process along the whole line of educational achievement. The children throw themselves on the floor, kick with their feet, hammer with their fists, scream at the top of their lungs, and then suddenly turn "good" again, peacefully suck their thumbs or get up as if nothing had happened. It means that they have returned from the sensible active attitude possible for the growing individual to the helpless and despairing passivity of their infant stage.

Abnormal Withdrawal of Emotional Interest from the Outside World. On the basis of our present experience we expect the state of homesickness to last any length of time from a few hours to several weeks or even a few months. When this period is over, the child finds himself attached to new people in his new surroundings. The new ties may be less solid and more superficial than the original ones. As already described, the child starts his new relationships on a more primitive level, and some valuable achievements are lost during the process of adaptation. But however big or small that loss may be, the fact remains that normally the withdrawal of emotional interest will be temporary and the child will return sooner or later to good relations with the outside world. It is different in cases where through a series of unlucky circumstances the child has to change hands more than once or twice so that his new attachments are again wasted, and he is deprived of his new objects as soon as they are found. His relations to people will then become more and more superficial, and abnormal reactions of some kind will certainly follow. We were able to observe two cases of this kind.

We use as the most instructive example the case of Tony, who had changed his place of living several times between the age of 2 and 3 (see Report 9). As described in his mother's letter, Tony had never been separated from his mother up to the age of 2 and spent 14 months of that time alone with her after his father had been drafted into the army. His wanderings began when his mother fell ill with tuberculosis and went into a hospital. She once returned from the hospital because she heard that he was unhappy in the place where she had left him. She took him home to her relatives in the hope that she would be able to leave him there.

Since all her sisters had gone out to do war work, there was nobody to leave him with, and she again found a private billet in the country. She left him there to return to the hospital. In the meantime he had developed bed wetting so that the billet would not keep him. Again he began to wander until he landed in our Country House at the age of 3.

Observation showed that as a result of his experiences

he had become completely and frighteningly impersonal. His face, though very good looking, was expressionless; a stereotyped smile would appear at times. He was neither shy nor forward, was ready to stay where he was put, and did not seem afraid of the new surroundings. He made no distinction between one adult and another, clung to no one, and avoided no one. He ate, slept, and played, and was no trouble to anybody; the only abnormal feature about him was that he seemed completely devoid of all emotion. For several weeks it was very difficult to get nearer to him in any way.

The ice was broken at last when he fell ill and was isolated with one nurse. Whenever his temperature was taken the nurse held him on her lap and put her arm around his shoulders to keep the thermometer in place. Until then he had been indifferent to every kind of fondling; this special position evidently aroused in him memories of being in his mother's arms. He became attached to the nurse, asked repeatedly for "his temperchure," and found the way back to his feelings with the help of this incident.

The second case, Evelyn (3½) (see Report 7), showed even worse abnormality. She holds the record with six different billets between the age of 2 and 3. Her parents are highly skilled war workers who sent her to the country at the beginning of the war with her older sisters' evacuation school party. She was unhappy in some billets, not well treated in others, and had to leave one place after the other because her foster mothers fell ill, went to the hospital, etc. In the end she became completely confused and failed to recognize her own mother, though both parents visited her very regularly.

Her emotional withdrawal from the outside world was the same as Tony's; all her other reactions were exactly opposite. Where Tony showed complete lack of emotion, she had emotional outbreaks of a hysterical type—fits of crying alternated with fits of laughing. Where Tony was easy to handle, she was impossible. When she came to our Nursery, she would not go to bed, could not sleep, would not eat, fought against being bathed, washed, dressed or undressed. She had fears of going downstairs, of leaving the house, of entering again through the front door. Sometimes she wanted to play with other children, at other times she screamed with fear when they approached her.

When she returns from a visit to her parents' home where she is now sent regularly, she tells fantastic tales about the events which happen there. Everybody pushes everybody else, her sisters hit her on the head, she is pushed into the fire and everything burns up. There are no bombing experiences at the root of Evelyn's fears. She is one among the few of our children who escaped the London air raids through early evacuation to the country.

As a consequence of the shock of her repeated separations she has developed a neurotic illness which is so far difficult to diagnose. Hysterical symptoms alternate with phobic behavior and compulsive mechanisms. The main feature is her withdrawal from the interests of the real outer world. Her expression is always worried, her glance fixed and stony. There is little hope that, like Tony, she will find a natural return to normality. She is ill enough to need and receive psychoanalytic treatment for her neurosis.

PRACTICAL CONCLUSIONS

At first glance it seems from this material that small children had little chance to escape unharmed from the present war conditions. They either stay in the bombed areas with their parents and, quite apart from physical danger, get upset by their mothers' fears and excitements, and hardened and brutalized by the destruction which goes on around them and by shelter life. Or they avoid these dangers, are evacuated to the country, and suffer other shocks through separation from the parents at an age which needs emotional stability and permanency. Choosing between two evils seems to be all that wartime care is able to accomplish for them.

Yet we should not be too quick in drawing such conclusions. That evacuation under the present conditions is as upsetting as bombing itself is no proof that methods of evacuation could not be found which guard the children's lives and bodily health and at the same time provide the possibility for normal psychological development and steady progress in education.

Our case material shows that it is not so much the fact of separation to which the child reacts abnormally as the form in which the separation has taken place. The child experiences shock when he is suddenly and without preparation exposed to dangers with which he cannot cope emotionally. In the case of evacuation the danger is represented by the sudden disappearance of all the people whom he knows and loves. Unsatisfied longing produces in him a state of tension which is felt as shock.

If separation happened slowly, if the people who are

meant to substitute for the mother were known to the child beforehand, transition from one object to the other would proceed gradually. If the mother reappeared several times during the period when the child has to be weaned from her, the pain of separation would be repeated, but it would be felt each successive time in smaller doses. By the time the affection of the child had let go of the mother, the new substitute object would be well known and ready at hand. There would be no empty period in which the feelings of the child are turned completely inward and, consequently, there would be little loss of educational achievement. Regression happens while the child passes through the no-man's-land of affection, i.e., during the time after the old object has been given up and before the new one has been found.

Two of our children have expressed this state of mind in their own words: Georgie (3¾), when he said, "I don't like you, I don't like anybody, I only like myself"; and John (5) when he said, "I am nobody's nothing."

Mothers are commonly advised not to visit their children during the first fortnight after separation. It is the common opinion that the pain of separation will then pass more quickly and cause less disturbance. In reality it is the very quickness of the child's break with the mother which contains all the dangers of abnormal consequences. Long-drawn-out separation may bring more visible pain, but it is less harmful because it gives the child time to accompany the events with his reactions, to work through his own feelings over and over again, to find outward expressions for his state of mind, i.e., to abreact slowly. Reactions which do not even reach the child's consciousness can do incalculable harm to his normality.

Objection might be raised that emergency war conditions do not allow considerations of this kind to carry weight. Still, it seems possible to base plans for "evacuation in slow stages" on psychological convictions of this kind.

If children under 5 have to be evacuated unattended like their bigger brothers and sisters, they should at least not be sent out under harder conditions than the older ones. School children, even if they lose the connection with their homes, will at least retain the relationship to their school friends and to their teachers who go out with them. Under-fives who are sent to nurseries go into the complete unknown.

One could conceive a plan under which all small children would be collected in day nurseries. They would get attached to their nurses and teachers and know the units in which they spend their days while they still live at home. In times of danger these day nurseries would be converted into residential nurseries and would be evacuated collectively. Mothers who refuse to part from their small children could be offered the chance to go too as paid domestic staff. Experience has shown that only a small percentage of all mothers would choose to do so.

Under such conditions evacuation would lose its horrors for the young child and abnormal reactions to it would become extremely rare. To maintain the remnants of the parent relationship so far as possible and simultaneously to prepare the way for the return of children to their homes after the war, parents' visits should be considered all-important. There should be little or no restriction through visiting rules. (In our houses parents come and go whenever their occupations leave them free to do so.) Provision should be made for the possibility of such visits, as it is made for all the other bodily and educational needs of the child so far as they are considered to be important.

It will be still harder to devise proper means of evacuation for small babies. If infants have to be separated from their mothers in the first weeks of life in the interest of war work, they best go to crèches near factories where mothers can deposit and collect them. This again does not solve the problem of shelter sleeping in times of danger. If babies go to residential homes, these should be situated as near to the outskirts of the town as possible to encourage frequent visiting. With infants there are no "remnants of a mother relationship" to maintain, and no memories to keep alive. The baby will have to make the acquaintance of his mother during the hours or days of visiting. There should certainly be some relation between the frequency of visits and the ability reached by the infant to retain remembrance.

Artificial War Orphans

If precautions of this kind are disregarded, it should be realized that evacuation of small children will necessarily bring many failures. The children are saved from one dangerous situation only to be exposed to another one. Children whose parents are actually killed as a result of enemy action are generally objects of pity. Under the conditions of indiscriminate evacuation thousands of artificial war orphans will be added to the smaller number of children who are really orphaned by the war. It is true that these children's loss is only one of feeling and attachment. But so far as their inner stability and their further psychological development are concerned, the consequences may be just as harmful.

13

Monthly Report
February, 1942

STATISTICS

The number of children has been raised to 120; 78 of these are resident, 5 are full-time day children, several of the 37 nonresident children are waiting for admission to the Country House.

Two children left Netherhall Gardens and 3 young babies were admitted in their stead: one pair of twins, Bill and Bert, 4 months, and little Jennie, 6 weeks old.

HEALTH REPORT

The scarlet fever in the Country House has at last run its course. When an interval of 6 weeks had elapsed without a new case occurring, the house was fumigated. After a further week the bigger children resumed school and the house was once more reopened for visitors.

In Netherhall Gardens 31 children (from 10 months to 3 years) were inoculated against diptheria. Fifteen babies were vaccinated. Four mothers refused permission for vaccination.

There were no real illnesses during this month. The sick room in the Country House is at the moment entirely empty.

SOAP RATIONING

The rations which are rather hard on private people are slightly more favorable in an institution. The amount allocated is based on the amount used during the last 6 months. We are trying hard to reduce consumption, but have to be careful at the same time not to lower our standards of cleanliness and hygiene which we value highly. We hope that our quota, together with the amounts deducted from the personal rations of the trainees who live in the house, will prove sufficient for all cleaning purposes.

COUNTRY HOUSE

So far as parents and children are concerned, the event of the month was the ending of the quarantine. The parents were notified in time; a bus for which we had made an official application long ago was available for transport on Sunday, February 22nd. Thirty parents visited, spent the whole day in the Country House, had meals with their children in the big nursery, took them for walks, and were shown whatever there was new or improved in New Barn.

The visit was on the whole most satisfactory. None of the children, except one, failed to recognize the parents after the 3 months' interval. Some of the younger children took a few hours to become really familiar with their parents. On the whole the efforts we had made to keep up relations with the absent parents with the help of letters, parcels, and messages showed a very good result. There were hardly any scenes at parting and all the children fell asleep at their usual time on Sunday evening. By now they seem to have managed the difficult task of maintaining a double relationship, to the parents on the one hand and to the staff on the other.

There were, of course, several inevitable disappointments and difficulties to deal with. Bertie (5) had been carefully prepared for the fact that his mother, who is still in an insane asylum, would not come. He affirmed this to himself repeatedly. It affected not only himself but also other children. When all of them stood at the big nursery window to watch for the arrival of the bus, Jim (5½) turned around and asked: "Is it really true that Bertie's mother is not coming?" The disappointment of his friend seemed to overshadow his own joyful expectation. Luckily, the mother's cousin was able to come with a friend of hers and Bertie seemed content to have at least "visitors."

Bad news was brought about the two tuberculous mothers who were, of course, absent. Tony's (3) mother is on the point of dying. Her sister came instead, but Tony had hardly ever seen her and was deeply distressed and upset. All the progress which he had made in the nursery suddenly disappeared and his face again assumed its former half-empty and wholly tragic expression. Georgie's (4) and Marion's (5) mother also was reported to be worse; there seems no hope for her recovery. Their aunt and grandmother visited instead, and the children were comparatively happy with them.

All the parents seemed satisfied and some of them quite excited about the progress which their children had made.

FINANCIAL REPORT

So far as the staff and management are concerned, the month was filled with financial worries which toward the middle of February assumed the aspect of a financial crisis. The London Office of the Foster Parents' Plan received a cable from New York which said that due to the American war situation all organizations dealing with foreign relief had to anticipate reductions. They left the final decision to their London representative, but suggested closing the house which would save most funds.

Since the Hampstead Nursery is without doubt the most expensive venture of the Foster Parents' Plan, this concerned us acutely. We feel that our work has just got under way; that all the parents have full confidence in us; that all the children feel at home and develop very satisfactorily, and that, as our Annual Report suggests, our efforts to make observations and collect material show some results. If we were forced to close down now in the middle of the war, our work would be rendered more or less valueless. Our 78 resident children would be homeless again, equally the 7 mothers who are now living with us. Forty or 50 mothers would be prevented from going out to work. The children, now over 5, who had originally come to us as billeting failures would have to resume their wanderings through private billets. The young babies would have to return to their East End houses or to shelters since it is hardly possible to find nursery places for young children in the country. Our staff, whom we selected carefully and who now have the opportunity to use their abilities to the fullest, would be scattered; the training of the young probationers would be interrupted. All our attempts to collect material and acquire knowledge about children in wartime would come to an abrupt end.

We are naturally distressed to think that our efforts should lead to such a negative result and quite determined not to accept this fate unless it proves entirely inevitable. We consulted with the London representative of the Foster Parents' Plan to find ways out of our difficulties. We tried to reach by cable all our friends in America and asked them to consult with the Foster Parents about continued support for our institution. We are at the same time making all efforts to raise at least a percentage of the necessary budget here in England.

The main problem for the moment is to live on a reduced budget until the situation in America is stabilized again or until one of our other efforts may bear fruit. This is made possible by a move from the side of our staff. The workers in all three houses offered to work without wages for the next four or six weeks to give us and the Foster Parents' Plan time to revise and perhaps to save the situation.

14

Monthly Report
March, 1942

STATISTICS

The total number of children has remained stationary at 120, i.e., 79 resident children, 5 full-time day children, and 36 nonresident children.

APPLICATIONS, VISITORS, ETC.

During March we have received an increasingly large number of applications for the admittance of children whose mothers want to take up war work and for children whose mothers are ill and have to go to the hospital. We have further received a great many requests for training, partly from very young girls who want to do some months of practical work in our houses before they go into other war nurseries, partly from fully trained nursery workers who want to make themselves acquainted with our ways of dealing with the current problems so as to apply this knowledge in their own work.

We were visited further by a large group (90) of teachers from infant schools and elementary schools in Essex as part of a course about nursery work in wartime.

HEALTH REPORT

The state of health during March was unusually good and the sickrooms were empty except for a few colds and slight digestive upsets.

FINANCES

Since our last report we received notification from the Foster Parents' Plan that they would be able to continue with two thirds of our former budget. This provided us with a firm basis for our decisions for the future. The alternatives were: to close down one of our houses, which would have automatically reduced the budget to the necessary extent; or to try and reduce expenses in all houses; or to keep all our activities alive and look for added support from public institutions or interested friends in England.

We chose a middle course between the latter possibilities. We carefully revised the arrangements in each separate department. Dismissals of household staff were made possible by the readiness of our trainees to take over some of the cleaning, the shelter hygiene, and some of the laundry work in their off hours. A circular letter to the parents had the effect that all their contributions were raised to the limit of their possibilities. Several English friends sent single donations of varying size to add to the money which we receive from America. Several of our attempts to get grants have had negative results, other attempts are still under way and may meet with better luck. The main point is that after four weeks' interruption, we have again started to pay wages to our staff and that we have avoided reducing the number of children under our care.

CHILDREN'S PROBLEMS

In spite of a certain feeling of insecurity about the future we could not help adopting a new arrangement of work with our nursery children in Netherhall Gardens which influenced their life in a decisive way. Since these children receive frequent visits from their own mothers, we had expected that they would not be searching for real mother substitutes and could be satisfied with a more impersonal and diffuse attachment to the various nursery workers dealing with their group. We had neither assigned specific children to specific workers nor divided the group for other purposes than the practical ones of play graded according to age. All the children knew all the workers in their group and were handled by them indiscriminately for the purposes of bathing, dressing, going for walks, etc.

There were two factors which induced us to change this arrangement. The one was that certain children suddenly showed strong preference for certain workers, followed them about, did not want to be separated from them, and demanded attention of a very personal nature. Since the workers felt that no favoritism should be shown, this led to all sorts of disappointments and denials for the children. The second factor was that certain steps in development were slow in coming; that in spite of all opportunities provided, some children were reluctant to grow out of their baby habits and others took too long to overcome reverses in their development, such as wetting and soiling, which were due to separation from home. We attributed these difficulties to the lack of a stable mother relationship.

The step taken was the subdivision of the large nursery group into six small "family groups" of about four children each. In assigning the children to their new substitute mothers, we followed the signs of preference shown on the one hand by the children, on the other hand by the young workers. Each "mother" now has more or less complete charge of her family. She alone bathes and dresses the children in her group, is responsible for their clothes, and offers them protection against all the current mishaps of nursery life. There is no necessity anymore to refuse a child special attention of a motherly kind.

The result of this arrangement was astonishing in its force and immediacy. The need for individual attachment with the feelings which had been lying dormant came out in a rush and in the course of one week all six families were completely and firmly established. But the reactions in the beginning were far from being exclusively happy ones.

Since all these children have already undergone a painful separation from their own mothers, their mother relationship is naturally burdened with all the effects of this experience. To have a mother means to them equally the possibility of losing a mother; the love for the mother being thus closely accompanied by the hate and resentment produced by her supposed desertion. Consequently the violent attachment to the mother substitutes of their own choice was anything but peaceful for the children. They clung to them full of possessiveness and anxiety when they were present, anxiously watched every one of their movements toward the door of the nursery, and would burst into tears whenever they were left by them for a few minutes.

Jealousy developed alongside with the mother attachment. There were two types of jealousy to be seen, one directed against the children of the same family group who actually shared the attention of the mother substitute; or when the children succeeded in accepting these brothers and sisters who were forced on them, they directed the full impact of their jealousy against the children outside their family group and would not allow their worker to have any dealings with them.

For a while we really thought that our grand innovation had been a great mistake. The formerly peaceful nursery reverberated with the weeping of children whose "mother" had left the room, for instance, to get something from the next room, and whose absence was mourned as if she would never return. Fights among the children multiplied in frequency and intensity.

Luckily, this state of affairs did not last longer than two to three weeks. With the realization that their new mother substitute really belonged to them, reappeared as often as she disappeared, and had no intention to desert them altogether, the state of frenzy subsided and gave way to a quieter, more stable, and more comforting attachment.

At the same time the children began to develop in leaps and bounds. The most gratifying effect was that several children who had seemed hopeless as far as the training for cleanliness was concerned suddenly started to use the pot regularly and effectively.

Bathing times in the evening have now become times of special intimacy when each child is certain of the full and undivided attention of his favorite adult. This, again, has had a remarkable effect on the development of speech. All the children in the group have greatly enlarged their vocabulary. And several children who were rather backward in their speech development due to nursery life have now, under the influence of this new stimulus, made up for these arrears. There is every hope at the moment that the speech of all the children will reach the level of development which it would have attained under the conditions of home and family life.

Real families were of course left together in our family groups.

There is the possibility that these newly formed attachments might have consequences for the relationship of the children to their visiting real mothers. Curiously enough, no signs of such changes have so far appeared on the surface.

The happenings in this group are at the same time a clear demonstration of the known fact that children transfer their early relationship to their families onto all the people who later play an important part in their lives. This transference of feeling is responsible on the one hand for the stormy and conflicting nature of the attachment of the child to the nursery worker, for the mixture of love and hate, possessiveness and jealousy; it explains on the other hand why the consequences of such attachments are so far-reaching where education and development are concerned. With the full return to the type of attachment which had been interrupted by the separation from the family, the child resumes his steady progress toward the formation of a normal personality. He overcomes his childish habits and unfolds the functions which belong to that particular stage of his individual development.

15

Monthly Report
April, 1942

STATISTICS

The total number of children stands at 121. Of these 78 are resident, 7 full-time day children, 36 nonresident or extension children.

In spite of this apparent stability of numbers, there has been a good deal of coming and going during the month. Our oldest child (11 years) was transferred to a place where she can find companions of her own age. Two babies, one 5 months, one 11 months, were admitted as resident visitors for three days and eight days respectively during an unavoidable absence of their parents from home. Jennie (5 months), who had been with us nearly since her birth, was legally adopted and left us in very good condition. She has found an excellent home with every hope for a good future. A baby of 4 months was temporarily admitted as completely homeless. She had been promised a place in a new nursery which hopes to open within the next few weeks or months and no other accommodation could be found for her during the waiting period.

One of our nonresident children was admitted to the Country House. We further admitted as full-time day children two sisters whose mother has found employment in our neighborhood while their father is serving a term of imprisonment as conscientious objector.

Again, numerous applications for babies had to be refused, sometimes to the extent of two or three a day. The age of these children now mostly ranges from birth to 2 years. Reasons given for the latest applications were the following: father in the army, mother wants to do full-time war work; father in the army, mother cannot look after his business and the baby at the same time; father and mother working, live in rooms quite unsuitable for the child; baby on waiting list for a day nursery to be opened in the near future, mother has to stay off work during waiting period, afraid to lose job; baby minded by neighbor while mother does factory work, neglect during 6 months of minding, has been in the hospital once, suffers from recurrent colds; mother working, had placed baby with friends who cannot keep her because no children allowed in their new flat; mother deserted family, father left helpless with small baby; delicate babies with feeding troubles from birth, lady almoners from hospital looking for place where they can receive some extra care, etc.

FINANCES

There has been no change in our financial situation since the last report.

HEALTH REPORT

The state of health during the past month was very good. One child in the Country House was suspected to have mumps, but this did not develop and no further cases materialized.

The excitement of the month was provided by Hilda (3 years) in the Country House. She contracted a toxic flu. For one day her temperature went up and down, in the middle of the second morning it suddenly rose sharply to 105; she had a collapse and was pulseless for a while. The trained nurse in charge of the sickroom frantically tried to reach the two doctors in the neighboring villages, but failed since both were out on rounds and not expected back for several hours. She notified our London house immediately by telephone, our own doctor left at once and within two hours had reached the child and given the necessary medical help in addition to the stimulants administered by the nurse; she brought the child back to London to have her under close observation while applying for a place in a children's hospital. The last step proved unnecessary, Hilda's temperature went back to normal and she recovered her usual health completely after a very few days.

PROBLEMS

In our last report we described our attempt to start "artificial families" in our nursery, i.e., to assign three or four children to one young worker as their special "mother." These remarks interested some of our readers and led to further discussion of the subject. This again was a welcome opportunity to review once more our observations about the attitude of the real mother toward the child who is separated from her and the reactions of the child to the expressed or unexpressed emotions of the mother.

In trying to trace the numerous failures of the billeting system to their sources, a great deal of attention has been paid on the one hand to the attitude of the foster mothers, on the other hand to the difficulties of the children which often seemed to make the task of foster mothers an impossible one. Less has been said about the inner attitude of the mothers themselves. But it remains a fact that children are taken out of billets and nurseries and brought back to danger areas even when billets and nurseries are satisfactory and when the children themselves are perfectly easy to handle; they are taken home in a great number of cases because the mother cannot cope with the conflict aroused by her own contradictory feelings. Her conscious wishes for the safety of the child contrast with other, only dimly perceived or wholly unconscious feelings which lie at the basis of the mother-child relationship.

Ambivalent Attitude of Mothers toward Separation from Their Young Children

We generally overestimate the strength of the mother's sensible wish to have the child removed from danger. Even in the middle of air raids a mother may show a double reaction in this respect. She wishes on the one hand to have her child well out of danger, on the other hand to keep him near her, where she can personally care for him, watch over him, and can know just where he is at the moment. She feels no one could protect her child as she can and therefore is reassured by his presence.

Reason and emotion definitely work against each other at these times. This may explain some of the continuous to and fro of evacuation. While one wish of the mother is active in sending the child to the country, another, purely emotional one, is the agent to bring him back again to her side.

Expression of the Same Ambivalence on Visiting the Child

When the mother visits the child, she will come with her emotions of longing, augmented by the doubt and worry whether she has done the right thing for the child. It would gratify her in one way to find that the child is worse off away from her than with her, and therefore she will be very ready to find fault and will examine the child for signs of neglect and ill treatment and will observe the nurses or foster mother with critical eyes. On the other hand she of course wants to find her child well and content. A sensitive child, besides having his own emotional reactions, will feel this tenseness and conflict in the mother. He will be aware of her critical attitude and feel torn between his allegiance to her and the beginning liking for his new surroundings.

These emotions which exist as undercurrents during the whole length of the visit then create violent disturbances when the time for leave-taking arrives. This is generally a most painful experience for the mother as well as for the child. The child will cling to the mother, scream, and show his misery in a noisy manner. The mother would certainly not want her child to let her leave gladly, but she cannot stand these upsetting scenes. She reacts to them by trying on her next visit either to fool the child by pretending that she is not leaving when she really intends to do so or by saying good-bye to the child over and over again. After a mother has experienced such scenes repeatedly she will acquire a new conflict: she feels that her visits only add to the unhappiness of the child, and she is now torn between the desire to stay away so as to spare the child further unhappiness and the desire to reassure herself by coming to visit the child again as soon as possible.

The situation is, naturally, even worse for the mother if the child reacts to her coming and going with apparent indifference. She is unable to understand such unfaithfulness; she will be hurt, jealous, unhappy, and probably will lengthen the intervals between her visits. She suspects the people who take care of the child of "turning him against her." Mothers in this state will at one moment be cross, at the next overaffectionate with their children. If not helped over this difficult moment, the most likely way out for them will be to take the child home again.

In the Hampstead War Nursery we avoid the worst of these complications by keeping open house for the mothers. They are reassured by the feeling that they have easy access to their children, that their visits are no disturbance to the routine or household, that they can take their children out for walks and home for nights whenever they are free. Nothing which goes on in the Nursery is hidden from their eyes so that their worst suspicions are allayed.

But even with the best intentions these conditions cannot always be kept up. We went through a difficult time when the Country House was in quarantine for scarlet fever and had to be closed to visitors for three months. Mothers who, under ordinary visiting conditions, felt very placid about their children's stay with us, would suddenly call up by telephone in an excited manner, complain that they had not received an answer to some imaginary letter of theirs which had never reached us, that they "worried day and night" about their child, that they "did not even hear whether the child was alive or dead," etc.

Several mothers took their children home on visits after the lifting of the quarantine to make up for lost contact, but these visits did not prove too satisfactory. Some mothers complained that the children did not seem the same to them, one of our fattest girls was considered too thin by her mother, Little Sonja (3) refused to look at her father whenever he tried to approach her, whereupon he telephoned us in an excited manner and declared: "I do not like the goings-on in that Country House." But, luckily, Sonja cried when the parents visited next at the moment of parting from them, and that completely helped the situation and restored her father's confidence in us.

Many of these reactions of the parents are fully conscious. The mothers especially are well aware of their double feelings: they would like to have their children stay with us in safety and under favorable conditions, and they would also like to have them home again. They also are aware that it is the changed behavior of the child which upsets them and strengthens the wish to have him return home. What they do not realize, however, is that the criticisms on which they pretend to base their decision are unreal or displaced; nor do they realize that the child's reactions are often increased by the conflict in the mother's mind.

In the long run even these irrational factors in the parents are open to influence. The pride in the development of the child, his concrete gains in health and knowledge, the loss of bad habits are very real factors in deciding the outcome of the conflict.

Undisturbed Positive Reactions of Mothers to Their Babies, Even After Separation

In Netherhall Gardens there is a good opportunity to observe the various attitudes of visiting mothers to their small babies. Here the mothers know when they leave their babies that even with frequent visits, they cannot expect recognition from them before they are a few months old. Some mothers visit daily, some weekly, and only a few less often.

There are some very natural, very possessive mothers who behave in much the same way on their visits. They enter the room and make straight for the cot where their baby is lying. They immediately pick him up and handle him in the most confident manner.

One mother of twin girls, for instance, placed the children with us when they were 4 months old; they have now been with us for a period of 9 months and during that time she has never failed to visit them daily in her off hours from work. At times our nurses were shocked at her apparent rough treatment of them; they worried, as time went on, why she did not learn something from their much quieter handling of babies. This mother seizes one twin after the other out of her cot, hugs her, holds her firmly in her hands, and squeezes her; both children react to this rough handling with evident pleasure. Now that they are older she even slaps them, to the horror of the nurses. But the twins show more contact with the visiting mother than with the nurses who are constantly with them. This is shown very clearly at their feeding time. Whenever a nurse feeds one of the twins, the other waits more or less patiently in her bed. But when the mother is feeding, the twin who is kept waiting screams and makes impatient noises all the time to call the mother's attention. There is no doubt about her jealousy. The rough treatment given by the mother is rightly interpreted by the children as an expression of her possessive love.

A similar situation can be observed in another baby who entered the Nursery at the age of 6½ months. He had been in unsatisfactory billets for 4 months, was taken home by the mother, and came to us after weeks of home life. The mother is a huge woman, extremely pleasant, a most motherly type with an immense lap. The baby fell ill after arrival and the mother could not visit for the whole first week because her husband at home had fallen ill as well. When she came at last and found him with a bad cold she was worried, she picked him up, cuddled him, crooned over him, rocked him, rather jerked him back and forth, held him very close, and finally soothed him to sleep. She put all the emotions which she had withheld from him during this week of separation into this short space of time. There is no doubt about it that some of her feelings imparted themselves to him. When she came a fortnight later he seemed very shy with her, felt strange, and did not recognize her until she held him again tight in her arms and crooned and rocked him as she had done before. He then cuddled down and was a real picture of contentment.

The same feelings can also be expressed in a completely different manner. We have a baby, Ivy, who entered the

Nursery at the age of 10 weeks. Her parents visit regularly once a week and nearly always together. They lean over the child's cot, handle her delicately and adoringly, somehow afraid to touch her except in the most gentle manner. Now that Ivy is 10 months old, her mother has a certain way of sitting on a chair with Ivy on her lap facing the father, who often feeds her in that position. This worshipping attitude of the parents surely also makes some lasting impression on the child.

This possessive handling as well as the adoring one certainly go far in outweighing the comparatively unemotional, even, and gentle treatment which the children receive from the nurses who take care of them.

Ambivalence toward Babies

All the mothers mentioned so far are very motherly types, possessive, affectionate, sure of themselves, and in no way torn by conflicting emotions in regard to their babies. But there are other mothers who, in contrast to them, show the well-known signs of double feelings toward their children.

A good example of this type is Sophie's mother, who brought the baby to us when she was 12 days old. At first she visited regularly every week, then she began to come less often. When the child was 4 months, she did not appear for several weeks; when she finally came again, she failed to recognize her baby. Sophie had lost a lot of her black hair in the meantime. The mother would believe that the child was really hers only after inspecting all the other children in their cots. After this visit she again stayed away for several weeks. When she visited next she went straight to the cot, probably in order to prove to herself and to us that she knew her baby. She picked Sophie up, hugged and kissed her, but Sophie did not like it and shrieked with terror. It took hours to quiet her again. While the nurse was holding her and trying to calm her, the mother paced up and down the room looking tense and worried. Every time she approached, Sophie started shrieking again. It was quite evident to us that the child reacted to the mother's violent emotion. The next time when the mother came, after barely a week, she approached Sophie's cot very quietly; she did not try to kiss her or to pick her up, but played with her as she lay in the cot, and Sophie seemed quite contented.

The mother's feelings on these visits are not difficult to discern. Sophie is an unwanted and illegitimate baby; the mother's interest in her is uncertain and unreliable to the highest degree. Her unconscious wish against the baby betrays itself in the failure to recognize the child. The child felt this negative emotion and reacted with terror. On the other hand there is also conscious love and affection, which urge the mother to visit and determine her reactions to a certain degree.

Purely Negative Reactions toward the Baby

The situation is much less involved where the mother only has the straight and undisturbed wish to get rid of her child. An example of this was Hubert, whose mother delivered him to us at the age of 3 weeks. We had no vacancy at the time, but accepted him since it was evident that the mother would otherwise leave him on the next doorstep. She weaned him immediately and left the same day against all urging to stay at least a few days. She visited a few times and then stopped. The next news came from an Adoption Society with which the mother already had made arrangements before his birth. In this case it seemed quite impossible to detect any conscious or unconscious leanings in the mother toward the child.

Summary

Observations of this kind may be useful for explaining some of the puzzling behavior of mothers during the evacuation of their children. With the recognition of unconscious wishes and their conflict with conscious attitudes, "puzzling behavior" usually can be explained as an unsuccessful attempt to combine an expression of both sides in one action or to satisfy the two attitudes one after the other in two sets of actions.

Under the conditions of normal and legitimate family life the only feelings toward the child of which the mother is conscious are positive feelings of pride and possession, love and affection. It is true that every mother also has emotions of another nature. The baby is also a burden to her, sometimes a disturbance in the relationship to the father, sometimes felt as a threat to her own body, sometimes a disturbance in enjoying herself, etc. But under favorable conditions feelings of this kind are usually barred from consciousness. Whenever they appear on the surface as impatience or exasperation with the child, outside reasons are found to explain their existence. In this way we get an interplay in the mother between conscious positive feelings and repressed negative feelings toward the child. The unconscious feelings may remain dormant under the conditions of normal family life.

When mother and child are forcibly separated, as they are for the purpose of evacuation, the mother may suddenly feel the separation as a fulfillment of her unconscious desire to get rid of her child. In that case she will be unable to stand the situation. She will disregard all reasons against it, will use the slightest pretexts to explain her decision to herself, and will enforce reunion with the child so as to be reassured about her own love for him.

Under unfavorable social and economic conditions and with unwanted illegitimate children the emotional situation of the mother is completely reversed. Her whole conscious mind is filled with the desire not to have the baby before it is born or to get rid of the child after his appearance. Natural motherly feelings toward the child cannot fail to be present as well, but they are felt as a threat to the mother's own existence and therefore banned from consciousness. Here the conscious wish of the mother and the necessities of evacuation coincide. Mothers of this kind present no difficulty in the beginning of evacuation. Their attitude becomes a danger only when they fail to visit and completely lose touch with the nursery or billet where their children have been placed. These mothers will certainly be untraceable when their children are supposed to return home at the end of the war.

Among our 80 mothers there are at present 4 mothers who belong to this type. But even with mothers of this type the unconscious attitude, in their case the positive one, has to be reckoned with and can be brought into play by a change of circumstances. When the mother's hostility has been expressed in the initial separation from the child, when, further, the economic threat which the child means to her has been removed through the outside help represented by the billet or nursery, the motherly feelings can in their turn rise to consciousness. Since under the new conditions they meet no condemnation from the conscious personality of the mother, it is sometimes possible against all expectations to establish good relations between these mothers and their children just under the conditions of nursery life.

16

Monthly Report
May, 1942

STATISTICS

The total number of children was kept more or less stationary slightly above 120. Inside this limit quite a number of changes occurred during the month.

Dismissals

(a) *Permanent children:* 3 children, among them Sophie, returned home under favorable conditions.

Our results with Sophie can be considered especially satisfactory. When she came to us at the age of 12 days, she was a curiously scraggy, unhealthy-looking baby, mostly hair and bones; she left us as a beautifully rounded, rosy-cheeked child. The mother, who had definitely not wanted this illegitimate baby at the beginning, had, through her frequent visits, grown to love and admire the baby and finally persuaded the family to accept her in their home.

(b) *Temporary children:* 3 boys returned home when their mothers returned from the hospital. They had stayed with us on earlier occasions and are on the list of children whom we receive whenever their mothers, through work, illness or childbirth, are prevented from looking after them.

Admissions

(a) *Permanent children:* we admitted 5 new boy babies, their ages ranging from 3 weeks to 8 months. Two of them are younger brothers of children who already live with us in Netherhall Gardens and whom we had promised admission even before they were born.

(b) *Temporary children:* a small girl of 18 months, Amy, was temporarily admitted to Netherhall Gardens at the urgent request of the lady almoner of the hospital where the mother is undergoing a surgical operation. The child had been left in the care of an 11-year-old sister who looked after her with the utmost devotion. But since the older girl stayed home from school for the purpose, the school authorities protested and a temporary home for the little sister had to be found. Little Amy, when she was taken away from her sister, suffered as much as other children suffer when separated from their mothers. When with the beginning of the Whitsun holidays, the school girl began to visit our house, the reunion between the two children had in every way the character of a reunion between mother and child, only without the resentment which is never absent in the child when a mother reappears.

A boy of 4 years was admitted for convalescence to the Country House.

The resulting numbers of children are: 81 resident, 8 day children, and about 35 outside children.

HOLIDAY SCHEME

If no infectious diseases disturb our plans, we intend to send groups of children for periods of 4 weeks of country life from Netherhall Gardens to New Barn all through the summer. The first children to go were 5 little boys from our bigger nursery group. They went with their own trainee "mother" who will stay with them and return with them. They therefore experience no new shock of separation and hardly any change of routine and can enjoy the new experiences and the many adventures of country life without any setbacks. One of the south-faced ground floor nurseries in New Barn is set aside for their exclusive use and we expect very good results both for their bodily health and for their mental development from this summer holiday.

There was surprisingly little time needed for their adaptation, except with Nick (2¾ years), who is separated for the first time in his life from his sister Susan. Since they have lost their father in the war and their mother had to break up their home to earn money, she is particularly anxious to keep the children in one place. We had purposely urged her this time to give her consent to this separation of the two since Nick is constantly under the domination of his older sister.

Susan is now 4 years old, very strong willed, and passes on to her brother whatever harsh treatment she may have received from her mother in former times. He has to do as he is told by her from morning till night; she orders him to be her dog, her baby, her sick child; she doctors him, dresses him up, and generally does not allow him to call his soul his own. Though at times he revolts against her, it took him more than a week to overcome his longing for her tyranny.

FINANCES

There has been no change in our finances since the last report. The parents of the Babies' Home have all raised their contributions.

HEALTH REPORT

The state of health in both houses was excellent. The sickroom in Netherhall Gardens kept itself busy with one case of eczema, one of indigestion, two impetigo spots, and one child who had lost weight instead of gaining. The sickroom in the Country House was completely empty for three weeks and the sicknurse went around lending voluntary help in all other departments.

PROBLEMS

We were notified in the middle of May that the mother of Tony C. had died in hospital, which brought the problem of Tony very much to the foreground of our minds.

Tony came to our Country House in September, 1941 at the age of 2¾ and has since been mentioned in our reports repeatedly. He was a bed wetter and therefore an acute billeting problem for whom no further foster mother could be found. Report 9 describes Tony as a delicate little boy of graceful, charming appearance, friendly but noncommittal, obedient and rather lost, and without emotional contact. It further brings in full a letter from his mother, written from the sanitarium where she was lying ill with tuberculosis and from where she had answered our questions about the child's past experiences.

The letter shows the mother's strong attachment to the boy and her vain attempts to combine doing the right thing for him and for the cure of her own illness. It shows how in the end she had been forced to leave the child to strangers so as to try and regain her former health. The father, as a private in the army, was unable to be of help in this situation; he came on leave for a very few days every few months, but this, of course, was not sufficient to do anything either for his wife or for his child.

In Report 12 we cite Tony as an outstanding example of those cases where children pass through too many hands, receive one shock of separation after the other, and in the end withdraw into themselves and completely lose their emotional contact with the outer world. We also describe there how in our house Tony first regained some of his feelings in contact with a nurse who held him in her arms while she was taking his temperature. In Report 13 we mentioned how much Tony missed his mother's visit on the day when, after the scarlet fever quarantine, the first official visitors' bus brought all the parents out to New Barn. Up to that time we were in correspondence with the mother, sent her several letters and reports about Tony's progress, and heard from the father, who visited twice while he was on leave, that she received them with great pleasure. Her answers stopped when she was not allowed anymore to write. We heard nothing more until the information came that she had died.

Tony, who is completely ignorant of all these happenings, has in the meantime formed a violent attachment to our sicknurse. His liking for the first nurse who had, as he called it, "given" him his temperature passed and he gave no visible signs of upset when she left us. But in December he came down with scarlet fever and spent weeks in the sickroom under the care of our Sister Mary Simon. He began to like her very much and this attachment deepened when again a few weeks later he returned to the sickroom with some minor illness. At the same time he began to lose his impersonal behavior, and all sorts of very vivid and passionate character traits started to appear.

The first period of his love for Sister Mary was by no means a happy one, He treated her as his possession, but his early experience had already taught him how easily possessions can be lost. This tinged his affection for her with a continual fear and insecurity. He would cling to her desperately, would be violently jealous whenever he saw her handle other children, and would demand her sole attention which he could not get. Once, on a walk, when other children took her hand, he called out excitedly: "That is my hand!" Curiously enough, he restricted this demand to the left hand only. Sister Mary was allowed to give her right hand to the other children, but he himself would then not touch that hand anymore. He wavered continually between expression of his devotion for her and of anger and resentment. When she gave him his evening bath, he would throw his toys and his teddy bear into the tub and then accuse her that she had done it. In the middle of the night he would wake up and scream for her. But, in spite of all this violent display of emotion, he was at that time not yet able to run toward Sister Mary when he saw her. He would only look up at her and smile shyly. Only when she lifted him up would he throw his arms around her neck and then look suddenly completely happy for a moment.

The most conflictful time for him was always bedtime. From the moment of undressing on he would cry quietly. Whatever he was asked, he would answer: "no. I do not like my Teddy; my car and I do not like you." He would order Sister Mary out of the room when she stayed with him, and he cried for her return when she was gone. She usually had to take him out of his bed once more, and only after he had cried quietly to himself for a few minutes in the bathroom would he, suddenly peaceful, allow her to tuck him into his bed.

He was no bed wetter at this time. The symptom had completely disappeared the moment he entered our house.

This period was certainly not easy, either for him or for the Sister, who at times had serious doubts whether the attachment to her was not more harmful than helpful to the child. Onlookers were especially worried by the disappearance of all the superficial adaptation which he had previously shown. His obedience was gone. The "good" little boy who was ready to fit in with every routine had changed to a violently demanding child, quite able to upset a whole bedroom full of children.

The Sister's own patience and interest and some encouragement offered from our side helped her to see the situation through. She met Tony's stormy outbreaks with unfailing kindness and affection. The result was that his reactions changed after a surprisingly short time. He now became very intimate with her. He performed all sorts of small tasks for her and he even told her something about his very few scraps of memory: "You know, Mary, my daddy carried my mummy in his arms." He can now feel more sure about her even when he is separated from her in the house. He plays in the nursery while she is busy in the sickroom. He only has to know where she is and to be given complete freedom to run and look for her at any moment.

When he has been dressed in his nursery in the morning, he now rushes over to her part of the house, throws his arms around her to say good morning, and then, like lightning, rushes off again to get his breakfast. Instead of accusing her of committing all his misdeeds, as he did before, he now shares with her the glory of his actions. Once, when he was helping her in the sickroom, a young nurse played with him and he, in fun, pretended to be strong enough to knock her over. He shouted with delight and, after she had left the room, turned to the Sister and said: "Didn't we kick her, Mary, didn't we?" Whenever she passes him in the house, he will just quietly look up and then say: "That was my own Mary."

There are interesting signs to show that with growing security his attachment has a tendency to become unselfish. When she told him one day that she was leaving the house to post a letter in the village, he just nodded without complaining and said to the other children:

"My Mary has her off today." When she went to London for a few days on leave, she prepared him carefully for the separation and found him eager to help her pack her bag. He stood quietly on the steps of the house to wave good-bye to her. And when the car which was supposed to take her moved forward a few yards to another position, he suddenly screamed out in great excitement: "Mary, Mary, you must get in or they will go without you." At that moment he had quite forgotten his own longing for her in the desire to see her plans fulfilled.

This progress in his return to normal emotions and affections cannot be expected to run along smoothly and uninterruptedly. He still returns to more difficult moods. He then is restless in his sleep and suddenly wakes up weeping: "My Mary has not said good night to me." He is more clinging on these days and less ready to remain with the other children. Bed wetting now reappears at times, usually when he has experienced some disappointment during the day. But even on these more troubled days he remains open, affectionate, and in good contact with his surroundings.

He was extremely shaken one day when another soldier father came on leave. He saw a man, very much his father's height and in the same uniform, come up the drive and rushed out to meet him. When he realized that the face he looked up to was that of a stranger, he stopped in his tracks and began to scream. He was carried back to Sister Mary to be comforted, but he sobbed for hours, and then, rather compulsively, repeated to himself over and over again a sentence which she had used to quiet him: "All soldier daddies look alike in their uniforms."

We only need to compare the extreme violence and liveliness of his emotions with the complete lack of emotional response which he had previously shown to realize what forces of repression had been at work in him.

He is an unusually beautiful child and he looks healthy. But to our concern he does not gain weight or loses shortly whatever he has gained. His examination for tuberculosis was negative before he came to us. But we intend to have him X-rayed again in the near future.

Tony has so far not been informed of his mother's death. When his father is on his next army leave, he will have to tell him. Consciously, the news may mean little to him by now. He has not seen his mother for 18 months and he did not recognize a photo of her shown to him the other day.

On our urging his father now sends him postcards with messages which Tony enjoys greatly and carries about with him.

17

Monthly Report
June, 1942

STATISTICS

The total number of children is at the moment 127, though, really, we intend not to raise our numbers above 120. But there are always circumstances of one kind or another which make an urgent admission necessary, where a temporary admittance cannot be refused or where a bed has to be filled before its former owner has actually been dismissed.

(a) *Holiday Scheme:* 4 children returned to Netherhall Gardens after a month's holiday in the Country House; 8 children, all about 2 years of age, went in their stead, accompanied by two young student nurses.

(b) *Dismissals:* 2 temporary babies returned home after a stay of one to two weeks. One day baby returned home permanently. One of our first children was unexpectedly taken home by his mother.

(c) *Admissions:* we admitted 3 babies (4 weeks, 6 weeks, 6 months), 2 of them with their mothers; 2 day children (15 months, 4 years), and 1 resident child (4½ years).

FINANCES

There has been no change in our finances since our last report. Our application for additional support made to the Lord Mayor's Air Raid Distress Fund has been answered in the negative.

The parents of the Baby House have again voluntarily raised their monthly contribution.

HEALTH REPORT

Babies

All the recently admitted babies are quite delicate but begin to show signs of improving. One of these, a small baby girl of 6 weeks, was successfully put back on the breast, though the mother had interrupted breast feeding to look for outside work two days before the child came to us. Since the mother still had some milk, we decided on the spur of the moment to keep her as well as the baby. In spite of difficulties in feeding, the child was exclusively fed on the breast for two days and the milk returned by degrees so that by now there is enough milk for three full feedings a day.

Rupture

The Country House had again an exciting incident, this time with Henry (3). Henry has for some time had an inguinal rupture and is on the waiting list for an operation in the Children's Hospital. Since the waiting period was expected to be rather long, he had been sent back to the country after a first visit to the hospital. One evening the rupture got incarcerated and he developed all the usual symptoms including vomiting. After a quick consultation over the telephone with our doctor, the sicknurse put him in a hot bath and the rupture was pushed back into place. The next day he was taken to London, his application to the hospital was urged, and his operation may now take place any day.

Threat of Measles

Three days after little Rose from the baby room in Netherhall Gardens had visited at home, her brother was reported to have come down with measles. Since we are always afraid of getting measles into our Babies' Home, we took rather elaborate precautions. Rose was protected by a human convalescence serum which we were able to procure thanks to the Medical Officer of the Hampstead Borough Council. Besides she was isolated outside our house with a young assistant. Her three weeks of isolation expire tomorrow and so far she is perfectly all right.

A few days later we were notified that measles had developed in the school in Hampstead, where our oldest child attends. Again, she was sent out of the house for the duration of her incubation period. She went to a private family who very generously invited her to join their own children who had just recuperated from measles themselves.

Threat of Whooping Cough

Two children in the Country House are suddenly under suspicion of developing whooping cough. They are isolated within the house and garden and will be watched carefully until the diagnosis is certain.

PROBLEMS

At a time when the most contrasting statements are made about the attitude of war parents toward their children, we should from our own experiences be able to form some judgment of the situation or at least contribute some material which might help to clarify the problem.

The *News Chronicle* of June 25th, for instance, publishes a statement about foster mothers of evacuees billeted in Northamptonshire being in revolt because they consider that London mothers are "getting rid" of their children while they earn good wages and "have a good time." Wellingborough Rural Council complains that their area has had to receive evacuees who have been sent from London on five or six occasions, that some children have literally toured Great Britain (and that many are unclean).

The *Evening Standard* of the same day reports that a factory in a western suburb of London which employs 2,000 married women has been losing them at the rate of 10 a week. The reason given is that there is no day nursery in the neighborhood to care for their children and that the neighbors who acted as unofficial "minders" are themselves going to the factories. They go on to say that the case of the nightshift workers is even worse. There is no provision at all for the children of these women.

At the same time it is still possible to hear statements that inquiries have been sent round in certain boroughs whether a day nursery or crèche was wanted and that the response has been completely negative. Last month there was even some insistence on the fact that day nurseries opened by certain boroughs had not filled up according to expectations. Other nurseries on the other hand are so full and the pressure for new admittances is so great that it is not possible to retain the places for children who are absent temporarily for reasons of infectious diseases.

A careful survey of the financial and personal circumstances of our own parents certainly does not create the impression that anybody is having a good time. A very few of our parents only are highly skilled war workers and receive big wages; all the others, especially the mothers, are unskilled workers in munitions factories. Inquiring into the situation of the one couple where both are highly skilled and hold responsible positions revealed the circumstances of their life as very trying ones. The father is mostly on night duty, the mother on day shift; they sometimes do not meet for a whole week and communicate by little notes left on the kitchen table. Buying and cooking are difficulties which can hardly be solved. There are no home comforts for the father and no rest for the mother when they return from work. Of their six children, one is in the army on the point of being sent abroad, four are evacuated to various places in the country, one is in our Nursery; all free time and much of the available money are spent on visiting the children in their billets. In this family there is, besides the satisfaction about the work done and the money earned, a good deal of resentment and bitterness. The children feel deserted by their parents, the husband rather feels that he has lost a wife. The mother's pride in her work is tinged by feelings of regret and guilt toward the children. Their youngest child, after a visit home from our house, said to the nurse: "Other mummies like their children to be home; mine doesn't."

The main areas in the situation of the parents where difficulties can arise and where solutions are hard to find seem to be the following ones:

Mothers with Newborn Babies

There are the young mothers with newborn babies and their husbands in the army who are in a great hurry to go back to work to earn. They hunt about for day nurseries where they can leave their babies, but are in most cases unable to find them. They wean their babies very suddenly or never start breast feeding since they feel that there will be no chance to continue.

We have in the last month received innumerable applications of this kind, were able to admit a few, and urged the mothers to stay, for a while at least, whenever weaning had not been completely carried out. All these mothers are extremely conscientious in visiting their babies and spend a good part of their earnings on their voluntary contributions and on clothing for the child. All these young mothers want to keep their babies near at hand and would not be willing to evacuate them to the country even if residential nursery places for newborn babies were available in evacuation. They seem to realize that full separation at this stage would destroy their own tie and attachment to the child.

Fluctuation between Town and Country

Another difficulty is presented by the mothers with slightly older children. They apply for evacuation to country nurseries not for reasons of safety but because there is no day nursery available and they want to be free for work. These mothers will invariably fetch the children back to London whenever their working conditions change (ill health, change of work, part-time work) and they find time again to look after their children themselves. They will apply for re-evacuation when they get tired out by the double strain or when their working conditions get harder. We have witnessed several cases of this kind.

It is a regular and justified procedure that mothers will have their children back in London when they have to give up work for longer periods because of pregnancy. Since they stay home anyway, they feel it only right to care for their own child. Two of our children returned to their mothers for this reason, and a third may do so in the near future.

Problems Left Unsolved by the Day Nursery

As far as we can observe the situation with our own day children, a number of problems still are unsolved. Mothers who are on full-time work find it very difficult to buy the rations and to do the most necessary amount of cooking, washing, and cleaning, not to mention the times when they are on night duty or when a child is ill, but not ill enough to be admitted to a hospital. It is not easy to keep these mothers from rushing off in the morning before the daily medical inspection of their child has been performed. They are always afraid that there might be something wrong, that they might be forced to take the child home again and so miss their work. It is due to reasons of this kind that mothers prefer residential nurseries to day nurseries. They always look for residential nurseries in London where they might at least visit their children in their off hours. But few places of this kind are available since the government from the beginning has discouraged the setting up of residential nurseries in danger areas.

Life on the Army Allowance

Some mothers decide the conflict between work and children by giving up work to live on the army allowance. This is an unsatisfactory solution from various points of view. They mostly find that they cannot manage and their situation compares very unfavorably with the women next door who continue to go to work and earn "good money." We had one example of this kind lately when a young mother decided to take her two children (aged 4 and 2) home after more than 1½ years' separation. She had planned it all carefully and tried to do her best for the children. But her weekly allowance amounts to 45 s. only, and she very soon found herself in trouble. In the intervening 18 months the children had become used to the good food in our house and were always hungry; she herself had become used to the ready money from her own earnings. She always ran out of money before the end of the week, saw the children lose much of their good health, and now implores us to take them back again. Apart from the money situation the children greatly missed the nursery toys and the space to move about in freely. The mother tried to find at least for the older girl some form of community life and occupation which she missed so badly, but this, of course, was not feasible; she was too young for school and, since the mother was staying home with the younger one, was not eligible for a war nursery.

There are other mothers, more practical than this one, who are somehow able to manage on their allowances without going out to work.

Parents' Criticisms

It is an interesting fact that mothers show more discrimination between well-run and badly run nurseries than the authorities allow for. We have at least 5 or 6 cases in our house where children had been removed from nurseries which did not satisfy the parents and where both mother and father had been hunting about for weeks to find a new satisfactory place to put their child in. None of these parents are specially demanding or "difficult" people.

War Distress

Apart from these situations which are created by the war work and which certainly do not provide "a good time" for either mothers or children, there are all the many unhappinesses which are the direct result of enemy action and which have come more into the foreground again since in the last few months the war in the East has been intensified. At present the situations of the mothers again resemble those during the blitz in the beginning stages of our work. At that time most of the families had suffered some loss or other; now again many families are threatened by new bereavements. Very many fathers have been sent abroad, some are feared missing or reported prisoners.

The father of two of our children whose mother is dying in a hospital from tuberculosis has been torpedoed three times; he is at the moment supposed to be in a hospital abroad after the last experience.

Conscientious Objectors

Two families are in difficulties since their fathers have gone to prison as conscientious objectors. The women have taken up work immediately and are doing their best to provide for the family during the fathers' absence. One of them is due to be released from prison in a few weeks, but as he was rejected by a tribunal while in prison he will certainly be taken immediately by escort to his army unit; and there the performance—command, disobedience, and reimprisonment—will be repeated.

Crime and Illness

Besides the unhappy circumstances created by the war, there are the usual tragedies caused by crime and illness:

One of our fathers was sent to prison for 15 months on a charge of bigamy. The mother is most bitter about him and says that he has ruined her life and the child's.

It is sad to report that of the four mothers who were in hospitals when we took their children, not one has since improved. Bertie's mother is still in the same psychotic state in the mental hospital; the mother of two other children is reported worse, she has tuberculosis of the larynx and is given up; baby Violet's mother, who always sent hopeful letters from the tuberculosis hospital, has had a relapse. Tony's mother died, as was described in our last report.

18

Monthly Report
July, 1942

STATISTICS

The total number of children is 122, 84 of these are resident. Two temporary babies returned home; two children who had returned to their mother in May, were readmitted.

FOOD PRODUCTION

The bright spot during the month is our successful production of vegetables in the gardens of New Barn. In autumn 1941, our prospects in this respect looked rather bleak. The old local gardener whom we had taken over with the house could not be brought to understand the vast difference between the needs of a small private family and an institution which feeds at least 100 people daily.

His conception of a vegetable garden was 2 dozen tomato plants, grapes in the greenhouse, a plot of potatoes, a few rows of lettuce, etc. We, on the other hand, had the ambition to put as much land as possible under cultivation and to keep our three houses in vegetables not only for the summer but also for the coming winter. A second elderly laborer from the village did not mend matters.

Our plans would have come to nothing if we had not been lucky enough to find a lady gardener, Miss Coupe, interested in wartime food production and in social work who joined our staff and very soon improved the situation. She succeeded in making the two men understand the needs of the moment, ideas were changed, and methods revolutionized. The available space in the garden was divided up between potatoes and summer vegetables. A big field which so far had yielded only poor grass was successfully cultivated and cropped with various green vegetables so as to give a succession for use from the coming September until April, 1943. The greenhouse was given over to tomatoes and all the necessary plants were raised in our own seed beds. During April and May we went through all the various stages of hope and fear which all English gardeners in England experienced. The long drought during spring considerably delayed all growth and for a while seemed to threaten the whole crop. The welcome rain remedied matters completely so that the present situation is most satisfactory.

During May, June, and July the following vegetables were provided for the kitchens of New Barn: rhubarb, lettuce, radishes, spinach, carrot thinnings, onion thinnings, turnips, spring cabbages, broad beans, peas, cauliflowers, and potatoes. The kitchen of Netherhall Gardens was provided with some vegetables and with lettuce. The orchard yielded cherries and the berry gardens gooseberries, strawberries, red and white currants, black currants, and raspberries. Of these the strawberries have been used for the children as fresh fruit, gooseberries and raspberries to make up several sweet dishes, and the currants mostly for preserving. Netherhall Gardens has already received the first 30 lbs. of red currant jam.

Our new gardener has been especially successful in enlisting the help and interest of the children. They were totally unused to gardens in the beginning, had to be prevented from entering the greenhouse, and were apt to cause damage of all kinds through ignorance. By now all the bigger children from 4 to 6 have small garden plots of their own where they grow flowers and vegetables according to their own choice. They all enjoy helping at the time of berry picking and most of them pick carefully and without eating; they know that they will get berries for themselves when they wish to stop. The children watch the seeds growing and can now be trusted to enter the greenhouse in the right attitude of curiosity, respect, and pride in whatever grows there. Wherever the gardener goes, she is usually followed by several children who watch whatever she is doing and gather a great deal of information without any formal instruction being given.

Altogether there are about 3 acres of land under cultivation at the moment.

MEDICAL REPORT

From January to June, 1941 we were completely free of infectious diseases and almost free from illnesses altogether. In July our luck broke, and it seems to us that we get more than our fair share of trouble.

Whooping Cough

Some Country House children were suddenly under the suspicion of developing whooping cough from unknown sources. While they were isolated in the house and watched, most of the other children started coughing as well. In spite of separation and prophylactic vaccine injections, the infection spread all over the house within a fortnight. Eleven of the children (most of them over 5) had had whooping cough previously, all the others, 21 in number, came down with it. At the same time 2 bigger children in Netherhall Gardens who had returned from their country holiday a fortnight previously started coughing. They and all cases that followed were immediately sent to the Country House, which at the moment presents the aspect of a big whooping cough station, with 42 children, 31 coughing and 11 well ones who already are immune. One of the 31 (Keith, 3 years, 8 months) developed whooping cough pneumonia and had to be sent to the local fever hospital where he seems to make a good recovery. The other 30 cases are fortunately very mild and the general state of health remains good.

The attitude of the children is interesting to watch. Only one child who was always subject to hysterical fits of coughing showed fury and anxiety when the attack was upon her. While the attacks were developing, she would kick and scream and fight against the nurse who tried to comfort her; but this behavior ceased when the illness was fully established. All the other children behave in an extremely sensible and quiet manner. They turn to the grownups for help and comfort when the attack is on them and they immediately run off and continue what they have been doing (play or meal) when the attack is over. There are no signs of anxiety that can be seen. One of the smaller children (2) says in the middle of her attack, to comfort herself and the nurse who holds her, "Soon over, soon over."

The Country House has so far been able to manage with one night nurse, though the night nurse herself has developed whooping cough. The illness with the added attention needed by the children is of course a strain on the members of the staff who luckily bear up under it very well. The bigger children also prove extremely helpful in looking after the little ones and in the household. The children are kept out in the open from morning till night and have their afternoon rest on camp beds on the lawn.

In Netherhall Gardens the situation got rather complicated. Since the first "coughers" belong to the group of bigger nursery children, this whole group was taken out of the house and settled in Wedderburn Road to be watched for further developments of the illness. Several of these have since been taken out to New Barn, but there is still a group of 7 left in the old house. This evacuation made it possible for the 35 children who remain in Netherhall Gardens to be spread over the whole house in a convenient way. Shelter sleeping has stopped for the time being, and the children remain upstairs at night in their airy rooms. Every trace of coughing is watched and every suspected case separated. With the babies the prophylactic vaccine injections so far seem to be helpful.

Here as well the general health is not affected and gains in weight are as good as ever.

Mumps

In the middle of the month while all this trouble was in progress Shirley, aged 4, developed mumps and was isolated in one of the sickrooms in Netherhall Gardens. On the same day one of our workers who lives outside came down with it. Twelve days later 3 more children and 3 more grownups developed mumps. All the children are now isolated in one sickroom where they enjoy life in a small group, entertain themselves extremely well, and laugh and play the whole day long. They seem to feel very little pain and discomfort, whereas all the grownups feel very miserable.

Threat of Measles

The threat of measles last month had no further consequences. But on top of all other troubles it was repeated again in the middle of July. A worker in the baby room, after missing for two days, notified us that she had developed measles. As whooping cough and measles are rather a bad mixture, we were anxious to protect all our babies by injections of human convalescent serum. We are extremely grateful to the Hampstead Fever Hospital which supplied us generously with the large amount necessary. At the moment we are still in the incubation period, but we hope to be able to report good results in our next report.

Vaccination against Smallpox

Reports about some cases of smallpox having occurred in Glasgow prompted us to discuss the question of vaccination with all those parents whose children had so far not been vaccinated. It was gratifying to notice that in spite of their former reluctance all the parents declared themselves agreeable with whatever our doctor thought best for the welfare of the children. Even an Indian father who so far had pleaded religious objections to vaccination gave his consent. Our doctor therefore has a free hand to proceed with vaccination whenever she sees fit.

PROBLEMS

It is one of the instructive aspects of a residential nursery that it provides opportunity for uninterrupted observation of the children not only during the various stages of their development but also during the changing states which belong to any one phase of their lives. Home conditions which would offer the same possibilities usually do not include trained and, above all, objective observers. Schools and day nurseries present only one side of the picture; hospitals again show a completely different side. It is rare for teachers and nursery workers to see how the children, whom they know so well when they are healthy, behave when they are really ill. Doctors and nurses on the other hand can only have a hazy conception how their young patients behave when they are in good health.

In a residential nursery like ours where the doctor, the nurses, and the nursery workers are equally in daily contact with the children, there is the possibility for valuable observation about the interrelation of bodily illness and psychological development, about compatibility or incompatibility of educational and medical measures, about the reaction of children to a physical pain and hurt, and, in a wider sense, about the whole attitude of the child toward his own body. We hope to have other opportunities to report observations made about these various subjects. The events of the last months have brought one of these themes, the reaction of the child to bodily hurt and pain, rather forcibly to our notice.

It is one of the main principles of modern education that children should be spared the shock which invariably results from moral compulsion or from bodily force being used in dealing with them. Whatever happens to them in the hands of a grownup person, their cooperation should be asked for and, where it is slow in coming, waited for. Wherever they resist violently, educational demands should be postponed for more favorable moments. Under the conditions of health and normality it is not too difficult to comply with this principle except in situations of extreme danger, where the child has often to be very forcibly and unwillingly snatched back to safety (danger of fire, deep water, boiling water, heights, street accidents, etc.).

Similar conditions naturally exist in times of illness. Though many modern pediatricians and nurses have learned to adopt the modern educational ways with children, they cannot spare them shocks and cannot wait for their permission when necessary medical actions have to be performed. This applies not only to operations when anesthetics may ease the situation, though narcosis often acts as a shock in itself, but also to preventive measures like injections, vaccinations, etc. Our children, for instance, from babies to school age underwent in the last months injections against diptheria, measles, whooping cough, and some of them were vaccinated. Injections against diptheria and whooping cough are, as is well known, repeated several times.

Our children at all times undergo a daily routine examination which certainly holds no terror for them. After a few days the doctor is well known to them, they willingly open their mouths to have their throats examined, they enjoy the extra attention to any small ills, and they compete about being first at the examination or about assisting the doctor in her task. They like to carry the spatulas, to handle the stethoscope, and in time learn quite a number of details about medical matters. (A little girl of 4, when she saw the doctor going upstairs, asked, "Why, is anybody coughing up there?") This familiarity with the doctor naturally takes one sting, the factor of the unknown, out of the situation.

Reaction to Injections

The babies normally react to injections only when they feel pain. Since they have no understanding of the situation beforehand they remain unmoved until they feel the prick of the needle. Many of them do not react to the prick either. They cry with pain according to the amount of fluid which enters under their skin, or the absence or presence of a stinging sensation, that is, they hardly cry for the whooping cough vaccine and more when injected with measles convalescent serum, where a large amount is given. Normally, the crying hardly lasts a minute, which means it stops together with the pain. It is usually toward the end of the first year that a reaction of anger, rage, or shock may follow after an injection—which means that the psychological reaction persists even after the bodily sensation is completely gone.

The situation is completely different with the older children whose bodily and psychological reactions intermingle. There again the first injection differs from the later one insofar as the children do not expect anything unusual and approach the doctor in their usual confident and friendly manner; from the second injection onward the sight of the hypodermic needle gives rise to disagreeable expectations. The doctor takes pains to explain the situation to the children and prepares them for a hurt. It is interesting to note how widely different their reactions are, though the setting of the situation is the same for all.

The variations in the individual reactions are determined by the relative proportion played by fear and pain respectively. There are the children in whom fear plays hardly any part; they react in that sense nearly like the babies: a very short period of disagreeable expectation is followed by an outcry at the pain, and this again is followed by full relief as soon as the procedure is over. The children take the chocolate offered to them after the injections and smile again at the doctor before they leave the room.

At the other extreme are the children in whom the fear of the whole situation is so overwhelming that there is hardly any attention left for the pain. The period of anxious expectation beforehand and the period of angry remonstrance afterward are more important than the reaction to the prick itself. With the children of this type, too, the psychological reaction usually does not outlast their stay in the surgery. Among 20 children there are usually about 2 who will refuse the chocolate offered because they are still angry.

There are all the possible variations between these two extremes. Furthermore, there are the older children (from about 4 onward) who have the same psychological reactions of anxiousness and fear, but are already able to combat them actively. Their understanding of the situation and their affectionate contact with the doctor enable them to control their fears and to cooperate intelligently.

It is further interesting to observe how the children behave toward the doctor and the nurse on the day following injections. Nearly all of them resume their former friendly and confident relations and are shaken again only when they see the hypodermic needle in the doctor's hands or are taken to the surgery; i.e., they react negatively to the instrument or to the setting, not to the people concerned.

In the beginning we were surprised to see that several children behaved in contrast to all logical expectations. Instead of avoiding the doctor, they turned toward her and, in a few extreme cases, seemed fascinated by her nearness and followed her or the sicknurse faithfully about like little dogs. It would be wrong to assume that such unusual behavior is based on the child's gratefulness for the care taken of him or on his complete understanding that the doctor and the nurse were acting only for his "good." Such affectionate devotion after being hurt is, on the contrary, due to an unhealthy trait, which is nevertheless to some degree present in all children.

Children very often do not hate and dislike people who

hurt them even if the pain is not inflicted in a good cause as it is here. Everybody knows that children can be devoted to very strict and even cruel mothers, nurses, or teachers. Their reaction may be based on fear, but this need not be so. Every child has masochistic tendencies which influence him toward not revolting against pain; this reaction, which is slight in normal children, may be quite considerable in others.

It is especially instructive for all people who work in education to observe this last-named reaction of children to pain inflicted on them. It is an exact parallel to the way in which many children react to corporal punishment, explains the so-called "good effect" of it, and warns all thoughtful pedagogues not to base any educational measures on this masochistic side of the child's nature.

19

Monthly Report
August, 1942

STATISTICS

The total number of children is 120; 83 of these are resident.

AIR RAID WARNINGS

Shelter sleeping, which had been given up on account of the various illnesses, had to be resumed in the middle of the month. On a succession of nights the sirens sounded between 2 and 3 in the morning. This caused a good deal of disturbance in the two nights when the children still slept upstairs and had to be carried down and put in their bunks in a hurry. Some of the babies woke up and two of our older children (orphaned by raids and therefore always excitable on such occasions) had to be quieted. The following nights, after shelter sleeping had been reinstated, the sirens, and the gunfire which followed them, remained unnoticed by the children.

There always is of course a fire watcher on duty in the house. When an alarm is given, the fire watcher goes up on the roof where he is joined by two of the resident members of the staff. The other resident members of the staff join the children in the shelter. Mothers who sleep in the house stay with their own children in the shelter. So far no bombing has occurred in our district during this period. But if planes should be overhead, our male pacifist helpers who live outside in the neighborhood will immediately run to the Nursery to relieve the nurses on the roof for duty with the children and help the fire watcher with whatever may be necessary.

COUNTRY HOUSE

In addition to its normal function, the Country House has during this month done excellent service as an open air station for all our whooping cough cases. The number of resident children was raised to 48; the generosity of the members of the staff who gave up their own rooms and suffered all kinds of inconveniences made it possible to find sleeping room for this unexpectedly large number of children; the lawns, the playgrounds, and the orchard could provide space enough for even larger numbers during daytime. Through a lucky chance we have now been able to secure some extra staff accommodation in a neighboring farmhouse.

FOOD REPORT

Due to the vegetable and fruit production in Lindsell, described in our last report, the greengrocer's bill has disappeared from the budget of the Country House. In addition to its usual functions and the extra work caused by the influx of whooping cough cases, the kitchen of the Country House has now turned to preserving. Up to the present date 150 lbs. of jam have been produced.

Since our last report on these matters, rice and biscuits have gone on the list of foods which are bought on points only. Fresh eggs are almost exclusively given to the children (ration for adults: 2 eggs per month).

CLOTHES REPORT

One of the pleasures of the month was the receipt of a large gift of clothes directly from the London headquarters of the Foster Parents' Plan for War Children. Nearly all the clothes were presents sent over from America; one large parcel, a gift from a working party in Zululand, South Africa, sent directly to the Foster Parents' Plan for War Children. This very welcome gift will relieve nearly all the clothing worries for the coming year.

Our bigger children have by now grown out of last winter's supply of clothes and everything which has been handed down to the younger ones has lost much of its original freshness and attractiveness. Our babies especially had just begun to look slightly shabby in spite of the most careful washing of the woollies and the best effort to preserve as much as possible the original shape and color of the garments. Nappies in spite of our large supply are always insufficient in number and if the laundry delivery is ever late, there is considerable trouble in the baby rooms. Shoes get worn out, and after repeated repairs become unmendable. The winter coats which the parents have supplied are often made of bad material, though comparatively expensive; they never last as long as one expects them to.

The new supply of clothes is therefore greeted with real delight by children, mothers, and staff alike and can be certain to receive good treatment. The bigger children who will now be given their individual clothes have learned to be really careful of them. They are proud and appreciative of nice colors and materials and try on their own to make everything last as long as possible. All the bigger children distinguish strictly between those parts of their wardrobe bought by their parents ("my very own"), those given to them by the Nursery ("my own"), and direct gifts from America ("from my American Foster Parents"). Our experience shows that children treat their clothes much better when they are marked with their own name and looked on as their own possession instead of being handed out indiscriminately sometimes to one and sometimes to another child out of the general supply.

MEDICAL REPORT

Luckily, the items to be reported are less exciting during this month than for July. The incubation of measles passed and no case developed. All the whooping cough cases of the Country House are well past their climax, and real attacks have become relatively rare. During the whooping cough period in the Country House some 20 cases of mumps developed. By now these cases too are well on the decline.

PROBLEMS

As mentioned in the description of our Training Scheme in Report 10, regular meetings were set aside all through the year for the single purpose of discussing child development and nursery school work in its practical and theoretical aspects. These discussions were followed by a series of papers written during these same meetings during June, July, and August. The following questions were set and answered by all the members of the staff (organizers, heads of departments, assistants, trainees).

Questions Concerning Instinctual Development and Its Disturbances

1. Think of a small child who enjoys sucking his thumb. Try to imagine the various possible fates and developments of this particular instinctual pleasure.
2. A child in your department refuses his midday meal. State the possible reasons and explain which actions on your part are correct in the various situations.
3. A child in your department does not fall asleep in the evening until 10 or 11 o'clock. State the possible reasons.
4. You are given the task of making one particular child "perfectly happy" for a period of 24 hours. Choose your child and state how you would go about it.

Question Concerning Character Development

1. At what periods of life would you expect the following qualities to appear in a child: generosity, disgust, boastfulness, shyness, sense of responsibility.

Questions Concerning Nursery Routine and Means of Education

1. State a few simple essential reasons and rules for our buffet breakfast in the nursery.

2. You have to train a group of nursery children on your daily walk to stop at the corner of a busy thoroughfare and not to cross the road alone. How can you go about it?

3. Imagine that you are the head of your department. Which changes of routine would you wish to bring about immediately and for what reasons?

Questions Concerning the Role of the Teacher or Nurse

1. How far is your attitude toward individual children in your department influenced by purely irrational elements? Try to become aware of some of these elements and describe them.

General Questions

1. The educational value contained in the nursery routine (suggestions for a lecture held at the Summer School of the Nursery School Association of Great Britain in Oxford).

2. Try to group your daily actions in the nursery according to whether they are directed toward
   (a) the bodily development of the child (growth and muscular control);
   (b) the intellectual development of the child (sensory development, thought formation, speech development);
   (c) transformation of instinctual drives (sex, aggression), i.e., character formation.

In every instance the writing of the papers was followed a week later by a summary and lively discussion of the answers given.

20

Monthly Report
September, 1942

STATISTICS

The total number of children is at the moment 116: 83 children are resident, 38 in Netherhall Gardens and 45 in the Country House.

AIR RAID WARNINGS

There were only two daylight alarms and one night alarm in London during September. Neither the day nor the night routine were much disturbed by them. In consonance with the warnings issued by the Government we keep up all precautions, which means that all children continue to sleep in the shelter dormitory, with the exception of those who are kept upstairs because of whooping cough.

The Country House had one night full of excitement. A

German airplane dropped bombs in the neighborhood and was chased by British fighters. The children heard the noise of bombs, which appears to be much more frightening in the open country than in London. There were flares and guns, and everybody listened to the fight. All the younger children slept through the noise, but most of the older ones were awake and anxious and needed soothing.

FOOD REPORT

Our garden at New Barn has produced well over 2,000 lbs. of vegetables and fruit. This appears to be a large amount, but in view of the fact that during one year Netherhall Gardens served 50,628 main meals to children, staff, and parents, it is easy to see that we could do with even larger quantities.

MEDICAL REPORT

During the last week of the month both houses finally got clear of the mumps infection; and all the bigger children are well past the climax of their whooping cough.

PROBLEMS

The following stories record some recent sayings of our children concerning the subject of war. After three years of war the idea of fighting, killing, bombing, etc., has ceased to be surprising or extraordinary; the existence of these activities is now accepted by the children as an essential part of their picture of the world.

There are still some little ones to whom war means nothing, for example, Hilda (3½), who looks up into the sky and says: "Look at the nice airplane, I'd like to have it for Christmas." But even at this age such lack of understanding is exceptional.

David (3½) complained when the alarm was given in the last daylight raid: "The sirens are eating me up." The remark shows his sensitiveness to the sound which for many adults also holds something of the threat contained in the howling of a wild animal. His friend Dick of the same age explained in answer: "The sirens are in the balloons," which sounds like a reminder of the many theories about the role of the balloons which many adults held at the beginning of the war.

During one of the recent night raids all electricity was cut off. The nurses who were sitting up with the children lit a few candles. In this very disturbed night, one of the children asked: "Is this my happy birthday?"

Whenever new alarms occur, the older children now come out with memories of past experiences. John (6) relates one evening: "After the last war there was one street where my aunt lived and there were no houses left, all are bombed, only the house of my aunt is left. And now they build new houses." The term "after the last war" refers in the children's language to the period of the blitz before John came to us.

Janet (5) also likes to speak about her past experiences. She says: "Once there dropped a bomb next to our house and we had no shelter. So we all had to lie on top of each other. First was my little sister, then I, then my mummy and daddy. I did not like it at all." Then she continues, smiling: "Do you remember the first night here when we were all so noisy that the Germans dropped a bomb on our house? But it was very far away. Do you know it still?"

The first part of Janet's story is probably a correct report of what had happened to her nearly two years ago, when she and her family had their house destroyed above them. The second part of the story contains a mixture of real and imaginary elements of what happened last year. There actually was a stick of bombs; it was not dropped on the Country House, but fell in its vicinity; this event occurred not on the first night, but a little more than a week after the arrival of the children there.

This is a good example of a child's interpretation of such a happening: in Janet's mind the bomb was dropped as punishment because the children were too noisy. Her smile and the contradiction in the story itself ("on our house— very far away") prove that Janet herself is well aware of her own additions to the truth. She herself had at the time commented with evident relief after the raid was over: "It was a kind German; he did not drop the bomb on our house." Although this sounds like a rather alarming new conception of kindness (to drop bombs on other people's houses only), it means to Janet something completely different: the German bomber had, in her conception, behaved as she had often known her parents to behave: he had threatened punishment, had frightened her, but had in the end not carried out the threat.

The night raid over the Country House mentioned earlier in this report produced an anxiety attack in Jim (6½). We describe his state in detail because Jim is mentioned in Report 12 as a typical example of anxiousness in a child due to the nervousness of the mother. His mother had developed states of anxiety during the raids, had never gone to bed while an alarm lasted, had stood at the door trembling and insisted on the child's not sleeping either. Jim, then 5 years old, had to get dressed, to hold her hand, and to stand next to her. At the time he developed extreme nervousness and bed wetting. He had quickly improved after separation from his mother and not shown any unusual behavior in raids.

Now, after an interval of more than 18 months, he has attacks of anxiety which definitely resemble those of his mother in all details. During the last raid he woke up, was frightened, trembled, and looked very pale. He said: "I don't like bombs, why do they drop bombs? Where are all the children?" He was taken out of bed and shown the children. "Where is Irene? Is Bertie in his bed? Is Georgie asleep? I want to see him!" Back in bed he suddenly whispered: "Is big John still alive?" When asked why he worried about him, Jim said: "I saw his face." (He meant that he imagined seeing his face; John was not in the room in reality.) He continued to ask: "Is Sophie in the kitchen?" After the all clear he still wanted to be told what was going on outside.

When he learned that British fighters had been hunting a German plane and had probably got him, he was not relieved. His worries finally transferred themselves to the German pilot. "I would not like to see a dead man, would you?" When told that the German airman might have been taken prisoner and not killed, he protested: "He is not an air-man, he is a Ger-man." (For Jim, probably two very different kinds of man, one good, one bad, and not to be confused with each other.) He demanded to have his hand held and needed much comforting and soothing before he found sleep again.

We knew that Jim's mother in her attacks of anxiety

had fears of her own death. Though we have no direct evidence of it, Jim's behavior makes it very likely that she also expressed vivid anxiety concerning the various members of her family, especially her grown-up sons serving in the army. She may see their faces in her attacks as Jim sees big John's.

The children vary a great deal in their reactions after such alarming night experiences. Some regain their high spirits remarkably quickly and appear if anything more unconcerned than before, These usually are the children who feel things very deeply but succeed in denying their discomfort after a short time. Others may remain subdued and thoughtful for a longer time.

After the night described above, for instance, all the bigger children talked about the attack on their way to school. Only Katrina (8) skipped along happily in front of the others and related a conversation she had just had with an old gentleman whom the children meet every morning. "He said: 'Lovely morning,' and I told him, 'School is nice again.'" Katrina reports this and runs off again. Mary (10), the oldest girl of the house, shakes her head moodily at such gaiety. She says: "I do think Katrina forgets that there's a war on."

An absolutely practical and matter-of-fact comment was made the same morning by Janet (5). She said: "What is the good of the Country House? They drop bombs in London and they drop bombs in the country."

An endless subject for talk which never fails to excite the imagination of the bigger children is Hitler's badness. The figure of Hitler is vivid to them not as that of a powerful enemy but as the incarnation of evil, i.e., a new edition of the devil. They never mention the British fighting against the Germans, but always talk about a conflict between

God and Hitler. They are at the age when their own conflicts between good and bad are very vivid to them, when at one moment they are completely "bad" and at the next swing over to "goodness" and intolerance of the small misdeeds of the younger children. These inner conflicts form the basis of their interest in world affairs.

Katrina (8) has a restless evening and starts a long conversation before falling asleep. She says: "Teacher says there are angels and once when we were in an air raid shelter, the Germans dropped bombs on us and we were very frightened. There was a lady in the shelter and she said there is a man sitting in heaven and he puts his arms out and he hides the people so that the Germans cannot bomb us. It is God. No German can do anything to us. Who made God? Who made everything? How did everything start?" She settles down to sleep, but after a few minutes she is heard to laugh quietly to herself and then she whispers: "Could God get wicked one day? Wouldn't it be funny if God got wicked one day and Hitler good?" It is easy to see that her own thoughts about God come from another source and have little or nothing in common with the teaching she receives in school and the religious consolation heard in the shelter.

Jim (6½) worries about the same problems. After a series of evenings when the group of school children had disturbed the younger ones with their noise, he asked: "Why are we naughty? Who tells us to be naughty?" He answers with a smile: "God tells us to be naughty!" When somebody answered that this surely could not be so, Jim said promptly: "But He made the Germans!" Why did He make them nasty Germans?"

The same question of responsibility, this time not for

the naughtiness of the children but for the outbreak of the war, is repeated in another conversation between John and Katrina: "I think God said to Hitler that there should be a war." Katrina answers very quickly and angrily: "Oh, no, John." John notices that he has said the wrong thing, is frightened, and asks Katrina very humbly, "What did He say then?"

The same idea of God being responsible for everybody, good or bad, is reflected in another conversation between Mary (10) and Katrina (8). They ask: "Whom will God help to win the war, Hitler or us?" Before anyone else can answer, Katrina answers: "God will help both, Hitler and us, because he likes all people."

On the other hand, this idea of bad people being liked is insupportable to other children. When Marion (6½) in a happy mood on the way home from school sings a little song of her own, "I like my Georgie and I like my Alice and I like everybody, everybody is good!" Janet interrupts her: "You don't like everybody, you don't like Hitler." Marion this time is too happy to argue it out. She says simply: "But Hitler is so far away," which means that at this moment her mind is not troubled by the dangers of badness.

These stories record the children's thoughts about only one special subject. Their minds are equally busy with the difficult questions of death, birth, marriage, and religion. They even become conscious of the fact that they are thinking. Janet (5), who is always the most explicit, remarked the other day: "Whenever I think, I think with my head, isn't it funny?"

21

Monthly Report
October, 1942

STATISTICS

The total number of children is still only 112. At the moment 40 resident children are in the Country House and 40 in Netherhall Gardens.

WAR EVENTS

There were very few incidents of a warlike nature during this month. Three daylight alerts followed each other in London one morning, but only the oldest children, who were out in the street, took any notice. The children in the Country House are getting more used to disturbed nights since air activity above them is pretty regular. Several times groups of our children who were out picking blackberries were disturbed by enemy planes. Since low-flying enemy planes have been known lately to machine-gun children playing in the fields, we have had to teach the children to be careful. They are called in immediately if they are in our own grounds and kept near hedges for protection when they are too far away to reach home quickly. Encounters of this kind naturally provide subject matter for talk for several days.

MEDICAL REPORT

The last whooping cough cases in both houses are approaching full recovery, and so far no new illnesses have appeared on the horizon. There are a number of slight colds, but on the whole the state of health is extremely satisfactory.

WORKSHOP

To save expenses for furniture repair and to assure the necessary supply of toys we have opened workshops in Wedderburn Road and in the Country House. The work done includes: heavy woodworking such as building a cart to facilitate transport between the London houses, i.e., a strong, well-joined box fitted on the undercarriage of a disused pram; painting of nursery tables, chairs, playpens, and toys of all descriptions; light woodworking, i.e., using scrap material for all sorts of toys and toy mending. An essential branch is the replacement of all missing wheels, of parts of Montessori material, and of the extremely important educational toys for all ages.

The workshop of the Country House is used at the same time for handicraft teaching. Each one of the children over

4 years of age was given one nursery toy for repair. For this purpose they learned to saw, to make wheels, to screw, to nail, and finally to repaint it. The child then remains responsible for this particular toy in the nursery. All children have started to make new toys such as ducks and dogs on wheels, puzzles, cubes; ashtrays, paper stands, candlesticks for friends and relatives. They are also able to help with the furniture repair, mainly by scrubbing and painting.

The younger children (3 to 4 years) make small toys for their own use, prepared for them by grownups or by the older children, such as little boats, bricks, animals. They drive in nails and rub with sandpaper. They paint and help the big boys to mend toys and chairs; they also help to screw and saw.

PROBLEMS

The last report recorded examples of the attitude of our children toward war and related problems. Since it met with considerable interest we continue the series. The subject chosen this time is the children's attitude toward death.

Understanding of Death

Under normal conditions young children have no real conception of death. To be "dead" is for the young child synonymous with being "gone"; the idea does not contain anything about life having ended. In this respect our children differ considerably from children of normal times. Many of them have been in close contact with death at a very early age, especially those who have lost their fathers through enemy action. In one way this has ripened their understanding and lifted it to a stage beyond their years;

in another way their normal infantile lack of understanding of death stands out in sharp contrast to this familiarity with it. At one moment they seem to know all about it, and then again they puzzle about the problem, they deny the existence of death and try to undo its consequences with the help of their fantasies.

Cruelty and Pity

We have one child, Jane (4), who is a great killer herself. She steps on worms and insects whenever she gets the chance and sometimes will kill quite a number of them if not prevented. At other times she is full of sympathy for animals and for inanimate objects which, as she imagines, have to die. She said "poor piggy" when she learned for the first time that ham comes from the pig and that, as her friend Harry (4) explained, the pig has to be "deaded" for the purpose.

Another time, playing with a box of matches, she stroked them carefully with her finger, saying, over and over again, "Poor little matches." When asked why she felt so sorry for them, she said: " 'cause they must die so quick." This double attitude is perfectly normal for her age when cruelty is just in the process of being changed over into pity. The child has free access to both reactions alternately. With Jane it will probably not take long until her desire to kill is relegated to the unconscious and strong reactions of pity are substituted for it in the upper layers of her mind.

Childish Death Wishes

Jane, who is usually extremely fond of her mother, said when her mother smacked her: "I am going to push you under a bus and you'll be all dead and you won't come back and it doesn't matter. I've still got my Ilsa" (her teacher in the nursery). In the same way Susan (4½) said to Jane in a quarrel: "I'll kill you! Right now, and you won't come back for a long long time. They'll keep you in hospital." Or Teddy (5): "My daddy is going to bring me a big gun next time he comes on leave. I won't shoot you! I'll shoot Dick" (2½). (Why Dick?) "Because he bites and kicks and takes the toys I want. When he is killed, I'll keep him dead a long time, then I'll send him to the hospital to be mended, much later when he comes back perhaps he won't bite anymore."

These death wishes, serious as they sound, are of the infantile type where the idea of coming back to life is closely linked with the idea of death. Susan and Teddy kill for limited periods only; death is a punishment for their enemies like being sent out of a room for a short time. The child is momentarily angry with his mother or his playmate; so he kills them. But his anger is of short duration, and therefore the loved person is brought back to life.

Return of Dead Parents

The same idea of the return of the dead acquires a different aspect in those cases where not the child's wish but some outside agency has actually killed a loved person. As we describe in Part II, all our war orphans are firmly convinced that their dead fathers will return at the end of the war and they extend this belief from their fathers to all other people about whose death they hear.

The child who is most concerned about the problems of

life and death is Bertie (now 5½), whose previous history we described at length in Report 5. He is the only one among our children who lost father and mother nearly simultaneously. His father was killed in the raids of November, 1940 and his mother, who developed an acute psychosis as a result of the shock, was certified and sent to an insane asylum 4 weeks later. It took Bertie a long time to admit that his father was dead. When he did so, his thoughts began to busy themselves with the idea of his return, with general theories about death and rebirth and his own possible part in them. At times he can discuss the subject simply and sensibly as, for instance, in this conversation with a grownup.

He said: "Will you be old very soon?" (Yes, I suppose so.) "Will you fall down dead then?" (Yes, I think so.) "Will I fall down dead very soon?" (No, not yet. You are very much younger. Are you afraid of it?) "Yes, I am and my daddy fell down dead and my mummy is in hospital."

Another time he flew into a rage because a helper had momentarily mistaken him for another younger child. He refused to joke about it and screamed. "No, I am not Henry, I am not Pat [both smaller boys], and I see you going littler and littler and your feet are going to be littler and littler." The implication evidently is that big people become smaller and smaller until they die. To be mistaken for a smaller child sounds to him like being threatened with death.

Another time he called late in the evening from his bed for the Nursery Superintendent to whom he is greatly attached. He said: "I want to tell you something. When my old father was killed I got another one and [hesitatingly] he is in London. Do people never come back if they are killed, did nobody come back from Heaven?" (I don't know anybody who came back.) "Can nobody see God? So if God would come to us, nobody would know Him and they would all fight Him." He pondered for a while and continued: "Why can't all the killed daddies come back and be little babies and come to the mummies again?"

Bertie's fear that people will not know God when they meet Him appears to deal only with a religious subject. In reality, he fears that he himself will not know his own father on his return. An old hostility against his father, which has long since been overlaid by his love and mourning for him, appears in consciousness in this surprising manner. The idea of rebirth contained in the same fantasy stands in contrast with other simpler fantasies of reparation where thoughts of God and childlike conceptions of wartime restrictions are mixed up with each other.

He said one evening in his bed: "God can make my daddy alive again, can't He? Why can't God put people together again if they have been killed and send them down from Heaven? I know why! Because He hasn't got the things together, all the stuff." And after a little while: "You see after the war God will have everything again, we have to wait until after the war, then God can put people together again."

Frequently Bertie himself assumes the role of rescuer. He said, for instance, when talking about his future: "I am going to be a fire-engine driver when I am grown up. I will put the fires out and rescue the people. If they are dead, I will make them alive again and take them quickly to the doctor."

Another conversation shows that he imagines the process of coming back to life as a gradual recovery of all the faculties. He had been visited by an aunt who evidently discussed his family history with other parents in front of him. When the parents' bus was gone, John (6) told the Superintendent in great excitement: "You know, Bertie's father is not dead, he only cannot move, but he can turn his eyes already." A moment later Bertie rushed into the room: "My auntie said my daddy is alive, he only cannot move, but he turns his eyes and is perhaps better at Christmas." When told that this could hardly be true, he threw himself on the floor and covered his ears with his hands: "I don't want to listen to you, I don't believe you." In all probability he purposely mistook bits of information about the catatonic state of his mother and applied them to his father.

Acceptance of the father's death is rendered especially difficult for those children whose mothers, for reasons of their own personal grief, do everything to keep their fantasies alive. The children know the truth and are at the same time not allowed to know it. They resent their mothers' lying to them, but at the same time are only too glad to find support for their wish-fulfilling ideas.

Susan, whose father also was killed in the London blitz, said when she was 4: "My father has deaded, he has gone far away to Scotland, he will come back, much later when I am quite big." At another time: "My father is in the army now, my mother says he is not dead anymore. The army is far away." Again at another time: "My daddy is in the navy now, he can't come back, there is too much water." And then another time triumphantly: "My daddy is coming Sunday. Yes, yes, he is coming Sunday. You will see, he is bringing me the biggest bit of chocolate you have ever seen."

The last instance shows how the missing father is slowly turned into an ideal figure who is the bringer of everything good. This development is strongest in evidence in little Peter, whose father was also killed in an air raid. He said: "My daddy is killed. Yes, Pam [his bigger sister] says so. He can't come. I want him to come. My daddy is big, he can work and he can do *everything*." With Peter fantasies frequently turn into confabulations. He says: "I have seen my daddy in the street, he has a nice uniform. Yes, yes, it was him; mummy says he will come back." Another time: "Daddy is taking me to the zoo today." (How do you know?) "He told me last night, he comes every night and sits on my bed and talks to me."

The same conflict between wish fulfillment and reality is lifted to a more conscious level in Peter's sister, Pam (5½), who said to one of the nurses: "My daddy is in the army now and he will bring me lots of sweets when he comes back [and then, in the same breath, into her ear]; "no, it is not true, my daddy is dead, he does not come."

It is only natural that these children who have met death in its most violent form can conceive of no other way of dying than by violence. To our great sorrow the head of the kitchen of our Babies' Home died in the hospital some weeks after a sudden operation. She had been a great friend of the older children, who were informed of her death. Pam's instantaneous response was: "Who killed her?" When told that she had not been killed, Pam explained the matter to herself very carefully. She said: "She died because she was very ill, she couldn't eat anymore and she got weaker every day, then her heart stopped beating and then one is dead. My heart won't stop. I thought a bomb or a fire bomb killed her. Like my daddy."

We went all over the house where he was, but we did not find him."

Susan (4) said about the same occurrence: "I used to go to Elsa's room, but now I can't, 'cause she's dead and she can't cook anymore, but it doesn't matter, she'll come back and she will do the cooking again."

Acceptance of Death

In contrast to these fantastic elaborations we are surprised to find at other times that these same children use the thought of death in a realistic manner and connect it with the ordinary facts of their everyday life. Susan (4½), for instance, had overheard that her favorite nurse was not feeling too well after an illness and had been warned not to lift heavy weights. Susan caught her when she did not keep to the doctor's orders and lifted children into their shelter beds. Susan turned on her in a very grown-up manner and said: "Don't lift children, do you want to go to the hospital? They can get into bed with the steps, and you don't get ill. People die in hospital. Elsa didn't come back, she was in a bed there, and then she died and I cannot see her anymore. My daddy can't come on Sunday."

Susan is quite ready to make friends with others on the basis of her loss. She said, again to her favorite nurse: "When is my daddy coming?" (He cannot come, you know he died and people who are dead don't come back, but we can think of them a lot and remember how nice they were.) "Yes, let's think of daddy, he was nice, very nice, I'll tell you about him every day. Does your daddy come on Sunday?" (No, my daddy died too, he cannot come.) "That's good, so I have no daddy and you have no daddy and Pam and Peter and Michael and Harry. Why has Sally got one?" She had suddenly reversed reality again for her own comfort. It had become normal to have no father, and presence of a living father was turned into an exception.

Again, as in the last report, it is little Janet (5½) who remains practical and level-headed even in these complicated and worrying matters. She said: "Rosie [her little friend] might die tomorrow. Perhaps all the people will die tomorrow. But I don't think God wants us all at once."

22

Monthly Report
November, 1942

STATISTICS

The total number of children is 113; 81 are resident, 48 in Netherhall Gardens and 33 in the Country House; 3 children are at the moment in the hospital. We admitted 3 small babies of 2, 5, and 7 weeks. One mother now works in our household and breast-feeds the baby. Two children left.

WAR HAPPENINGS

London had three short daylight alerts during this month.

FINANCES

The Lord Mayor's Air Raid Distress Fund has finally refused our second application.

FOOD REPORT

There are few changes in the food situation, except such as are due to the change of season. The efforts to grow vegetables have given way to efforts to store and preserve.

Both kitchens do their best to make egg powder replace fresh eggs. Distribution of eggs has been cut considerably during the last month: children under 5 now receive hardly more than 1 per week, adults 1 every 4 weeks.

Milk has been fixed at 2 pints weekly for adults; the children's ration has fortunately not been affected (1 pint daily).

The sweet ration is now 12 ounces per 4 weeks.

MEDICAL REPORT

In Netherhall Gardens, 3 senior toddlers came down with scarlet fever. Since it is impossible to isolate the London nursery, all three children had to be sent to the fever hospital. During the incubation period all visiting has been stopped, which is a severe blow to our parents, some of whom are used to seeing their children daily.

PROBLEMS

After a 6 months' interval we continue the story of Tony who has by now reached the age of 3 years 11 months. Tony and his problems were repeatedly mentioned earlier. Report 8 recorded his admission to our Country House. At that time he was a bed wetter, an acute billeting problem for whom no further foster mothers could be found.

Report 9 included a letter in which his mother described the wanderings of the child from his second to his third year of life while she was treated in a tuberculosis hospital. Report 12 cited Tony as an outstanding example of those children who pass through too many hands, receive one shock of separation after another, and finally withdraw completely into themselves. Report 13 described Tony's distress when his sick mother failed to appear among the other mothers in the parents' bus on a special visiting day. Report 16 tried to give a full description of Tony's adaptation and development in our house. When he arrived, he appeared to be reasonably well-adjusted, but he showed complete lack of feeling for anything or anybody. During the first 6 months he slowly regained his lost emotions, attached himself temporarily to one nurse and then permanently to the sicknurse Sister Mary. His love for her changed him back into the charming, affectionate, willful, jealous, and passionate little boy that he had been before his mother's illness. Report 16 ended by saying that we had received the news of his mother's death in the hospital but that we would leave it to the father to tell Tony about it on his next leave.

Tony's father visited him in July. The child was friendly but rather shy and quiet and in no way demonstrative. He did not react to whatever his father may have told him until a few days later when he and Sister Mary went for a walk together. He waited until they had left the gate and then he said simply: "Mary, I have not got a mummy anymore." She asked who had told him and he answered: "Nobody did, I know it." They walked further and he began to talk a great deal about his father. Sister Mary asked: "Why did you talk so little to your father?" (His father had naturally minded that the boy was shy and always hung his head instead of answering.) To this question Tony said promptly: "I did not talk because I did not want to." On the way home, Tony said: "I came here with my daddy and my daddy chucked a big stone at me and I cried and I do not like my daddy anymore and I will never like him again." Sister Mary listened to his tale and then asked whether he had not invented this story about his daddy and the stone. Whereupon he laughed and said: "Yes, I did."

But the feeling of resentment against his father which had expressed itself in this fantasy would not be denied. He took the same subject up again when he was in bed in the evening. He said: "Do write to my Daddy, I don't want him to come here, I don't want to have lunch with him; somebody else can have my daddy." Sister Mary, who felt worried by this display of hostility against the father, tried to soothe him by telling him stories about other fathers who also had no time to visit their small sons because they were in the army. Tony listened with interest and pleasure, but it did not change his feelings. When the stories were finished, he always returned to the same sentence: "I do not like my daddy anymore."

Incidents of the same kind recurred during the weeks that followed. Tony often wanted to hear "a story about daddy" before he fell asleep, but he used every opportunity to assure Sister Mary that he disliked him. This sudden display of hostility may have been due to various causes: it is possible that Tony felt resentment against the bearer of the news about his mother's death because he resented the news. He may have felt the father's attempt to make up to him for the mother's absence and resented it, as children resent substitutes which are offered to them. The fantasy about his father having "chucked a stone at him" points to the further possibility that Tony blamed the father for the mother's death; the father might have killed his mother just as in the fantasy he had attempted to hurt Tony. It is difficult to decide without further investigation which of these explanations comes nearest to the truth.

For nearly four months after this incident Tony had no opportunity of seeing his father, who had returned to his army unit. He had visitors at times, mostly unmarried younger sisters of his mother whom he hardly knew, and also a married aunt who came with her husband because she had promised her sister before her death to show some interest in Tony and possibly to bring him up with her own child after the war. Tony naturally showed no affection for these relatives, was always rather shy at the beginning, but quite ready to joke and laugh with them after a few hours. He definitely preferred uncles to aunts and showed them off proudly to the other children.

Once when the parents' bus left he cried, though the visitor had been an aunt he had never met before. When Sister Mary asked him later why he had cried, he only laughed. When asked again he said: "I did not cry because my auntie left, I cried because the bus went away." After this he met his little friend Ralph and inquired whether Ralph had cried when his mummy left. Ralph said: "No, I did not," whereupon Tony said proudly: "But I did."

Tony developed normally during this period, took part in all the indoor and outdoor activities of the nursery, and formed a firm friendship with Ralph, aged 4.

His relationship to Sister Mary remained unchanged and

was tacitly acknowledged as something special by all the children in the house. Once when Sister Mary tried to settle Tony to sleep in the late evening, Beryl (4½) was rather noisy nearby. Sister Mary asked her to be quiet, to which Beryl answered crossly: "Don't boss us, you can boss Tony!" Bella (8) even suggested that Tony's father should marry Sister Mary so that Tony need not be separated from her after the war. Although in other respects his behavior was normal, he developed one peculiarity during this time: a tendency to lose all the possessions which he held precious, postcards from his father which he carried around proudly for the first few hours, little photos and cigarette pictures which he collected. He would first treasure them, then lose them and expect Sister Mary to find them for him. This symptom is not unusual with children who feel abandoned by their families and somehow "lost" in the world.

Toward the end of the third month Tony's father was expected home on leave, and we invited him to spend at least two nights with Tony in the Country House. Tony's dislike of his father was by then a thing of the past. He was beside himself with pleasure and excitement and made preparations for the visit for days on end. He went over and over again into the room where his father was to sleep, put flowers on the table, and finished the preparations by setting out an extra little chair where he planned to sit waiting for his father to awake in the morning. He talked incessantly of the visit and lived through it all in anticipation. It was a terrible disappointment to him that his father failed to appear. News came instead that his father had had a minor accident: he had fallen off an army lorry, injured his foot, and was lying in a hospital.

From then on his father was hardly out of Tony's mind. Whether it was the unfulfilled expectation of the visit or dread of the hospital which he had heard mentioned so often in his mother's case, all his thoughts now centered around his father. Whereas in earlier times he had discussed his father only when he was alone with Sister Mary, he now mentioned his name continually and to several people. When he was out on a walk he picked blackberries, flowers, leaves; whatever they were, he wanted to keep them safe for his father. When a small child fell down and cried, he said immediately: "My daddy did not cry when he fell out of the lorry, did he, Mary? My daddy is much stronger than anybody else. You are big, Mary, but my daddy is much bigger, isn't he?" When he saw a child running: "My daddy can run much faster." Sometimes the blackberries were too high for him to reach. On these occasions, the other children say, "No one can pick them, but God could pick them." Tony said: "My daddy could pick them."

When Tony was ill in the sickroom for two days, he spoke almost incessantly about his father. He remembered an occasion when his father had visited him in the sickroom 9 months before. He said: "You know, Mary, how my daddy came to see me in the sickroom? He laughed with me and picked me up and brought me chocolates with pink stuff in them, and he took my photo and I had my own blouse on." All these memories are correct in every detail. When Sister Mary bathed him in the evening, washed his hair, and cut his nails, he again talked about his father. He dislikes having his hair washed. He said: "Does my daddy cry when his hair is washed, Mary?" She answered: "No, Tony, soldiers do not cry." He said in his bath: "My daddy can die in the water, can't he?" (He means *dive*, but it is quite possible that the mistake betrays his fears for his father.) When his toenails were cut, Sister Mary by chance started with the little toe, whereupon he cried out excitedly: "First the daddy one, Mary." He thought the big toe was by far the most important. At mealtimes he would eat greens, though he is not too fond of them. He said: "So that I will get strong like my daddy." Out on a walk he met a row of army lorries and cried out: "That is the samest lorry that my daddy is going on."

So far as reality was concerned, Tony's father was a most elusive figure at the time. After his accident he stopped writing, gave no further news about himself, and it was difficult for us to discover his whereabouts. It seemed as if he had suddenly lost interest in his child. Then at last, after several weeks had passed, he again announced that he would visit him.

We did not want Tony to have a second disappointment, but we also did not want Tony to be surprised by his father's visit. Therefore Sister Mary talked with him about the possibility of his father's coming, but explained at the same time how soldiers cannot always keep to their plans. Tony asked frequently: "My daddy is nearly coming, isn't he?" When the father did arrive, Tony was out on a walk. He was fetched back, came running, and called out from afar: "Now my daddy has nearly arrived." This time he showed no shyness and did not hang his head. He rushed toward his father, jumped into his arms, and threw his arms around his neck with the happiest expression.

The father had not come alone, he was accompanied by a very charming girl whom he introduced as his girlfriend and his future second wife. She stayed only a short time and was quiet and tactful in her behavior toward Tony. The father introduced her to Tony as "the young lady." Tony seemed to like her, sat on her lap, and answered her questions, but without addressing her directly. He did not appear jealous, though he had often been jealous when his father had come accompanied by one of the aunts. When the young lady was gone, he talked very freely with his father.

He said: "I have not got any mummy, I have only you first and then my Mary." Then he wanted to know all about the army, army lorries, soldiers, airmen. He was immediately ready to sleep in the same room with his father. He said to Sister Mary in the evening: "You do not need to sit with me, my daddy is staying with me." He shared his whole life with his father, ate his meals with him, went for walks with him, learned boxing from him. But he did not mind his father being nice to other children, and he slept quietly at night in spite of all the excitement.

Tony was present when his father telephoned the young lady, and father and son discussed the future as if they were two adults. The father said about his girlfriend: "She likes you very much, Tony. Would you like her to stay with us? We are both coming to see you next month." Tony turned to Sister Mary and said: "The lady is coming to see me, Mary. She is nice, isn't she? My daddy says so." When the father bathed the child for the last time before leaving, he was heard to say: "You wait, son, till the war is over. Daddy is going to get a nice new woman. As a matter of fact, daddy has one." Tony said: "She?" The father said "yes" and Tony laughed.

It is difficult to understand why Tony is not jealous, but we have seen him react in similar ways with Sister Mary (see Report 16) when he suppressed his own sorrow at seeing her go to London in the desire to see her wish fulfilled. His attachments to people are evidently so passionate that he feels entirely one with them, and finds satisfaction for himself in the fulfillment of their wishes. He therefore likes the lady in identification with his father, but it is quite uncertain whether he himself really thinks of her as a new mother. He announced a few days later when his father was gone again: "My daddy says he is going to buy me a new mummy." But when asked whether it was the lady his daddy had brought with him, he said definitely: "No, I don't want a lady, I want a mummy." When left to himself, the new woman meant nothing to him and he can conceive of a new mother only in terms of the old.

Tony did not cry when his father left. He was so full of thoughts of him that the real parting seemed a minor detail. Whereas, before, he made up for his father's absence and fought his own hostile thoughts about him with the help of fantasies about his wonderful qualities, he now keeps the image of his father alive in himself by imitating him, i.e., by identification. Tony's father, for instance, used to cough in the mornings. Now Tony coughs after waking. He says: "I have got a cough like my daddy has." At breakfast he stirred his cornflakes with his spoon a long time and said: "My daddy did this when we had our breakfast. All the children should do it like my daddy."

On the evening after the father had gone, for the first time he did not ask Sister Mary for a daddy story. He simply said: "My daddy is going to buy me an army lorry," and fell asleep.

He was greatly impressed by his father calling him "son" and asked: "Mary, will you call me 'son' like my daddy does?" When she said that she would rather not, because he was really not her son, he agreed that she might continue to call him by his pet name, so long as no one else was called by it. A name to him seems to mean more than to other children. He always addresses Sister Mary by name as if he expressed his possessiveness in that manner. The continual repetition of his father's name evidently means the same. This is most clearly expressed in the November letter which he dictated for his American foster parents:

> ... I tell you about my daddy, he is always calling me "son." He has been here a lot of days. We had breakfast and tea and dinner together. When my daddy came back with me in the dark, and all the trees were dark in the sky, we couldn't even see them. My daddy carried me over the bridge. My daddy's gun was standing in the corner where my daddy slept, and when it started to rain my daddy's hair got wet because I had his soldier cap. When the war is over, but first I must have my birthday, it will be nice in my house with my daddy.

23

Monthly Report
December, 1942

STATISTICS

The total number of children is 117; 83 are resident, 46 in Netherhall Gardens and 37 in the Country House; 1 child is at the moment in the hospital. We admitted 4 new children to the Country House, among them a pair of twin girls aged 3 years and 7 months. Two little sisters departed.

PROBLEMS

Planning for postwar conditions, which is going on in educational circles everywhere, has directed our thoughts to our own future or rather to the more general problem of what—apart from financial possibilities—is to be the position of a residential nursery in a postwar world. We assume, as we have done in our Annual Report, that our Nursery presents a fair average of the circumstances met with in other establishments. A collection of facts based on our figures of the present moment may therefore serve a useful purpose in providing a forecast of the position in which all residential nurseries may find themselves at the end of the war.

We should like to use this and the next reports to consider the following three main questions:

1. How long will it take to dissolve residential war nurseries; i.e., what are the prospects of reuniting the families which have been disrupted by the war?

2. If large numbers of children are left homeless, how could residential nurseries be reorganized so as not to produce the "institutional child"?

3. Can residential institutions like ours serve other purposes besides that of caring for homeless children?

Disbanding of a Residential Nursery

PROBABLE REUNIONS WITH FAMILY: 49 (59%)

Careful consideration of the family circumstances shows that, present conditions remaining unaltered, of our 83 children 49 could without much further trouble return to their families as soon as their fathers are demobilized and their mothers stop war work. The families of these children are more or less complete and the parents legally married; in some cases mothers, though alone, are independent wage earners and will be able to make a home for the child, especially if the child is over 3 and if day nurseries are available.

Complications of all kinds are present even with these 49 cases: in 3 families the marriage of the parents broke up through war conditions, but there is reasonable hope that some adjustment will be made later; in one case a baby was born from another man during the husband's absence in the army and it is still uncertain whether he will be accepted as a member of the family; in the case of the girl twins, aged 3 years 7 months, who were admitted this month, reunion with the family has already been tried and has failed.

PERMANENTLY HOMELESS FOR VARIOUS REASONS: 34 (41%)

After these 49 children have returned to their homes, there will still be the serious problem what to do with the remaining 34. The causes of their being without a home can be grouped as follows:

i. Illegitimate children: 14

All these children have never had a home. Twelve of them are babies born illegitimately during the war whose working mothers have very little prospect of setting up homes for themselves. Though all of these 12 mothers are hardworking and have every intention of supporting their children, they will be unable to do so the moment the young child is returned to them, All they would be able to afford would be cheap private foster homes of a low type. Two older illegitimate children, now 4 and 4½, have already had that experience with disastrous results between birth and admittance to our house.

ii. Return home undesirable because mother unfit to care for the child: 5

We should be very reluctant to return these 5 children to their families because of physical or mental illness and general neglect.

iii. Return home impossible because of mother's illness: 4

At the present moment 3 of the mothers are unfit through

illness to take care of their children and will in all probability remain so.

iv. Return home impossible because of mother's death: 4
v. Return home difficult because of father's death: 7

Summary

Total: 83
A. 49 (59%) Probable reunions with family
B. 34 (41%) Permanently homeless after the war
    i. 14 illegitimate children
    ii. 5 with unfit mothers
    iii. 4 with invalid mothers
    iv. 4 whose mothers have died
    v. 7 whose fathers have been killed

(To be continued in subsequent reports.)

24

Monthly Report
January, 1943

STATISTICS

The total number of children is 124; 91 are resident, 52 in Netherhall Gardens and 39 in the Country House. We admitted 4 new babies and 2 toddlers. In addition, 3 children who had gone back home to their families during December and January promptly returned after the night raids on London and were readmitted.

MEDICAL REPORT

The organization of work was complicated during the month by an epidemic of flu among the staff. Altogether about 15 members were affected by it. They came down with temperatures of varying degrees, colds, bronchitis, and 2 cases of pneumonia. This time the infection did not spread to the children among whom only the ordinary number of winter colds occurred. The Country House had several more cases of chicken pox, the babies' home a few very slight cases of German measles.

PROBLEMS

We postpone the discussion of questions 2 and 3, which were left over from Report 23, to return once more to the psychological problem of air raid anxiety. The new raids on London and the countryside during January furnished added material for observation.

There were 5 raids on London during January.

Sunday	17th	8:30 P.M.—10 P.M.
Monday	18th	4:45 A.M.—5:45 A.M.
Wednesday	20th	12:30 P.M.—1:15 P.M.
	20th-21st	2 short alarms during the night

The Country House shared the same raids and had some additional warnings.

During the day raid on London all the children went down to the shelter dormitory, and baby feeding went on in the shelter without disturbance of the usual routine. In the night from Sunday to Monday, though the noise was rather terrifying, all the children with the exception of one slept through it. In the Country House, where the children sleep in ordinary rooms, there is of course not the same protection against noise so that they wake and worry even with less serious reason for disturbance. Taken as a group, they have by now become extremely sensible. But anxiety is always apt to spread quickly from one child to the others. An example of such group disturbance is the following.

One Child Frightening the Others

On January 18th, when the sirens sounded about 9 P.M., rather heavy gunfire was to be heard. The group of children in the sickroom of the Country House included a girl of 9 who was temporarily staying with us for convalescence. This child had on other occasions already proved that she found it tempting to frighten the others. When lights are out in the bedroom, she often begins to tell ghost and murder stories and enjoys feeling the power she has to upset the younger ones. On the ocassion of the air raid Katrina (8), who usually keeps her fear well in check, got very excited. She complained: "I said to Sally that we will not have any bombs here because Germans are not interested in single houses, but Sally says that they *only* come to bomb the country and certainly also our house, and now I am frightened."

The example shows how thin the layer is which covered Katrina's fear. When she gets anxious, she repeats to herself the consolations which she has heard from grownups: that the German airplanes look for airdromes, factories, etc., and are probably not interested in unimportant single houses like ours. But consolation of this kind is little help and if anybody attacks it from outside, the fear underneath is only too ready to rise to the surface.

Confidence in the Adults

As we have often stated previously, the children are as easily influenced by the quiet and confident behavior of a grown-up person as they are susceptible to signs of fear in others, grownups or children. On the same evening of

January 18th, Tony (4) woke up and said to Sister Mary: "I heard the siren, go and fetch big John because the Germans are dropping bombs." He was quite confident that big John, who is in charge of the A.R.P. work, will deal with the Germans and the bombs.

In the same way Katrina quieted down as soon as she was assured that the grownups would stay awake and watch so long as the raid lasted; she promptly left waking and worrying to them and dropped off to sleep. But we are glad to note at the same time that this reliance on the grownups does not breed overdependence in the children. After waking in this same night, Tony had asked Sister Mary to stay in the room. A little while later when he saw her still beside him, he said: "Why are you still sitting here?" She answered: "You wanted me to stay." Whereupon Tony said shortly: "Go downstairs and finish your supper." His own dependence on her did not outweigh his consideration for her comfort.

Observation of an Anxiety State in an Individual Child

The following is again, as in Report 20, a detailed account of a state of aid raid fear in a given child, this time a girl of 6 who had previously experienced bad raids and the shock of losing her father in one of the worst nights of 1941. The account is given by Dr. Ilse Hellman, the Superintendent of the Nursery, to whom the child is greatly attached.

On January 17th-18th (there were two air raids during the night. Anne did not hear the first one at 9 P.M. and slept right through it. When I came down from my attic room shortly after the second warning at 4:45 A.M., Anne was awake and crying. I climbed up to sit on top of the step-ladder in front of her bed, as she sleeps in a top bunk, and she stopped crying almost at once, stretched her hands through the netting in front of her bed, and held my hand tightly between her two.

She said: "I cried, I am very frightened of the siren, the airplanes come and want to kill us." She then told me the whole story of her father's death in the same words as she had told it often before. She spoke very excitedly and quickly: "There was a siren and daddy had to go and he said he would be back soon and he never came back. And there was a fearful noise and we waited, and he never came back, and he said he would cook the breakfast in the morning and he never cooked it because he never came back. And we looked out of the door and it was all red. And we looked for him with mummy in the morning and the house [where he had been fire watching] was all to bits and we couldn't find him."

The story was interrupted twice by loud gunfire which made her stop, squeeze my hand and say: "I'm glad you came down from your room, it's more comfy when you are here. You shouldn't be in a room high up in an air raid." Later she said: "You shouldn't sit on those steps; look, the blast would get you, you are just in-between the door and the window. One should never be between a door and a window." When the story of her father was finished, she told it over again.

Then, as it was quieter, I suggested that we might try to sleep. She said: "Yes, I would like to, but I can't find the right position; I could try and hold my arms right over my head so I wouldn't hear the guns"—and she tried it. "It's no good like that, it makes you feel stiff and you hear the noise just the same; I could try to cross my arms over my tummy, that would make me feel comfy." She tried this and said I should lie down in the bottom bed, so she could still hear my voice if she wanted to. I did so, but after a few minutes the noise was much louder and she said: "Come up again, I am so frightened, but it's nice to be in bed, I wouldn't like to be outside." When there was a very loud noise, she turned toward the wall and said: "You should always lie near an inside wall, not outside, come into my bed and let's both lie near the inside wall."

Then it was quieter and she said: "When I shut my eyes, I see nice colored rings; do you see colored rings?" I said, that I just saw colors. She thought that rings were nicer than just colors and said: "Now I shut my eyes again and see something lovely, I see two lovely white horses pulling a cart." Then she opened her eyes and cried suddenly in great fear. "I think that door behind you is made of glass, yes it is, I am sure." I reassured her and reminded her how dark the shelter was in daytime and that there was no glass through which to see the garden. She shut her eyes again and said: "Oh, the nice white horses have gone and I see nasty ones running down the street and treading on all the people."

She seemed annoyed that all the other children slept, occasionally called them by name, and was rather quiet and depressed, She said that she knew I was right and that the door was not made of glass, but she thought the workmen had left the top of the door made of glass when they removed the rest. She asked whether I thought the house would be bombed. I said that one could never know this ahead, that I very much hoped not, to which she said: "After all, if they want to bomb, they could bomb one of them empty houses." After a while: "But they want to kill people." She then said she wanted to tell me a secret and whispered: "Ich liebe Dich" ["I love you"] into my ear, which she does frequently when she wants to show that she quite specially likes me to be with her.[1]

I asked whether she would like a story or whether we should again try to tell each other what we see with our eyes closed or anything else, but she could not be distracted

---

[1] Anne has picked up these German words and uses them to show special intimacy with her friend, the Superintendent, whose mother tongue is German.

from listening to the noise. Once, when it was particularly loud, she asked: "Was it a bomb?" I said it sounded more like a gun. She said: "Perhaps it was a time bomb, they sound different, or maybe we will find lots of bits in the garden tomorrow." She suddenly sat up and seemed much more cheerful and began to copy the various sounds: "Listen, they are singing a song—pom, pom, pom," she laughed, then went on, "Ping, ping, ping; now listen to this one, it is a funny old cart going over a bumpy road."

When the all clear sounded, she lay down at once and said: "Now, it's all over, I'll try to sleep. If there is another siren, will you come down again?" I reassured her and she was soon asleep.

The next morning she told all the children about the "awful air raid," and that she had cried. She was very excited all day, ran about and made a lot of noise, cried occasionally for reasons that would not make her cry otherwise. She must have told the children a great deal more than we actually heard, because all the children, who had slept right through, kept on playing bombing and shooting most of the day.

The discussion of this report could start at various points. Questions of interest are: How much of the fear which the child experiences is related to the actual danger of the moment, how much of it comes from past experiences of the same kind, or from other, inner sources? What method does the child use to fight her fear? How far is her fear helped or hindered by her emotional tie to a grown-up person? What are the consequences of such an anxiety attack on her general behavior?

FEAR OF REAL DANGER

We are surprised, as on many previous occasions of the same kind, at the large amount of detailed knowledge which this child of 6 possesses. "Fear of the unknown" certainly plays no part in her state of anxiousness. She is clear about the war situation, the identity of the enemy, and his intention to kill. ("But they want to kill people.") She is clear about the weapons used on either side. ("Was it a bomb?" "Perhaps that was a time bomb, they sound different." "Maybe we will find lots of bits [of shrapnel] in the garden tomorrow.") She is familiar with all the usual warnings and precautions. ("You shouldn't be in a room high up in an air raid." "One should never be between a door and a window in a blast." "You should always lie near an inside wall not an outside." One should never be near a glass window.) All these warnings she probably heard more than 18 months ago during the London blitz and before she came to us, i.e., when she was hardly more than 4. But she understands every word and uses them intelligently.

There is proof of the close correlation of her fear with the real danger: her fear rises and falls with the rise and fall of the noise of the raid. With less normal individuals whose air raid anxiety is of the neurotic kind we can often observe the opposite. They find a lull in the noise harder to tolerate than the noise itself, fill the quiet intervals with anxious expectation of the next outburst, and are unable to sleep after the raid is over. With them the situation of real outside danger has started up an old inner fear out of the individual's intimate life, which naturally does not stop when the outside provocation ceases. Our Anne is on the whole an excellent example of "reaction to real danger." It fits in well that she drops off to sleep immediately the all clear has sounded.

ADDITIONS FROM THE PAST: REPETITION OF TRAUMATIC (SHOCK) EXPERIENCE

But even the most normal individual never responds with his emotions exclusively to the actual stimulation of the moment. Whatever new experience the child encounters carries with it the significance of similar experiences of the past, so that the child transfers past feelings to the present event. Anne, who is a brave and clever child, would probably withstand a dangerous situation of the kind described without crying if this event were to her really only the air raid of January 17th, 1943. But the event is multiplied many times in her mind.

To her, it means above all the repetition of a past occurrence of the worst kind. Whenever sirens sound, whether in daytime or at night, whether accompanied by gunfire or not, a compulsory repetition is always set going in Anne's mind. Exactly as with another child, described in Report 12, she relives the events and feelings of the night of her father's death with all the tragic details which she guessed only through the medium of her mother's despair. It is characteristic of such states of repetition that the story is always retold exactly with the same details and the same words, and accompanied by the same feelings, but it is always told as if it were new. There is no abreaction noticeable in the sense that the experience loses force through repetition.

This type of reaction is certainly the reason why people who have experienced an actual loss in an air raid are less able to withstand repeated raids than others who have not had traumatic experiences of this kind. Popular explanation would probably say that the unfortunate experience of the past has raised fears of future damage. In reality, this reaction has nothing to do with fear of any future happening: its sole significance is the automatic return of an undigested emotional experience of the past. Secondarily, this of course weakens the ability of the individual to deal with the new danger of the moment.

"NEUROTIC" ANXIETY

Owing to that repetition, there is one point where Anne's fear blots out reality. She knows that the emergency exit from the shelter to the garden is closed off by a door made of solid wood. But it seems to her suddenly that the door is made of glass. ("I think that door behind you is made of glass, yes it is, I am sure.") When reminded that she cannot see through the door in daytime, she shifts her fear from the door to the transom. (She said she knew that the door was not made of glass, but she thought the workmen had left the top of the door made of glass when they removed the rest.) She is "quiet and depressed" during this dispute about the glass. Her good sense of reality and her confidence in what she is told fight against the overwhelming inner conviction that something will happen to her valued grown-up friend. This time the inner fear wins and reality has to give way: the door, or at least part of it, is, as far as Anne is concerned, made of dangerous glass.

METHODS USED BY ANNE TO FIGHT HER FEAR

We realize that the difference between courageous and cowardly behavior is determined not by the quantity of fear which the individual feels but by the methods which he is able to adopt in regard to it. There are some children who give in to a slight amount of anxiety and cry helplessly; there are others who will fight their fears with all sorts of means at their disposal. Although Anne is in this respect at a great disadvantage, because of the compulsive repetition described above, she is not helpless. It is interesting to note what methods she adopts.

The simplest is an attempt to shift bodily positions; the successful shutting out of exciting noises tempts her as a means to shut out the accompanying emotions. This is the method most commonly used by children who just creep under their bedclothes and stuff their fingers into their ears. It is simple and primitive and based on the child's impulse to shut out and *deny* whatever is unpleasant. ("I could try and hold my arms right over my head so I wouldn't hear the guns. . . .")

But for some reason this method fails Anne. She is probably so afraid and, at the same time, again sensitized by the former shock, so convinced of the presence of the noise, that she stiffens with the tension. ("It's no good like that, it makes you feel stiff and you hear the noise just the same.")

Her next idea is an equally age-old childhood device: to give herself bodily comfort and thereby shut out the disagreeable outer world. ("I could try to cross my arms over my tummy, that would make me feel comfy.") But again this method fails; it is on the whole more helpful in situations of pain and disappointment than in fear.

After a while Anne tries a new way which reminds us of parental advice often given to children when they are anxious before falling asleep. Mothers will say: try and think of something nice. Anne, obedient to her own advice, sees colored rings and, proud of her success, gets bolder in her imagination. ("I see two lovely white horses pulling a cart.") It is impossible to say without further investigation what this picture means for Anne; we can only guess that it is a symbol for something connected in her own mind with beauty, happiness, and strength.

Again she is unsuccessful. Her fear is stronger than her fight against it, and her lovely picture is turned to one full of destruction and violence, as if two peaceful persons of her imagination had suddenly changed to raging devils. ("Oh, the nice white horses have gone and I see nasty ones running down the street and treading on all the people.") But again she picks up courage and tries a new method.

Children in the grip of a fear often belittle the person or power that attacks them by making fun of it; their fear can be measured by the noisiness of their jokes ("pom, pom, pom, ping, ping, ping"). Her attempt at humor even changes the horse and cart over into a new picture; it becomes a "funny old cart going over a bumpy road." The three returns of the horse and cart in three different aspects make it quite certain that this is not a chance picture but an important symbol derived from Anne's earlier life, the significance of which is surely unknown to Anne herself.

EMOTIONAL RELATIONSHIP TO THE GROWNUP

It is interesting to realize that Anne, in her state of fear, never once asks for her absent mother or worries about the safety of the mother and her brother and sisters. She is concerned only with the past and so far as she is concerned with the present she thinks of herself and one grownup, who at the same time plays the role of helper and protector but also that of the person for whose life she fears.

Fears for herself and fears for the grown-up person alternate; her warnings are equally directed toward the safety of both. ("You shouldn't be in a room high up in an air raid." "You shouldn't sit on these steps; look, the blast would get you." The frightening glass door threatens her protector.) She sends her down from the steps to be in safety and calls her to come up again when her fears about her own person grow beyond consideration of the other's danger. The height of comfort would be to be in bed together and in safety. ("Come into my bed and let's both lie near the inside wall.")

It is an important point to note that not for a moment does she lose contact with her protector on whom she has transferred all her emotions: that means that she has no moment of panic. Panic develops only when all feelings are withdrawn from contact with the outer world, and especially from people who represent loved authority. Quite the contrary, at a moment of intense fear Anne whispers "I love you" into her friend's ear, as if such an offer of love were the most powerful method of ensuring protection from authority. The Superintendent evidently represents for Anne a double figure: on the one hand the father who was threatened and killed by a raid, but at the same time also the parents of earlier times who were powerful enough to guard the children against all dangers.

AFTEREFFECTS

Anne is not, as children often are, ashamed of having been afraid. Instead of hiding it, she alludes to it in daytime. This is in keeping with the fact that she shows little inhibition or repression where bodily or mental qualities are concerned. She is always glad to show to others what she can do, whether it is school accomplishments or gymnastic stunts. But at the same time she belittles the importance of the event by talking about it. Its aftereffects are nonetheless shown in various ways. She suddenly refuses to go to school alone, though she had just learned gladly to go unattended. When urged, she runs off, half crying with her head averted. She cried with terror on that same day when a dog barked at her on her way home.

25

Monthly Report
February, 1943

STATISTICS

The total number of children is 121; 89 are resident, 53 in London and 36 in the Country House. We admitted 2 children of 3 and 2 for temporary stay while their mother is in the hospital to be delivered. The girl of 3 has been in our house twice before on similar occasions. We also admitted a 14-year-old girl, eldest of a family of 11, whose two little sisters (3½ and 2½) have been with us since 1941. She will stay with us temporarily for the double purpose of feeding her and of teaching some simple housework. During this month 2 resident children and 3 temporary children departed.

MEDICAL REPORT

The event of the month was the appearance of measles in two children of 3 and 4 at Netherhall Gardens. To safeguard the younger children we decided to immunize all babies under 2 with convalescent serum and simultaneously to evacuate all children over 2 to Wedderburn Road. This meant that Wedderburn Road had to be rearranged so as to provide two good sickrooms for children with measles and two nurseries with sleeping accommodations in the shelter for all the other children who are still well but who have been exposed to the measles infection. So far five children have contracted the illness, two of them extremely mild cases, one a severe case with high fever and a slight pneumonia.

PROBLEMS

[Many of the problems discussed in this and subsequent reports form integral parts of the original book on *Infants Without Families*, which is here included as Part II. In order to avoid unnecessary duplication, they are omitted from the Monthly Reports. In this report the discussion of the position of residential nurseries in the postwar world (which was stressed in Report 23) is resumed. See Part II, ch. 1.]—*Editor's note.*

26

Monthly Report
March, 1943

STATISTICS

The total number of children is 122; 90 of these are resident, 52 in London and 38 in the Country House. There has been comparatively little coming and going during March. We have accepted triplets and have admitted 2 of them at the age of 22 days. The third, who was born with a weight of only 2 lbs. 13 oz., has to remain in the hospital until strong enough to join the others. Further admissions were impossible owing to the spreading of measles to Netherhall Gardens.

AIR RAIDS

There were four air raid warnings in London during March. One of the evening raids produced a new and changed outbreak of excitement in the girl of 6 whose air raid fear was described in Report 24. After further observation of her anxiety attacks we shall communicate the material (see Report 27).

MEDICAL REPORT

Nearly all the older children whom we had transferred to Wedderburn Road last month to await their turn of measles came down with it; five may still get it. All the children over 3 were mild cases; among those between 2 and 3 years, one developed an otitis and two a slight bronchopneumonia; all responded well to Sulphapyridine. The most serious case was a little girl of 2 years with a spreading bronchopneumonia; usually a lively and happy child, she developed a state of intense distress with withdrawal of interest from her surroundings, accompanied by violent rocking. She is now recovering slowly.

In Netherhall Gardens, where all babies under 2 had been inoculated with convalescent serum, measles did develop, but in a very different form. Nothing at all happened for thirty days. After this prolonged incubation period the first two children fell ill and were followed at intervals by seven others. All these young children are especially attenuated cases, developed only slight temperatures for two days, and showed no complications whatsoever, although among them was a delicate baby of 5 months. These children too were taken over to Wedderburn Road, which has done good service as our measles hospital. The number of measles cases so far nursed in the house has reached 27.

The state of health in the Country House is especially good. There have been no colds, sore throats, etc. The sickroom has been empty for two months except for one extremely delicate little boy who has returned from the hospital after pneumonia and now spends his days as an open-air patient in his crib on a sunny terrace.

REMARKS ON TRAINING

Several of our students have now reached the stage when, as part of their training, they work elsewhere for a short period. This gives them an opportunity to apply what they have learned and to collect new experiences or bear greater responsibility than our Nursery can offer. They return after the end of these periods to continue their training in a different department. At present four students are on such work; three, who have finished their training in the baby department, have taken over newborn babies after the mothers' return from the maternity hospital; and one student, who has worked for 18 months in the nursery of the Country House, has been admitted as a voluntary guest worker to an I.C.C. infants' school.

PROBLEMS

[See Part II, ch. 2.]

27

Monthly Report
April, 1943

STATISTICS

The total number of children is 122; 89 of these are resident, 50 in London and 39 in the Country House. In this month too there has been little coming and going.

AIR RAIDS

Up to the writing of this monthly report five air raids have occurred in London, two in daytime and three at night. The children in the Country House have had frequent opportunity to see enemy planes and to hear machine gunning, for instance, on their way to school. Many children mention incidents of this kind in their Foster Parents' letters.

MEDICAL REPORT

The London nursery is still in quarantine for measles; the last cases are coming at longer intervals. All the later cases are mild and of short duration. The number of cases so far nursed in the house has reached 35.

As mentioned in the last report, the state of health in the Country House is excellent. The sickroom has remained unused for nearly 2½ months.

PROBLEMS

Since air raid alarms have become more frequent, we return once more to the subject of war reactions.

1. Dick, a rather backward boy of 2 years, 11 months, has only just reached the stage of talking about absent things; hitherto he had only named objects or activities which he actually saw or carried out. One of his first "stories" was the description of an air raid which he remembers: "Warning come . . . naughty warning . . . naughty warning . . . warning all gone . . . Dick sleep." We were especially impressed with this story, which, in spite of its primitivity, describes all the essential elements of a night alert: surprise in the beginning, disapproval of the happening, relief at the all clear, and return to sleep.

2. Maurice (2 years, 9 months) and Sonja (23 months) were returning from a walk on Hampstead Heath when a warning sounded at noon. Ivy, who sat in a pram, looked up and around and seemed very perturbed. After a little while she smiled faintly and said "car." Maurice, who walked beside her, remained undisturbed and said "car

talking." A little later he added: "Big noise, not wow-wow, but car talking." Both children satisfied themselves with the explanation that the unusual noise was really only that of a much admired "big car."

3. Two days later Maurice (2 years, 9 months) and Carol (3½ years) were out on a walk when a company of soldiers marched along with their gas masks on. Maurice gave a terrified look at them, screamed, and rushed in the opposite direction. Carol said: "Oh look, they look like bogeymen, don't they?" Then she went to Maurice, put her arms round him, and said: "It's all right, Maurice, they are only playing at bogeymens."

4. It happens frequently that children comfort each other on such occasions. Another day when the sirens started, Dan (3¾ years) was very frightened and began to cry: "I don't want the warning." Keith (4 years), who was playing with him, said: "Don't cry, Dan, I'll jump into the sky, I'll shoot the warning, and it will fall down into the water, won't it, Dan?"

Children are taught to adopt various precautions in regard to air raids which they understand only imperfectly. Occasionally their remarks throw light on the distortions and fantasies to which such rules give rise in their imagination.

5. Dan (3 years, 8 months) never liked to have the netting around his shelter bed hooked up. But on a certain evening, a day after an air raid warning, he said: "Shut the net, so that the guns can't come in. There was a 'warder' [warning]. There were many airplanes which made bomb-bomb-bomb. Naughty airplanes."

Without hearing that remark, it would never have struck us that Dan mistook the netting, which was meant to safeguard him from falling out of bed, as a safeguard against bombs.

6. The children in the Country House were told that they must not use loud whistles outdoors, since people might mistake them for the whistles of air raid wardens. Sometime later they found some small whistles among their toys. Marion (6 years, 1 month) asked: "If you whistle in Germany, will Hitler come at once and kill you?" She evidently remembered that there was some danger connected with whistling, but its nature had changed in her imagination.

7. Paul (4 years), lying in his bed in the evening, said: "Don't forget to do the blackout. once my mummy forgot to do the blackout and a policeman came to our house and that was why my daddy was killed."

8. One of the evening raids in March called forth another anxiety attack in Anne (6 years), whose air raid fear we described in detail in Report 24. Readers are asked to refer back to that report and to compare the accounts of the two anxiety outbursts. Those who know something about the development of anxiety attacks will not be surprised to find that some elements remain static (the repeated story of the father's death), whereas others change in a significant manner: what forms the hidden background of one attack is brought into the foreground of the next.

In this particular instance something important had happened in the child's life between the two incidents: her mother had had to undergo an operation and was in the hospital for several weeks. Anne showed on several occasions that the mother's stay in the hospital reminded her of former occasions when her younger brother and sister were born in the hospital. She even might have expected a renewal of such happenings, though she knew at the same time that, since the family is fatherless, this could not be the case. However this may be, the air raid described connected itself in her imagination with fear of blood, violence, and all the various elements of her sexual knowledge. We may remember that the raging horses in the first attack already pointed in a similar direction.

The following account is given by Dr. Ilse Hellmann, the Superintendent of Anne's nursery department.

I arrived at Wedderburn Road a quarter of an hour after the sirens had sounded and found Anne sitting up in her top bed in the shelter, looking very worried. I was told that she had woken up as soon as the warning sounded. Anne took my hand, held it very tightly, and said: "Why did you come from Netherhall? They have a shelter there, you should have stayed there. You shouldn't have come, you could have been hurt, or killed." I said that I had wanted to be with the children and that it had been fairly quiet in the street. She asked me to come into her bed; I took her down to the bed below hers and sat beside her. She cuddled down, leaning against me, and appeared more comfortable and quiet. Then she suddenly got very excited and shouted: "The guns aren't loud enough, I want big guns and lots of bombs." Each time there was a new noise she shouted: "Louder, louder, that's not enough." Then she went on: "I want them to come down right here and to make a big hole in the wall and the house will be all open and I'll bleed and everybody will bleed."

This outburst was followed by the story of the night when her father was killed, in exactly the same form as I have often heard it: "He went out in the evening—he said he would cook the breakfast the next day, but he never did—we waited, mummy opened the front door, it was all red outside." There was a new detail on how they were all lying close together under the staircase, her little brother covered with a carpet so he couldn't hear. When the story was finished she said: "I must tell you a secret" and she whispered: "I am terribly frightened."

She looked round and went on whispering: "Do you know, this shelter is made of wood, what will you do if it burns?" I said I would ring the fire station, and she wondered if they would be here in time and if they would be sure to come. I said she knew where the depot was and that it wouldn't take a car long to get across, also that Mr. Spender knows us and would certainly come. (The reference is to Stephen Spender, the poet, who does duty as an Auxiliary Fire Service man at our nearest fire station and who is a friend of our Nursery.) She seemed quieter and tried to make jokes, singing, "Spender, Spender, suspender, my mummy has got suspenders on her pink rubber belt."

Then a young nurse came in from the street, looking very frightened, and the night nurse made her lie down on a bed. Anne said: "Is she hurt? I think she is; look, she is lying on her face, she is crying." She discovered a dark patch of iodine on the nurse's hand and was sure that it was blood. I told her that I had seen it on her hand this morning, but she obviously did not believe me and kept on watching her. Evelyn (4 years, 10 months) was awake too and holding my other hand, but Anne took little notice of her; she looked at her only when there was a loud noise and Evelyn made frightened sounds.

After a specially loud noise she continued the story about her father: "The next day mummy took Janet, Mary, and me into a taxi and we went to look for daddy. Mummy cried and Janet and I cried, but Mary laughed because she didn't understand." I asked where her brother was. "He wasn't born then, he was born after daddy was dead." I said I didn't think that possible as he is much bigger than Mary, but she got very cross and said I couldn't know as I had not known her at that time.

She insisted that her brother was born long after her father's death, and went on: "Do babies come out of the belly button?" I said she had asked me the same question only a few days before and added: "Have you forgotten what I told you or didn't you believe it was true?" She laughed, said she hadn't forgotten: "You say it comes out down there, my mummy calls it bobbins down there, my mummy says boys have whistles and girls have bobbins. You say that's where the babies come out, but Janet says it's the belly button, a big girl told her." She became much more restless after this talk, did not say anything but watched the young nurse and began to wish once more that the house would be bombed, that it would burn, and that she would be hurt: "If I am hurt perhaps my bottom will be cut off and all bleeding and I'll go in an ambulance and there will be a grumpy sister and she will shout at me."

She held on to me all the time and, although she wanted a drink, was too frightened to let me go as far as the kitchen. When it became quiet outside, she quieted down too, got rather sleepy suddenly and asked if her mother was in a safe convalescent home. As soon as the all clear sounded, she climbed into her bed, sent me home, and fell asleep within a few minutes.

It is interesting to note that Anne's anxiety attack is by no means an uncontrolled outburst. When during another noisy night raid the Superintendent was absent, the nurse on duty sat with Anne to comfort her if necessary. But Anne remained silent and did not betray whatever was going on in her mind.

28

Monthly Report
May, 1943

STATISTICS

The total number of children is 120; 82 of these are resident, 44 in London and 38 in the Country House.

The third of the baby triplets has at last joined the other two. A baby boy of 24 hours was also admitted temporarily. This is the youngest baby we have had so far.

Seven children were able to return home, some of them with promises of further help from us, or promises of readmittance in case of further air raids, at holiday times, etc.

AIR RAIDS

London had 19 air raid warnings since the last report, 2 in daytime and 17 at night.

MEDICAL REPORT

We have at last finished with measles, and the sickroom of Netherhall Gardens is at the moment empty, as the one in the Country House has been for 3½ months.

PROBLEMS

[See Part II, ch. 3.]

29

Monthly Report
June, 1943

STATISTICS

The total number of children is 121; 82 of these are resident, 44 in London and 38 in the Country House. We admitted two babies, one of them with his mother. Two young children returned to their mothers.

FINANCES

We have not reported about our finances since November, 1942, when the Lord Mayor's Air Raid Distress Fund had refused our application for financial help. Since then we have received refusals from all other authorities, funds, etc., whom we had asked for grants. We are thus still faced with the task of finding a monthly supplement to the money which we receive from the Foster Parents' Plan for War Children, Inc., New York.

AIR RAIDS

London had 10 air raids since our last report, all of them at night.

MEDICAL REPORT

Apart from a few light cases of German measles, the state of health in both houses was excellent.

PROBLEMS

[See Part II, ch. 4, pp. 599-612.]

30

Monthly Report
July, 1943

STATISTICS

The total number of children is 119; 81 of these are resident, 42 in London and 39 in the Country House.

AIR RAIDS

London had only 6 air raid warnings since our last report. The Country House has so many at times that for the moment we have given up counting. The children are now thoroughly used to the noise of low-flying airplanes and no disturbances have been noticed lately.

MEDICAL REPORT

There are still a few mild cases of German measles. Otherwise the state of health in both houses is very good.

WORKSHOP

The workshop of the Country House has completed a series of new toys, specially attractive insets, and a set of animals made from scrap material. The workshop is a great attraction to the older children and is open for work all day long. We hope to develop this side of our activities.

PROBLEMS

[See Part II, ch. 4, pp. 612-634.]

31

Monthly Report
August, 1943

STATISTICS

The total number of children is 121; 83 of these are resident, 45 in London and 38 in the Country House. We admitted 5 new babies. Two little girls who had lived with us for more than 2 years were able to return to their mothers; and 2 temporary children returned home.

MEDICAL REPORT

The state of health in both houses is very good, but a new worry has arisen. A few of our London children are suspected to have ringworm and are being strictly isolated.

TRANSPORT

The Country House is losing the pony and trap which had been most generously lent by a lady during her absence in

America. She has now returned and since she too lives in an isolated place, she needs the pony herself. It is still uncertain how we will make up for this loss. The pony has done essential work for us whenever the petrol rations had given out, as, for instance, getting the food rations, conveying people with luggage to and from the bus stop, and other emergency trips of all descriptions.

PROBLEMS

[See Part II, ch. 6, pp. 650-655.]

32

Monthly Report
September, 1943

STATISTICS

The total number of children is 122; 83 of these are resident, 46 in London and 37 in the Country House. We admitted 4 babies and 3 babies departed.

MEDICAL REPORT

Seven of the smaller children were found to have ringworm and to our great regret had to be sent to the hospital for treatment. Otherwise the state of health in both houses is very good.

HARVEST

The orchard of the Country House had the most marvelous crop of apples of enormous size and beauty. Winter apples are of course stored for winter use. The perishable ones are being eaten, cooked, canned, sold, and given as presents to friends of the Nursery. The children are thrilled and now divide their time between picking blackberries and collecting apples. They feel that they shared in producing this crop because they withstood the temptation of picking or shaking them off the trees while they were still unripe.

PROBLEMS

[See Part II, ch. 5, pp. 635-641.]

33

Monthly Report
October, 1943

STATISTICS

The total number of children is 123; 85 of these are resident, 49 in London and 36 in the Country House. We admitted 5 babies, 2 of them for temporary stay. The 2 babies we admitted last month for temporary stay returned home.

MEDICAL REPORT

One more child was found to have ringworm and had to be sent to the hospital. One of the children from the Country House was sent to the hospital to have her tonsils removed. Otherwise the health in both houses is excellent.

AIR RAIDS

There were 9 air raids in London since the last report, all at night.

SHOE REPAIR SHOP

The repair of our children's shoes had lately become one of the major difficulties of the Country House. Owing to the excellent state of health in the house, the sick nurse, Mary Simon, decided that she lacked occupation and undertook to learn shoe repair. The essential tools and odd pieces of leather were bought and in the course of a few weeks she acquired enough technical skill to resole, to mend heels and minor defects. By now all the boots and shoes of the children are in excellent repair. An application for more and better leather made to the Board of Trade brought an immediate visit from the Regional Technical Officer for Leather Control. He was extremely appreciative of the quality of work done, declared it to be equal to the standard of an official repairer, and promised an adequate further leather supply.[1]

PROBLEMS

[See Part II, ch. 5, pp. 645-649.]

---

[1] For the children's reactions to their sick nurse's new occupation, see Report 51.

34

Monthly Report
November, 1943

STATISTICS

The total number of children is 121; 81 of these are resident, 46 in London and 35 in the Country House.

Admissions and Departures

Our population has remained very stationary. Admissions and departures occurred mostly among the youngest babies. We have now set aside a few beds for the purpose of admitting newborn babies whose mothers are detained in the maternity hospital because of breast abscesses, etc., or slightly older ones during a period of temporary illness, operation, etc., of their mothers. We admitted 2 cases of this type during November and discharged 4.

The only other child who left us was Mary, 11 years old, the eldest of all our children. She returned to her parents where she now can be of real help to the family while the mother goes out to work. During her 2 years with us she played a very important role as senior, and her steady character, her even temperament, and her good sense had gained her everybody's love and respect. She used her time with us to the best advantage and learned a great deal about housekeeping, cooking, sick nursing, and the care and upbringing of young children. It was of special interest to us to see how her ideas about "discipline and educational methods" were modified and softened while she was watching our own efforts with the children. She has now returned to the Council school which she attended before her evacuation and will work for a scholarship to gain admission to a secondary school. We shall keep in close touch with her and she has a standing invitation to spend all her school holidays with us.

MEDICAL REPORT

The state of health in both houses is very good. Colds and flus have so far affected the staff more than the children.

AIR RAIDS

There were 15 air raid warnings in London since the last report.

PROBLEMS

In Report 23, we began to discuss the effects of residential life on young children and to collect material for answering the question whether residential nurseries can be reorganized so as not to produce the "institutional child." Eight further reports were then used for the purpose of comparing the development of children under family conditions on the one hand and residential conditions on the other hand (See Part II).

We came to the conclusion that there are realms in the infant's life where the residential nursery, very much on the lines of the day nursery school, can be very helpful by creating excellent conditions for development (health, hygiene, development of skills, early social responses). But we tried to impress our readers with the fact that there are other realms (emotional life, character development) where the residential child is at the gravest disadvantage.

The absence of the family constellation has far-reaching consequences for the unfolding of the child's instincts and emotions and consequently for the development of his whole personality.

We realize that the continuance or discontinuance of residential nurseries after the war will probably be decided by social and economic needs and not on the basis of psychological requirements. In spite of this it may be helpful for future developments to have the psychological circumstances of a residential nursery outlined in one's mind. If the organizers of residential nurseries recognize the limitations of such institutions, they will then face and more effectively fight the consequences of such limitations. [The remainder of this report, which is omitted, contains the general outline of *Infants Without Families*.]

35

Monthly Report
December, 1943

STATISTICS

The total number of children is 123; 85 of these are resident, 47 in London and 38 in the Country House.

MEDICAL REPORT

We have been very fortunate so far as the influenza epidemic is concerned. In London there were many cases of colds and slight temperatures among the children, but no child was seriously ill. Influenza among the staff was more noticeable and made working conditions rather difficult for those who remained healthy. The Country House had similar difficulties owing to a short wave of colds and flu among staff and children. But at the moment the sickroom is again completely empty.

AIR RAIDS

There were 9 air raid warnings since the last report. Our people in the Country House spent one very uncomfortable night with fighting going on overhead. Three parachute flares were dropped in our garden, and to the children's great interest one parachute was recovered without damage and handed over to the proper authorities. All the children behaved well, the older ones with full understanding of the danger of the situation.

PROBLEMS

It may be of interest to our readers to follow in detail the development of one particular child under the conditions of our Nursery. The little girl Sally, whose case is chosen for this purpose, is a typical "war case" so far as her outward circumstances are concerned. Her homelife, like that of large numbers of other children, was broken up by the war. Her father died shortly after the beginning of the war, and her mother had to go out to work to maintain herself and her child. An attempt to do this while Sally attended a day nursery failed, since the hours of the day nursery did not coincide with the mother's working hours, and illness of the child interfered with the mother's ability to earn.

Like many other mothers, this little girl's mother was completely unaware of any difficulties and problems in her child's life. Though very fond of her, Mrs. S. dealt with the child in a cool and unemotional manner and expected the same attitude from Sally. For her a child was naughty or silly when she cried, and good when she did not cry. Her main concern at the time of separation was therefore that Sally should not give way to crying. It was, for instance, impossible to persuade her to stay with Sally until bedtime on her first day in the nursery; she was quite convinced that her child would be reasonable even if not comforted by her. The arrangement was that Sally should go home to her mother for weekends and that her mother should continue to provide for her clothes.

When Sally visited her mother, she often met a particular man who has helped the family in times of difficulty. Whatever his role may have been in reality, he played an important part for Sally, who referred to him as "my new daddy."

Sally entered the Nursery shortly before her fourth birthday. She was a charming and refined-looking child with beautiful, dark, curly hair. At the day nursery she had been attending, she had been nicknamed the "little princess." She had better manners than most of the children and was clean in her habits; but an usually deep and harsh voice formed a striking contrast to her appearance.

It took some time before we realized that this fairly typical history and unusually charming exterior belonged to a complicated personality with numerous behavior problems, inhibitions of activity, and difficulties of development. Sally was then given into the charge of a senior student, Miss Kut. The following is the report of Sally's development written and compiled by Miss Sara Kut under the supervision of Dr. Ilse Hellman, the head of Sally's nursery department. Sara Kut writes:

The observations of Sally during the first four months were collected in the same manner as those of the majority of our nursery children. Each worker notes on cards what she thinks worth recording about any given child; it may be progress, or return to former habits, an unexpected reaction, or a behavior that seems to illustrate a well-known fact particularly clearly. The following observations therefore contain essentially what seemed to us most striking about this newly arrived child and do not give as many details as it was possible to collect later, when I had taken special charge of her.

What struck us most about her was her entirely stereotyped talk concerning the subject of her father's death. At all times of the day, whatever she was doing, she would sooner or later say: "My old daddy is dead, but he will come back, my mummy says so; when the war is over and they don't need the airplanes any more, then he can come down from heaven." She would go around from one person to the other, asking: "Do you have a daddy?" If the answer was "yes," she would say that hers had died, and express the hope for his return in the usual manner. When told that the grownup she had asked, or other children in the Nursery, had lost their fathers too, she would assure them that after the war or "in a long, long time" their fathers would return.

She changed the subject mainly to ask about her mother, wondering whether she would *really* come back, and obviously seemed to fear that she had left forever. She asked everyone of us where we were going, whether we would come back, and why we could not stay in the room. All this was the main subject of her play as well; she continually enacted a game of getting lost and we had to search for her and be very pleased at finding her. In the beginning she was really hiding, while later she would just cover her face with her hands and say: "I am all gone now, you can't find me."

This behavior became more stereotyped still when her mother had to go to the hospital and was unable to visit her for several weeks. She frequently asked for her, and repeated literally what our doctor had told her about her mother's illness. At times she suddenly came with a quite cheerful face and said: "My mummy is all gone, she won't come back." When she was finally told a definite day when her mother would at last come to see her, she developed the following fantasy, which she repeated frequently during four days: "When my mummy comes, I will be lost; she will look for me everywhere and she won't find me." She really enacted this scene when the mother came; and when the mother finally did find her under the table, she let herself be picked up, clung to her, and cried. The mother was very affectionate, but said: "Don't cry, don't be a baby. I'm here now."

Sally's own fear of crying was so great that for many weeks whenever she was sad or angry she would shout: "I'm nearly crying, I'm going to cry now," and she did so only when she had been expressly told that she should cry whenever she felt like it.

During the first few weeks Sally formed sudden violent attachments to one or the other of the workers in the nursery, clinging to her the whole day, wanting to sit on her lap, saying, "I like you, I will kiss you," innumerable times. At the slightest criticism or refusal of her wishes, but often also without apparent reason, she would suddenly change over to threatening and shout: "I don't like you, I'll kill you," or: "I'll chop off your head, so it rolls into a corner and you can't find it," or once: "I'll kill you like my mummy killed my daddy."

She made little contact with the other children; she watched them, but did not join in their games. She played with dolls, and they too were either dying or getting lost. She was unable to concentrate on any nursery school activity, she did not draw or do any other constructive play. She refused to do anything for herself like dressing and washing, and made continual demands on people, being extremely cross when they were not fulfilled at once.

Since Sally's longing for a grownup's affection and her

inability to maintain a relationship, owing to her immediate attempts to hurt and upset people, became more and more apparent, we decided after six months that I should try to win her affection and keep her in my "family" of children in spite of all her probable attempts to break away from me.[1]

From the time when I took Sally under my special care, I began to keep weekly notes about her while the other workers continued their observations as they had done before. My family then consisted of two boys, Jeffrey (2) and Donald (3), and now Sally (4 years, 3 months). Sally showed great jealousy of Jeffrey from the beginning, but soon became fond of Donald. She surely felt that I was fonder of Jeffrey than of Donald; moreover, Jeffrey, being so much younger, needed more care and always was a center of attention in the Nursery.

Sally soon understood and accepted the fact that I was now to do everything for her. Her pleasure about it was visible at times, but more often she would suddenly stop me and say: "You have bathed me, now somebody else can dry me." When this was done, she turned to a third person and said: "You can do my hair today." If she was in a pleasant mood, then she sometimes said to me: "I don't mind if you finish me today." This repeated itself in innumerable variations and in connection with most activities right through the day.

When Sally was alone with me, she would invent and repeat games in which she suggested our taking turns, in a kind of aggressive interplay. She formulated this, for instance, as follows: "If you make me cry, I'll make you cry," or: "If you kill me, I'll kill you." She also derived pleasure from being forced and showed this in the following way: "If I say no, and you say yes, I'll do what you say." One

[1] As was indicated in Report 14 and others, all children at the Nursery are divided into so-called families. Each worker has 3 or 4 children in her care, for whom she becomes a mother substitute during the time of separation from their mothers; we bathe our children, put them to bed, we take them for walks and give them special treats whenever possible.

day, when Sally was cross with me, she said: "You can't take me to Regents Park now!" I said how sorry I felt about it, but she exclaimed: "If you say yes, then I'll go to Regents Park with you." Many times she refused to make use of her freedom to act, but insisted that I should *make* her do a definite thing. She was quite unable to do anything for herself, and any encouragement to do so was taken as a sign that she was not loved.

At this time she would react with aggressive behavior to any criticism I made: "You don't like me anyway, I am not your friend anymore," were replies heard frequently. Sometimes she tried to swear at me, but without using bad language; e.g., she shouted at me: "You chair, you wardrobe," or the name of any other object.

As soon as our relationship had become more firmly established, Sally showed me that her interest in the difference between boys and girls was very great. Looking at people she would enumerate all men and boys she knew and insist on their really being girls; she said, on the other hand, that all girls were really boys. But she herself always remained what she really was, a girl.

During the same period Sally began to show fears at bedtime: she would not be left alone and when she had fallen asleep, she would wake up after a short time, crying, having wet her bed. She repeatedly gave an explanation of her fear of being left alone, in the following way: "You stay with me, I don't want it dark. Then I am frightened and the dog and the mouse and the rat will come and bite me all up." After she had repeated this on several evenings, I suggested to her to make the dog, rat, and mouse of plasticene. She immediately accepted the proposal and reminded me of it the next morning. I made the animals for her and Sally wanted them to be put into three little cages, which had to be kept on the mantelpiece in the nursery. She very rarely took them down, but made sure every day for the next three weeks that they were still there. At this time her nightmares ceased.

Sally often referred to her "new daddy." She told me that

he had visited her and her mother the last weekends and brought her lots of sweets. She said he was a wonderful daddy, he played with her on these occasions, and she described these games with great excitement. She often asked to be swung through the air or tickled, just as her new daddy had done with her. If a Sunday passed without a visit from him, Sally would be very disappointed. Her questions about other people's daddies continued, but now instead of the usual conclusion: "Your daddy will come back, as my daddy will," she said: "Never mind, if your daddy is dead, you get a new one. I have got a nice new daddy."

During this whole period Sally exclusively used all play material to give expression to her fantasy world; she was still unable to use the equipment in the nursery in a constructive way. She did not make friends with the children. Whenever she was asked to join in group activities, she either declined to do so or got very cross, and the children did not care to play with her either. She continued to ask for help for every little thing and would call us nasty or silly when her wish was not fulfilled immediately.

In the following part of the observations the nature of the material and the way in which it presented itself showed definite changes; especially her relationship to me showed some improvement. She began to tell me stories every night as soon as she was put into the bathtub. In great excitement, her voice sounding hoarser than usual, and constantly breaking out into violent laughter, she shouted, pointing to the drain: "Down there lives a man, his name is Peter Bumibum. Peter Bumibum, because he come from the bumibum." She said Peter was talking to her, enacting this in an unintelligible, violent language, and then she answered in the same manner. I listened to this daily story and sometimes asked why she and Peter had to shout at each other so much. However, she gave no explanation.

Her conversation, when alone with me during the following weeks, sooner or later inevitably turned to the difference between boys and girls. She would say: "Jeffrey has got a doodle. David has got a doodle. Sybil has a wee-wee. All girls have a wee-wee, only boys have a doodle. Mummy and my aunty have a dick and I have a doggy." Sally, until two months ago, always kept to these differences in the names which she had given to the genitals of boys and girls, women and herself. At this time, she began to masturbate openly and was seen trying to hold a clothes peg between her legs.

She began to provoke the other children to play aggressive and sexually exciting games with her, but met with repeated rebuffs, for instance, from her friend Sybil, who told her "not to be rude." Her friendship with little Donald was also based on similar games. She wanted him to visit her in her bed, either morning or evening, wanted to play with him and tickle him. When she was told to leave him in his bed, she answered: "But Donald does like me to tickle him, he always laughs."

During this time she was particularly keen on stories in which animals or people died. She was delighted with a story told by a visiting student, in which a fox cut off many other animals' heads. She herself then told me: "There is a mouse in my mother's kitchen, it jumped on the table and lost its tail."

The former game of taking turns lost its character of aggressiveness. She substituted for it an exchange of pleasant things: I had to sing my favorite song and she sang hers, or she would say: "You kiss me, and I kiss you." Bedtime became peaceful, and she was now able to express her affection.

Sally began to take part in the other children's activities, but her general behavior during this period became especially difficult. She remained aggressive toward the workers, at the same time wanting their love. She often persuaded the other children to do forbidden things as soon as the grownup had turned her back. Once, for example. playing in the garden, she called to Sybil and some other children: "Come let's go on the coal, she's gone into the house"— "she" being the nursery assistant. When Sally now wanted to swear, she no longer used inoffensive words but adopted truly bad language, frequently and freely. She did not yet show any wish to do anything for herself, but insisted on my doing everything for her. There were no attempts at constructive play during this period either.

Her mother continued to take her home regularly and Sally always awaited her impatiently. With her she continued to be the good little girl whom her mother liked to see. The "new daddy," about whom we heard so much before, still appeared in her conversation, but she seemed less excited when she mentioned him and less preoccupied with the whole problem of the death of her old and the presence of her new daddy.

During the following months, the second half year of her stay with us, great improvements could be observed in every respect. Her relationship to me was so well established that the fact that I went on a three-week holiday did not have any negative influence on it; she could maintain it throughout the period of separation. During this time she chose a friend of mine as a substitute, saying: "It will be my Hanni, while my Sara is away." Sally seemed quite content and showed fewer problems than before. Soon she told Hanni the first of a series of stories at bathtime: "There is a new man down the bath, his name is chocolate creamy-creamy man. He has a brown overall, black buttons, quite a black face, and very white teeth." She put her mug on the drain: "I am putting my mug on his bum!" This story was again told almost every night, with great excitement and accompanied by sudden outbursts of laughter.

On my return, I was given a great welcome. Sally now was able to give expression to her affection for me, without destroying it at once, in her former ways. As a consequence of this she began to accept my criticism and tried to please me.

On my first evening with her, and on many subsequent ones, she told me stories very similar to the one mentioned before. In telling them her pleasure in the use of "funny words" and repetitions became more and more evident. The stories began to be repetitive in content and increasingly assumed the character of "nonsense talk": "Today, there is a nasty chocolate bumibum-creamy man in the bath. In my house there are lots of them. My house is lovely, many toys and lovely clothes. Sometime, when you are very nice, I will take you to my house." A few days later: "There is a new man in the pipe. He has got lots of children and they are all good. They have got paper in their bum. Micky Lollipop called up the chimney and went up the pullipull. A chopper came down and cut his mummy's head off and then they danced together." Another story: "Peter Rombi-Rombi and John Jahihaiji have got 11 children, Mr. Man came and danced with them. Mr. Man came and sat on bumy." And another: "There was a little man who had 2 gigies called Sybil and Boxer. And the horse jumped on the man's head and on his bottom; and a glass broke on his jungiabumbia." And a last story in this series: "There was a little man and he had a little juviake. a tummy, and a little vomiake. He hurt his juviams and he had a daddy."

At this time she constantly carried with her a bottle filled with sand, and, holding it in front of her, used it as a weapon with which to attack us.

She then turned to a different kind of story: "I am thinking that the doggy, what is in the garage, is eating me all up and my mummy is running away with a white doggy and left me alone." On one occasion Sally suddenly burst out crying: "You don't like me, do you, nobody likes me anyway! I am not a nice girl, Mummy doesn't like me either." Then, rather distressed: "Where do the children get their faces from?" I told her then that they were in the mummy's tummy, whereupon she burst out: "Don't be silly, I am not in my mummy's tummy and I never had nappies!" The subject has not been mentioned since.

The talk about sex differences ceased and Sally showed in many ways that she tried to make the best of being a girl. Her interest in clothes became very great. She would choose in the evening the frock to wear next morning. She dreamed of red velvet and actually persuaded her mother to have a coat made for her of such material. She was found standing in front of a full-length mirror. It was bad weather and no chance to go out for a walk, but Sally had dressed herself in the new coat, gloves, and a little gray fur beret. She stared into the mirror admiring herself. When she noticed me, she turned around and said: "Aren't I a smart girl?"

In the evenings a new game made its appearance. With her beautiful hair undone, she tripped up and down in front of the mirror, making some dance movements. She called it a "fairy dance" and had to be watched and applauded by all of us.

Her former attempts to break off a relationship changed into attempts to regard everything one did as a sign of one's affection for her. At table, for instance, she asked: "Why do you sit next to me?" When told that there was a free chair next to her, she countered, "No, I think you chose this chair because you like me and want to sit next to me." Or she would ask: "Why did you put the jam jar there on the table?" When told it was simply placed there to be within everybody's reach, she would say: "But it is just a little nearer to me than to the others. I think you put it there because you like me."

At this time, at last Sally's attitude toward the other children underwent a complete change. She began to take care of the little ones in a motherly way and did so not to earn praise but because of the pleasure she derived from it. Her friendship with Donald lost its aggressive and provocative character; she now looked after him in every respect, for instance, dressed him, sat with him at mealtimes, and always remembered him when she had sweets. When Jeffrey had to go to a hospital, Sally at first seemed relieved, but then constantly inquired about him and insisted that I should send him parcels with sweets. Presently, Sally began to share sweets with her friends, often keeping one of her mother's sweets for the one or the other. Previously, she used sweets to upset children by boasting about them but never giving them away. She herself was always greedy for sweets, begging from every person in the house, and even once asked a man in the street who was feeding a horse to feed her instead of the animal.

During the following months Sally became quite independent. She dressed and undressed without help and also liked to bathe herself. One day she surprised me by being ready before I had even turned to her. She took pride in being "nearly a real school girl" and tried to live up to it. She became very helpful in the house and good at scrubbing and tidying. She easily learned to sew and became especially clever in making little bags or handkerchiefs for herself and others. A corresponding change took place in her play in the nursery school, where she settled down to painting and puzzles and joined in group games.

A spell of almost perfect behavior was followed by a more difficult one, but with the difference that she now worried about the consequences of her behavior and immediately tried to make good what she had said or done wrong. Once when she rushed across a crossing, knowing how very forbidden that is, she turned around, asking: "You aren't really cross with me, are you?" When I happened to knock against her with a pram, she did not, as formerly, become angry, accusing me of having hurt her badly and on purpose, but she said: "You haven't hurt me, it was the wheel."

At this time the distinction between right and wrong played an important role in her thoughts. This did not yet prevent her from doing what was forbidden when she thought herself unobserved; but instead of becoming aggressive when she felt that she had been naughty, she tried at least to excuse herself by pretending that she meant to do right. For instance, when being reproached for playing with an important document which she had removed from its accustomed place, she said quickly: "Oh, yes, I only meant to bring it to you."

The latest worry which I could observe in her concerned a completely new subject. She cried very unhappily in her bed one evening. When questioned about it, she finally said: "If my mummy doesn't stop growing, I can never be as big as she is. She is sooo big." She was pleased to hear from me that her mother had actually ceased growing long ago, but this relief did not last long. She returned to the subject twice during the same week.

The foregoing report by Sara Kut covers a period of eleven months, i.e., from Sally's 4th birthday to the age of 4 years, 11 months. Doubtless Sally has made good progress during that time, and has actually changed from a real "problem child" to a fairly well-adapted member of the nursery group. We expect that she will have no great difficulties when she enters school after her 5th birthday.

Her development in the Nursery, as described in the report, went through various phases.

During the *first* phase, which lasted about six months, Sally was busy with one central problem, the death of her father and the separation from her mother. She was unable to react to these events with a free flow of emotion, either of sorrow or of unhappiness or of simple longing. This estrangement from her own feelings was probably due to her mother's strict suppression of emotion. She was able to express what was going on in her only with the help of compulsive actions, which became very monotonous. The problem of death and separation weighed on her mind to an extent which limited and inhibited all her activities. Her achievements in practical matters and in the nursery school were consequently far below her intellectual standards.

A new factor was added to the situation by the introduction of the substitute mother, Sara, and the development of an attachment to her. This attachment revealed in living repetition the ambivalent character of Sally's feelings, which swung continually between love and hate, aggression and submission, accusation and self-accusation. Again, these emotions expressed themselves largely in her behavior.

In a *second* phase these problems receded far enough into the background to make room for a new interest: Sally's curiosity about the difference between boys and girls. She revealed considerable knowledge about sex differences. Night fears, which made their appearance at the same time, showed that she attributed the difference between boys and girls to some violent assault, i.e., biting (the dog, rat, and mouse). It seemed to give her some reassurance that she was able to confide her anxieties to Sara, who, by modeling and caging the symbols of danger, took over the role of protector in Sally's fantasy. Her interest at this time widened somewhat, but merely to the extent in which the scope of her fears and fantasies widened.

A decisive change occurred in her reaction in a *third* phase, when her fantasies began to express themselves in real "stories," instead of being acted out and thereby distorting her daily behavior. Her stories revealed the level of her sex development, namely, her interest in anal, dirty, and aggressive matters. Her attempts at sex play with other children bore out this assumption. The possibility of expressing such fantasies openly gave her, to a degree, freedom from them; this showed in a new ability to feel positive affection.

An interesting *fourth* phase showed Sally trying to accept her femininity, Instead of comparing herself unfavorably with boys, or thinking out reasons why girls are mutilated and handicapped, she began to feel pleasure in her own appearance and developed real feminine vanity concerning her hair and clothes. But she was still not convinced of being really intact and likable, as shown by her exaggerated search for proof that she was loved.

These steps in development so far show beneficial results in four main respects:

in her emotional relationship to the mother substitute, in which her ambivalence has lessened and positive reactions are permitted free expression;

in the development of normal social relations to the other children;

in a better functioning of her conscience; instead of torturing herself with self-accusations, she has begun to let herself be guided by its moral prescriptions;

in her intellectual development which, freed from the pressure of her fantasies and problems, expresses itself in the normal achievements of her age.

36

Monthly Report
January, 1944

STATISTICS

The total number of children is 121; 81 of these are resident, 44 in London and 37 in the Country House.

MEDICAL REPORT

We have been less fortunate with the influenza epidemic during the last month. Though the sickroom in the Country House is again empty and all the bigger children in London have got over their colds, some of the younger and youngest babies were seriously ill. Three had to go to the hospital from where, we hope, they will soon return. The others are by now on their way to recovery.

AIR RAIDS

There were 9 air raids since the last report. Our shelter

PROBLEMS

After more than a year's interval we continue the story of Tony, who is now 5 years, 1 month old and goes to school since the autumn.

The problem of Tony has recurred in our reports repeatedly since his admission to the Country House in September, 1941. The last detailed account of his development was contained in Report 22. At that time Tony's problems seemed very near to solution. The symptoms for which he had been sent to us (bed wetting and a lack of emotional response) had disappeared. He had formed a warm and personal relationship with the sicknurse, Sister Mary, and he had developed a deep and loving attachment to his father, whom he adored unrestrainedly. These two attachments helped him to overcome the loss of his mother, who had died after a severe illness. Report 22 ended with the news that Tony's father was engaged to marry a very charming young woman and had introduced her to the child as a future mother. Tony seemed to like her very much, and all his plans and wishes turned toward the pleasant prospect of a new "home" after the war, with parents of his own, as in the old times which he still remembered.

During and after this period he showed improvement in various directions, above all in a greater independence with regard to his mother substitute, Sister Mary. He was able to do with less signs of affection and his behavior in the evenings, which had always been the times when he was most demanding, changed considerably. He ceased to be fussy about his bath, and instead of begging Sister Mary to stay with him until he fell asleep, he sent her away himself. He would say after a short talk with her: "Mary, now you go and have your supper; you can stay away a long time. Go quickly to bed if you are tired, just come and look at me before you go to bed. Now go, I'm going to sleep." He would fall asleep quickly and peacefully.

His general interests at this time widened. He formed firm friendships with other boys and took active part in all the occupations offered by the nursery, the workshop, and the garden. On the basis of his great admiration for his father's strength and manliness, he was apt to form similar relationships to other boys who were stronger or bolder than he was. He imitated and obeyed them to the point of being easily led into mischief by them. He was eager to enter school and did so even before he had reached the compulsory age.

His development might have proceeded on these comparatively peaceful lines if fate had not had another shock in store for him which once more threatened to unsettle his hardly won stability. In the middle of April, 1943 Tony's father appeared unexpectedly. Tony ran downstairs to meet him, but suddenly stopped dead in his tracks when he realized that his father was accompanied by a strange woman. His father greeted him as always and added immediately: "Go and kiss your mummy." This was all the notice and explanation Tony received of a complete change of plan in the father's life, and consequently also in Tony's.

The father had married this woman a few days previously and they both came to visit the child during his remaining leave. Neither of them seemed to expect anything but pleasure on Tony's part, and they were astonished when he suddenly burst into tears. He soon controlled himself and, with his usual obedience toward his father's wishes, greeted the new mother and silently sat beside her. He even went so far as to laugh about his father's jokes and, by the time they left, seemed to have regained his usual cheerfulness.

As a result of this experience Tony regressed to many of his former habits and became once more clinging and dependent on Sister Mary. After the parents had gone, he succeeded in expressing his disappoinment clearly. He said at bedtime: "Mary, I don't want this mummy, I want my daddy to myself. My daddy said once that he is going to make me a new mummy, but he has not made this one."

In the following days he became very troubled and unable to express himself. He would say whenever he met Sister Mary in the house: "I want to tell you something, I want to tell you something." But when asked what he wanted to tell, he could not think of anything and only said: "I want to give you a kiss," or: "I want to go to the lavy," or: "I'm hungry." He developed a rather frightening habit of slipping down on the floor every so often. He would call out: "Mary, I'm falling, I'm falling, pick me up." Or "I want to be your baby, carry me around." He refused in this period to work in our nursery school, saying: "I want to be silly. I want to be a baby." Longing for his father alternated with the expression of negative feelings. He would ask innumerable times: "When does my daddy come?" and say a few minutes later: "I don't want him to come at all;" or: "Mary, you can have my daddy and my mummy." "I don't want this mummy." The new mother had brought him chocolate as a present. He offered Sister Mary some, saying: "Here, Mary, I give you a sweet from my mummy." The sweets which his father used to bring he had always kept jealously for himself.

A second short visit by the parents took very much the same course and, though outwardly more successful, brought little change in the child's behavior.

During the summer months which followed Tony seemed to digest his new experiences very slowly. He was invited "home" on his father's next leave and went apparently willingly and with great expectations. He returned, pale and rather difficult in his behavior and unable to communicate anything about his experiences. He became more quiet again and after a short while resumed his evening conversations about his father, as in former times, without mentioning his mother. He joined again in all the children's interests and conversations. One evening, in a very troubled mood, he wanted Sister Mary to tell him when the war would be over and whether he would then go home. When told no one could foretell the exact date but that he would surely return home at the end of the war, he said: "But somebody told me that lots of soldiers will be dead when the war is over and then my daddy will be dead too and where shall I go home then?" He cried and cried and could not be comforted.

During the autumn months when he began to go to school, his development progressed again and we hoped that he had once more settled down. But these good times did not last and, though he seemed perfectly all right during the day, he developed regular disturbances around bathing and bedtime. He did not want other children to be bathed before him; he dragged out his own bath endlessly, but cried when as a consequence he was late for supper. He demanded to be carried down to his supper, but did not like anything that was put on his plate. He seemed hungry, but was unable to eat, did not touch his supper, and asked for bread before going to sleep. He developed an endless ritual of saying "good night" to Sister Mary, calling her back from the door over and over again and not looking at her when she was beside his bed. When asked what it was that he really wanted, he would say only: "I am tired." Once at such a time he asked unexpectedly: "Do I grow small or big?" When told that he would grow to be a big boy, he answered: "You know when I was a baby I was ever so good." A few days later, when all the children wrote letters, he wrote a letter to his father which began: "Dear Daddy, I am good."

The night nurse reported that he called her to his bed regularly in the middle of the night asking her questions like the following: "Where is Mary?" "Has she gone away?" "Why does she go to bed so early?" "Did she look at my face before she went to bed?"

The same ritual with its difficulties then extended to his leaving for school. He suddenly asked Sister Mary to "take me to the gate of the drive and say good-bye." When she did it, he repeated his bedtime behavior down to the last detail. Unable to say good-bye, he stood there stiffly until it was late for school. When at last made to go, he cried despairingly: "I don't want to go to school. I did not say good-bye to my Mary."

Sister Mary's attempts to find a reason for this disturbing and so far unexplained behavior remained unsuccessful until last week when Tony suddenly opened up in the following way. Sister Mary had invited him to have supper in her room and in the course of a conversation asked him to tell her why he cried so often. He first evaded the question and talked about school. Then he asked to sit on her lap and sleep. After a silence of ten minutes, he suddenly said: "Mary, I have a baby in my home." Sister Mary thought that he was referring to his aunt's baby and asked for details. Tony said: "No, it is my baby and the baby of my mummy and my daddy. It is like Violet" [the youngest child of the Country House, about 2 years old], and it says to mummy, 'Mum,' and to my daddy, 'Dad,' and my daddy says I have to share my daddy with my baby and, Mary, is daddy still my very own daddy?" He added further: "My granny is keeping my baby because my mummy is always working and her name is Rosy."

We have so far no verification of this surprising piece of news. It might, of course, be a fantasy of Tony's, namely, an expression of his jealousy or of the fear that a child of the new marriage might deprive him of his father's love. But it somehow did not sound like a fantasy. Tony's account of the baby, its age, its behavior, and its position in the family seemed precise and real. If the baby is a reality, this fact might contain the key to Tony's difficulties of the last half year. His account refers to his last visit to his parents six months ago. It would mean that he kept this, for him overwhelming, experience secret for all this time, unable to communicate it and forced to express it instead through highly disturbing behavior.

37

Monthly Report
February, 1944

STATISTICS

The total number of children is 121; 83 of these are resident, 45 in London and 38 in the Country House. We admitted 2 children with their mothers, who have joined our staff. We further admitted 2 babies and a little boy for temporary stay.

MEDICAL REPORT

The influenza epidemic is passed, and our 3 babies have returned from the hospital. Of our 83 children only 1 is at the present moment in the sickroom.

AIR RAIDS

There were 10 air raids since the last report. As everybody knows, the character of the air raids has changed lately and one of the recent February nights felt like a reminder of the beginnings of the London blitz. There is little to choose between the nights in the Country House and the nights in London. If anything, the London children sleep more quietly due to the shelters. We can only hope that our precautions for the children will prove adequate.

PROBLEMS OF ADMISSION

In Report 17, we attempted to make a survey of the circumstances which had forced the parents of our children to break up homelife and to place their children in a residential nursery. In the intervening time we have received large numbers of applications for admission and have had ample opportunity to observe the various problems and emergencies which arose consecutively in close connection with the various phases of the war effort. The need for residential nursery accommodation has certainly not diminished since the outbreak of the war, though the reasons for it have changed periodically. We attempt in the following pages to give a picture of the circumstances as we see them reflected in our own work.

Applications Due to Air Raids

Since air raids on London had been considered negligible by the population in the last two years, very few of the applications which reached us during that time stressed the idea of danger and the need for evacuation. On the whole more parents applied to have their children placed in the London house than in the country, so as to make further contact with the child easier. This situation has changed very suddenly in the last few days. While writing this report we have received two urgent applications to admit bombed-out children and various requests from mothers who want to be evacuated with their babies. We expect several of our children who returned home during the last year to apply for readmittance or re-evacuation; sleeping in deep shelters has again become the habit and the children stand it badly.

Reasons for Applications Prior to Air Raids

Before this latest emergency began, the constant stream of applications which poured into our office could on the whole be divided up into three big groups: (1) children of mothers engaged in war work; (2) children of mothers in ill health or during childbirth; (3) children of unmarried war mothers.

The extracts quoted from applications are taken from letters written by the mothers themselves, not from the many others which reach us through charity organizations.

CHILDREN OF MOTHERS ENGAGED IN WAR WORK

Many mothers who are on strenuous war work do not succeed in combining their hours of work with the use of a day nursery. There are hardly any foster mothers available now in the London area, and child minders are naturally scarce and very unsatisfactory. Some mothers who have an older child evacuated are looking for accommodation for a younger one. A recurring phrase in the mothers' letters is the "worry" which they feel when they are torn between the necessities of earning money on the one hand, and "doing the right thing by the children" on the other hand, many of them with an eye on the absent father who might blame them for neglect of the children. The following quotations are meant to illustrate those specific circumstances.

London, S.E.19

Dear Sir or Madam,
I wish to enquire whether you have a vacancy for a baby boy aged 3 months. The position is that I am in the National Fire Service and my baby is at present with a foster mother with whom I am very dissatisfied. My husband is serving overseas and I cannot trust another foster mother and certainly cannot stand any more worry, wondering whether the foster mother is looking after my baby properly.
An early reply will be very much appreciated.

London, S.W.7

To Matron; Dear Madam,
I am serving in the F.F.F. and my husband is a Polish Flying Officer. I have a small son aged 2 and want with all my heart to have him near me in London. He is in a nursery school at the present, but is pining terribly for me and he must be surrounded by love and kindness. If you cannot take him immediately, would you put his name on your waiting list. I know you will do all you can to help.

London, N.W.6

Dear Sir,
I called on you about a fortnight ago re my little girl, entering your Rest Center, and you told me to write to you in 2 weeks or so. I am anxious to get her settled as I am on war work (aircraft) and I won't have too much time off to get her fixed up. I am a widow and another child to keep, who is by the way evacuated. So if you would be kind enough to do something for me or recommend to somewhere, I would be greatly obliged to you. Trusting you will favor me with a reply.

London, S.E.20

Dear Sir,

Our Woman Supervisor has sent me your address to see if you can possibly help me to get my children fixed up in one of your nurseries or if you can't fix my oldest child who is nearly 3½ years, maybe you can my baby 2½ years.

I am on the buses and I have to be up very early and I work sometimes until midnight. At the moment I have someone who comes in, but only for the time I am at work, and I am afraid she does not look after the children very satisfactory, and I find it very hard having all the worry of the shopping and the children to look after as this person does not do anything—only sit with them. They were in a private nursery, but the person had to close down as she was not registered: they have been home a while now and I have tried very hard to fix up but have not been successful. I do hope you can help me as it's an awful worry to have to go to work knowing your children are not being cared for. I shall be most grateful if you can help me.

London, N.W.6

Dear Madam,

I have been recommended to your nursery in Netherhall Gardens, and I am writing to ask you if it would be possible for my baby girl age 4½ months to reside at that nursery. I have been widowed since 7 months just after I knew I was having baby, and since I find I can't manage I have to go out to work. I have a boy nearly 3 which I take with me but cannot find anyone suitable to mind baby. Trusting there is a vacancy.

South Chingford, E.1

Dear Madam,

I am employed as conductor and Miss X. wrote to you regarding my two children aged 5 and 2½ years. She said maybe you could find room in one of the nurseries in the country for them. I have no one to mind them. I have to work all late duties, so my mother can mind them when she comes home from morning work. This late work and the worry of leaving them sometimes alone if I have to go into work before 1 o'clock, it's making me ill. I do not want my son put into private billets as he cannot write home and tell me if he's not being looked after properly. I know they will get every attention in a nursery with trained people to look after them—and as my husband is in Africa I want to make sure I am doing the best thing for the children as he'd never forgive me if they were not given every care. So please will you do your utmost to help me in this matter as I am certain I could not do better for them no matter how hard I tried. So hoping you will let me know as soon as possible what you can do to help me.

If you can arrange for them, try and get them right into the country, so I will not worry then in case of air raids.

CHILDREN OF MOTHERS IN ILL HEALTH OR DURING CHILDBIRTH

Under the present conditions when no domestic help can be found for the middle classes and family or neighborly help is not available for the working classes since most women are out working, every illness of a mother creates a real emergency situation for the child. Applications of this kind rarely come from the mothers themselves, but come mostly through the almoner of the hospital where the mother has applied for treatment. Operations on women often have to be postponed until residential accommodation can be found for the child.

Since only the minority of maternity hospitals can supply accommodation for the older children of pregnant mothers, the occasion of childbirth is one of the most frequent reasons for applying to us.

As previously reported, we receive many requests from

hospitals to admit newborn babies for temporary stay while their mothers are kept back in the hospital with breast abscesses or some other postpartum trouble.

Mental breakdowns of the mothers are a not infrequent reason for application.

General ill health of the mother, which renders her unfit to cope with the difficulties of a home and children, constitutes the reason for many further applications.

Essex

Dear Madam,

The Medical Officer of Hampstead suggested you might help me with the problem of what to do with my small son while I am in hospital. There is no place here to leave him and we shall be moving to Hampstead very soon. I cannot postpone this operation any more so I would be so grateful if you could take him for just the two weeks.

Will you please let me know at once about this? And the earliest the baby could come? My husband is on Active Service and it is a worry. My son is nearly 2, very intelligent and happy and gets on well with other children.

Enclosed is envelope for your reply. I do hope to hear soon.

York

Dear Madam,

I wonder if you can recommend either a good residential nursery in the Hampstead district or some kindly and competent person who could take charge of a 17 months baby boy for three weeks or a month?

I am expecting a second baby early in June, and I am rather at a loss how to arrange for the welfare of the first, as I want to keep him as near home as possible, so that his father can keep an eye on him, and I have nobody who could be with him in his own place. The period would probably be from the end of the first week in June. But I should be glad to make the arrangement for the one month, or even longer. I am not really concerned about the expenses.

This request is, I know, a difficult one to meet, and I also know that you do not exist as a bureau of information in these matters, but as I meant to do the best I can for my small son at what may be a difficult time for him, I hope you will be able to help.

London, N.W.6

Dear Madam,

I am in ill health and have never recovered after childbirth and I am still under treatment. I respectfully ask you if you possibly could take my baby under your care for about 4 weeks as I must have a complete rest for at least this time as you can see from the Dr's. certificate.

My baby is 1 year old and in excellent health. I am quite prepared to pay for her keep.

I would be much obliged if you could give me an interview.

London, E.1

Dear Madam,

Having heard of your Hampstead Home I am appealing to you to allow one of my children to enter your home for the duration of the war.

The circumstances are that my husband is in the Army and that my condition of health is so bad that I find it extremely difficult to bring up 3 young children the eldest being 4 years of age. I can assure you that the Local Welfare nurse and Officer strongly advise finding a home temporarily for at least one of my children. I can also assure you that all of my children are and have been well cared for.

To prove condition of my health my husband was discharged temporarily for 3 months so that he may assist me, he has now returned to his unit for duty and service, I am sure the welfare and myself would greatly appreciate all that can be done for me.

I am now living in a very badly blitzed area and the change of atmosphere is needed and very necessary. Please reply and hoping that you will assist me. If you care to visit my home you are welcome at any time.

UNMARRIED WAR MOTHERS

It is common knowledge that a very large number of babies are at present born illegitimately as a direct result of war conditions. The fathers are young men in the Forces; many of the persons who have applied to us are members of the Dominion or Allied armies now in this country. The mothers are usually young war workers or were in the Forces. In all these cases the mothers have been extremely anxious to place the babies as quickly as possible and to resume their former occupations. Many mothers have already registered their babies with adoption societies and only ask for temporary admission; in cases of mixed (half foreign) parentage, where adoption is not easily obtainable, the plight of the mothers is very great.

We have on the other hand met a number of unmarried war mothers who are eager to keep their children but unable to cope with the problem where to place them, or how to find lodgings where they would be permitted to keep them. Applications of this kind are usually made personally or through social workers.

London, N.W.1

Dear Sir,

I phoned you Saturday about putting my expected baby in the Nursery. The reason I want to do this is because I have no home to take it to when I come out of hospital, only one room and the landlady does not allow babies. I will pay for it money well in advance, till I get back to work, and find a flat where I can take it. Hoping you will help and give answer to the bearer, as my condition would not allow me to call personally.

London, E.5

Dear Sir,

Please could you take my baby in your home for a while. I am not married and my baby boy is 3 months. I have no father or mother, so I have no one to turn to. I have a small furnished room for my baby and myself and I have to do everything in it. Drying wet washing at night. Which is not good, with the baby in the same room. I have to take him to a day nursery every morning in the fog and rain, and fetch him again at night in the blackout. I do not earn very much money, and the time I pay my rent, buy coal and gas, and keep myself, I have hardly any money left. If only I could get my baby properly cared for. I could get a job outside London with more money. So please will you help me.

Hoping to hear from you soon.

We are sorry to say that all the applications mentioned above had to be refused because of lack of vacancies. It is evident that at present the need for residential accommodations for these three types of cases is overwhelming. The illegitimate war babies especially present a problem which will have to be dealt with after the war within the framework of more comprehensive social schemes.

38

Monthly Report
March, 1944

STATISTICS

The total number of children is 122; 85 of these are resident, 45 in London and 40 in the Country House. We admitted a pair of twins, aged 3 months, and 4 of our former children who had returned home during the last year and whom we had promised readmittance in the event of new air raids. We also admitted a boy, 2 years, 1 month, made homeless by the raids, His mother is in the ninth month of her pregnancy; his father is overseas (see Report 40). Four children departed.

MEDICAL REPORT

The state of health in both houses was very good. All the babies who had not so far been vaccinated were vaccinated against smallpox.

AIR RAIDS

There were 15 air raids since the last report.

In conversations with many of our parents we have made a point of warning them against putting too much trust in the safety of our shelter. We asked them not to miss any opportunities to send their children to the country. These talks had little effect. Altogether only 2 children were evacuated. In spite of many noisy and disturbed nights, nothing happened in the immediate neighborhood of the Nursery.

PROBLEMS

We have often stressed the fact that young children are comparatively little disturbed by air raids and that anxiety shown by them is most commonly due to infection through the fear shown or felt by the adults. We were able to confirm this impression during the raids of the last two months. Of the 50 children sleeping in the shelter of Netherhall Gardens, not more than 2, or at the most 3, woke up even in the noisiest raids. Not more than 2 children showed signs of anxiety. The proportion of waking up and fear is naturally much greater in the Country House, where the children are older, have more real knowledge of the danger, and are exposed to the full noise of the raids without the protection of a shelter.

But this comparative immunity against air raid anxiety is in many young children offset by a special sensitivity to the noise of raids. The following observations attempt to trace in detail the anxiety reactions of a delicate and sensitive child between the ages of 15 months and 2 years, 10 months.

Rose was admitted to the Nursery in July, 1941, at the age of 10 weeks, with severe intestinal disturbances. Her weight had fallen to 6 lbs., 11 oz., she looked emaciated, pale, and ill, was sleepless, cried constantly, and vomited frequently. During the first two years her lack of appetite and her delicate constitution gave rise to constant worry. Although her gain in weight remained unsatisfactory, her development was normal in other respects. Though tiny, she grew into a beautiful little girl, charming and dainty in her ways, intelligent, passionate, and attached to her surroundings. She walked and talked and completed her toilet training at the normal time.

The history of Rose's war experiences began before her birth. Her father had left for the army and her mother slept in an Anderson shelter during the whole pregnancy. Her older brother (4 years) was afraid of raids since a night when all their windows were blasted and their ceiling came down. He urged the mother to use the Anderson shelter even in quiet nights. Five months after the first incident, shortly before Rose's birth, a landmine dropped in the neighborhood and once more damaged their flat. This history was probably responsible for the baby's and the mother's delicacy. The mother was able to breast-feed Rose for only one month. Then she fell ill and lost her milk. Rose's feeding troubles dated from this event.

At 15 months Rose showed the first disturbance in a very noisy raid. Due to an infectious disease of the other children, the babies were not sleeping in the shelter dormitory and had to be taken down hurriedly two nights in succession. Rose merely showed interest the first night, but was intensely upset the second night, crying for almost two hours during the raid. It was difficult to determine whether the cause of her upset was the raid itself, or the noisy and disturbed atmosphere in the shelter, or merely lack of sleep.

At 20 months Rose had improved so much in her general development that her mother decided to take her home. The experiment worked very well for three days. In the fourth night there was an air raid. Since the mother's flat was situated between two railway lines, with antiaircraft guns and sirens very near to the house, Rose was shocked by the simultaneous sound of the sirens and guns. She was rushed into the Anderson shelter, where she had to stay for two hours. During the small hours of the morning another raid occurred and Rose cried for hours. She was quiet during the day, but demanded continually to be cuddled and petted. She trembled with fear when the sirens started up again in the evening. The mother decided to return her to the Nursery so that she could have the protection of the shelter. She showed no special signs of anxiety and seemed to be pleased when placed in her shelter bed. When the sirens went off again the next day at lunchtime, together with noisy gunfire, she began to cry helplessly. She ceased crying when she was put into her shelter bunk, finished her lunch there, but looked frightened. She remained excited all afternoon. Each time when a door banged or when the bigger children were especially noisy, she cried. She cried and looked afraid when she fell, though she did not usually mind falling. She even cried when something was dropped on the floor, though there was no real noise.

She slept through the next two alarms during the following night.

A few weeks later Rose had another shock when a

storm blew down the Nursery chimney and all the bricks fell near the window of the room where she was playing. Her fear was not as great as during alarms.

At 21 months Rose was being dried after her bath when the sirens went off. She immediately stood up and anxiously looked toward the window. While she was being dressed to be taken to the shelter, she stood silently and looked intently in the same direction.

When the sirens were heard in the distance the next day, Rose was immediately taken to the shelter before any noise was heard in the neighborhood. She had apparently not heard anything and remained undisturbed. But upstairs again after the all clear, she suddenly ran away and squeezed herself into a corner between cupboard and wall, furthest away from the window. She cried constantly "ou ouh" in real fear and looked more frightened than ever. There was no noise at the moment except the rumbling of a train in the far distance. When attempts were made to calm her, she sobbed and allowed herself to be cuddled. But when the next train passed, she immediately ran again to the same corner and cried as before. She quieted down when she was taken to the shelter in the evening.

She continued to show this fear of train noises in the following days. When taken out for walks, she showed fear every time a milk cart passed and would pass a standing cart only when she felt herself protected. At that time this fear seemed to extent to horses in general.

At 21½ months there were no raids, and Rose seemed to overcome her fear of trains. She was able to pass standing carts, but still showed fear of moving vehicles. When placed in a pram in the garden for her nap, she did not react to the noise of trains. Sometimes she would look in the right direction, shake her head, and laugh.

At 22 months Rose did not wake during an evening raid. During the following morning raid she quietly continued her breakfast.

At 2 years Rose was alone in the garden in a pram when the sirens went off. She did not cry, but picked up her belongings and stood in her pram with arms outstretched waiting to be fetched. Since her fear and the frequency of air raids had lessened at this time,[1] her mother took her home again and kept her for six months until the birth of a new baby. This time the experiment was successful: Rose showed no excessive anxiety during alarms. She was taken to the Anderson shelter many times without showing any disturbance.

She returned to the Nursery for six weeks while her mother was in the hospital.

At 2 years, 9 months Rose's air raid anxiety returned when she was home again with her mother and the newborn baby. When sirens or guns were heard, she cried bitterly for her nurse in the nursery. At other times she remained quiet, merely lost color, and squeezed herself into corners. She asked for cotton wool for her ears and pushed it into her ears herself. She showed similar anxiety when visiting in the nursery. She entered the surgery to have her weight taken, discovered the sunlight lamp in use, squeezed herself into the corner between desk and wall, trembled, but did not cry.

At 2 years, 10 months, when the raids got worse, Rose's mother asked for permission to return the child to the

[1] During eight weeks there were 10 night raids and 2 days raids of which Rose took no notice.

Nursery once more. She arrived in February in good condition and without any visible signs of anxiety. During the next month she went through 10 night raids and alarms, some of them very noisy, without waking once in the shelter. On March 22nd, she had the worst attack of anxiety which she had shown so far. The raid was an average one, the noise rather loud, but not worse than many times before. But unluckily there was some commotion and loud talking in the shelter. Rose woke up with the noise inside and outside and cried, "Them guns, them guns." She ceased crying when taken out of bed to the night nurse's arm chair, but had a fit of violent trembling. She quieted down when her favorite nurse comforted her, played with the nurse's belongings, and watched her. Her shivering returned from time to time. She said, "Nasty guns, dirty guns," and once she said gently: "My Sophie" [the nurse's name]. When the noise died down, somebody offered her cake and, although it was not one she usually liked, she ate both hers and the nurse's.

It was not easy to comfort her during her shivering attacks. The nurse tried to play with her in several ways. Rose reacted well to one of them: the nurse imitated the noise of the raid, saying, "Boom, boom." Whenever the noise outside followed on the nurse's sounds, Rose looked up, nodded her head, and later on even smiled a little.

She showed no aftereffects from this anxiety attack during the following day.

In Rose's case the possibility cannot be excluded that her first outbreaks of air raid anxiety were provoked by her surroundings: the hurry and disturbance in the shelter; the anxiety of her older brother when at home. After these first incidents her anxiousness seemed completely a reaction of her own. At a certain, very favorable time of her development, she remained undisturbed even when in the company of her anxious family. At a later period her air raid fear returned, and remained even in emotionally quiet surroundings.

39

Monthly Report
April, 1944

STATISTICS

The total number of children is 124; 86 of these are resident, 44 in London and 42 in the Country House. We admitted 2 children of 4, with their working mothers; 2 children of 10 months and 19 months, one of them readmitted after absence in the hospital.

MEDICAL REPORT

The children's state of health in both houses is very good. In contrast to this, there have been several cases of sore throats and jaundice among the staff of the Country House. Eight of the adults have been ill so far, which created rather difficult working conditions for the others.

AIR RAIDS

There were only 7 air raids since the last report.

PARENTS' PROBLEMS

We have heard from several of our readers that they were interested in the extracts from parents' letters which we included in Report 37. It may be of similar interest to follow an individual case in greater detail. The story of this family is a good example of the wartime difficulties of a mother of young children and of her incessant struggle to do what she considers the "right thing by them."

Mrs. X's husband, a night cleaner in a hospital, was killed in an air raid in September, 1940 while he was on duty as stretcher bearer. Her two children, Susan and Nick, were at the time 2½ years and 1 year, 2 months. The pension she received for herself and the children was about £2 weekly. She found that she could not live on the pension with the children and decided to look for factory work, which at the time was possible only under full-time conditions. She applied to us through the Friends' Ambulance Unit and we admitted the children in July, 1941, and kept them continuously until April, 1943.

Though gruff and unfriendly in her manner and rather harsh in her handling of the children, Mrs. X is really a very conscientious mother. She evidently adores little Nick, who is an outstandingly beautiful child, and shows herself very critical of Susan, who is in many ways like her. She visited the children absolutely regularly during the years when they were with us. She supplied nearly all their clothes, sewing and knitting for them, and paid 12/- weekly to the Nursery toward their keep. She never wanted them to be evacuated to our Country House so as not to lose the weekly contact with them. Even though Susan was very often in tears at the end of a Sunday because of her mother's preference for Nick and unfriendliness toward her, the tie between the members of the family was really very close.

When part-time work was introduced in war factories, Mrs. X immediately decided to have the children live with her again. Susan by that time had reached school age and Nick was admitted to a nursery class in the same school. She was full of hope that things would work out very well that way.

In March, 1944 she suddenly contacted us again and asked to have the children readmitted. She vaguely said that we "could now have them for a long time." She is an extremely independent person and not given to lengthy explanations about her private affairs. But her manner betrayed that she had some serious reason for her request, and we accepted the children. Susan was eager to return, but Nick withstood the renewed separation very badly. He cried for hours every evening and sat listlessly in daytime without showing interest in anything. He clung desperately to Susan and even had to be allowed to accompany her to and fetch her from the school near us. Mrs. X was distressed when she saw his state and when he begged her to take him home when she visited. She stood it for one Sunday, but when he had not improved during the next week, she decided to take the children home again.

In the excitement of the moment she became more

talkative and disclosed the dilemma she found herself in. Her actual reason for bringing them back had been that she had found it impossible to combine her part-time work with the school hours of the children. The Labor Exchange had offered her work from 8-1 or from 2-6. To accept either had meant that the children should do one school journey, either in the morning or in the afternoon, unescorted. Since there are two bad crossings on the way, she had not dared to take the risk and had made up her mind to manage on the pension of £2 per week. With rent 9/-, coal 4/-, gas 6/8, insurances 2/-, this had proved impossible and she got behind with rent.

Our social worker, who is very friendly with her, then visited her in her home and tried to help her to arrange matters. He got her to accept a weekly allowance of 7/6 for three months to pay off her debts and give her time to look for suitable part-time work without being pressed by real privations. He also supplied shoes for the children from the stocks of the Nursery, though Mrs. X refused assistance with clothes, which she is proud to be able to supply herself.

A very few days after this, things took a turn for the better. She phoned our social worker in great excitement to tell him that the foreman of her former factory had sent for her and that, as he was short of staff, it had been arranged that she could work from 10-3, allowing her to escort the children to and from school, where they also would get their dinner. Her wages for this work are 25/- so she asked for the weekly payments to be discontinued.

40

Monthly Report
May, 1944

STATISTICS

The total number of children is 122; 81 of these are resident, 43 in London and 38 in the Country House. We admitted 2 temporary babies, the younger one accompanied by its mother. Two little sisters who had lived with us since February, 1941, went home at last to rejoin their mother. Four children whom we had readmitted temporarily during the air raids departed.

MEDICAL REPORT

The state of health among the children in the Country House was uninterruptedly good. The London House had three light cases of scarlet fever who were sent to the hospital. The quarantine passed without any further cases.

AIR RAIDS

There were only 3 air raids since the last report.

PROBLEMS: REGRESSION AS A DISTURBING FACTOR IN CHILD DEVELOPMENT

In our earlier reports and in *Infants Without Families* [Part II], we have repeatedly mentioned the fact that the normal development of a child may be arrested or seriously interfered with whenever the outward circumstances of the child's life undergo a sudden and serious change. Not only do children cease to develop further for a while after such an experience, they even regress instead of progressing, i.e., they return to infantile habits and modes of behavior which they had outgrown and apparently left behind forever.

Such regression of development may concern only the child's instinctual drives. Wherever this happens we see children revert from later phases of infantile sexual development to earlier ones, from the first manliness of the nursery child to the aggression and dirtiness of a toddler, or even to the biting and sucking pleasures of an infant. Or the regression may concern the child's emotional relationship. When this happens we see children lose their more adult, considerate, and human attitudes toward grownups and return to the egoistic exactingness of the small infant; or they may lose their human ties altogether and concentrate wholly on pleasures derived from their own body: masturbation, sucking, rocking, and head knocking. Where, on the other hand, the process of regression extends to that part of the child's personality which we call his "self" or "ego," the child may lose all those acquisitions which have been made gradually under the influence of education: the child becomes dirty again where previously he had acquired habits of cleanliness; he reverts to cruelty where he had learned to restrain aggression, and pity his victims; he reverts to greed and lack of shame; and he loses whatever moral and ethical ideas he may have been on the point of building up.

Whenever we have described this process in former reports, we have illustrated it with cases where such changes in the child's life (separation from the family) were brought about too suddenly, without proper consideration for the child's feelings, or without allowing sufficient time for the child's reactions. In dealing with new cases of this kind we have attempted to work out a process of "separation in slow stages" so as to mitigate its consequences for the child. Although this has proved beneficial with children from 3 or 4 years onward, we have found that very little can be done to prevent regression where children between 1½ and 2½ are concerned. Infants of that age can stand sudden changes and separations of a day's length without any visible effect. Whenever it is more than that, they tend to lose their emotional ties, revert in their instinctual pursuits, and regress in their behavior. Their developmental acquisitions are all the more easily shaken, the more short-lived and therefore less stabilized they are.

The following case of a 2-year-old, whom we admitted last March (see Report 38), may serve as a practical illustration of these theoretical remarks. In the case of this particular child it was possible to take nearly all the precautionary measures against undue shock which we had worked out while observing other cases. He was not torn away from his mother all at once but introduced to the Nursery with her help and active cooperation. He was not pushed into a large nursery group without preparation, but, at least for the first days, kept with a small number of children entrusted to the same young nurse. His mother lessened her visiting gradually so that there was no abrupt change; when she disappeared completely, she still kept her link with him alive with the help of parcels and messages. The complete separation from her lasted only about two weeks; and he returned home again after seven weeks. In spite of all these precautions and the fullest cooperation of mother and staff, the child went through a distressing period of regression, as described in the following detailed report written by Dr. Ilse Hellman, who handled the case in her department:

Bobby's Previous History

Bobby M. was the child of young and intelligent working-class parents. His father, who is in the Army, was sent to India when Bobby was 18 months old and his mother pregnant with the next baby. On Bobby's second birthday, the mother's home was badly damaged in a heavy raid on London: their windows were blown in and their ceilings brought down. Unluckily, Bobby developed chicken pox the day after, so that no one would shelter mother and child for fear of infection. The mother therefore managed to stay in the damaged premises until he had recovered. While he was still ill, she took the child in a pram on a daily round of inquiry to find some place where he might be cared for during the time when she would be in the hospital for the birth of the new baby, then due in four weeks. After many fruitless attempts, a social worker put her in touch with us and we admitted the child as soon as he was noninfectious.

Bobby's State of Development at the Time of Admission

When Bobby came to us he looked the picture of health, and he seemed advanced in every respect in comparison with many other children of the same age. His mother told us that he had always been an "easy" baby, sleeping well, enjoying his food, and that she had had very little trouble with his education so far. He was independent, having started to feed himself early, and his training in cleanliness had been completed at about 18 months as far as daytime was concerned. For the last three months Bobby had also been dry at night, having responded well to the mother's potting him late in the evening and early in the morning.

Bobby spent the first afternoon and evening with his mother and a young aunt in a small room in the Nursery and was keenly interested in the toys, using them cleverly and talking about what he saw in a jolly manner. His language development was especially advanced compared with that of our nursery children. His mother had a very charming way of dealing with him; she was most concerned to do whatever we thought best to help him to adapt, and although she lived far and was rather tired— only a few weeks before the arrival of the new baby— she immediately agreed to stay with Bobby until he was asleep, and to come and visit him as soon and often as possible within the first days. A young nurse who was to have charge of Bobby helped the mother on the first evening and he was friendly with her. He fell asleep in the shelter without any difficulty, obviously tired out by the many new experiences.

Gradual Weaning from His Mother with First Regressions

The next day he was very cheerful, played with two other children in a small room, as we wanted him to adapt himself very gradually to the large group in the nursery. Whenever he wanted something, he turned to his nurse rather than to anyone else. His mother visited him daily during the first week. He was delighted to see her, did not specially cling to her, but played beside her, showing her all the toys. However, he cried a great deal when she had to leave. She had at first intended to continue coming in the late afternoon so as to be there at bedtime, but as he could not settle down to sleep as long as she was there, she came earlier after the first few days and left before he was in bed. He slept well except for the nights when there were air raids and the sound of the siren and guns aroused great anxiety in him. Bobby was wet during the night from the beginning of his stay with us.

When in the second week the long Underground journey became too difficult for the mother, she decided to come only twice. At this time Bobby had his first "accidents" in daytime and was less active. While previously he had not minded the aggressiveness of many children in the group and had been able to hold his own without being too aggressive himself, he now started to whine a great deal, running to his nurse for comfort and at other times attacking other children. He started sucking his fingers in daytime.

Complete Separation with Loss of Bowel and Bladder Control and General Infantile Behavior

As her confinement was coming too near, the mother stopped her visits. She asked whether I thought sending Bobby parcels and picture postcards would help him over this time and promised to keep in touch with him in this way. When she had not visited him for several days, Bobby changed a great deal. He became listless, often sat in a corner sucking and dreaming, at other times he was very aggressive. He almost completely stopped talking. He was dirty and wet continually, so that we had to put nappies on him. He sat in front of his plate eating very little, without pleasure, and started smearing his food over the table.

At this time the nurse who had been looking after him fell ill, and Bobby did not make friends with anyone else, but let himself be handled by everyone without opposition. A few days later he had tonsillitis and went to the sickroom. In the quiet atmosphere there he seemed not quite so unhappy, played quietly, but generally gave the impression of a baby. He hardly ever said a word, had entirely lost his bladder and bowel control, sucked a great deal. On his return to the nursery he looked very pale and tired. He was very unhappy after rejoining the group, always in trouble and in need of help and comfort. He did not seem to recognize the nurse who had looked after him at first.

His mother had kept her promise and had sent many parcels and pictures which she had drawn for him herself. Bobby understood that they came from her, brightened up whenever he was given one, but seemed to lose the cards very quickly.

The change he had undergone during these few weeks was very striking, and the mother was worried when she saw him for the first time. She visited him as soon as possible after the birth of the baby on the eleventh day. Bobby seemed to take her first visit in a matter-of-fact way, appearing to be neither pleased nor upset. He sat next to her, played with her as before. He was quite desperate when she left. Ten days later the mother took him home for good.

Mother's First Report after Bobby's Return Home: Appearance of Air Raid Shock

Three weeks after the birth of the baby the mother very courageously undertook the task of taking complete charge of both children and simultaneously attempting to clear up and put in order a groundfloor flat underneath the one she had been bombed out of before. She herself carted bucketfuls of glass and broken slate from the backyard to a nearby dump while workmen all around were busy with the rubble. In a letter she described Bobby's state, which is an instructive mixture of the combined effects of belated air raid shock, reaction to separation, and jealousy due to the birth of the new baby.

Extract from mother's first letter:

> Bobby, I am sorry to say, is not very well. He has tonsillitis again, and has eaten nothing since Sunday. He also has terrible nightmares, and seems to go almost mad for a bit, and screams and throws himself about. He also is afraid, and always screams if someone knocks at the door or rattles anything. When he was standing outside the other day and the workmen threw some rubble on the pile, I thought he would go into a fit almost, he was so frightened. The doctor at the Welfare said she thought he probably has some sort of memory of the bombing, as it is the same house, and this flat is exactly the same as the top floor where we were.
>
> Also, Bobby is worried when I feed the baby, and once or twice has cried and said, "And me." Apart from that, though, he seems pleased with the baby, and strokes his hair and kisses him good night, and gives him pencils to play with! It is a pity he should be not well again, because he seemed to get on so the first week, and was getting fat and rosy-cheeked again. Still, I expect he will soon find out that things are all right in spite of everything.

Readaptation to Homelife: Improvement in Cleanliness

Extract from mother's second letter a fortnight later:

> When I wrote a fortnight ago, Bobby was not at all well. Now, however, he has picked up and is very well in

every way. He is fat again and his cheeks are rosy. He is really happy, I think, and laughs and enjoys himself all the time. The nightmares have stopped and the fears have disappeared, except that he is still afraid of falling and of dogs. I cannot understand why he is afraid of dogs.

His behavior toward the baby is far less hostile and he is now interested in the baby's hair, eyes, and legs, and wants to pick him up and play with him. He is also much improved in cleanliness, we have not had a wet bed for a week. He eats enormously. The difficulties that still remain are sucking fingers, putting anything and everything into his mouth, telling people to go away, sometimes for apparently no reason, and destructiveness. He will sometimes deliberately tear a book and pull the leaves from bushes. However, apart from this he seems to be getting on well, talking a great deal and doing a great many things every day.

Summary

The combined efforts of the mother and the Nursery were unable to spare Bobby the consequences of his threefold traumatic experience: bombing, breaking up of homelife, and arrival of the new baby. He reacted to the first of these experiences with anxiety symptoms of various kinds, to the last one with very natural jealousy and some aggressiveness. The bulk of his symptoms consisted of regressions: return to destructiveness and sucking; undoing of bowel and bladder control; loss or deterioration of the new faculty of speech; lessening of emotional contact with the outer world; states of dreaminess with withdrawal into himself.

Further reports from the mother will show how much time is needed to do away with the last remnants of these symptoms, and to start the child once more on a path of progressive development.

If our efforts combined with those of the mother were unable to prevent this abnormal phase in the child's development, they at least were able to minimize the harmful effects as much as possible and to prevent the child from getting firmly fixed to any one of the above-mentioned symptoms.

41

Monthly Report
June, 1944

STATISTICS

The total number of children is 119; 83 of these are resident, 14 in London and 69 in the Country House.

MEDICAL REPORT

There are 5 cases of whooping cough among the older babies in the London house. The cases are, so far, mild ones; but under the present conditions of life the various precautions against spreading of illness were much more difficult to maintain than usually.

AIR RAIDS

Due to the present postal censorship regulations we cannot give the usual statistics of "air raid warnings since our last report." We can only say that, owing to the new air attacks on Southern England, our conditions of life have reverted to those under which the Hampstead Nursery began its existence in 1940.

PROBLEMS

The problems discussed in this report will hardly be of interest to readers in England. The tasks of the past month were practical ones and are only too well known to all those who are responsible for the welfare of children under the conditions of air attack. Our friends in America, on the other hand, may be interested in a description of the present phase of the war, seen strictly from the point of view of nursery life and nursery routine. We are very conscious of the fact that it is the realization of what modern war may mean for children which prompted the Foster Parents' Plan for War Children to create and maintain institutions like the Hampstead Nursery.

Since the existence of our house in 5 Netherhall Gardens is based on its spacious shelter dormitory, which is in regular nightly use, night raids are of no consequence for the nursery routine. A decisive change in the life of the children begins only when night alerts continue into the morning. This means that 40 children have to be washed, dressed, and served or fed with breakfast in the shelter. Dressing and washing, usually spread over eight different rooms, takes place on a single dressing table and one washstand. Space, which is ample for the night, becomes more than crowded as soon as the children are awake and want to move about.

The only solution for this emergency is to "take turns."

The bigger children are served with breakfast in their bunks, during which time the babies are taken out of their carrier cots or baskets and cleaned with oil to replace a morning bath. This finished, they are put back in their cots and fed, which means that the bigger ones can be released from their bunks to wash and dress. The oldest children are waiting impatiently for an all clear to go to school; the nursery school children are equally impatient to set off for Wedderburn Road; the junior toddlers begin to be very fretful when their usual crawling time arrives and restriction of movement continues. The all clear signal is followed by an immediate surge of the whole shelter population upstairs. The household staff immediately descends for the usual energetic cleaning and airing of the shelter, a very necessary procedure in a place where 40 infants (in various stages of their toilet training) have spent a long night and morning.

Air raids in mid-morning make themselves felt less, though there may be some excitement if they occur while the school and nursery school parties are still on their way. Once arrived, the children are taken care of. They sit in the shelter of their school, or they continue their nursery school work in our shelter in Wedderburn Road. Plasticene, colored pencils, toys are taken downstairs; our shelter even has room enough to set up some small tables and chairs. The shelter dormitory in Netherhall Gardens, once aired after the night, affords ample and even quite pleasant accommodations.

It is more disturbing when the children's meals begin upstairs and suddenly have to be transferred to the shelter, though it is astonishing how many of the usual methods and habits of serving and feeding can be maintained even under these conditions. But air raids during the lunch hour carry another disadvantage of a more serious nature. They coincide with the off hours of a number of the nursing staff. When all the members of the staff are present, it is, with practice, possible to have every child removed from the house, terrace or garden to the shelter in less than two minutes; at favorable moments the garden and terrace are completely cleared of children while the sirens are still going. This quick removal to safety is more difficult during off hours, though the house and kitchen staff fill the gaps as best they can.

For a while we continued afternoon naps in the rest rooms upstairs during all clears, even though the children sleep more peacefully when put to rest in the shelter, without any necessity to be awakened and carried down in the event of a warning. In this respect, as in similar ones, we have been guided by weighing the disadvantages of sudden disturbance and removal to the shelter against the disadvantage of too many hours spent underground. The same consideration holds good for short intervals of all clear inserted between long periods of alert. So far as the comfort of the children, especially the babies, is concerned, the removal to the upper world is often more disturbing than a continued existence in the peacefulness of the shelter. But our attempt (as everybody else's) has been throughout not to let the children miss any chance of getting to the daylight or to the garden, even if such periods last only a few minutes.

The whole nursery becomes indifferent toward all clears and warnings when evening with the usual routine of undressing, bathing, and going to bed draws near. Since this means return to the shelter in any case, it is of little importance whether it happens a little earlier or later. Once in the shelter, nearly all the children are remarkably unaffected by the noise of raids. Arrangements have been altered only insofar as a subsidiary night duty has been installed. Some of the mothers who work in the house now sleep in whatever shelterbeds are available for adults.

Baby Department

In the baby department the alterations which are caused by the raids are more strenuous for the staff than for the children. Life in this department is complicated by the whooping cough infection. Every attempt is made never to let the five youngest babies, who are so far free of infection, come into contact with the others. An isolated part of the shelter is allotted to them and every care taken that they should not meet the other children, even in the general rush downstairs when an alarm is given. It remains to be seen whether these precautions will have the desired effect of restricting the whooping cough to one department only. The continual carrying of heavy babies, upstairs and downstairs, indoors and outdoors, following on warnings and all clears, is heavy work for the students and the older staff. Many alterations of routine rules are necessary. Feeding is often interrupted. The strapping of bigger babies into their prams on the terrace has to be discontinued, since it takes too long to undo so many straps in the event of a warning. The older babies now spend their time on the terrace in playpens instead of in prams, much to their liking.

The babies themselves have, so far, remained remarkably unaffected. They look well and have retained their good coloring in spite of the short hours spent upstairs, and in spite of the whooping cough. Even those whose mothers get excited by the raids remain quite peaceful themselves. They resent it, of course, if they have to travel downstairs in the middle of a meal; but nearly all of them settle down to feeding again after a short upset.

There are many signs that the various air raid precautions simply mean a new kind of nursery routine to them which they accept as simply as they accept other matters of routine. They now begin to show signs of restlessness when left on the terrace too long, without the interruptions which have become usual. And on one day, when hardly any sirens went off and the babies had what the adults called a "perfect day" without being carried about too much, they all suddenly were distinctly bored and fretful. We concluded that babies finally adapt to everything, whether pleasurable or unpleasurable.

The air raid arrangements contain one definite advantage for the older babies. Under ordinary conditions they are kept separate from the nursery group and see the bigger children only in the distance. During daytime in the shelter, their cots are placed well in view of the playing space of the bigger ones. All those babies who are old enough to sit up and look, use that opportunity to the best advantage.

Junior Toddler Department

The children of this age group (1-2 years) have spent a very difficult month. The change of outward conditions has been extremely trying for them. All their favorite occupations are connected with movement of some kind, and shelter life for them has meant above all restriction of movement. Their part of the shelter dormitory is a bay with three-tier bunks on both sides. They either had to sit in their bunks, behind their shelter nets, secure against falling out as at night, or—with an obstruction placed at the end of the bay—they could be permitted a short run in the alley.

This, naturally, was not sufficient for them, and attempts to escape from their part of the shelter had to be watched for continually. To give them at least some exercise a chair was placed for them at the end of the alley, so that they could all have jumps off it. This was considered a great pleasure, but, again, did not last for long. Their only happy moments were those when they could be allowed to explore the shelter further. Whenever this was impossible because of the presence of the other children and the whooping cough precautions, unhappiness reigned among them. They had frequent temper tantrums, accompanied by violent head banging and were difficult to comfort. Even children who are usually gentle and quiet became irritable and aggressive under these conditions.

Certain significant changes in their behavior could be observed. They lost nearly all their pleasure in eating. Usually, their waiting time for meals is full of pleasurable excitement. In the shelter they waited for their food in silence. They ate their normal quantities, but treated the meal as a matter of routine, not as a pleasure.

The regularity of their motions was affected. During a certain day of shelter life only one child out of the group of six had a motion.

As happens in times of separation, illness, and frustration (see our Report 41), their behavior regressed in various ways. Several of them had just learned the meaning of "taking turns." While waiting for their turn, they had recently acquired the habit of running about wildly and joyfully in anticipation, or of sitting and kicking their legs. This ability to "wait" disappeared under the new conditions. Whoever had to wait for a turn (for instance, for jumping) in the shelter, fell into a temper and could not even enjoy his turn when it came.

One little girl (22 months), who had just acquired the ability to let her mother depart after visits without tears, fell back into crying again on such occasions.

The most outstanding manifestation of this kind was a reverting to the worst table manners imaginable when meals were taken upstairs during all clears. This group of children had shortly before acquired fairly good eating habits, with a certain amount of cleanliness and tidiness in handling spoons and food. This acquisition disappeared to a large extent. The children still ate in the former manner while their hunger was great. But, after the first few minutes of a meal were over, they messed about with their food, smeared with it, licked it, emptied their plates onto the tables, etc. After meals of this kind, taken upstairs (not shelter meals), their feeders looked as they used to look half a year ago. But whereas then the mess had seemed largely due to their inability to handle the food, the same actions now had the character of deliberate "smearing."

It is difficult to say whether, in addition, the children were actually afraid of the sound of the sirens. On two occasions two of the little girls (22 months) ran to the nearest adults at the sound of the sirens, and lifted their arms with anxious expressions on their faces.

When the raids showed signs of continuing for a while the staff of New Barn, Lindsell, offered to vacate two big rooms in the old farm house which serves as a staff hostel. The adults went into emergency quarters, doubled up with others, and the rooms were given over to the junior toddler group. At the moment they lead a very happy existence there, temporarily evacuated with their own staff, and isolated from the other New Barn children since they are in whooping cough quarantine. They are extremely happy with their new freedom, crawling and running about in the high grass. They show great fear of horses, cows, and chickens, so far unknown to all of them.

Nursery Group

The behavior of the bigger children (2-7 years) was a pleasant surprise for us during this time. We had often wondered how our children, who are in no way trained to be "implicitly obedient," would stand up to emergencies in which rules have to be followed without questioning and restrictions accepted as necessary evils. We found, to our satisfaction, that all the nursery children, who were at all old enough to have some understanding of the situation, were on the whole cooperative, helpful, and easy to handle. They seemed to realize that the confinement to the shelter, the hurry indoors from the garden, or downstairs from the nursery, the smallness of playing space, the interruption of meals, etc., were due to conditions over which the adults had as little control as they themselves.

Although blitz conditons were new to all those who had been mere babies in 1940-1941, they quickly adapted themselves to them. After the first few days many of them showed definite signs of fear in their expression when surprised by a warning in the garden; they seemed to appreciate the shelter as a place of safety. From the second day onward, there was really no need to urge any child to hurry into the shelter. When the sirens went off, the whole group would start running toward its entrance, the older children calling out, "Warning, Warning!" the youngest lifting their arms to show that they wanted to be carried. It was very much easier to occupy them in the shelter than with the junior toddlers. They would bring all their sitting occupations with them, chairs and tables would be set up so far as space permitted, the gramophone played, or nursery school continued quite successfully underground. Provided that the confinement did not last too long, there was no real unhappiness.

On the other hand, the whole group seemed like drunk when they came up the shelter stairs after having stayed down for several hours. They ran around the nursery at high speed one after the other, singing and shouting; later they tumbled over each other and rolled about on the floor. Several times on these occasions, when out in the garden again, the whole group imitated the noise of the sirens. They would have gone on for hours with great satisfaction, if it had not been necessary to stop this useful outlet for the sake of the neighbors.

The children were much less concerned about the planes or bomb explosions than about the sirens themselves. The noise of the sirens was to them not an announcement of danger but the danger itself. They hated it and abused it in various ways. Several children said: "The warning is naughty, it is doing big job, high in the sky."

Nearly all the children personified the warning in some

form or other. Dan (4 years, 3 months), when told that he could return to the garden after an all clear, asked: "Where has the warning gone? What does it look like? What color is its dress and what sort of shoes does it have?" When asked how he imagined it, he said: "I do not know whether it is a man or a lady, I think it is a nasty lady, a nasty shouting lady."

The question where the warning is, or where it goes to when it is over, puzzles many children. Bridget (4 years) said repeatedly: "There is a warning in the garden." "There is no warning in the shelter." "Is there a warning in your house too?" "Was there a warning in the meeting?" Joan (3 years, 2 months) asked: "Where is the warning now, who killed it? My daddy with his gun?"

When Dan once again asked: "Who makes that noise?" Olga (7½) answered in fun: "Don't you know, it's old Hitler shouting because he is cross that we have so many planes." Dan took the answer seriously and said: "He has a very loud voice, he must be very, very cross."

The younger children of the group were naturally confused by the technical terms which the older children used quite glibly. Some of them called the warning a "warming." The all clear was for them an "all Clare" (the name of our former sicknurse). Larry (3 years) called all clears "all clear warnings." He said, quite logically in his own terminology, when an all clear was sounded: "The warning is all clear again."

For one of our difficult problem children (3 years, 1 month), the warning with its consequences became confused with her own sense of guilt. Whenever she had to stay in the shelter she felt as if she had been punished. She showed the expression which she always has after doing something forbidden. She sat in corners quietly or walked about aimlessly. She changed at once when out in the garden again, ran about cheerfully until the next warning. She cried each time when she had to return to the shelter. She definitely suffered, not from the real danger or the real restrictions, but due to the meaning which they assumed for her.

After a period of this life, the whole nursery group of 20 children went to New Barn as temporary evacuees. The nursery at New Barn had always seemed filled to capacity. But in this situation emergency conditions were established, the big playroom fixed up as a dormitory, and staff and children of the nursery group of Netherhall Gardens were made very welcome by the staff and children of New Barn.

New Barn, which had a population of 38 children last month, now has a total of 69 children.

42

Monthly Report
July, 1944

STATISTICS

The total number of children is 117; 87 of these are resident, 13 in London and 74 in the Country House.

MEDICAL REPORT

There are 7 cases of whooping cough among the babies in London, none of them severe ones. Our efforts to restrict the infection to the baby department were successful. The junior toddler group, so far isolated in the Country House, is now out of quarantine for whooping cough.

AIR RAIDS

Air raid conditions in London have remained unchanged since our last report. The 13 babies who are left in Netherhall Gardens still divide their time between upstairs and downstairs, with a large part of the day usually spent in the shelter. Against all expectations they have not suffered in health or in spirits. Since they are now the only inhabitants of the big house and shelter, they live in great comfort. The best parts of the shelter are at their disposal, as well as ample crawling space upstairs. But life in Netherhall Gardens has become rather dull. For the first time since the opening of the Hampstead Nursery there are no visitors; there are no courses and lectures since most of the students are working in the Country House; and there is only a skeleton staff. Variety is provided only by the air raid warnings and by the tales of bombing and blasting brought in by visiting mothers. Some of our mothers have now been bombed out or blasted out for the third time.

EXTERNAL PROBLEMS

Since June our Country House has admitted 37 additional children. Thirty of these are the juniors and seniors from Netherhall Gardens; the rest are former New Barn children who had returned to their parents during the comparative peace of the past year and have now been re-admitted. This doubling of numbers in a house which had always appeared to be filled to capacity raised a number of problems. The task was not merely to create the necessary number of "billets" in the house, but, while doing so, to maintain the standards of the pre-emergency period. This meant thinking in terms of individuals rather than in terms of age groups. The general aim was to give every newcomer the feeling that his arrival was expected, planned for, and welcome, and thereby to reduce the possible harmful consequences of evacuation to a minimum.

Sleeping Arrangements

New Barn has safe and extensive grounds and a very large day nursery, formerly a studio. But its drawback from the beginning was a lack of sleeping space. All that is available for beds or bunks are two middle-sized rooms upstairs and two big south rooms on the ground floor, the latter used as combined bed and living rooms. In each of these rooms the children moved nearer together, and emergency cots were placed beside the regular beds.

The only further possibility seemed the conversion of the day nursery into a dormitory, in the hope that good summer weather would make up for the lack of a playroom. In a general staff meeting this solution was turned down and an alternative substituted for it. The big playroom is now being converted into a dormitory every evening, and reconverted into a day nursery every morning while the children are at breakfast. This means the daily transport of a number of stretcher beds, cots, and their accessories, and a special effort at cleaning, airing, etc. But the arrangement works to everyone's satisfaction, and both appearances of the former studio fulfill their purpose admirably. The household workers remark that they feel like stagehands with a circular stage, where the setting of the next scene has to be completed while a play is in action.

The junior group from Netherhall Gardens, as mentioned in Report 41, found accommodation in two ground floor staff rooms of the old farmhouse.

A further difficulty was presented by the placing of the nursing staff from London. Since the village is small and crowded and offers no possibilities of accommodation, the staff of New Barn had to receive their London colleagues in their own rooms. Since rooms were turned into double ones, double rooms now house three or four people. The sewing room was converted into sleeping quarters; the same happened to half of the workshop. Two chicken houses were adapted for human use, the sitting nests now serving as built-in bookcases.

Household and Maintenance Departments

These departments are naturally working under double pressure. Apart from the constant transportation of beds mentioned above, 50 additional beds have to be made, and all the existing children's and staff rooms are more difficult to clean since they are more crowded. The laundry has assumed huge proportions, and sewing and mending have become hardly possible due to lack of space. Huge parcels of mending are transported back and forth to Netherhall Gardens to keep some of the remaining staff busy there. Clotheslines and drying space have become very precious; on rainy days it is a great problem where to dry the sheets and nappies of the youngest children. Visitors have to be put up for single nights, since the train connections with London have become more difficult.

The boilers need more attention than usual to provide sufficient hot water for a daily bath for 74 children. Repair of toys and furniture never ceases since everything is now in short supply and used to the utmost.

Kitchen and Garden Departments

A great deal of thinking, arranging, and planning has become necessary to cope with the new conditions. The kitchen has been given one additional helper, at times two.

But neither the kitchen range nor the little calor gas stove have grown larger, and kitchen and larder space is extremely limited. The kitchen still serves as a dining room for the whole staff. There is no refrigerator since the electric plant is still under repair; and with weekly food deliveries, to keep supplies fresh is an unending problem. The garden department does its best to cope with the demands. But crops were not planned to satisfy the needs of both houses, since the transport difficulty usually makes it impossible to send large quantities to London. This means that vegetable supplies, meant to cover two months, have run out in one, and that the same will be true of all further gatherings until the apples are ripe. From then on there is good hope that there will be plenty for all.

The kitchen department now receives regular help from the nursery children who, as part of their nursery school work, appear in groups with their teachers to prepare the vegetables. They shell peas and beans with great competence and with real pleasure. And even those children who have no interest in cleaning vegetables are suddenly seized by an urgent desire to work when the morning task consists of preparing fruit. Everybody wants to top and tail gooseberries and red currants.

There is a constant demand for homemade biscuits, which is luckily paralleled by the eagerness of the children to help in making them. The kitchen gives out the dough and the necessary tools, and the children roll and cut them ready to be baked.

During July the kitchen had its peak day on Parents' Sunday, when two big buses brought 70 fathers, mothers, and relatives, who received morning and afternoon tea and lunch. On this day the kitchen catered for 185 people. The main meal was given out in cafeteria fashion and eaten on the lawn.

CHILDREN'S PROBLEMS

Since the incoming children outnumbered those who were living in New Barn, time had to be allowed for the two groups to merge into one, neither to give the New Barn children the feeling that they were dispossessed, nor to leave the newcomers in a situation where they were guests without real right of possession. This adaptation was greatly helped by various factors: in spite of the necessary rearrangements of staff, the Netherhall children arrived with their own group mothers, and the New Barn children kept theirs; this mean that the main attachments of the children remained unbroken. The children who came directly from their parents were all oldtimers, which meant that they were familiar with the habits of New Barn. And many of the Netherhall children found either brothers or sisters or former friends in New Barn, who took them in hand, made them familiar with the place, and introduced them to everything that was strange. The juniors in their isolated farmhouse found at least their own toys, their slide, and their own tables and chairs which had preceded them. They treated these as fixed familiar points in an otherwise strange world and, starting out from them, slowly explored the new and bewildering country setting with unknown birds, chickens, horses, cows, lawns, and sheds. All the older children were gratified to find their corners for washing and dressing complete with hooks with their names or signs on them, ready on arrival.

On the whole the studio-dormitory was treated as a

reception room where all the Netherhall children slept on arrival. As they found friends and acquaintances among the New Barn children, they slowly moved on into the other bedrooms. The same happened concerning group work, group walks, etc. The new children were given their choice where to attach themselves, until the distinction between New Barn children and London children became less recognizable.

Behavior Shown by the Evacuated Children

REACTION TO NEW EXPERIENCE

Certain children, of a specially happy and outgoing nature, treated the whole experience as a pleasant adventure. This was particularly noticeable in Jeffrey (3 years, 8 months). He is one of our happiest nursery children (brought up in Netherhall Gardens from the age of 4 months); he is a sturdy and well-developed boy, a big eater, who relishes new experiences as he relishes his food. He is full of energy and curiosity and makes friends wherever he is. From the moment the children knew they were going to be evacuated, he was full of the idea of the "country" or the "Country House." He could not wait for the ambulance to arrive and from then on concerned himself exclusively with whatever belonged to the new house. He wanted a "country breakfast." He said, when the tables were laid: "Sit next to me, in the country." And when tired and in need of comfort, he even demanded to be taken on a "country lap," i.e., the lap of a member of the staff of the Country House.

Other children, in spite of finding former friends in the Country House, and in spite of many satisfying incidents, still showed that they were troubled by a sense of strangeness. Several of them (Jessie and Bessie, 3 years; Ivy, 3 years; Bridget, 4 years) avoided using the names of the New Barn children in the beginning. If they had a fight with one of them, they would come and complain: "Somebody hurt me!" even in cases where they were perfectly familiar with the names of the accused ones.

Bridget (4 years), a Netherhall child, was found standing in front of two little sisters who had just returned from their parents in London, studying them in silence. When asked what troubled her about them, she said seriously: "The two little girls don't like it here. Do they know me? Lilian [her New Barn friend] knowed me when I came to the country." Her own sense of strangeness and bewilderment on arrival had obviously made her understanding of what went on in the newcomers.

On her first afternoon, in the intervals of running about happily with her friend Lilian, Bridget had always returned to her group mother from London and said quietly: "You know, I do not know my friends anymore" or "I do not know this country anymore." She had actually been in New Barn on holiday when she was 2 years old, but could not remember her experiences. The knowledge that she herself "was known" to somebody had to serve as a reassurance against her general sense of strangeness and insecurity.

PERSISTENCE OF AIR RAID WORRIES IN THE LONDON CHILDREN

The London children were on the whole well aware of the reasons for their evacuation. Freda (3 years, 1 month), who had herself been evacuated from Netherhall Gardens, asked a member of the staff who arrived in the country a few days after her: "Has the warning sent you?" Bridget (4 years) often asks whether she will stay in the country "for good" or whether she will go back to London when "the warnings are over." In a lively discussion with her friend Lilian she was overheard to explain carefully that she would stay only so long as "the warnings" were on, which was not really "for good," whereas Lilian would not even then go back to London.

Some of the London children missed "a shelter" on their first night in the country. Bridget, on her first night, though she could not say enough what a "nice country" it was, was restless until asked what it was that she missed. She urgently wanted to know who was "on shelter duty tonight."

A group of four junior toddlers (20-22 months) was playing very happily on their second day in the country, loading a pram with hay and pulling it off again. Suddenly all four of them rushed to their nurse, frightened, and demanded to be lifted up. The nurse was at a loss to understand what had happened to them until she noticed that a blackbird had begun to sing quite near to the children. They had obviously mistaken the singing for the familiar sound of the sirens.

Though New Barn is fairly untroubled by bombs, a great deal of flying goes on overhead. Low-flying airplanes sometimes shake the whole house or, seen from outside, appear to touch the chimneys and treetops. Two of our younger London children reacted with great anxiety to noise of this kind, Terry (2 years, 2 months) and Jack (2½ years). Terry, on his first day in the country, was obviously afraid of every plane which passed over the house. He did not cry or shout in fear, but placed both hands in front of his eyes and did not remove them until the sound of the engines had died down. After his nurse had seen him act in this way several times, she urged him to watch out for the planes together with her and to watch them go by. After doing this for about an hour, Terry ran toward her whenever a plane appeared and shouted excitedly: "Look, look!"

Jack reacted in a very similar way. He began to cry whenever a plane drew near, rushed to the nearest adult, and called out: "Airplane is hurting me!" He also was taught to look out for the planes, to recognize them in the distance, to follow their course, etc., until his fear of planes gave way to an active interest in them.

A fortnight after Jack's arrival the following incident gave evidence of his change of attitude. He was most interested in watching a number of pigs in a pigsty and ran to his nurse to tell her that all the pigs were "in the shelter." A few minutes later, when an airplane was heard overhead, he ran to the sty and shouted into it: "Airplane's not hurting you!" and then informed the nurse that "the piggies are frightened." He had by then exchanged his role of being frightened himself for that of protector and comforter for the pigs to whom he ascribed his former anxiety.

A week after their arrival in the country, a group of Netherhall Gardens children were observed to play the following game: they all crawled under the cots in their bed-living room and imitated the sound of an all clear. Dan (4 years) called: "All children come out of the shelter!" All the children crept from under their cots. This game was repeated several times.

Jeffrey (3 years, 8 months) asked to have a house drawn for him. As soon as it was finished, he scribbled over it wildly, covering it all up in black. When asked why he did this, he said: "The airplane has spoiled it all to bits, no, the big bad wolf has done it." The "airplane," like "the warning," like "Hitler," or "the bad Wolf," are now equally convenient symbols for everything that is considered evil.

The air raid fears of the older children are very different from these fantastic anxieties of the younger ones; they are based on an awareness of the real dangers. Mary (12 years), when she returned from her parents in London, had wild outbursts of fear for their lives. She knew that they remained exposed to danger and was afraid that she might never see them again. John (12 years) wanted to return home as soon as he heard that part of their house had been damaged by blast. He very naturally remarked that he would rather be near his mother.

Fears for the safety of parents are the topic of endless conversation in the bedrooms of the big children every evening.

Reactions of the New Barn Children

It was not easy for the New Barn children to receive so many evacuees, and to have whatever "home" they had established for themselves invaded by the newcomers. The young nursery children reacted to this experience with an immediate and frank jealousy, which died down after a very few days and changed into an easy acceptance of the new companions. The school children went through a longer period of adaptation. Their first reaction was one of enthusiasm. They competed in helpfulness with the adults, who gave up or shared their rooms with the Londoners. The big children, in their turn, offered their tuck boxes to serve as receptacles for the possessions of the London children. They renounced their right to a special "Sunday breakfast," which had always been served to the school children in their bedroom as a special treat. They introduced the newcomers to their village school and their school friends, etc. They were so happy in the carrying out of all these acts of generosity that it took some time for their natural jealousy to appear. When it broke through, it did so rather violently, but then again died down and gave way to acceptance of the new situation.

INSTANCE OF JEALOUS BEHAVIOR

Dudley (4 years) asked why two buses were arriving on this Parents' Sunday instead of one, as before. When told that this was due to so many children living in New Barn now, he said simply: "Me do not like London children. Them must go away."

George (7½ years), who is by nature a sensitive and retiring child, said: "I do not like these many people here, I do not like such a crowd."

Isabel (7 years, 1 month), herself a rather excitable and noisy child, accused the London children of her own failings when she began to be jealous of them: "I do not like that crowd; they are too noisy."

Bella (9 years, 8 months) is at all times a very jealous girl who has never overcome the aftereffects of her position as the middle child in a family of three girls. The arrival of the London children brought this jealousy into the foreground with full force. She had a violent outburst about missing her special Sunday breakfast. She shouted: "Why must all these children be here? I don't want them! I hate them! I do not mind if there are bombs in London, I do not care what happens, I do not want them here!" She wept loudly and passionately and it took her a long time to understand and master her feelings.

A characteristic conversation was overheard by the night nurse when she passed the bedroom of the 5-year-olds at 6 A.M. about a fortnight after the arrival of the evacuees. It concerned the children's "shop," one of their most valued and beloved institutions. Since the village itself possesses no shop, and Dunmow, the next shopping center, is eight miles distant and out of reach of the smaller children, a little shop is opened for them in the Nursery on Sundays. The Superintendent displays and sells to them small articles, sweets, toys, pencils, booklets, seeds, etc., which they can buy with their pocket money. The decision what to buy next Sunday, whether to save up for bigger articles, etc., plays an important part in the children's conversations.

On this morning one of the boys was heard to say: "Do you remember the time when we were alone still?" An enthusiastic answer came from another bed: "Yes, and do you remember when we had our shop alone?" "Now the London children buy everything. But when the bombing stops in London, then we will have our shop to ourselves again!" In reality, of course, the London children have no greater buying power than those from New Barn. The larger numbers of children, naturally, make for longer queues and some anxiety is created whether the most desirable objects will have disappeared before one's turn arrives.

It is interesting to note how closely this reaction of the New Barn children resembles the attitude of numerous people in the towns and villages of England to the influx of London evacuees. In our case it is impossible for the children to have copied the attitude of the adults in their environment. There is, as mentioned above, no shop in the neighborhood where observations of this kind might have been made.

INSTANCES OF ATTACHMENTS SHAKEN BY JEALOUSY

One of the student workers of New Barn, who acts as group mother to five children from 4 to 6 years, reports that the children of her group became very difficult to handle after they had received several London children as guests in their bedroom. Dressing in the morning, supper in the bedroom, settling at bedtime, which had always been pleasurable times, presented many conflicts. She felt for a while as if she had lost all influence on her children. The children did not behave badly toward the newcomers but, instead, turned against her, as if she had wronged them or betrayed their confidence in some way. She quotes the following instances of behavior observed in her group:

Jim (4 years) is a very affectionate and possessive boy, usually in excellent contact with her. In ordinary times he is easily led and tries hard to please her. About two weeks after the arrival of the Londoners the following incident occurred which shed light on the state of his feelings concerning her and the consequent revolt which became apparent in his actions. He and two other children had been taking green apples from the trees. When the gardener reproached them and told them what a waste it was not to let the apples ripen, the two others were repentant and promised not to do it again. But Jim turned a deaf ear to reasoning which he otherwise understands very well. He turned on the gardener and his group mother and said fiercely: "I shall go on stealing green apples. I know a secret place which you do not know, from there I shall still take them. I do not care if nobody else gets any apples when they are ripe. And I do not even care if you will tell my mummy of me, or Alice [Goldberger, the Superintendent]. Tomorrow I am going to steal some more. I do not like anybody here, so they do not need any apples. And you, Elizabeth [his group mother], are the nastiest girl here, you must never have an apple."

Percy (6½ years) has always loved what the children call their "late supper" in their own bedroom. It is actually no real supper, merely a last snack taken in a small group in intimacy, while conversations, storytelling, etc., are going on. Usually Percy asks immediately on his return from school, in the afternoon, "Will there be supper in our bedroom?" A few days after the arrival of the London children he said suddenly: "I am going to have supper in the hall. I do not like it in here anymore; it is too crowded." He was deeply hurt and disappointed and did not return to his group until a separate supper table was specially arranged for the three biggest boys of the room.

Andrew (6 years), Jim's elder brother, behaved in a very similar manner. Two days after the arrival of the first evacuees in the house, he said: "I do not like this place anymore; it isn't what it used to be: the doll's house is locked, the children are not allowed to get their socks by themselves, and the nursery is painted the wrong color." His discontent was, at that time, still vague. The evacuees had not yet invaded his own room, and he attributed the dissatisfaction due to their arrival to all sorts of minor incidents and changes, even to the painting of the nursery, which had been carried out many weeks previously.

When London children were admitted to his own bedroom, his discontent turned into fierce aggression against his otherwise beloved group mother. He called her the worst names of which he could think and insisted that he would like to "chop her head off." He threatened every evening: "I will not go to sleep, I will make a noise in the bedroom." He did not pay the slightest attention to her demands, behaved very badly at suppertimes, otherwise the time of the greatest intimacy and friendliness, mimicked everything that she did, made the other children laugh at her, etc. But he was not aggressive toward other children and adults, apart from such vague threats as "I'll hit you. . . ."

This behavior lasted about a week and then broke down suddenly. He cried before going to bed, and when his group mother sat with him for a while, he suddenly said: "Are you still sad about me? If I tell you that I am sorry, will you still be sad? I do not like to go to sleep when you are sad." He then talked at length about his bad behavior during the past week and said: "I do not like Christopher [a London boy]; he says all these nasty things and he makes me say them too." From then on friendly relations were established again, and on the following days Andrew was very helpful and tried hard to be good.

HELPFULNESS TOWARD NEWCOMERS

The instances of helpfulness toward newly arrived and specially toward younger children are innumerable. The older girls took special pleasure in going over to the farmhouse to help with the juniors, who are now out of quarantine. They are very skillful in handling the little ones, helping with washing, feeding or in playing with them.

Katrina (10 years) often asks to be left on duty with them during staff meetings and can always be relied on to replace an adult worker at such times.

Helpfulness of this kind is especially apparent at breakfast time when the children choose their own places. Paul (5 years) is always sought after as a neighbor by the youngest children. He serves them milk and bread, generally looks after their needs, and does not care how late he himself finishes his own meal.

REUNION OF TWO SISTERS

The fusion of the two houses led to an unexpected reunion of Katrina (10 years) and Anne (7½ years), two sisters who had lived separated from each other in our Nurseries for several years. They are the eldest of four children who were admitted in July, 1941 after the tragic death of their father in an air raid. Up to that time Katrina had been a devoted eldest sister who looked after her three young brothers and sisters. Once in the Nursery, her long-suppressed jealousy broke through and assumed such proportions that it was considered wise to separate her at least from Anne, who was the special object of her jealousy. Since then the two girls had often been together for short holidays, but had never taken much notice of each other, except to quarrel and to compete with each other.

Anne's arrival in New Barn as an evacuee from London created a very different situation. They unexpectedly became great friends. Katrina was ill for a while and Anne kept her company in the sickroom. They entered into long and intimate conversations with each other, reminiscing about their past childhood which so far had never played a part in their relationship. Anne said to Katrina: "I must ask you something I have wanted to ask you for a long time, can you remember when daddy tried to sit in Lilian's little pram in Hampstead Heath and he fell over and we all laughed?" Katrina did remember and immediately asked Anne if she remembered an incident when daddy had kept them waiting outside a shop and they had run away. For nearly half an hour they reminded each other of their memories, getting more and more excited,

They all concerned little tricks their father had played on them, or things they had done for which they had been punished. Katrina remembered the time when her mother was in the hospital having Lilian, and a very grumpy lady from upstairs looked after them. They had been so sorry for this lady's daughter to have such a horrid mother. They remembered an incident when Lilian dirtied her chair and they were quite helpless about how to clean it. Katrina remembered covering Lilian's face with a blanket so that she could not breathe and her mother scolding her for it. They seemed very happy while they were talking and in the end Katrina said: "It is nice having someone to talk to about things nobody else knows."

43

Monthly Report
August, 1944

STATISTICS

The total number of children is 113; 83 of these are resident, 8 in London and 75 in the Country House.

MEDICAL REPORT

The state of health of all children under school age is excellent; the juniors especially have benefited greatly from their stay in the country. A number of children of school age have come down with a short attack of flu.

All cases of whooping cough in the baby department have recovered. Two older babies now are under observation for signs of a beginning cough; and the three youngest babies have been transferred to a three weeks' quarantine in Wedderburn Road, prior to their departure for the country.

AIR RAID PROBLEMS

Air raid conditions in London have changed little since our last report. Since we cannot count on transferring the children back to London before the onset of bad autumn weather, we are busy planning improvements in the existing accommodations of New Barn. We have received visits from the Medical Officer for Maternity and Child Welfare, Regional Offices of the Ministry of Health in Cambridge; the Senior Medical Officer for Maternity and Child Welfare, Essex County Council; and the Medical Officer of Health for Dunmow. It is still uncertain which of our various projects for creating additional space either inside or additional to the Country House will materialize.

CHILDREN'S PROBLEMS

Readers of our reports will readily understand why we do not want to solve our practical difficulties of space by either having our school children billeted or by placing some of our nursery children with other institutions. They will remember that almost all our older children, who came to us during the bombing period of 1941, were so-called billeting failures, i.e., children who had been unable to bear the sudden separation from their homes and had failed to adapt themselves to new surroundings. They have by now peacefully settled down in our house, have chosen their substitute mothers, made their emotional attachments, and overcome their problems; they have developed on normal lines and have adjusted easily to the village school. To uproot them now, perhaps only a few months before they can finally return to their future peacetime homes, would bring their old difficulties to the surface and might easily turn them again into what they have been before: namely, problem children.

Our young children, on the other hand, many of whom were brought to us by their mothers soon after birth, have so far been spared the wanderings of other war children. It would seem a great pity to let them begin now with the shock of separation, various experiences in other billets or nurseries, or a complete change of environment and educational method. Their mothers, or their absent fathers, expect us to give them a stable home for the duration of the war.

In many of our monthly reports and especially in our Annual Report and *Infants Without Families* [Part II], we have brought forward evidence of the depth and strength of a young child's attachment to his parents and the vital importance of these emotional ties for the child's mental and moral development. In what follows here, we quote instances of children who have formed a similarly strong tie to a substitute mother. In most cases it takes a long stay in the Nursery before a child forms a new attachment of this kind; it happens sometimes after a few months, sometimes after more than a year. Occasionally, a first choice is made by the child and the loved object discarded again and exchanged for another, more stable, or more suitable one.

These new ties are often more violent in nature than the original mother relationship was. The child has experienced separation and disappointment once, expects their repetition unconsciously, and thus clings all the more passionately to the loved person. If outward circumstances permit such a relationship to develop without further disturbance, the child will benefit from it for his emotional and moral development in the same manner as children benefit from the early attachment to their parents; that is, he will derive real help for his whole life, not merely passing satisfaction. In due course the child will outgrow this attachment, as children normally outgrow the relationship to their own mothers.

Where such relationships are broken up, either by removal of the child to another place, or by removal of the adult due to change of work, marriage, illness or death, the child suffers in very much the same manner as he suffered originally when first separated from his natural family surroundings. If children choose more than one adult person for their attachments, or if adults come and go, according to the exigencies of work, difficulties arise between conflicting allegiances which, for the child, are as serious and painful as the conflicts felt in family surroundings between allegiance to father or mother, or between the former attachment to a mother who has died and the later one to a stepmother who has taken her place.

Our children are, on the whole, very outspoken, which means that they are often able to express in words what other children merely feel dimly. This refers to the whole range of feelings which originate from the need for a firm tie to an adult person. They express their craving for some form of substitute satisfaction when they are dissatisfied in their emotional relationships; their passionate enthusiasm about the individual people whom they choose as substitute parents; their bitterness, conflicts, and disappointments; and, step by step, the new growth of a stable and satisfying attachment.

Substitute Satisfactions of an Immediate and Material Kind

Charlie was placed in the Nursery by his mother at the age of 2 years, 1 month. When she left him for the first time, he was in wild despair, tried to get off the nurse's lap to run after her, and sobbed, "Mummy all gone," for a long time. He constantly asked for his coat and shoes and quieted down a little when his shoes were put on his feet. He then agreed to sit on the nurse's lap. She noticed that while he was crying his hand moved up slowly to his mouth, but that he quickly removed it as soon as his forefinger touched his lips. His mother had reported that she had had a "long fight about his nasty sucking." The nurse said to him: "You can suck your finger, Charlie." He moved it up quite slowly, always watching her face while it got nearer to his mouth. Then he violently sucked his forefinger, stopped crying, and did not cry anymore that night.

Bridget (2½ years) asked for a sweet before going to bed one night. There were no sweets. Then she asked for a cheese sandwich and for a biscuit. She could not have either of them, so she said: "But then I want my mummy!"

Bob (3-4 years), whenever he is specially unhappy about the separation from his mother, clings to some piece of clothing which he brought from home. When he first came, he could not be separated from his shoes and even wanted to keep them on when he went to bed. When his mother was unable to come for several weeks, he constantly wore an overcoat, and showed signs of the greatest despair when anybody tried to persuade him to take it off. When his mother was not permitted to visit him during a period of scarlet fever quarantine, he insisted on wearing a hat, sometimes all day and night. Once, when told that his mother would not come next Sunday, he began to cry, rushed to the drawer where the caps are kept, and called out: "My mummy does not come, me must wear a hat!"

Sucking, craving for sweets, neurotic fads connected with clothing, are very frequent reactions with which the child tries to combat his sense of distress and lack of satisfaction. From the point of view of the child's development, they are not helpful; their role is rather that of a drug taken to alleviate pain. Normally the child should dispense with them again soon after a new relationship to a mother substitute has been formed.

Overestimation of the Newly Found Loved Object: Reveling in Its Possession

Bridget (3 years, 4 months), who is a passionate and affectionate child, is always heard to comment on and count the people whom she loves. She insists on their possession and jealously defends her rights against the other children. It is only in moods of great generosity that she is willing to let somebody share her rights. Her favorite nurse used to be Jean; when Jean went to work in the baby department, she slowly accepted Renee as a substitute. It was at this time that her remarks about the whole problem were most frequent.

She met Jean on the stairs of the nursery and called out, "My Jean!" adding after a moment: "I have got my Jean and I have got my Renee."

She was bathed in the evening in a very noisy room to

where little conversation could be understood. When the younger children leave for the shelter, the room becomes empty and is suddenly very quiet. Into the stillness Bridget was heard to whisper to herself: "My Renee very own, my Renee very own, and my Miss Freud very own."

Sometimes she included her great friend Lilian in these relationships. Bridget and Lilian both wanted to be bathed in the evening by Renee, so Bridget said to the nurse: "You be Lilian's Renee too. Lilian's Renee and Bridget's Renee."

Sometimes her generosity went a step further. In the sickroom when her nurse came to visit her, she said: "You sit next to me because you are my Renee, my Renee and Lilian's Renee only." Then she threw a glance at Sidney's bed, which stood next to hers, and added: "And Sidney's Renee."

Dick (4 years, 4 months) said to Anne, a worker who was the friend of his new substitute mother Bertha: "My Anne, my Bertha, my everybody."

Jeffrey (3½ years) is extremely fond of his nurse, Elisabeth, and admires and idolizes her in every way. When he heard the wireless going in the next house, he said: "Listen, lovely music, it is my Elisabeth singing." When asked how he knew that it was her voice, he said: "Because it is so pretty and what my Elisabeth does, is always pretty."

When the children were told one day that there would be a picnic meal since the kitchen had to be closed for a short while due to repairs, he said confidently: "Oh, no, you wait, you will see, my Elisabeth will cook something for me."

One could be easily misled into believing that children who insist in this way on the possession of their loved people feel especially secure and reassured. But closer observation shows that the opposite is true. Children who feel really secure with their parents or with substitute parents do not remark on the fact. They accept what is offered to them as their natural right, without making any comments about it. It is the children who have experienced loneliness, loss, and longing and are afraid of repeating the experience who cling to their objects with overinsistence, as if they were constantly attempting to reassure themselves. The remarks quoted from Bridget, for instance, occurred shortly after she had been parted from nurse Jean, who until then had been her sole mother substitute; Jeffrey's love for Elisabeth developed to the extent described after his first mother substitute (a senior student who left the house after finishing her training) had left him; Dick's enthusiastic exclamation occurred a week after he had been transferred from London to New Barn where Bertha had received him as his new substitute mother to whom he turned very quickly.

Reactions of Bitterness and Disappointment after Separation from a Substitute Mother

Dan (4 years, 4 months) and Martin (4 years, 8 months) were among the few children parted from their special group mother when our London children were evacuated to New Barn. Instead of seeing her daily, being bathed and dressed by her, etc., they now see her only on long weekends when she still takes care of them. They both react very similarly to her partial absence. They do not mention her during the week, and are very affectionate when she arrives. At bathing time, however, they criticize whatever she does and accuse her of hurting them, putting soap into their eyes, rubbing them too hard with the towel, etc. Both said, independently of each other: "You do not know how to bathe me anymore, because you are not always here." Still, they insist on being bathed by her. But even after three consecutive evenings they both continued to express their anger with her in this way.

In spite of all efforts to keep our children under the guidance of their group mothers, there are some who, due to circumstances beyond our control, have changed hands too frequently and show the bad effect of such experience. One such child is Miles, now 3½ years, who was admitted to Netherhall Gardens at the age of 12 months. He made no firm attachment in his first year in the Nursery. His health was delicate, due to a babyhood spent almost exclusively in Tube shelters. He had several attacks of bronchitis and pneumonia and spent long periods in the sickroom with intermittent intervals in the juniors' department. He was transferred to New Barn for reasons of health at the age of 22 months.

There he attached himself to a student worker who looked after him for seven months and then had to leave him to take up her training in the baby department in London. He passed into the hands of a senior student who again left him after a period of eleven months to take up a position in London. His next attachment was a young student of whom he became extremely fond. But she too had to leave New Barn after four months to spend some time in London for her baby training.

Before this happened, she had a long talk with him in the evening before he went to sleep. She explained that she did not like to leave him, but that she had to go to

London for a time to learn all about handling small babies; that her friend Doreen, with whom he was well acquainted, would now like to do everything for him, to put him to bed every evening, to dress him, to bathe him, etc.; and that he could go and help Doreen in the garden or in the workshop, wherever she was busy. Miles listened to all this with an expression of disbelief on his face. When she had finished, he turned his face to the wall and said: "And when will Doreen go to London?"

He had by this time had the experience that all his attachments were transitory and not really worth making. The results of this attitude are clearly visible in his difficult behavior, his failure to adapt himself to the simple rules and regulations of the Nursery, and in a general slowing up of the normal process of becoming "social."

Conflicting Allegiances

Christopher entered New Barn at the age of 2 years, 4 months, a delicate, shy, and difficult boy who had been definitely neglected by his mother. His special problem was an alternation between insistence on overcleanliness and severe setbacks to wetting and dirtying. When he became more confident and able to express his feelings, he showed his disappointment with the way his mother treated him. He complained that she never visited him, never fulfilled her promises to bring him new shoes, toys, etc. He expressed jealousy of "baby dogs" which he thought his mother kept at home and of a baby brother of whom he had vaguely heard.

It took him a long time to make a definite attachment in the Nursery. When he at last found a substitute mother, his relationship to her was close and affectionate. Unluckily, it was interrupted after several months by a severe illness which forced that particular student to enter a sanitarium for a six months' cure. He suffered a great deal at that time and showed great longing for his "little Hilda" (as she was called to distinguish her from a senior student of the same name). His "little Hilda" became a legendary figure for him. All the good things which had happened in his life were attributed to her, all the bad things to other people, or to his mother. Whenever somebody failed to comply with his wishes or to do him a favor of any kind, he would remember, or rather imagine, similar incidents of his past where his "little Hilda" had satisfied his desires.

At the age of 5 he formed a new attachment to another student who took care of him, Edith. He was satisfied to be bathed by her and wanted her regularly to stay with him in the evening for a talk. He would tell her many stories about past events, and showed signs of jealousy when she was busy with other tasks or with other children. He did not want her to stay with anybody else, nor did he want anybody else to stay with him. When she said that she had to go into another bedroom to help there, he said: "Don't go into Elsie's bedroom. Elsie has enough people to help her, don't you help her." When she said that there was washing up to do in the kitchen, he said: "Tomorrow I shall throw all the plates into the bonfire in the garden, then you cannot wash them."

This new attachment to Edith did not prevent him from talking about little Hilda as often as before. He knew that she was ill in the hospital and dictated a letter to Edith, to send to her:

Say to my dear little Hilda, is she nearly better now? Say that she must come back. And will she bring a little toy for me? I want her to bathe me when she comes and to dress me. When she comes, she should see me in my bed and stay with me and wash me, always. When will she take me down to breakfast? And she must see me to the gate when I go to school. When I play out in the garden, she will come and look for me. She will find me for my bath. And write down that she must not go away, but bathe me another day; and put me to bed another time; and come to the tent with me sometimes. Tell her to take me for walks, and then bring me back here. Now put lots of love and kisses from her Christopher.

What had begun as a letter obviously developed into a fantasy of wish fulfillments in his mind. From then on he felt that little Hilda's return was drawing nearer and began to worry how to solve the problem of his double attachment.

A few days after dictating his letter, he again opened a conversation with Edith at bedtime. He said: "I know you are going to London tomorrow." She answered that she had not planned to do so and asked him why he expected her to go. He said: "Because my little Hilda is coming back." She explained that this would not happen quite so soon, but he kept on without taking any notice of her words: "When my Hilda does come, you will go to London and won't come back, won't you?" Again she said that she had no reason to go to London. So he said in a resigned voice: "But you could go into the kitchen and help Sofie [the cook], couldn't you?" When asked why, he explained: "When my Hilda comes back, I want her to bathe me and dress me, and there will be nothing for you to do here. So do go and help Sofie, won't you?"

In the following days he returned to the subject twice, asking her in a very friendly manner whether she would not like to go to London: that he would not make a fuss if she went and did not come back again.

His relationship to Hilda is obviously by far the stronger one. He clings to her memory with great faithfulness, though he accepts Edith as a temporary substitute. On the other hand, he is much too sensitive simply to discard Edith when Hilda returns. He worries about her fate and attempts to settle things for her, to arrange her future work, etc. His offer that she might go to London is well meant. He knows that she goes there at times to visit relations, and usually he takes her going very badly. The state of conflict in him is visible and absorbs a great deal of his interest.

Satisfying and Stable Relationships

In contrast to these disappointing and conflicting experiences, most of our children succeed in establishing satisfying and stable relationships to their group mothers, and with their help build up the foundations for a normal and social attitude to life.

A striking instance of this kind is Reggie (now 4 years), who came to Wedderburn Road at the age of 5 months. He once returned to his mother for a short period, was brought back to Netherhall Gardens, and later on transferred to New Barn. His first loving attachment was formed to a senior student who had complete charge of him until he was 3 years old, when she left the house to marry. He was deeply unhappy, violently jealous, and regressed in various ways. He made scenes at bedtime and gave up all bladder and bowel control. In the months which followed, he slowly attached himself to the Superintendent of the Nursery. He began to develop a dislike for his former mother substitute which he showed openly whenever she visited. He said firmly: "I do not like her anymore." His relations to "My Alice" began with a repetition of all his difficulties, which were now concentrated on her. While he was still insecure in his attachment, he would trail after her all day long and could not bear to be separated from her at all. Once, when he could not find her in the house or garden, he wandered off into the village, which is two miles distant, and was found in the village street, all alone, dragging a little toy behind him. He had thought that "My Alice" might have taken the school children to the village school and that he would find her on the way.

When this phase passed, his development once more resumed its normal course. He became clean again, though he suffered many setbacks before this was finally accomplished. He became quiet, confident, and showed the more normal possessiveness which boys of that age display toward their mothers. He felt certain that she could help him out of all his difficulties.

When she warned him once not to stand on the widowsill, so as not to fall off and hurt himself, he answered confidently: "You could mend me." When another child worried whether his group mother would return from London at the appointed time and bring him the promised toy, Reggie said to Alice: "When you come back, you always bring me something. Last time you brought a big duck and two little ducks, because you promised, didn't you?"

The problem whether she can like him in spite of his

many defects occupied his thoughts a great deal. The following conversation dealing with this subject took place, as usual, in the evening in bed. Reggie said: "You do not like me when I am wet." Alice answered that she did like him, but thought that he was too big now to be wet. He pondered about this problem and then continued: "But you do not like me when I run away?" She answered that she did like him, but that it made her very sad when he wandered away all alone. After this he took her hand, pulled her nearer, and whispered gratefully: "You are my secret! I climb up a high tree and pick two big apples, one for you and one for me!" After a moment he added: "No, I pick three, two for you and one for me!"

But, though he worried about her reactions to his wetting, he did not admit it in front of others. When the night nurse once reproached him for wetting his bed again and not being a "big boy," he looked at her triumphantly and said not quite truthfully: "Didn't you hear what Alice said? Even if I am wet, I am still a big boy!"

He produced the following fantasy in relation to her, which most children at one time or another produce in relation to their parents. He looked at her and said: "When I shall be Alice, I will stay with you a long time. I will grow as high as the ceiling and you will be very little." She said: "You will be a very big Reggie then." But he answered very firmly: "No, not Reggie, I will be Alice then. When I am Alice, I shall bathe you always in the big bathtub."

As happens in all normal attachments of this kind, the child, under the influence of the loved adult, not only puts up an active fight against all his difficulties and defects, but also unfolds all the constructive qualities which lie within his possibilities. Reggie, for instance, became very generous and protective in his relationship to his Alice. At a period when all the children were very keen on competition and attempted to beat each other in running fast, climbing trees, dressing quickly, etc., he suddenly turned around on a walk, when walking in front of Alice, and said to her: "I do not beat you. I do not want to beat you; I walk very slowly."

Developments of a similar nature occur in the majority of children. The following instances are quoted from one of our most problematical and demanding boys, a child who lost his mother and whose homelife was completely disrupted by the war. He made life for his substitute mother very difficult, with endless scenes and temper tantrums, due to his violent clinging to her. After one and a half years in New Barn he showed the first signs of "settling down." He was ill in bed when he asked the worker who cleaned the room to call "My Alice." She said that she would do so in a minute, when she had done the room and would go downstairs anyway with the brooms. For the first time he did not show his usual demanding impatience, but said quietly: "Oh, yes, I can wait."

Half a year later, Alice warned him one evening that she would be off the next day and that he should not make his usual fuss, asking for her. He answered to her surprise: "I do not care a bit. I know, when I come home from school, you will be here anyway,"

It takes a surprisingly long time to build up a child's relationships again after they have been destroyed once. Educational development on the other hand does not really progress until this has happened. The foregoing examples will have served their purpose if they succeed in illustrating the point that these attachments made by children in a nursery are worthy of consideration and of preservation.

44

Monthly Report
September, 1944

STATISTICS

The total number of children is 113; 78 of these are resident, all of them in the Country House.

MEDICAL REPORT

The state of health of the children is good, except for a few isolated cases of chicken pox and a slight flu which began among the younger children in the last days of the month.

AIR RAID STATISTICS

In Reports 41, 42, and 43 we were unable to send our American friends the detailed accounts of our living conditions which might have interested them. Postal censorship regulations prohibited not merely, as usual, the naming of places and dates where incidents had occurred, but equally the figures about the frequency of air raids, which we usually mention in our reports as an indication of the strain (or absence of strain) under which children and staff are living. These latter restrictions were lifted on September 7 when official statistics were published regarding the flying bomb raids prior to that date.

We hope that the following figures will be a belated help to our readers to visualize the state of affairs in Netherhall Gardens prior to the evacuation to New Barn.

The flying bomb attacks, as revealed in the official statements, began in the middle of June. From then onward there were:

96 air raid warnings in the second half of June;
194 air raid warnings in July;
117 air raid warnings in August;

which makes a total of 407 air raids for these three months.

The life of the Nursery was naturally determined not only by the frequency of raids, but still more so by the varying length of the individual air raid periods. The following figures serve as illustrations in this respect:

The longest night alert lasted 12 hours without interruption.

The longest daytime alert lasted 9 hours (see Report 41 concerning continual shelter life of children).

The greatest number of alerts on a given day was 15 (see Report 41 concerning the carrying of babies to and from the shelter).

The greatest number of alerts in the shortest time was: 6 raids in 4 hours on one day, and 6 raids in 3 hours on another.

On a certain date, when all the children were still in Netherhall Gardens, the only raid-free period in 24 hours was 2 hours, 35 minutes.

CHILDREN'S PROBLEMS

Soon after our London children had settled down to a peaceful country life, the atmosphere of the Nursery was once more disturbed by outside events. Two official announcements were made by the Government at the beginning of the month: (1) that "the battle of London was over," (2) that the blackout regulations were changed to a mere dimout. Our bigger children misunderstood these announcements to mean that the end of the war had come, and an intense wave of excitement immediately swept through the whole house. Everybody began to talk about going home, the arrival of parents to collect their children was expected with impatience, and even those children who have no parents began to make their preparations for an imaginary homecoming. Children who are more than ordinarily attached to their group mothers, as, for instance, Marion and Reggie, started to cling to their adults and worried about the expected separation.

The return of air raids on London after a week's respite, the first disappointment that the dimout was followed by an immediate alert and readjustment of the blackout curtains, and the Government warnings against return to London because of the possibility of V-2 raids, all worked as an antidote against these anticipations. The children settled down once more to their wartime existence. There is, at present, even less feeling of "peace" in Lindsell than ever before. Whereas London has many quiet nights, the population of New Barn is often troubled by raids.

The feeling that the end of the war might be imminent, which for a short time the adults of the Nursery shared with the children, induced us once more to look into the future prospects for our children. During the last three years our social worker has made incessant efforts to keep in close contact with all the parents, to improve relations with them wherever they were indifferent, and to trace and recapture contact whenever it had been lost or was on the point of getting lost. Due to his efforts, many more of our children will be reunited with their families at the end of the war than we had thought possible at an earlier date.

At present we are making special efforts to help some of our unmarried mothers toward future independence, i.e., toward the possibility to earn sufficiently to make a home for their children. Such attempts are best begun while the children are still with us, either as residents or as day children, or while the Nursery is still there to fall back on. One of these mothers, who took evening classes in sewing while working in the household of the Nursery, has good hopes to obtain a position in the sewing room of a big deparment store.

Contact between children, parents, and Nursery was further greatly helped by the monthly, or bimonthly, Parents' Sundays in New Barn. These Parents' Sundays have in time become an essential item in the life of the Nursery. Since we tried to turn them into very pleasant occasions for the parents, with three free meals per day (tea on arrival, lunch, and tea before departure) and all the amenities of outdoor life, with deck chairs, open air performances, etc., they quickly lost all character of duty visits. There is now little need to urge parents not to miss a visiting day. Every Parents' Sunday is declared to be better than the last one; the highest praise was given by a mother who declared after a specially bright and successful summer Sunday visit that it had been "beautiful, like a wedding." According to circumstances, each of these Sundays has some special feature: this month, with its big apple crop, each parent was permitted to pick and take home as many apples from the orchard as he or she could carry.

At the same time we have provided possibilities for the visit of near relatives and children of the family whenever there is no infection in the house. These details may seem trifling, but they are, in the long run, a great help in keeping the link between children and parents and in excluding some of the discomforts and consequent estrangements which mass visiting in such long intervals produces only too easily.

All these preparations and precautions naturally do not prevent the occurrence of awkward situations between parents and children. On the last two or three Parents'. Sundays Reggie (4 years) has created special difficulties. He has steadfastly refused to meet or greet his mother, for fear of being taken away by her. On her last arrival he hid under a big bush in the garden and had to be searched for. The mother, who shows little interest in the child, is naturally offended by his behavior, which makes her conspicuous in front of other parents. She answers his dislike by throwing out hints that she has little inclination to "take him home after the war." She has separated from her husband during his absence in the army and considers her children as a burden and a hindrance in remarrying.

45

Monthly Report
October, 1944

STATISTICS

The total number of children is 110; 75 of these are resident, 14 in London and 61 in the Country House.

MEDICAL REPORT

The cases of chicken pox have increased in the Country House. Nearly all children who have not had it in previous years are by now down with it. Simultaneously there are some cases of flu among the older as well as among the younger children. Since the number of patients exceeded the number of beds in the two sickrooms, the whole upper floor of the Country House was turned into a sick bay.

The junior group in the farmhouse escaped the chicken pox infection.

AIR RAID PROBLEMS

There were only 20 air raid warnings in London since the last report. The Country House on the other hand had many anxious nights. Since the house has no shelter, the bigger children suffered a good deal from the alarming noise of low-flying bombs. Repeated experiences of this kind prompted us to divide the risk once more by bringing a number of our London children back to Netherhall Gardens. Their evacuation to the country had lasted four months, nearly to the day.

CHILDREN'S PROBLEMS

In the past month we reported that the thoughts and plans of our older children in the Country House are now turned toward the future and the ending of the war. Many of them have lived in evacuation, and separated from their homes and families since 1940, that is, the greater part of their lives. All those who still retain a memory of family life long for its renewal, for privacy, intimacy, and the absence of a crowd.

"Peace" or the "end of the war" have acquired the quality of magic words for the children. They imagine the world after the ending of the war as a kind of paradise with wish fulfillment and no frustration, and they expect everything from it, from freedom to "scribble on the walls" (one of the prohibitions in the Nursery) to the return of dead parents. They are thus completely oblivious of all the obstacles which will have to be surmounted before they can really return home.

REPORT 45

We promised in Report 44 to give a more detailed account of the efforts of our social worker, whose dealings with the parents are meant to pave the way for the homecoming of the children. During the existence of our Nurseries, his work has continued without a break, as an essential accompaniment and corollary to the educational work done directly with the children.

Mr. James Robertson writes as follows:

Throughout the war it has been the Nurseries' policy to encourage close contact between the children and their parents or next of kin, partly in the hope of facilitating the children's ultimate return to family life.

Yet, in only a few instances will there be no difficulties in the way of the children going home. However, in the case of 25 children we are optimistic that the difficulties can be overcome with our assistance. In the main these are children whose family life can be resumed after the cessation of air raids, because their fathers and mothers are at home, although their economic position will probably not improve. In addition, there are the fatherless children whose mothers have worked in our Nurseries. These mothers are now being helped to set up homes of their own and to find work which will carry them through the postwar period. In some measure these 25 children, who have been with us throughout the war years, present the simplest placement problems. Among those who will still be with us even after London is declared safe are children whose family life has been destroyed or seriously disrupted by the war or other circumstances, and whose future is very uncertain. Furthermore, children whose fathers are in the army will stay with us until the fathers return home and the mothers are able to give up work.

But the problems in the way of placing these 25, while relatively simpler, are nevertheless real enough. Among these are external problems caused by the destruction of housing and the lack of new building during the war. Many families lost their homes altogether; others need larger flats or live in badly damaged accommodations that are quite unsuitable for children. The repairs, though being hurried, will take a long time; hardly any flats are available; rents are extremely high; and many landlords refuse families with children. Moreover, many of the poor families lack beds, bedding, and furniture for children. The Nurseries can help overcome this difficulty from oddments of furnishing which we have in stock.

In other cases, where such material difficulties do not exist, it would seem that a child could simply go straight home once the danger of air raids has passed. Yet some of these parents are tempted to procrastinate. They cite obstacles after obstacles which are not genuine but merely represent rationalizations of their unwillingness to resume full responsibility for their children. While they have not lost their attachment to the children, the wartime separation from them was compensated for by the freedom it gave the parents; a freedom that many of these young parents are somewhat reluctant to give up.

Further details of our efforts to resettle the children under our care will be given in Report 52.

46

Monthly Report
November, 1944

STATISTICS

The total number of children is 110; 60 of these are resident, 22 in London and 38 in the Country House.

MEDICAL REPORT

The state of health in both houses is very good and the sickrooms are empty. There are no further cases of chicken pox, though the quarantine has not yet expired.

AIR RAIDS

There were only 17 air raid warnings in London since the last report. Occasional excitements about alerts and flying bombs, or rocket explosions without previous warning, are equally divided between both houses. On the whole the older children are much less interested in these happenings, and much more indifferent to the noise caused by them, than they were a month ago.

CHILDREN'S PROBLEMS

[In this report James Robertson reviews the social problems of several children. Since many of these have been summarized in previous reports and are again taken up in Report 52, they are omitted here.]

47

Monthly Report
December, 1944

STATISTICS

The total number of children is 109; 60 of these are resident, 27 in London and 33 in the Country House.

MEDICAL REPORT

The state of health in both houses is good and both sickrooms are empty. The London children are beginning to show the first signs of winter colds, due to the exceedingly damp and foggy weather, but so far nothing serious has developed. The New Barn children live in fog, rain, and dampness but seem to stand it very well.

AIR RAIDS

There were only 8 air raid warnings in London since the last report, but as the main threat are now rockets and not flying bombs, the number of warnings has ceased to be an indication of comfort or discomfort. The London children are not troubled by thoughts of V-2s, which to them remain a vague threat. But the New Barn children are extremely troubled by low-flying V-1s which make a great noise reverberating through the high roof of the house. They are most affected by it when it happens at bedtime in the evening. These flying bomb raids, coupled with the constant sight of American and British planes, keep the minds of the children very much on the war.

PROBLEMS

[This report deals with the development of a pair of identical twins, Mary and Madge. It has been omitted because this material has been published by Dorothy Burlingham in her book on *Twins* (1952).]

48

Monthly Report
January, 1945

STATISTICS

The total number of children is 109; 59 of these are resident, 25 in London and 34 in the Country House.

Two little brothers, one of whom had been with us for four years, have left us to go home to their mother. Their homecoming was planned and worked for by our social worker for several months. He helped the mother to set up a flat of her own again, to provide some essentials for the children, to secure a place for them in the local day nursery so that she can continue with part-time work. Jeffrey, the older of the two boys, came to us as a sickly baby of 5 months. His foster mother could not keep him because of alleged epileptic fits; he grew into a big, strong, and good-looking boy with lively sparkling eyes, one of our happiest and healthiest children.

MEDICAL REPORT

There were three cases of scarlet fever among the London children. They all went to the hospital, made a good recovery, and were dismissed after three to four weeks. The youngest one has been taken home by his family for further convalescence: the other two are isolated in one of our staff hostels for a further period.

New Barn has one case of whooping cough which has gone to the hospital.

AIR RAIDS

New Barn had a narrow escape when an American fighter plane, the pilot of which had bailed out, cleared the roof of the main house, the adjoining staff house, and the treetops of the garden, crashed into the next field, and burned up. There was great excitement in the neighborhood with police, soldiers, and airmen coming to the rescue. The children were very upset, especially the big ones, who had heard the noise across the field in school. The general opinion was that the crash had been on New Barn. Since it was near school closing time, they all came rushing home to see whether the house was still standing. Their next concern was the pilot, who was for a while believed to have perished with the plane. Each child felt certain that it had been his particular airman, the one who had entertained them at the Christmas party at the American airdrome. There was great relief when the pilot was reported to have landed safely.

Netherhall Gardens and New Barn hear fairly equal

numbers of V-2s and occasional V-1s. So far both houses have escaped all damage, but many of the London parents of our children were less fortunate during the past months and reports about their flats or rooms being bombed or blasted again are coming in continually. On Parents' Sunday in New Barn, though it was otherwise as pleasant a parents' day as ever, it was painfully clear that some of the mothers were in low spirits due to fear of the rocket bombs and anxiety for relations in the Forces who are involved in the battles now being fought in Europe and in the Japanese war.

Jim's mother, who was always badly affected by the raids, is again in a bad state. She wavered between sleeping in the shelter, where she caught a bad chill, and staying home, where she is upset by the explosions. Due to her nervousness, she and her husband both feel at their wits end.

Janet's and Gladys's father has been sent to the Pacific and their mother is upset and unhappy. She lived in a district of London which has suffered badly during the blitz from flying bombs and rockets. She herself had been bombed out or blasted five times. A fortnight ago workmen of the borough finished at 5 in the afternoon with the repair of her windows. At 7 in the evening a rocket blasted most of the windows again and brought down a ceiling. Two days later a rocket damaged the remaining windows.

Miles's mother was blasted out two weeks ago in a badly damaged flat in which she was living. She went to live with her parents where a few days later she was blasted again.

Bertha's and Reggie's mother lost her flat and some of her furnishings due to a rocket.

Tilly's mother lost a house which she had just taken and furnished in the hope of taking in lodgers and maintaining herself and the child in the near future. Since she was absent at work when it happened, she escaped injury, but the shock of finding her house in ruins made her ill.

PROBLEMS

[In this report the development of the identical twins, Mary and Madge, is continued. See Dorothy Burlingham (1952).]

49

Monthly Report
February, 1945

STATISTICS

The total number of children is 108; 59 of these are resident, 26 in London and 33 in the Country House.

Our baby room has been reopened as an emergency department for young infants. The first two arrivals are 2 baby boys of 4 and 6 weeks respectively, who will stay with us while their mothers undergo operations in the hospital. Further arrivals are expected shortly.

AIR RAIDS

We have been asked by several readers in what ways our children react to the noise of the rockets (V-2s), whether they find them more, or less, frightening than the flying bombs or the ordinary bombs of former times.

So far as the older nursery children (from 3 to 5 years) are concerned, the rockets play a very insignificant role in their daily lives. The absence of air raid warnings with the consequent lack of preparations (being taken to shelter, etc.) is felt as a great relief, all the more so since many of the children had always regarded the warning as the main threat. But whereas these bigger children often disregard the noise of rockets, the younger ones are markedly affected by it. The following observations, made when a rocket crashed during the play hours of a group of junior toddlers, may serve as an example of their usual reactions.

Daniel (17 months) seemed oblivious of the noise. About two minutes later he seemed to notice that the other children were talking about something which had happened outside; it was only then that he looked toward the window.

Jill (23½ months) did not react for a few seconds, then began to hit the air repeatedly, to look toward the window, and to talk fast in baby language.

Renny (23½ months) sat down immediately and turned pale.

Louis (2 years, 4 months) cried for a second and then began to talk about "naughty bom bom." He repeated these words many times during the day and was still heard talking about it in the shelter when going to bed.

Sophie (2¼ years) turned pale and after some time joined in Louis's "naughty bom bom." Several times during that day she rushed toward the window, saying, "Stop it, naughty bom bom."

Lily (2 years, 4 months) began to cry after a few seconds and mentioned the incident several times during that and the next day.

Zeeta (2 years, 5 months) clung to the nurse in fear for a second. She then talked about the bang repeatedly during that day and mentioned it several times during the next four days. At another time, about half an hour after a rocket had crashed, she rushed to the window and shouted as loud as she could, "Naughty bom bom, I don't want it." Later on, when she was sweeping, she took her little broom, rushed again to the window, and banged against it; then she said proudly: "I hit the naughty bom bom."

Louis and Zeeta, who are the oldest children of this group, seemed to be most impressed, or rather most fascinated, by the happening, as shown in the following observation. Louis is going through a time when he finds it rather difficult to fall asleep in the evening; he jumps about in his shelter bed, calls the other children, and he and Zeeta, who sleeps in the neighboring bed, giggle for a long time. One evening, he seemed to quieten down at last but said in a chanting sleepy voice innumerable times: "Naughty bom bom all gone now." Zeeta joined him and they both continued to chant this sentence until it became more slow and dreamy and they both fell asleep.

Among the older nursery children Joan (3 years, 11 months) is the one who is most impressed by the rockets. She is a day child who sleeps at home and is brought in by her mother on her way to work and fetched in the evening. Her mother reports that she never tires of talking about the rockets and that she will do anything which she otherwise refuses to do when promised "a story about rockets." She prefers such stories to the usual fairy tales. She pays special attention to slight vibrations of blast which other children fail to notice, and feels herself in every way to be an expert on the subject. When, on their way home, her mother pointed at something in the sky and said: "Look, Joan, there's an airplane on fire," she answered: "No, Mummy, that's no plane, that's a rocket." When the crash followed, she began to run, calling: "Quick, Mummy, or we'll be killed." When subsequently she heard people in the street discuss the rocket, she said proudly: "See, I said it was a rocket."

MEDICAL REPORT

There were no further cases of scarlet fever in Netherhall Gardens. New Barn had one further case of whooping cough; otherwise all the children are in very good health.

CHILDREN'S PROBLEMS

In this and the following reports we propose to discuss, in greater detail than has been possible so far, the principles of early upbringing which underlie our dealings with our various children.

Handling of Difficult Children

Most of our older children, who came to us in 1941, 2 to 5 years old, many of whom are still living with us, presented definite behavior problems on arrival. As described in Report 12, they had suffered severely owing to various causes. Some of them had lost one or both parents; many of them had been moved from billet to billet and failed to adapt themselves; most of them had been through experiences of severe bombing; and all of them had witnessed the complete breakup of their family life. These experiences had made them bewildered and insecure, had produced neurotic symptoms of all kinds, and turned many of them into so-called problem children.

Our task with them was, above all, a remedial one; it lay in an attempt to undo some of the harm which had been done. We had to restabilize their living conditions; to help them to re-establish emotional contact with the outside world where it had been broken; to try and understand their behavior and trace it back in detail to the traumatic experiences of their past. Accounts of our dealings with the children of this group are contained in many of our Monthly Reports.

For these children, normal development and normal upbringing had been interrupted by their war experiences. They needed a prolonged period of rehabilitation to regain their lost balance so far as their emotions and their instinctual development were concerned. With many of them it is only now, after an interval of three to four years, that they resume life as fairly normal human beings and can be handled and dealt with as normal children should be.

Children Admitted As Infants

Another group of our children was of an entirely different nature. They were born during the period of big air raids on London, their mothers being bombed out either during pregnancy or shortly after the birth of the baby. They had not experienced a breakup in their family life since no family life had existed for their mothers at the time of their birth. The fathers had mostly gone overseas, so that there was no home to bring them back to. After a few weeks or months of nightlife in shelters, they found a stable home with us, from the beginning of their conscious existence.

The same was true for a further group of infants who joined us directly from the maternity hospital where they had been born. They were the children of working mothers who were not able to maintain a home during the absence of the fathers. Some of them were illegitimate war babies whose fathers had gone overseas and could not be traced and whose mothers had no means to provide for them.

It was the problem of these two last-mentioned groups which prompted us to look more closely into the emotional situation of the homeless child, and to discuss the ways in which his development differs from the development of children under normal family conditions (see Part II). We did our utmost to preserve and strengthen the tie between these children and their mothers, so as to give them at least remnants of a family attachment. For that purpose we admitted some mothers for prolonged periods of breast feeding; we employed mothers in the household who wanted to remain near their children; we kept the London Nursery open for visiting at all hours of the day. For the country Nursery transport was provided at regular intervals prescribed by the Ministry of Transport, and there was little that we could do to enlarge on it. But we were always ready to house mothers or fathers who could travel out on their own and stay overnight or for a holiday; and we spared no effort to make the monthly, or bimonthly, communal visits in the parents' bus as pleasant as possible for the visitors.

This had the welcome result that children and parents did not lose sight of each other completely, and that the children remained conscious of the fact that they had people outside the nursery to whom they belonged and for whom they were important. Some part of their emotional attachment at least became fixed onto the mother and the father, though the picture of the distant parents in the child's mind was often distorted beyond recognition. But we could not alter the fact that the responsibility for the upbringing of the children in this all-important period of their lives rested completely with us. There was no possibility for most of the mothers to share this task with us. There was, consequently, also no possibility for them to object to, or interfere with, the way in which we were dealing with it.

Some Principles of Normal Upbringing

For parents, or other educators who have to deal with the early reactions of young children, it is usual to adopt one of two opposite methods. As described many times before, the infancy of every human individual is dominated by powerful instinctual tendencies, and by the wishes and qualities which originate from them. As the child grows from his first babyhood to the age of 5, he passes through successive stages of greed and dirtiness, of aggression and cruelty, of exhibitionism and curiosity; he adopts and develops autoerotic habits of various kinds (sucking, rocking, masturbation). All of these tendencies and activities run counter to the normal social behavior prescribed in the adult community, which the child has to enter at school age. All types of education have, therefore, one main aim: to rid the child of his antisocial behavior, and to redirect his wishes according to the norms of morality which exist in the adult society.

Conventional Upbringing

The more old-fashioned forms of education try to achieve this mainly by repressive methods. The expression of the child's early sexual and aggressive tendencies are suppressed as fast as they appear, and before they can extend and develop. The child who feels hostile toward the parents or their substitutes is not permitted to express either his anger, or his resentment, or his death wishes. Exhibitionism is overlaid with modesty. Curiosity remains permitted only on nonsexual grounds, and where it does not conflict with the parents' demand for discretion. Cruelty is pushed into the background, to make way for pity, as early as possible. Dirty habits are fought from the very beginning of life. Autoerotic habits are condemned as dangerous and abnormal.

It is not even deemed sufficient for children to refrain from giving active expression to these forbidden wishes; they are expected to eradicate the very wishes from their minds, to forget about them, and to overlay them with new and better ethical standards.

In their choice of educational methods, educators of this kind prefer those which have a quick, immediate, and lasting effect, as, for instance, material rewards, withdrawal of love, threats, and punishments. It is considered an educational success when children do not repeat a forbidden action after once having been punished for it, and when they estrange themselves from their crude wishes to the extent of barring them completely from their consciousness.

But early upbringing of this nature, though it may seem efficient enough in the beginning, is not as beneficial to the development of the child as is generally believed. Instinctual tendencies, once repressed, are beyond the individual's control. Though they have disappeared from the surface, or even been turned into their opposites, they continue to exist in their original form in the unconscious mind; they continue to influence and distort the child's behavior in more subtle ways, and they remain a potential threat to the individual's mental health. Just because they are repressed, they are also unalterable, and excluded from progressive development.

Aggressive tendencies, for instance, which, at an early age, have given way to repressive educational methods and have been turned into gentleness and compulsive pity, will remain fixed in that state and cannot be transformed and redirected into useful channels, for example, in the service of fighting the forces of nature or other enemies of mankind.

It appears as if the child had mastered the forces in his own mind; in reality he is restricted, not really able to exercise a sensible control over his instincts. Instead of being dominated by his wishes, he is dominated by his repressions and cannot alter their results with growing maturity. The same children who have, to the satisfaction of their parents, become "good," and socially adapted, develop in many cases, to the disappointment or to the despair of the same parents, into inhibited, stunted, and impoverished personalities.

Modern Upbringing

In some of the forms of modern education mistakes are made in the opposite direction. Many parents, nurses, and teachers have learned from modern psychology to assess infantile instinctual life according to its true value. They recognize in its crude expressions the raw material from which adult sexual life and adult activity are made. They realize that most of the child's troublesome activities and unwelcome asocial attitudes represent transitional stages which prepare the way for further steps in development. They realize further that most infantile wishes and feelings are limited in time; they belong to definite ages and, after a short existence, will give way to new manifestations. There is little sense in taking up the fight against them before they have run their course. After all, there is no more hurry to get rid of infantile immorality than there is hurry to get rid of all the other attributes of childhood.

These parents, or their substitutes, accordingly wish to give the child freedom of expression and adequate scope for the manifestations of his primitive activities. They feel hesitant to cause the child distress through frustration of his wishes, and they withhold their criticism and their interference so far as possible. They have learned to respect the child's instinctual life and, incidentally, learned to fear the consequences of too much interference, namely, the neuroses and inhibitions which can originate directly from childhood conflicts.

But they forget that, for the child, the task of outgrowing and overcoming his early instincts is an incomparably difficult one. Infantile instinctual wishes are much too powerful to be simply "outgrown." Free expression and scope for activity are helpful to the child, but without any check on them they can become dangerous. Easy satisfaction of wishes in preliminary stages of instinctual development may make the child reluctant to leave these stages, and what should be transitional (greed, dirtiness, aggression, exhibitionism) may be turned into a permanent position. Without definite help and continual guidance, the child is not up to the task of transforming and redirecting his instinctual forces.

Since there is always pressure from the surrounding world (whatever the educational attitude may be), and since many of the instinctual wishes are incompatible in themselves (love and hate, activity and passivity, etc.), the child feels that some stand against the instincts is demanded from him, but he is unable to cope with the demand unless adequate educational help is given. Consequently, children become afraid of their own instinctual forces and develop anxiety, dissatisfaction, and inner conflicts which do not contribute to their happiness and fail to lead to the desired final result: to their social adaptation.

Educational Attempts in the Nursery

In the dealings with our young children, whose upbringing lies completely in our hands from the beginning, we attempt to apply our psychological knowledge of infantile life: that is, we tried not to do away with education, merely to modify it. Our aim is to educate the children toward a mastery of their drives, not based on repression (so far as repression can be avoided in human development), but based on a very gradual transformation and redirection of instinctual forces.

Instinct education of this kind is a slow process; immediate results are neither aimed at nor welcome. Violent educational measures, which cause emotional upheavals with consequent sudden changes in the child's behavior, are discarded in favor of educative attitudes which further processes of growth and development. Just as there are no sudden leaps and bounds in the child's bodily development, so there should be no sudden conversions from "badness" to "goodness," from immorality to morality, from instinctual expressions to compulsive reaction formations against them. Each stage of instinctual development should find expression, should be lived through, and brought under slow control as it arises. Relapses into former habits, and certain breakdowns in controls that had already been established, lie within the normal.

In his instinctual life, as in his bodily and intellectual achievements, the child learns through battling with the difficulties of the task, and through his failures in accomplishment. It has been found possible, even for very little children, under the direction of certain modern nursery school methods, to handle dainty and breakable objects, as, for instance, glass and china, and to use dangerous tools, the handling of which used to be strictly forbidden in former times (knives, scissors, hammers, saws, etc.). Breakages and damage will occur occasionally, but not more often than they have always occurred in spite of prohibitions, and not to a greater extent than can be coped with, and that is amply paid for by the growing skill and freedom which the child acquires.

Similarly, the child can learn to cope in a sensible manner with the dangerous instinctual forces in his own mind, without being forbidden to remain in contact with them, and without coming to harm in the process. Young children can, though slowly and gradually, learn to manage themselves.[1]

In the next report we shall give more detailed accounts of such educational processes with regard to the various manifestations of instinctual development.

[1] [For the further development of ideas concerning psychoanalytically informed upbringing of children, see A. Freud (1946b) and especially *The Writings of Anna Freud*, Vol. V, ch. 16.]

50

Monthly Report
March, 1945

STATISTICS

The total number of children is 109; 61 of these are resident, 26 in London and 35 in the Country House.

MEDICAL REPORT

The state of health in both houses is very good. New Barn expects an influx of measles since there is a case in the village school and several cases in the villages around us.

AIR RAIDS

Apart from rocket explosions there have been 10 air raids in London since the last report and considerably more than that in New Barn. Since both houses are in the target area for rockets, the question of shifting the children from one house to the other has not arisen.

New Barn had one of its wartime excitements when a passing air convoy scattered numbers of parcels which were marked "explosives" among the neighboring fields; evidently, they were meant for another destination. The staff spent some anxious hours, fearing that our very adventurous boys might pick them up and blow themselves up. There was some excited telephoning back and forth, the local policeman standing guard until an army lorry came and the parcels were collected and removed. The Nursery settled down again to its usual routine after the reassuring message had been brought in that there was "nothing to worry about. It wasn't like bombs, it was only dynamite."

CHILDREN'S PROBLEMS

Toilet Training in the Nursery

The following detailed account of the methods of toilet training used in the Nursery has been compiled by Dr. Ilse Hellman to illustrate the points about instinct education which we discussed in our last report. Dr. Hellman writes as follows:

The earliest outside interference with the child's natural desires concerns his hunger. Satisfaction is regulated according to the opinions of the adults of what is good for the child and, as a result of the feeding rules and regulations, the child has to learn to bear a certain amount of tension. The child and the adult world remain, however, in agreement with regard to the ultimate satisfaction of this wish. This inevitable educational interference can at times endanger the original pleasure in the satisfaction of hunger (see Reports 53 and 54).

The educational task of training a child to become clean is of an entirely different nature. Left to himself, the child satisfies his need to eliminate whenever the tension in bladder or bowels makes itself felt; under the influence of training he again has to learn to bear tension, i.e., to inhibit his sphincters up to the time when he has reached the place where elimination is permitted and to relax his muscles there. But this is not the whole task.

We know that originally the child enjoys to touch and handle dirty matter and does not show any signs of disgust in regard to either taste or smell. In order to make the child socially acceptable in this respect, education has to interfere with his natural tendencies to a very large extent. His love of dirt has to be changed into love of cleanliness, disgust has to be brought about in accordance with the standards of the grownup world, and new means of satisfaction have to be substituted for activities which cannot be permitted in their original form. The time granted to a child to live through this phase, and the amount of satisfaction and frustration he experiences, are of far-reaching importance for his further development and the formation of his character.

Mothers' Attitudes to Toilet Training

For all who have to deal with the child's education for cleanliness, the ultimate aim is the same, namely, to get the child clean. Approach and methods in achieving this, however, vary widely. In our capacity of advisers on childhood problems in the correspondence column of the magazine *Nursery World*, Dr. Liselotte Frankl and I had the opportunity to advise a large number of mothers on matters of training and to note their reactions as revealed in their letters. We found that, apart from the purely practical considerations (reduction of work, laundry expenses, etc.), three factors were mainly responsible for their attitudes.

1. There are the mothers who, owing to their own childhood training, have developed strong reaction formations which make them intolerant of any form of dirtiness; they cannot bear to see the signs of their children's pleasure in dirt and have to suppress them as quickly as possible.

2. There are other mothers who cannot stand the child's opposition to their wish to control his bladder and bowel movements. A battle of wills develops between mother and child in which the mother can gain her ends only by using drastic methods.

3. Other mothers would, according to their own nature, be more prepared to be tolerant but do not dare to act on their own judgment for fear of outside criticism (on the part of neighbors, members of the family, etc.).

Those whose own tendencies go toward early suppression of undesirable dirty habits find theoretical support in mothercraft manuals, where earliest possible cleanliness is emphasized on hygienic grounds, and in educational books based on behavioristic psychology. A psychology that does not acknowledge the presence of instinctual forces in the child approaches training for cleanliness merely as a process of learning to inhibit and relax muscles in response to an outside stimulation. It therefore emphasizes an early onset of this training under strictly regulated circumstances.

In this country large numbers of nurses and mothers follow these principles and many children are conditioned to respond to the touch of the pot from the age of a fortnight on. But general experience shows that with the overwhelming majority, this automatic control, based on a conditioned reflex, does not outlast the end of the first or the beginning of the second year. Approximately at this time most of the children who are trained from birth have a breakdown, to the great disappointment of their mothers. The mothers feel in these cases that they have worked in vain and that something must be wrong with their children if they relapse into dirty habits just at the time when they expect them to become reliably clean. They often redouble their efforts and undergo considerable emotional strain in fighting what they believe to be an abnormal reaction of their child. In reality, this breakdown is a normal occurrence. It signifies that the child has reached the level of instinctual development when his interest becomes centered on the parts of the body which serve the excretory functions, and on the products of excretion themselves. The child's instinctual tendency to gain satisfaction from excretion and its products is strong enough to overthrow the effects of conditioning.

Factors Determining the Training in the Nursery

The time when toilet training is begun in the Nursery is determined by the following factors: (1) The child should be physically able to sit freely without undue strain. (2) The child should be intellectually able to establish the mental connection between his needs and our demands, to understand the word used for them, and to express his needs verbally not long after. (3) The child should have a good and steady emotional relationship with one adult. This relationship is the only possible basis for successful education wherever drastic methods are discarded, and where the use of material reward and punishment is not considered desirable. The child's wish to please the adult and to avoid her criticism, his efforts to gain her love, and his fear of losing it are the moving forces in this fight against the instinctual tendencies.

These three conditions are usually fulfilled at the approximate age of one year, with some children earlier. If children are changed from one department to the other at the age of one, it is better to wait with their toilet training until they are settled in their new surroundings.

Achievement of First Control

When training begins, we mostly find that the child does not take long to grasp what is expected of him. The first chance successes make it possible to give praise and to arouse in the child the understanding of the grownup's wish. Signs of disappointment when removing soiled or wet nappies are equally understood. Nevertheless, with most children the completion of the task extends over a very long time. There are only a few whose training can be described as an unbroken line of steady progress. What we commonly find is rather a continual swaying backward and forward of a conflict in which sometimes one and sometimes the other partner gains the upper hand.

In the first stage this conflict takes place between child and grownup. The child is still in agreement with his instinctual wishes, defends them against interference, and responds with resistance to their frustration. In spite of his wish to please the adult, refusals to give in to her demands show themselves over and over again by stiffening, running away, or withholding excrement while sitting on the pot. It is obvious that the child's wish to cooperate is closely linked to the existing emotional situation between him and the mother substitute. The response given to his refusals, the amount of displeasure shown, any inconsistency in the approach have an effect on further progress. Any worry or anger which the child feels toward the mother substitute finds its expression in resistance to her demands.

Even where the mother substitute maintains an unchanged, calm, and understanding attitude, she cannot help opposing and hurting the child's feelings. The child's evaluation of his excreta is still totally different from that of the surrounding adult world; what is waste matter and dirt to the latter is to the child at this stage a precious product which he would like to keep, to touch, to play with, to show off. Many children react with anger when their excreta are taken from them to be emptied out. It is easier for the child to overcome this stage when he is permitted to play an active part in it, to empty the contents of the pot or to pull the chain in the lavatory.

While so many obstacles interfere with steady progress even under normal conditions, it is obvious that violent emotional upheavals like illnesses or separations and, in family life, the arrival of a new baby mean the loss of recently achieved control and return to earlier modes of behavior. Under nursery conditions, where continuity of the relationship between child and worker is aimed at but not always possible, setbacks of this kind are more frequent than in family surroundings, and the final stage is probably reached later for this reason.

In the later stages of their toilet training many of our children are quite aware of the fact that their efforts are made for the sake of their favorite worker. They hurry to the lavatory because, as they say themselves, "their" nurse "cannot like them wet." And when their mother substitutes have their free days, or their holidays, they feel deserted and helpless and express the fear that they will have setbacks.

Development of Disgust

While in the early part of the training we find that children sometimes become well able to achieve control, especially where their bowels are concerned, there are as yet no signs of disgust, and they will cheerfully play with the content of their pot if left to themselves. The first sign that the child himself begins to turn against his dirtiness is usually shown not in his own actions but in his criticism of other children and grownups. Whenever such criticism makes its appearance, we can welcome it as an important step forward in the change of attitude which we are trying to bring about.

At the toddler stage it is not unusual for a whole group of children to stand around a puddle, pointing at it in horror and abusing the child responsible for it as "dirty" or "naughty," regardless of the fact that every member of this community is still quite likely to do the same himself without feeling especially guilty. When unobserved, the same children who express such harsh criticism are quite likely to put their hands into the puddle and play with it.

A child who has just wet himself quite unconcernedly may the next moment criticize an adult worker who has spilled some water from a bucket.

It would be wrong to assume that such criticism appears after the child has made a step forward in his development and turned away from his former instinctual pleasure. On the contrary, criticism seems to be directed outward before the child directs it toward his own actions, or rather, before such inward criticism actively interferes with the child's behavior. Gradually, everything connected with the subject of dirtiness becomes a center of attention; dogs and horses in the street are criticized; even the picture of a Negro was hit and called "dirty boy." Soon thereafter, the child begins to show disgust of his own excrement and worry about his own lack of control. Such worry can either be openly expressed or be disguised in various ways.

Records on a pair of identical girl twins, for instance, illustrate this stage particularly clearly. The twins, whose training was started at the age of 13 months, were able to keep clean all day at 18 months for the first time. No signs of disgust had been noticed until then, but soon thereafter it became obvious that both began to worry a great deal whenever an accident occurred. One twin showed this openly by making a disgusted face and sometimes even crying. The other reacted differently: she denied what had happened by walking away, laughing, or shouting, "Good girl"; or she said: "Not me wet" but accused a toy horse or her sister. Later she took a chair and, putting it over the puddle, said: "Chair done wee-wee."

Sticky hands are objected to and hurriedly wiped now. The cleaning of floors and tables becomes a favorite occupation; the pleasure at this stage still lies in the handling of the wet cloth rather than in the urge to do away with the mess, but it forms an important beginning in the line of sublimated activities.

Simultaneously with this we found that all children—even the greediest—refused all foods which reminded them in some way of excrement, especially chocolate and coffee-colored puddings, sometimes gravy or custard, sometimes sausages.

All this goes to show that a stage is reached in which the child himself has taken up the struggle against his instinctual wishes. While in the early stage the conflict takes place between the mother substitute and the child, or rather, between the child's impulses and his wish to keep the mother's love, the later stage shows us the child in conflict with himself. One part of him has taken over the wish to be clean, but is still many times overwhelmed by the strength of his instinctual drives.

In the further process we find all children going through a stage of anxiety which expresses itself in excessively frequent visits to the lavatory, and an anxious expression showing their worry about getting there in time. Their anxiousness to keep clean seems ever present and in many cases interferes for some time with all the child's activities. As in all other phases, the violence with which the conflict shows itself varies widely; while some cope with it in a few weeks and without showing a more general emotional disturbance, other children develop various transitory symptoms. While some children, for instance, anxiously ask to go to the bathroom four or five times an hour, approximately in the twentieth month, but otherwise continue to play as cheerfully as ever, others show their anxiousness to keep clean in a general restlessness, unhappiness, and irritability that prevents them from settling down to anything for any length of time. For several weeks, for instance, one child's face would suddenly show an anxious expression in the middle of a meal, a game or on a walk; announcing "It's coming" or "It comes so quickly," she appealed for help.

At this stage the child is fully aware of the desirability to be clean. He suffers from the struggle which goes on within himself and is distressed by his failures. When this phase is reached, it is important for the mother substitute to change her attitude. If she continues to criticize the child for his failures in cleanliness, which are now involuntary accidents, the child will feel that she is unkind and out of sympathy with his own struggles. Such a feeling will not help but will hinder his efforts. For the adults, on the other hand, it seems particularly difficult to concede the children the time necessary for this last phase of the process. They feel that the child now knows what is wanted and could achieve it if he only made the effort. As a result, they often show the tendency to become more strict at the time when they should confine themselves to encourage the child and share the pleasure in his successes and his disappointments in the inevitable failures.

When the child is given time to go through these stages slowly and when the need for satisfaction of instinctual wishes is recognized, the process of reaction formation against dirty tendencies will be accompanied by opportunities to satisfy the original impulses in different, socially acceptable forms. All nursery and infant schools realize the great attraction which play with sand and water has for young children. The pleasure in handling these materials and in using them for creative purposes is originally derived from the child's enjoyment of messiness and from the interest in his own excreta. Gradually, as the pleasure in cleanliness becomes more firmly established, satisfaction is derived from play with objects which are more and more remote from the original ones, as, for instance, with wet sand, clay, plasticene, pebbles, shells, shiny beads, buttons, coins. Where satisfaction is not denied, but displaced in this manner, a return to the original mode of satisfaction is less likely to occur. Similarly, the chance for free expression in play and speech serves the purpose of working through this phase in a healthy manner.

Our children, who are used to express their thoughts in a straightforward way, show that the subject still plays an important part in their mind even at a time when they have already achieved full control in the day and also at night. Dolls are continually dirty and have to be wiped and punished. The expressions of anger used for their dolls are far more violent than any they have ever heard themselves; they rather reflect their own angry inner criticism about their mishaps. Talk about "big job" occurs in fun or anger; anal words are the most common words for abuse.

Gradually, as the change in attitude becomes more firmly established and new instinctual wishes make themselves felt and gain importance, interest and excitement around matters of cleanliness diminish. However, achievements brought about under such difficulties have the tendency to give way under emotional strain and many instances of regression to dirty habits occur. The first control to be lost is usual cleanliness at night, the one that is the last to be established; wetting in daytime, dirtying, and actual return to play with dirty matter point to more and more serious disturbances.

Approximate Dates for the Completion of Toilet Training

In March, 1940 the magazine *Nursery World* sent out a questionnaire which was answered by 208 mothers and nannies and gave details of the training of 250 children. The results were published in the July number, 1940, under the title "Investigation of Habit Training." The results of this survey were as follows:

Reliably clean in daytime: 4 percent before 1 year
61 percent after 18 months
35 percent after 2 years
Reliably clean at night: 41 percent under 2 years
42 percent between 2 and 3 years
17 percent after 3 years

Our results compare with these in the following way. Children who have changed hands several time were usually not reliably clean and dry before the age of 3 in daytime, and 3½ to 4 at night. On the other hand, a group of toddlers who were brought up in the Nursery from the beginning and handled by the same workers throughout the whole time have now achieved reliable cleanliness in daytime and at night at the age of 2½.

Where training under Nursery conditions is delayed, two factors are mainly responsible: the unavoidable change of workers with the consequent breaks in attachment during the period of training; and the constant presence of numbers of younger children who still have a lower standard of cleanliness.

Individual differences are very marked. The strength of

the child's instinctual drives and the nature of his attachment seem to play the decisive role.

Consequences for Character Formation

It is by now commonly known that strict and forcible methods of toilet training produce severe repressions of the anal drives accompanied by the character trait of obstinacy. Under the conditions of training described above the sublimations of the instinctual drives are more marked than their repression; and obstinacy is remarkably absent in our children.

51

Monthly Report
April, 1945

STATISTICS

The total number of children is 102; 66 of these are resident, 31 in London and 35 in the Country House. We admitted 4 young babies for temporary stay. One of our former babies has returned from evacuation and joined his companions of old, now in the junior toddler group.

AIR RAIDS

There were 6 air raid warnings since the last report, evidently the last which we are going to have.

Since there is not enough sleeping space in the upper house in Netherhall Gardens, the shelter still serves as our dormitory. In spite of that, the children seem to be aware of the fact that the shelter is no longer necessary for purposes of security. The following incident shows how quickly wartime habits give way to peacetime behavior:

One of these mornings three children, all between 3½ and 4 years, were seen to run upstairs from the shelter, still in their dressing gowns, breathless and smiling. When asked what they were doing, they explained that they were playing: there was "a warming" in the shelter and they ran away from it, upstairs.

It had not taken them long to reverse the habit of their lifetime, namely, to hurry to the shelter whenever there was an air raid warning upstairs.

SICKROOM REPORT

We postpone the continuation of our more theoretical discussion of educational methods, so as not to lose touch with the actual happenings in the Nursery. The following is a short account of the measles epidemic which has kept the staff of New Barn very busy during the last month. So far 14 children (3 to 10½ years) have come down with the illness. There have been some high temperatures, the usual measles misery, some coughing, but no pneumonia, some ear trouble, but no serious complications of any kind. Four further cases are still expected. The rest of the children have had measles at earlier ages.

Sister Mary Simon, who is in charge of the Sickroom in New Barn, describes the reactions of the children during this period as follows:

The Role of the Sickroom in New Barn

Since our New Barn children have passed through most of the children's diseases, illness in New Barn has become a rare event, and a stay in the sickroom takes on the aspect of a change and an adventure to which the children look forward. They enjoy the greater privacy which the sickroom offers compared with the larger dormitories; they enjoy the special bodily attention which they receive, the special food, the opportunity for quiet and uninterrupted conversations, and, in the case of the school children, the welcome holiday from school. Life in the sickroom resembles family life as closely as is possible under residential conditions.

In the long intervals when there are no illnesses and when the sickroom is empty, it serves as a workroom where I have a special table for shoemending. When there are not more than one or two children in bed, with minor ailments, I usually continue shoemending, which the children watch with great interest from their beds. Once, when Isabel (7 years) came down with a high temperature, and I began to clear away my tools to give her a complete rest, she objected very strongly and said: "Why don't you go on shoemending when I am ill. I want to watch you."

When children are really ill, the sickroom takes on the aspect of a hospital room. They lie quietly in bed, stretched out flat, with their beds tidy, and the room immaculate. But this is, luckily, a rare event. As soon as their spirits return, the sickroom is turned into a department of the nursery school. Preferred occupations in bed are drawing and cutting out; the older children also do useful things like knitting and sewing. Sometimes a wave of helpfulness sweeps through the whole sickroom and the children combine their efforts to do some work in their beds which helps the kitchen or household staff. The older children like short periods of music on the wireless, and often ask for the news at 1 P.M.

All the children like me to sit quietly and talk to them.

They want to hear about my former work in children's hospitals and ask many questions about it. They take a very intelligent interest in their own illnesses and in those of the other children. They ask about their temperatures, the cause of their illnesses, the reason for their special diets. The discussions which follow offer the opportunity to explain many medical details to them. Because of this understanding of their own condition, they seem to suffer less than other children, even at times when their illnesses are really acute and disagreeable.

Measles

When the first cases of measles appeared in the house, the quarantine interfered with the various plans for excursions and short-distance travels which had been made for the Easter holidays. The children were very disappointed, and it took some time until alternative plans were made. Three of the older children, who had had measles before, were able to go to Cambridge, as planned, for sightseeing. The boys who had to remain home organized themselves into a group of builders and put up a new shed of their own in the boys' playground. A carpenter, lent to us by a great friend of the Nursery, repaired seesaws for the smaller children and erected a new swing out of old material.

Simultaneously the children began to lay their plans for our measles epidemic. They "booked" their places in the sickroom. Alfred (6), whose greatest friend is Jim (9), asked me: "Would it be all right for you if I get measles together with Jim?" Many of them seemed to think that in some way I could arrange and time their illness for them; they even looked forward to it, though I warned them that they might not find it at all pleasant, at least not for the first few days. When Alfred was actually put to bed, with a temperature of 103, he said to me: "Is it still like good old times in the sickroom, that one can choose what one wants for supper?"

When the measles misery was at its height, the sickroom was especially quiet, and the healthy children began to worry about this unusual state of affairs. At ordinary times, when there are only minor illnesses, there is a good deal of social intercourse between sickroom and house. The children shout messages up from the garden, little stones are thrown up against the sickroom windows to attract the attention of the patients, or things are thrown down into the garden to friends. This time the sick children did not react to these overtures, and I had to ask the others to stop calling so as to let the patients sleep.

The first child who was allowed to visit, since she had already had measles, was Bella (10 years). She was very upset about the flushed faces and sick expressions which she saw, and left the sickroom pale and disturbed. I had to explain the nature of the illness, its momentary effect, etc. She felt more reassured, and gladly accepted my invitation to visit daily and watch the improvement of the patients.

She evidently imparted her impressions to the other children, since from then onward great consideration was shown by everybody. Whoever was permitted to visit the sickroom was on his best behavior, quiet and gentle. As soon as the children were better, streams of letters went up, as well as bunches of flowers. In the sunny days which followed, the sickroom looked like a flower garden. Letters and envelopes lay on each bedtable. The general impression was that of a hospital ward at visiting hours.

Jim (9 years) was especially glad to receive a letter from Marion (9 years), who is his best friend. Since he seemed worried that I might read it, I gave him pajamas with pockets to keep the letter safe and assured him that there was no need to show his letters to anybody, that I also liked to keep my letters private. At that he blushed and seemed relieved.

Behavior of Individual Children

In general, all the children were very sensible and not difficult to deal with, even at the times when they felt really badly. Behavior, of course, varied according to their individual characteristics. The following are examples of three different children in the sickroom.

Bertha (7 years) was outstandingly helpful during the whole period. She was one of the early patients and spent a long period of convalescence in the sickroom before rejoining the healthy children. Her main pleasure during this time was to be my helper and assistant. She loved to help me with the clearing up and cleaning of the two rooms. When I came upstairs with the full lunch tray, she would meet me on the stairs, full of eagerness to fetch, to carry, to hand round plates. She sat down to eat only after the others had started. When her little brother (4¾ years) arrived as a patient, she was full of solicitude. When I fetched a nightgown for him and he undressed in his bed, she interrupted herself in the middle of a game, rushed to him, and wrapped a dressing gown around him. When he fell asleep suddenly, she quietly went to his bed, removed his tray, and covered him up. At bathing time she cleaned the bath, helped to remake the beds, and swept the room once more before going to bed herself.

Katrina (10½ years) was harassed during the whole period by her usual jealousy and was not easy to satisfy. She had looked forward to a great deal of individual attention during her illness and minded when more and more patients arrived, so that finally four girls had to share one of the two sickrooms. Her weapon was, as always, to hurt the other children by making unkind remarks to them. When she and Janet (8¾ years) had high temperatures and I asked them to keep very quiet, Janet once sat up for a moment. Katrina immediately shouted at her: "Lie down, you silly fool, you must not sit up!" She drew the picture of an ugly woman, showed the drawing to Janet, and said: "That is your mother."

Interestingly enough, her behavior got much better when she developed a painful ear. She had to have drops put in, and the other children watched this procedure attentively. She also had fomentations and aspirin, and again the other children watched the applications with interest. Instead of minding the pain, Katrina enjoyed the attention which, for a while, made her the most important person in the room. She was able to be much nicer to the other children under these changed conditions.

Tim (5 years) was a patient who presented me with difficulties and gave me much occasion to think and wonder about him. Two or three times every day he was overcome by a mood which he seemed unable to control. He was, for instance, looking forward to getting up. When it was time to do so, he suddenly did not want to put his vest on, stood stiffly, and did not move. Nothing could then persuade him to do it, neither explanations, nor kind words, nor firmness. If left alone, he would return to bed and lie quiet for an hour or more. When I took no further notice and said only much later that he should come and dress, he was all pleasure and eagerness, as if the whole former incident had been completely forgotten. Many small occurrences could induce such moods in him. His reactions were always the same: to lie quiet for a long while without moving. He could overcome the moods when left to himself; when I tried to oppose him, he would scream and be aggressive.

Occasionally it was very helpful, even at the height of such moods, when I offered him something very difficult to do. He is very keen on difficult occupations.

I had the opportunity to overhear some of his conversations with Saul (4 years), who is very attached to me. Saul said that he liked me. Tim answered: "I do not like anybody, I only like my food." When there was talk about the end of the war and about going home, he said: "I am not going home, I am not going anywhere." When I told him that he was well again and could join the healthy children downstairs next day, he said to me: "I shall come to visit you in the sickroom, not when you like; I shall come when I like."

He never expressed approval to me directly, but when Bertha's little brother appeared in the sickroom, he called out to him: "Come into the sickroom, you get all you want."

I assume that most of his behavior is due to a state of resentment and jealousy directed against his own family. He is one of four children, three of whom lived with us during the whole war. Some time ago, his parents took his elder brother home to live with them and his baby sister.

But they could not take him and his younger brother, since they live in very cramped quarters and have to wait for a bigger flat, which is promised to them but may still take a long time to materialize.

52

Monthly Report
May, 1945

STATISTICS

The total number of children is 100; 62 of these are resident, 28 in London and 34 in the Country House.

MEDICAL REPORT

The measles epidemic in the Country House has run its course, and the quarantine is over. All the children have returned to school and look fit and well. The state of health in both houses is very good and both sickrooms are empty. Two children will go to the hospital to have their tonsils removed.

VE DAY

With the ending of the war with Germany, the Hampstead Nurseries have entered into the last phase of their existence. The Nurseries were established in 1940 to help London parents to care for their children during the period of bombing, evacuation, and homelessness. With the return of more peaceful conditions, their main purpose is fulfilled. All that remains is the resettling of the individual children in their homes. We count on completing this task in slow stages until November 1, when the Nurseries will be closed.

The lease for 5, Netherhall Gardens expires one month after VE Day, the lease for New Barn, six months after that date; 13, Wedderburn Road, which is lent to us by a Swedish Committee, will, we hope, be open for us until October 1.

Our London children will therefore leave Netherhall Gardens within the next fortnight and will be settled in Wedderburn Road for the remainder of their time with us. The ordinary routine of the Nurseries, the training of students, the usual courses, lectures, etc., will be carried on as usual there and in New Barn until the autumn. Both houses will, as before, be open to visitors. There will be further Monthly Reports to continue the discussion of general educational problems that was started in Reports 49 and 50.

We can never be thankful enough to the Foster Parents' Plan for War Children for maintaining us throughout the long duration of the war, and now for giving us this additional period which will be of great value in deciding the final fate of the children.

PROBLEMS OF RESETTLING THE CHILDREN

The following estimate of the family situation of our 62 children, and of the time and manner of their leaving, has been made by Mr. James Robertson, our social worker. He groups the children as follows:

Group 1

There are 13 children among our total of 62 who will be able to return home almost immediately. Their sole reason for being in the Nursery was the bombing. Their parents have solved their wartime problems in one way or another. Several fathers are still in the Armed Forces, but the mothers can manage in spite of work since the children are old enough to go either to school or to a day nursery. In one case, where the father was killed, the mother has found work as a secretary and can have her two children with her for the first time in their lives. These little sisters have never met before since the elder sister was evacuated during the whole war and the younger child with us from birth. In cases where no day nursery is available, the children will continue to come to Wedderburn Road as day children until the autumn.

Group 2

There are 3 children who will leave us in about a month. Their two mothers have joined forces and after much searching and many disappointments have found a flat and received the necessary permits for utility furniture. Since the Utility Permits will take some time to come through, the Nursery will lend them sufficient furniture for a beginning. Both mothers are working, and the three little girls will come as day children to Wedderburn Road until vacancies can be found for them in a day nursery nearby.

Group 3

There are 10 children whose mothers belong to our resident staff. They will leave together with their mothers when we can release them and when they find other, adequate work.

Group 4

There are 17 children whose return home is assured, though the date depends on outside circumstances beyond the parents' control. In three of these cases the setting up of the home has to wait for the father's return, which is expected to take place in the late summer. Two of the children are of Czech nationality and will be repatriated as soon as circumstances permit. One child is of French nationality and will be taken home to France by his mother. Two children, a brother and sister, who lost their mother during the war and whose father, a sailor in the Merchant Navy, has remarried in Australia, will leave for Melbourne to live with their new stepmother as soon as transport facilities are available. One child is waiting for a vacancy in her London school. Another child is waiting until the parents, who live in an overcrowded little flat and are on a priority list for better accommodations, have room enough to receive him.

Group 5

There is a family of 3 children who, ultimately, will have to return to very poor slum conditions in the East End. They can return any time, but we shall delay their departure as long as possible. Two of the children are young and delicate, and another summer in New Barn will be of benefit to them. No real improvements in the home conditions are to be expected, though the local social worker is doing his best to push the claim for better accommodation with the authorities. The family ties are strong, and the parents are ready to receive them. There are six brothers and sisters in addition to the three who will return from us.

Group 6

There are 16 children whose future and date of departure are still uncertain. Plans have to be discussed with the charitable institutions by whom they were originally sent; in the case of a full war orphan, with the Children's Officer from the Ministry of Pensions; in the case of an abnormal child, we are applying for admission to a special nursery home. Three homeless children of school age will, we hope, find admission in a permanent English Home of the Foster Parents' Plan for War Children.

Two children, a girl of 7 and her little brother of 4, find themselves unwanted by their mother and have no home to return to. The marriage of the parents broke up during the father's long absence in the East. The mother has entered into a new relationship with a young soldier whom she expects to marry when the divorce is effected. She expects a new baby and has no affection left for the children of her earlier and unhappy marriage. The little girl is one of our nicest, most eager, and most helpful children (see Bertha in Report 51 on the measles epidemic); the little boy, Reggie, who has been mentioned in several Monthly Reports, is now passionately attached to our superintendent and as estranged from the mother as she is from him. The only solution for these children seems to be adoption, to which the mother agrees. We hope that it may be possible to find a good home for them.

CORRESPONDENCE

The following are two characteristic letters, written by one of the mothers of Group 1 to Miss Alice Goldberger, the Superintendent of New Barn.

Letter 1

Dear Alice,
  Just a few lines to you hoping that this will find Jim and all quite well. I hope that Jim is quite all right at school and doing his lessons very nice. Well, Alice, we are having good weather in London and I must tell you that it is good to be nice and quiet and go to bed and have a nice sleep. Well, tell Jim that I think he will be coming home for good the next time I come down, so would you like to see that he gets his hair done nicely and if there is any clothes you can give him to fetch back, I would be glad. I am sure I thank you all for your kindness to him in our time of trouble. But I do not know yet when the bus is coming down. I have been quite pleased with how you looked after him. Give my love to Jim and I will see him soon.
  Kind regards from Mr. and Mrs. X

Letter 2

Dear Alice,
  I thank you very much for the letter. I am sorry to hear that Jim has been in the sickroom with the measles. I suppose it is the changeable weather, but we are having

very warm weather in London now. I expect Jim is excited to think he is going home after all this time, I am glad he has been a good boy and I expect you will miss him after all this time. I expect they seem to be pleased that the war is over, it is a good thing for all of us. And also I thank you for trying to give Jim a nice outfit to come home with, as I have not got anything at home for him. I think Jim will be a comfort to me, but I think he will miss the nice grounds that he plays in down the country, and I have got his place ready for school. Well, Alice, I would have written before but last week I had a telegram from my son to say he was in England coming home from a German Prison Camp after five years, so you see I never got over the shock for a week, so you see it was just like a dream to me I could not realize it was true, so he was home for victory and we did enjoy it together. Well Alice, I shall fetch him down there to bring Jim home, you will have the pleasure of seeing him. I do not suppose that Jim will remember him after all this time. Thanking you for asking about him. I hope that Jim is getting well, and we will soon be coming down now. Tell him that his brother Gilbert sends his love. Kisses for Jim. I will close now.

Kind regards from Mr. and Mrs. X

53

Monthly Report
June, 1945

STATISTICS

The event of the month was the closing of 5, Netherhall Gardens. To make this possible the department which had received babies for temporary stay was closed altogether. Some of the babies had gone home before this date. The last three left in the first week of June, one of them to return home, two to go into other nurseries.

Further, all those toddlers left whose return home had been prepared for the beginning of June, or for whom some other, permanent arrangement had been made for this date. The remaining children were transferred to 13, Wedderburn Road, where they settled very happily. The shelter in this house has been dismantled and makes a big and convenient play and dining room. For the first time since they have been with us, our London children sleep upstairs in big and airy bedrooms.

In New Barn, where conditions otherwise remain unchanged, the first six children left to return to their families. Reunions seem to work out very well.

The total number of children is 80; 43 of these are still resident, 15 in London and 28 in the Country House.

MEDICAL REPORT

The state of health in both houses is very good.

SOCIAL WORK

Our social worker is busier than ever. Constant contact has to be kept with the families whose children are still with us; and the families to whom children have returned are visited. There are, naturally, obstacles of various kinds to overcome. Even families on priority lists have great difficulties in obtaining their flats. Places for returning children have to be secured in schools or nurseries. Foster mothers for the working days of the week have to be found in some instances. Our efforts to find favorable adoption for two children still continue and begin to look hopeful.

CHILDREN'S PROBLEMS

Feeding Methods in the Nursery

In Report 50, we gave an account of toilet training as it is actually carried out in our Nursery. We attempt to do the same in this and the following reports with reference to the feeding habits of our children and the feeding methods which are in use in our Nursery work.

General Importance of Feeding Methods

The feeding methods which are adopted by a mother or nurse when dealing with a child or, later on, with a group of children constitute the first interference on the part of the outside world with the instinctual desire of the child. They are, therefore, considered to be of supreme importance for the whole future adaptation of the child to the demands of the environment.

Trained mothers or nurses, according to the type of their training and knowledge, hold certain ideas of what kind of nourishment is wholesome for the child. These ideas concern the question of breast or bottle feeding, the introduction of supplementary foods, the problem of weaning, the balancing of liquids and solids in the toddler's diet, the proper balance between carbohydrates, proteins, and fats in the children's food altogether. Mothers who have had no training nevertheless invariably have certain fixed ideas about the respective value of meats and vegetables, sweet and savory foodstuffs, soups and teas, etc. All mothers, except the neglectful ones, hold strict ideas about the time when food should be taken, and when not.

From the toddler stage onward social conventions determine the manner in which food should be consumed. Thus, the young child is, from the beginning, confronted by various demands: that he should consume a certain, specified diet, at specified times, and that, while doing so, he should develop a certain specified set of behavior.

The Common Feeding Situation of the Baby

The clashes between the wishes of the child and of the adult already begin, in this respect, at the baby stage. It used to be the habit of untaught mothers to feed the child at the breast or from the bottle whenever he showed signs of unrest or dissatisfaction. Intake of food in unregulated quantities thus played the role of a general comforter without much regard to the digestive capacities. Stomach upsets and frequent intestinal disturbances were the logical outcome of this type of rearing.

The modern, medically supervised, regime of baby feeding prescribes feedings of a certain quantity with three hourly or four hourly intervals between feedings. This procedure evidently agrees with the child's digestive needs and therefore promotes health and regular gains. But it leaves the child without satisfaction at all those moments when hunger appears at other than the prescribed times; or extends beyond what the mother is supposed to give from the breast or bottle; or when the wish for food and satisfying stimulation of the mouth region through feeding arises out of the frequent, vague, and unspecified discomforts and dissatisfactions of a baby's existence. At all such times mother and child are in real conflict; the child urgently demands a gratification which the mother, for the baby's own good, is quite determined to refuse.

It is by now common knowledge that the success or failure to establish a satisfying feeding situation in the first year of life has far-reaching consequences, not only for the child's later attitude to food and for his bodily health, but also for the whole course of his instinctual and emotional development. Failure of breast feeding owing to reasons either within or beyond the mother's control, sudden weaning, periods of hunger and frustration owing to neglect, and periods of diminished nourishment and intestinal disturbances due to illness—all these upset the child's relationship toward this first and simplest form of instinctual gratification and create an attitude of distrust and uncertainty concerning instinctual satisfaction as such. Without realizing all the implications of these early happenings, mothers have always felt certain that a well-fed and well-feeding baby was a "happy" baby and had good prospects of growing into a good eater and a happy child.

The child thus emerges from the suckling period with certain definitely positive or negative attitudes toward food. The fate of all later feeding will be influenced by this basic atmosphere which has been established in the first year of life. But this does not mean that the right or wrong handling at the later stages is less important. The feeding methods at the toddler and nursery stages serve to aggravate or to correct former mistakes and mishaps, besides dealing with those elements which enter into the feeding situation at the later levels of instinct development.

The Common Feeding Situation of the Young Child

Conflicts between the wishes of the child and of the adult continue undiminished at the toddler and nursery age. Children, as is well known, do not always like the things which are good for them. Under conventional feeding conditions many young children refuse vegetables; some actively dislike codliver oil (though others love it); much disagreement exists between mother and child in the second year about food which has to be chewed; in some cases all new items introduced into the diet are treated by the child with the utmost distrust. There is, usually, happy agreement about such matters as orange juice, or other fruit juices, puddings, and sweets. Liquids, in many cases, are taken much better than solids; milk in its various uses is still a favorite with many children, but actively disliked by a few.

But even when the quality of food does not give rise to too much difficulty, conflicts invariably arise about quantities. The appetite of some children far exceeds what to the adult seems the norm. These toddlers would, or so it appears to the adult, never cease to eat if the decision were left to them. The appetite of others, on the other hand, is so quickly satisfied that the actual voluntary intake of food hardly goes beyond the starvation level. The children of the first kind object as violently to restrictions of eating as those of the latter type react to the urging of food by the mother or nurse.

Where the quantity of nourishment which the child demands coincides with the expectations of the adult, conflict may still arise about the child's preferences. Many toddlers want very little of certain courses of the meal (soups, meat dishes, vegetables) and much too much of others (potatoes, puddings, cakes, sweets). This leads to the practice commonly used in many families and institutions, that the child is not given what he likes before he has eaten what he likes less.

In all well-regulated families and institutions mealtimes are as firmly established and as unmovable as are the baby feedings within a well-regulated baby regime. But toddlers and nursery children have their own ideas about this matter. They often refuse food at mealtimes, though they would have been quite ready to eat shortly before or immediately after it. They are ready to eat certain things, especially sweets, at all times, whether immediately before or after a satisfying meal. They strongly resent the restrictions and prohibitions under which they are commonly placed in this respect.

As regards table manners, children certainly do not take readily to any of the conventional methods of eating. At certain stages toddlers strongly resent sitting through a meal. They cannot see why food should not be eaten while sitting, or standing, or running about; indoors or outdoors; with the use of implements or simply with the use of their own fingers. They do not seem to mind how much they dirty themselves with their food, or how sticky the substances are with which they smear themselves and their surroundings. It needs considerable educational pressure to keep a young child quiet at mealtimes. To keep a toddler clean while eating can usually be accomplished only by forbidding him to handle all liquid and soft foods. This implies that the toddler will still have to be fed passively at an age when he would really be clever enough to feed himself actively.

Much educational effort is commonly spent on this training of the child, often not less than on his toilet training. Most workers in education take the point of view that this effort is well spent. They expect that the training of the child in this respect will pave the way for future training in other respects. The toddler who submits to adult rule where food is concerned; who eats or drinks not what he likes best but what is considered best for him; who eats up what is on his plate whether he feels like it or not; who does not cry for more helpings than he is supposed to have; who does not crave sweets between mealtimes; who agrees to be fed passively without meddling and smearing; who waits patiently for the meal to appear; who sits quietly through a meal without leaving his chair—a child who has to this degree submitted to the interference with one of his most vital instinctual wishes has actually made a first and most significant surrender to the powers of authority. It can be expected that he will behave in a similar manner where future educational interferences with further instinctual desires are concerned (toilet training, the restraint of aggression, general control of emotions, etc.).

Objections to This Type of Training

Argumentation of this kind is correct so far as it goes. Interference with the instincts is all the more effective the earlier it happens. What happens to the desire for food may easily serve as a prototype of what will happen later to the other desires of the child. Nevertheless, there is one weighty objection to be raised against this way of handling the feeding situation of the young child. It can be proved that large numbers of children who undergo such training cease to enjoy their food. That means that they lose their appetites and become what it dreaded by all mothers: so-called "bad eaters."

54

Monthly Report
July, 1945

STATISTICS

The total number of children is 75; 40 of these are resident, 13 in London and 27 in the Country House. Admissions have been stopped, and departures have by now become daily events.

Whatever happens in the life of the Nursery, now happens for "the last time," as the children know very well. New Barn had its last Parents' Sunday, which was enjoyed very much, and very regretfully, by everybody.

MEDICAL REPORT

The state of health in both houses is excellent.

SOCIAL WORK

The efforts to resettle children in their homes and to help and advise parents about necessary preparations continue as before. The Children's Officers from the Ministry of Pensions are very helpful about plans for five of our war orphans.

To our great disappointment we have, so far, been unsuccessful in finding adoptive parents for the girl (7 years) and the boy (5 years) who have been offered for adoption by their parents. The two children are so deeply attached to each other that we are unwilling to separate them; and it seems difficult to find parents who are willing to adopt two children.[1]

CHILDREN'S PROBLEMS

We continued the discussion of feeding methods in the Nursery.

The Common Error of "Teaching" Children to Eat

In Report 53 we described various feeding situations of the young child and pointed out how the way in which they are handled may land mother and child in an atmosphere of struggle and conflict, and finally result in the loss of appetite on the part of the chid.

All mothers and nurses wish the children under their care to eat well and with pleasure. But they defeat their own ends if they work toward this aim by "teaching the child to eat," or "training the child to have proper feeding habits," very much in the manner in which they teach a child to "become clean."

[1] After many more months of repeated disappointments the two children were finally adopted by a Quaker couple.

Difference between Toilet Training and the Acquiring of Feeding Habits

In Report 50 on "Toilet Training in the Nursery" we stressed the basic difference in the role of education in the two instances. In toilet training, most of the struggles and relapses occur not merely because it is difficult for the child to achieve bladder and sphincter control, but because the demand to be clean interferes with an instinctual desire. At the period when toilet training has to be carried out, the child passes through the anal stage of instinct development in which he prefers dirtiness to cleanliness and feels strong urges to smear, to handle dirty matter, to be interested in his own excreta. Since there is no place for these anal pleasures in later life, education works against these trends. The child has to learn to reverse his attitude to dirt, to reject and repress his original wishes, or to transform them until they become acceptable (sublimation in the form of play with sand and water, plasticene, paint, etc.).

No such reversal is necessary or desirable where the child's attitude to feeding is concerned. On the contrary, the pleasure gained from the satisfaction of hunger, and many pleasures derived from stimulation of the mouth zone (oral pleasures), are expected to play a considerable role throughout life. It is, therefore, a mistake to interfere with these instinctual desires to a degree which might change the child's attitude toward them. The original relationship between wish and satisfaction should remain undisturbed where eating is concerned.

If the child is forced to keep to mealtimes which do not

coincide with his own appetite, if he is nagged about table manners, criticized for his taste preferences, and has to follow strict prescriptions as to quantity and quality, he loses his pleasure in food and becomes a poor eater. No amount of training and teaching can make up for this loss of natural appetite when it has once occurred. Eating, which should be an instinctual pleasure, is then reduced to a duty, a task which the child performs unwillingly under the pressure of education.

Some Necessary Modifications in the Child's Attitude to Feeding

Although no child needs to be taught to eat, all children have to outgrow or modify certain feeding attitudes in the course of their development. This should be brought about carefully, gradually, with the minimum of force, and always with the main object well in view: to preserve as much as possible of the child's original appetite.

TONING DOWN OF IMPATIENCE AND GREED

Many mothers and nurses are unduly worried by the impatience with which toddlers react when they have to wait for their food, and by the greedy way in which they eat when hungry. Such reactions are natural at this time of life and do not call for educational interference. At this early age the child is too immature to tolerate delay in the satisfaction of any of his instinctual desires. The distress which the child feels at such moments cannot be lessened or made to disappear however much the child is admonished to "sit still," to "wait quietly," or to "eat nicely."

To let children wait for their food does not teach them

anything and has no beneficial consequences; some children are even overwhelmed by their impatience and distress to a degree which makes it impossible for them to eat when the meal finally arrives. This reaction of the child changes, independent of any "training," with the growing age of the child. The infant of 1 or 2 years is completely at the mercy of his instinctual urges; the child of 3, 4 or 5 years can to a certain degree wait for his satisfactions, and therefore reacts with less violence.

ACQUIRING A SENSE FOR THE RIGHT QUANTITIES

Most mothers and nurses firmly believe that the young child would either overeat or starve if the right quantity of food were not measured out for him. This is not true, except for those children whose natural attitude to food is seriously disturbed either through organic or neurotic illness, or through wrong handling. Where children have always been restricted in the satisfaction of their appetites, they naturally use any free access to food to make up for lost opportunities; where children have always been urged to eat beyond the limit of their appetites, they are naturally glad to escape from the obligation to eat when such an opportunity arises for them; and where children have never been permitted to use their own discretion with regard to food quantities, they appear to be unable to judge how much is necessary for them. On the other hand, all healthy and normal toddlers whose feeding has been handled right from the beginning will need little or no guidance with regard to the quantities of their food. They will, in the manner of healthy animals, develop a natural sense for their own needs and be guided by it.

That children are the best judges of the quantity of

food needed by them has been proved by interesting experiments in America (Davis, 1928). The experiment can be easily repeated by any mother, nursery or institution. Our own experiences in the Nursery have shown that children, though they have been neither urged to eat, nor prevented from eating as much as they liked, have not suffered from digestive upsets and have gained satisfactorily without being overweight.

We cannot expect all children to eat equal quantities. Appetites vary according to the individual nature of the child, and we have to be prepared to find among children, as among adults, big eaters as well as small eaters. It is equally futile to expect individual children to eat the same quantities each day. Appetites vary with any given child; whatever is eaten less on one day, or at a given meal, will probably be made up for at the next meal or the next day if the occurrence passes without comment from the adult. Apart from fluctuations of appetite owing to the state of health, moods, emotional experiences or upsets, observation of behavior in the first year reveals certain fixed relations, for instance, between the amount of sleep and the quantity of food taken by the child. (Some of our babies were observed regularly to take more food when they had had less undisturbed sleep, etc.)

These variations and fluctuations naturally become more apparent where the child is given freedom to react with a minimum of interference.

ACQUIRING A SENSE FOR THE RIGHT TYPE OF FOOD

Under conventional feeding conditions it is not easy to make a child eat a balanced diet. Whoever has had to carry out that task will find it difficult to believe that the same children, if not "taught" anything and if given freedom of choice from the toddler stage onward, will arrive at the self-selection of a more or less balanced diet. A conclusive experiment of this kind has been carried out for several years in an American nursery organized for this purpose (see Davis, 1928). It can be repeated by any mother or nurse, wherever children are fed.

Children's tastes vary with their ages, and at each successive stage most children show a conservative tendency where food is concerned. They prefer the known to the unknown and are usually reluctant to make new additions to their diet. But this conservative tendency is by no means an insurmountable barrier. If new foods are not introduced at a time when the child is not ready for them, and if they are offered to the child, not forced on him, new appearances on the child's menu are, after a period of distrust, examined with interest, tasted, and accepted. The example of older children is followed in this respect, and the wish to share an adult's meal often serves to lead the child into adventurous experiments of eating new foods.

Children vary in their preference for either sweet or savory foods. Where the feeding situation has not been spoiled by enforced training, they do not exclude either kind for any length of time. Where they are given real freedom of selection, they seem to be guided by the needs of the body, an instinctive attitude which they lose completely under the influence of undue educational interference.

In our Nursery children are given complete freedom of choice at breakfast, which is laid out for them, with one nurse to serve, as a display of various foods and drinks on a low counter. They make their selection and carry their food back to their own tables in the manner in which it is done at self-service counters and cafeterias. They return for additional helpings of what they like as often as they like. They are admitted to this type of breakfast as soon as they are able to walk independently; in the beginning they sometimes have to receive some help with carrying.

At lunch and tea time they are served while sitting at the table. As soon as they are competent to handle a big spoon, food is offered to them in dishes from which they can serve themselves. They are free to refuse what they do not want and have additional helpings of what they like, so far as rationing permits. No conditions are attached to any single course of the meal. Pudding will be served without comment whether the child has had the first course or not. Occasionally a child will be so eager to have his pudding that he pushes his first course aside to eat the sweet; when that is done and when the child is partially satisfied, he will return to his first course and finish off his meat, potatoes, and vegetables with pleasure and without the former impatience.

All the children who have been treated in this manner from their first year onward become, without exception, good eaters of a well-balanced diet without any of the eating fads which make mealtime in a nursery a burden: they eat and drink with pleasure; they do not keep food in their mouths unchewed; they do not dislike vegetables, which they take either raw or cooked; and they show such a healthy appetite in front of nearly every kind of food that visitors once suspected us of having starved them.

55

Monthly Report
August, 1945

STATISTICS

The total number of children is 47; 20 of these are resident, 10 in London and 10 in the Country House.

Departures

In New Barn leave-taking has become the order of the day. Outfits are being prepared to last the children for at least a year. Boxes are packed, and farewell parties are given nearly every day. Students have to leave to take up work elsewhere. During August, 17 children left to return home under more or less favorable circumstances.

In Wedderburn Road the daily work has not yet diminished, though the number of resident children has become equally small. Seven former boarders are still returning to the Nursery in daytime to be cared for until the London elementary schools reopen after summer holiday.

MEDICAL REPORT

There are no ill children in either house, though there are colds and a slight flu among the staff.

CORRESPONDENCE

We are receiving a number of letters of thanks and appreciation from the parents, which we are collecting for further discussion. Interestingly, some of them lay emphasis not only on the "good manners," but also on the "healthy appetites" of the returning children.

CHILDREN'S PROBLEMS

We continue the discussion of feeding methods in the nursery.

Eating Disturbances

When we discussed the beneficial effects of self-selection of diet and noninterference by the adults on our children's appetites in Report 54, we did not mean to imply that such methods are sufficient to prevent the occurrence of the more serious eating disturbances which frequently arise during a child's development. Considerate handling of the child's daily feeding does a great deal to safeguard his appetite against all minor and more superficial upsets. Above all, it does away with the unnecessary day-to-day struggle about meals which exists in many families. Such handling minimizes, but it does not exclude, the disturbances and inhibitions which arise on all the points where the child's natural wish to eat is complicated by the interference of other instinctual tendencies and their vicissitudes. Such points of danger are: (1) the child's relationship to the mother; (2) the fate of the anal tendencies; and (3) the child's attitude to his own aggressive and destructive tendencies.[1]

---

[1] [The discussion of eating disturbances has been omitted here because it was published as "The Establishment of Feeding Habits" in *Writings*, Volume IV, ch. 21; see also "The Psychoanalytic Study of Infantile Feeding Disturbances" (*Writings*, Volume IV, ch. 2)—*Editor's note.*]

56

Final Report
September to December, 1945

Our last resident children left the Nurseries by September 1st. Twenty-three of them are still under the care of the Foster Parents' Plan as nonresidents.

At the end of 1945 the Hampstead Nurseries are handing back the last of their premises and are about to close their books, five years after the first two children entered their Rest Center in 13, Wedderburn Road. As the first weeks of the work had been spent without children, in building the shelter and general preparations, so the last weeks of this year passed with the dispersal of the furniture, the reconditioning of the various houses, and much office work in ending the manifold financial commitments. The correspondence of the Nursery, which consists largely of inquiries regarding vacancies for children and students, is still lively.

The organizers of the Nurseries cannot close this series of Monthly Reports without giving expression, in their own name, as well as in the names of the parents for whose children the Nurseries provided, and of the staff for whom the Nurseries constituted a unique opportunity for work and study, to the feeling of immense gratefulness to their head organization, The Foster Parents' Plan for War Children, Inc., New York.

The Hampstead Nursery began life modestly, sponsored by a small group of friends in England; a very few of these continued untiringly and faithfully with their moral and financial support to the very end, and continue even now to take an interest in the further fate of our children. But apart from this initial small group, the Foster Parents' Plan for War Children took over the full and complete financial maintenance of all the houses of the Nurseries, including the help to nursing mothers, to nonresident children, and toward the rehabilitation of those families to whom the children are returning.

We are aware of the fact that no other nursery establishment in wartime England has been provided for on an equally generous scale, or has been granted such freedom in determining which of the pressing needs in their sphere of work should have priority. It was this lack of restriction which made it possible to add a certain amount of family welfare to our main purpose of child welfare, and thus to keep families sufficiently together to assure the return of the evacuated child. The Foster Parents' Plan for War Children shared with the organizers one main desire: that all the children who passed through their hands should be spared as much as possible of the damage which a five-year war was doing to the child population of Europe. We hope to be justified in saying that for some of the child population of the Hampstead Nurseries the war years, in spite of many unavoidable deprivations, meant, in the final summing up, a definite gain.

The final statistics contained in this Report are meant to serve a double purpose: to give evidence once more to contributors to the Foster Parents' Plan of the type and range of work on which their money was spent; and to provide for all those readers of our Reports who are interested in the research and experimental side of the work the dates and figures concerning the case material on which our observations have been based.

RESIDENT CHILDREN

Length of Stay

It was the policy of the Foster Parents' Plan for War Children, and within their framework our policy in the Hampstead Nurseries, not to serve large numbers of children in a transitory manner, but to give a limited number a stable home during wartime. In contrast to the Government policy, our children did not have to leave the Nurseries and go into billets when they reached the age of 5. We considered 5 an age when children cannot break their attachment to the people who have brought them up without losing a considerable amount of the gains in development which they have made. We also believed that the necessary later readaptation from group life to a life in their own families would be rendered more difficult if they had to enter a strange family for a transition period of uncertain length. Accordingly, the children remained with us at school age and were sent to the nearest elementary school, in London as well as in the country.

To avoid changes for children who had already suffered overmuch from the initial separation from their parents, we refrained, wherever possible, from sending them to hospitals or to convalescent homes and instead made extra provisions for them within the Nurseries.

So far as possible, children did not leave the Nurseries to go to other institutions. This happened only in a very few cases where children were either too ill (crippled), or found too abnormal (mentally deficient) to benefit from their stay.

The Nurseries did not, like many similar institutions, experience that children were snatched away at a moment's notice and returned to unsatisfactory surroundings. Due to the efforts of our social worker, the relationship to the parents had developed satisfactorily. Parents were only too glad to have their children remain until the emergency for which they had been admitted had disappeared. In many cases this meant a stay for the duration of the war.

Even in cases where emergency admittances had been made for homelessness after air raids, for sudden illness of

LENGTH OF STAY

1-4 weeks	19 children
1-12 months	70 children
1-2 years	30 children
2-3 years	23 children
3-4 years	39 children
4-5 years	10 children
	191

a mother, etc., it was frequently impossible to limit the child's stay. Emergencies usually lasted longer than had been expected, and strictly temporary cases frequently changed to permanent ones.

These reasons explain why the Nurseries, in spite of a daily average of 80 resident children, have altogether handled a total of only 191 residents.

Age on Admission

During our Rest Center period in 13, Wedderburn Road (1941), young children were admitted regardless of age. Those sent to us as unfit for shelter sleeping and as failures in billeting were mostly between 2 and 4 years. They formed the bulk of our later school children in New Barn, Lindsell.

To avoid unnecessary hardship in separating families, we repeatedly admitted, and kept, older children whose younger brothers and sisters were with us. This mixture of ages, especially in New Barn with its wide scope of activities, proved very beneficial for the whole atmosphere of the house.

With the opening of our then so-called Babies' Rest Center in 5, Netherhall Gardens, we began to specialize in the admission of babies and nursing mothers, direct from maternity hospitals. Since many of these infants remained with us for a number of years, we had a good opportunity to test our methods of upbringing from the beginning, and over long periods (see the Reports 53-55 on Feeding, and Report 50 on Toilet Training).

To avoid overcrowding in the Nursery departments we had to limit new admissions of the 2 to 5 age group and reserve the Nursery places for our own babies who grew into them. From approximately 1943 onward admissions

were therefore restricted to newborn babies and urgent emergency cases.

AGE ON ADMISSION

Age Group	1	1-4 weeks	24	children
" "	1a	1-12 months	74	"
" "	2	1-2 years	33	"
" "	3	2-3 years	22	"
" "	4	3-4 years	14	"
" "	5	4-5 years	12	"
" "	6	over 5 years	12	"
			191	

LENGTH OF STAY OF THE ABOVE AGE GROUPS

		1-4 weeks	1-12 months	1-2 years	2-3 years	3-4 years	4-5 years	
Age Group	1	2	13	2	3	4	—	24
" "	1a	12	26	11	9	15	1	74
" "	2	3	14	5	3	6	2	33
" "	3	—	7	5	3	5	2	22
" "	4	—	2	3	3	4	2	14
" "	5	1	3	1	1	4	2	12
" "	6	1	5	3	1	1	1	12
		19	70	30	23	39	10	191

RESIDENT MOTHERS

Whenever a newborn baby was admitted to 5, Netherhall Gardens, we made a special effort to persuade the mother to remain with him for the first weeks to breast-feed him. Two to three beds in the house were set aside for this purpose. After the first period of breast feeding, the mother could choose either to find work and lodgings outside or to remain in the house as a paid household worker.

Other mothers, of toddlers, who did not want to be separated from their children or who wanted to be evacuated with them, were accepted as paid household workers in New Barn, Lindsell.

Beside sparing a number of infants and toddlers the usual painful wartime separation from their mothers, this scheme for working mothers effectively solved all the domestic problems of the Nurseries. In contrast to other wartime institutions, the Nurseries never lacked domestic help and never experienced a crisis of any kind either in their kitchen or any other household department.

The agreement between the Nursery and the working mother was as follows: the mother gave her full working time to the Nursery, but, if she so desired and if it was possible to arrange, she was given sufficient time to dress, wash, bathe her own child in the mornings and evenings. She had free access to her child whenever she wished, and, especially in New Barn, there was no restriction placed on the child searching for her in the house or following her about where she worked, or having certain meals with her in the kitchen. Some of the older children of working mothers had an extra small bed in their mother's room. The part which mothers played in the care and upbringing of their child depended on their own inclinations. While some of them took complete charge of their children's bodily care, their clothing, and general guidance, and spent their whole free time with them, others were only too glad to leave the work and responsibility to the Nursery staff and merely visited and played with their children when they felt inclined to do so.

The total number of mothers employed by the Nurseries as domestic staff was 21, their children numbering 28.

TRAINING ACTIVITIES IN THE NURSERIES

Full-Time Students

Apart from the Heads of Departments, who acted as the teaching staff, and three or four paid assistants who functioned during 1941-1942, the children's work in the Nurseries was done entirely by students who worked full-time for the training which they received, in addition to board, lodging, and pocket money. Three student hostels in London and a cottage and farmhouse in Lindsell provided accommodations.

The training scheme of the Nurseries did for the children's departments what the scheme for working mothers did for the kitchen and household side; it solved the staffing problem in a satisfactory manner. The Nursery never lacked working students; vacancies were in constant demand, and applicants frequently had to be refused or placed on a waiting list.

So far as the organizers of the Nursery are concerned, their interest in the training scheme went far beyond its practical wartime value. For them it created an opportunity to realize and thereby put to the test certain ideas concerning an all-round training for workers with children, i.e., a training which does not unduly stress either the bodily or the mental side of the development of children, but is based on an understanding of the interaction between the two sides.

Beside being guided to observe and understand the growth of the child's body and his intelligence, students were instructed in the principles of psychoanalytic child psychology, which led to an understanding of the function of the instinctual drives in early childhood and their role in character development. The habits of the child and the most common behavior problems were the subject of systematic lectures and discussions. All theoretical teaching was given in close connection with the practical work of the students in the various departments, and constantly illustrated by the living examples which the rich case material of the Nurseries provided. Advanced students were put in individual charge of problem children and received guidance in the handling of their difficulties.

Observations were recorded in all departments and furnished the basis for teaching and discussion. Charts concerning the development of the youngest children, with special regard to feeding, sleep, bodily development, served the same purposes.

It was considered necessary for a full-time student to remain three years to gain the full benefit of a training of this kind. The practical side of the Training Course consisted of work in the following departments: Babies from 10 days to 3 months; Babies from 3 to 12 months; Milk Kitchen; Junior Toddlers (1-2 years of age); Nursery (2-5 years of age); Nursery School; School Children (5-9 years of age). Added to this were periods of assistance in the sickroom department, and intermittent periods of night duty in the shelter dormitory with sole responsibility for the night feeding of the babies.

The length of time spent in the different departments was variable, according to the special interest of students, their previous training, and their plans for specialization in the future, with a minimum of several months in each department.

There were, further, in New Barn facilities for three-months practical training courses in institutional cooking for children, in vegetable gardening, and in toy making.

LENGTH OF TRAINING

25 students	1 month to 1 year
13 "	1-2 years
14 "	2-3 "
12 "	3-4 "
2 "	over 4 years
66	

Part-Time and Guest Students

Apart from our regular staff and student population, the Hampstead Nurseries also served as a training ground for numbers of part-time and guest students, such as expectant mothers, welfare workers, personnel from many of the voluntary services in England and on the Continent.

WAR HAPPENINGS

The war history of the Hampstead Nurseries needs no special comment; it is identical with that of the whole of England. The monthly records of air raids which we included in our Reports did not go beyond mere figures; for reasons of censorship they would never have reached America if they had done otherwise. Like numberless other houses, the Nurseries had many lucky escapes, and never suffered more than a bad shaking, or some broken windows, and collapsed ceilings. The shelters of both Wedderburn Road and Netherhall Gardens did satisfactory service. In their function as dormitories they assured the children's undisturbed sleep, even on noisy nights. Our evacuated children, though less exposed to danger, suffered on the whole more from nightly disturbances because of the absence of a shelter.

We kept count of air raids for the Reports from 1942 onward. Between September, 1942 and Victory Day there were 593 air raids. The longest confinement to the shelter which our London children experienced was on June 18, 1944, when there were only 2 hours and 35 minutes raid-free out of the 24 hours.

We are still too close to our war experiences to be able to judge how far the results of our experience in group education of young children were directly attributable to the war atmosphere in which the work was undertaken.[1] The emergencies which the war had created were powerful factors in the children's lives. Since they were the reason for the existence of the Nurseries, they formed the background for all other happenings. The times of danger in the blitz, and in the V-1 and V-2 periods, with the constant concern for the safety of the children, created a bond between staff and parents which might otherwise not have existed. The loss of relatives, the war shortages, the lack of quiet sleep, played their part in the lives of the adults, as a strain added to the exigencies of the work.

Apart from these factors, the daily work and study seemed to remain singularly unaffected by the big happenings in the outside world.

[1] For published follow-up studies of some of the children mentioned in these reports, see Kennedy (1950), Bennett and Hellman (1951), Burlingham (1952), Hellman (1962), Burlingham and Barron (1963).

Part II

Infants Without Families
The Case For and Against Residential Nurseries

by
ANNA FREUD
and
DOROTHY BURLINGHAM
(1944 [1943])

See Publishing History (pp. xxviii-xxx) for previous publications.

CHAPTER 1

Some Comparisons Between the Early Development of Institutional and Family Children

It is recognized among workers in education and in child psychology that children who have spent their entire lives in institutions present a type of their own and differ in various respects from children who develop under the conditions of family life. Knowledge about the nature of these differences has been gained partly through individual observation where such institutional children have in later life turned antisocial or criminal (see Aichhorn, 1925), partly through group observation of large numbers of children evacuated as babies to residential nurseries during this war. Superficial observation of children of this kind leaves a conflicting picture. They resemble, so far as outward appearances are concerned, children of middle-class families:

they are well developed physically, properly nourished, decently dressed, have acquired clean habits and decent table manners, and can adapt themselves to rules and regulations. So far as character development is concerned, they often prove—to everybody's despair and despite many efforts—not far above the standard of destitute or neglected children. This shows up especially after they have left the institutions.

It is because of these failures of development that in recent years thoughtful educators have more and more turned against the whole idea of residential nurseries as such, and have devised methods of boarding out orphaned or destitute children with foster families. But since all efforts of this kind will probably not succeed in altogether doing away with the need for residential homes for infants, it remains a question of interest how far failures of the kind described are inherent in the nature of such institutions as distinct from family life, and how far they could be obviated if the former were ready and able to change their methods.

Careful comparison of our own residential children with children of the same ages who live with their own families has taught us some interesting facts. Advantages and disadvantages vary to an astonishing degree according to the periods of development.

BIRTH TO FIVE MONTHS

Babies between birth and about five months of age, when not breast-fed under either condition, develop better in our Nursery than in the average low-income household. Their gain in weight is more regular, and intestinal disturbances are less frequent; their skin, coloring and general appearance are more satisfactory. In times of illness the absence of the tension and anxiety which the young mother invariably feels is certainly of advantage to the child. Mothers who reared the first children in their own homes and now have a third or fourth baby with us are usually full of praise when they compare the progress of this "institutional" child with their first "family" ones. The reasons are not difficult to find: more carefully prepared food, with variation in the food formulas whenever necessary; plenty of air in outdoor life, whenever the weather permits; less economy in laundry; skilled and regular handling and removal from the disturbances of a crowded household in restricted quarters.

Breast-fed babies are, of course, better off than bottle-fed babies wherever they are. Our best results are found in babies who are breast-fed by their own mothers in our home. They show the double advantage of mother's care combined with the careful hygiene of the nursery.

FIVE TO TWELVE MONTHS

In the second half of the first year the picture changes definitely to our disadvantage. Whenever we have an opportunity to compare our 5- to 12-months-old babies with family babies from average homes, we are struck by the greater liveliness and better social response of the family child. The latter is usually more advanced in reaching out for objects and in active play. He is more active in watching the movements of people in the room and more responsive to their leaving or entering, since whoever comes and goes is known to him and concerns him in some way.

A child of that age is, of course, unable to take in and differentiate between all the changing personalities in a baby ward or big nursery. For the same reason the baby's emotional response to changing expression, face or voice, of the adult may be slower to develop. His ability to imitate, which he develops from the 8th month onward, is stimulated in a lesser degree where contact with the grownup is less frequent, or less close, or has to be divided between several grownups as is inevitable in a nursery.

Even where our residential babies are stronger and healthier, these differences in intellectual and emotional development are sufficient to make the family baby appear more "advanced" and therefore more satisfactory. The comparative backwardness of the residential baby at this stage is due to the comparative unfulfillment of his emotional needs, which at this age equal in importance the various needs of the body. The relationship to the mother of the small newborn infant was based on the gratification of bodily needs. Emotional interplay between child and adult occurred exclusively during feeding, bathing, and changing, and was therefore no less frequent under nursery conditions than in the home.

Between 5 to 12 months emotional interplay, and the intellectual stimulation which results from it, is more or less distributed over all the waking hours of the child's day. Consequently, the nursery child, who receives individual attention only when he is fed, bathed, or changed, is at a disadvantage. The amount of further individual attention —play hour, outings in pram, baby gymnastics, etc.—which can be given to a child depends on the staffing of the nursery and other routine arrangements. Attention of this kind has of course to be given by a mother substitute to whom the child is attached. It is valueless when offered by visitors, strangers, or occasional "voluntary workers."

On the whole we can say that in the second half of the residential child's first year the loss in emotional satisfaction outweighs the gain in bodily care.

ONE TO TWO YEARS OF AGE

Muscular Control

With the beginning of the second year the scales turn again in our favor. The great event in the child's life is his new ability to move freely and to control his movements, an ability which progresses quickly from crawling to walking, running, climbing, jumping, and is continued with the handling and moving of objects, as pushing, pulling, dragging, carrying, etc.

Even where mothers fully recognize what intense pleasure the child derives from exercising these new functions, they are, because of outward circumstances, usually unable to give the child free play and thus further his development in this respect. There is in the ordinary household no space for the child to move in or no safety when he moves in the given space. Most mothers are only too well aware of the dangers from fires, boiling water, falls from heights or injury from furniture or falling objects which the child might pull down on himself. The result is that toddlers in their own homes remain in their cribs, or strapped to a pram, or at best confined to the narrow space of a playpen, at a period when in a nursery like ours they cover miles in continual movement about their room.

Some children at this period for a while disregard all

toys and show little interest in their companions; they behave as if they were drunk with the idea of space and even of speed; they crawl, walk, march, and run, and revert from one method of locomotion to the other with the greatest pleasure. These children mostly use toys where they can include them in the continual game of moving. Chairs and pots are not used to sit on but are propelled about the room. Soft toys and animals on wheels are "taken for walks," balls are followed, and some chidren, after they have once gained an easy balance, show special pleasure in moving a toy along in each hand while they move themselves. Sometimes for an hour on end the whole population of the junior toddler room is on the move, circling around, crossing and recrossing like people on a skating rink.

Handling is of course not confined to toys. Whatever is loose in the room (whether coal bucket, nappy-bins, pail, broom) is included in the interest and is handled and explored. If permitted, the children use to the full the newly developed functions of opening, undoing, pulling out, and especially unscrewing. It is easy to imagine that actions of this nature which, when several children are together, resemble those of a demolition squad, cannot be tolerated without damage and expense in a private household. It is not only the child whom the mother wants to safeguard from the objects, but similarly the objects which she has to safeguard from the child.

Freedom to use hands and legs in the way described has further advantages besides the intense pleasure and satisfaction which the child gains by exercising them. Handling quickly becomes more and more skillful under these conditions, so that the toddler of about 18 months of age can already help to set out tables and chairs for his own meal, feed himself, help at dressing or undressing himself, and generally cooperates actively in whatever happens, at an age when family children are often still fed on the mother's lap and handled as if they were passive objects. These differences in activity and earlier control of movement through exercise and opportunity create the appearance of enormous precocity of development of the nursery child.

Speech Development

But it would be a serious mistake to overestimate the advantages gained in this field and not to correlate them with retardations and disadvantages which occur at the same time in other spheres of the child's life. The achievement of muscular control is only one of the tasks reserved for the second year of life. An equally important one is the development of speech. Observations made by academic psychologists have established the fact that at 1 year the average vocabulary of a child is 2 words, and that at 2 years it may be any number of words from 40 to more than 1,200 with a wide variety of phrases and sentences. Whenever we compare our nursery children over 1 year with family children in this respect, we find that they compare unfavorably. The disparity in development does not start as early as the baby stage in talking. Many observations in our baby room prove that our children under 1 year "speak," that is, babble and chatter gibberish, extensively and certainly not less than other children. Some babies are, of course, more proficient than others in this respect.

The greatest talker of the baby room was a girl who, at

the age of 9-10 months, had developed great ability in producing a variety of sounds. At that time she showed little interest in the usual baby toys, but talked to herself nearly all day long. With her it was easy to distinguish between the various sounds and tones which seemed exciting in themselves: rrda, grra, irrga, daraa, dada, ida, and others, singsongs or melodies, which served to call certain people. Her pleasure in talking and her rising excitement while doing so were especially apparent.

But even though most of our babies possess the required two words at 1 year, speech development becomes slower and slower from then on. The good start made in babyhood is not continued in the same manner. When tested, at the age of 2, for instance, even those of our children who are well up to standard and forward in other respects show some 6 months' retardation of speech.

The retardation in the second year may be due to two reasons. The first is that the child at home is the only nonspeaking member of a community in which speech is the method of communication. In the nursery, where the junior toddler group is usually divided off from older children, the child lives in a community of nontalking playmates where speech would not be of immediate help to him. If speech is learned largely by imitation, then the opportunity to learn is certainly restricted.

The second reason is probably more important still. Though imitation of older brothers and sisters plays a great part, especially in extending the vocabulary, the beginning of real speech develops on the basis of close contact between child and parents. The child has empathic understanding of whatever emotion moves the mother; he watches her face and through imitation reproduces her facial expressions. It is the same emotional interplay with the resulting imitation which is a powerful drive toward expression in speech. With the restriction of this interplay in the absence of the mother there is a definite lessening in the urge to speak.

Some children develop a separate language or sequence of sounds to be used exclusively for contact with their mothers. This was apparent with one of our baby girls of 9 months, for instance, whose mother worked in the household of the Nursery and naturally appeared in the baby-room at all hours of the day. The child began to produce a special tone to greet her which sounded like the clucking of ducks. In the course of a month this sound had become completely different from all her other sound productions so that everybody knew from afar when her mother had entered the room. At 11 months the same baby went through a stage of dissatisfaction in which she found it especially intolerable to have wishes postponed or denied. She always wanted her mother to pick her up out of her cot as quickly as possible. At this time she stopped producing the pleasant clucking sound at sight of her mother and adopted a grumble which she kept up each time until the mother had fulfilled her wish. The substitution of the grumbling for the happy clucking sound designated a change in the relationship to the mother from satisfaction and acceptance to impatient demandingness.

Inquiries in other residential nurseries have confirmed the impression gained in our own. When children are home on visits, for instance, at Christmas or during their mothers' holidays, they sometimes gain in speech in one or two weeks what they would have taken three months to gain in the Nursery. Similarly, there are many examples of children brought up at home who lose their newly acquired ability to speak during an absence of the mother. Regression of this kind is further proof of the interrelation between contact with the mother and learning to speak.[1]

This difference of progress in the two stages illustrates the fact that two different factors are at work in speech development: one is the simple pleasure in the production of sound, a pleasure which is partly centered in the mouth itself and partly aroused by the volume and quantity of tone and sound production, rhythm, etc., a pleasure comparable to other early gratifications of the self-regarding or so-called "autoerotic" kind. The other factor is an urge toward expression and communication with the loved people of the outside world; the pleasure gained by its fulfillment might be called other-regarding or pleasure based on object relationship. The examples above show both factors at work side by side in an instructive way.

This differentiation explains why speech development progresses normally in the first year and is delayed in the second year under residential conditions. The first factor, i.e., the urge to gain oral autoerotic pleasure, is present in full force. Like all autoerotic gratifications of this age (sucking, rhythmic movements, masturbation), it is all the more active the more the child is left to himself. Speech development progresses on this basis, but only to the limits of baby talk. The second factor, i.e., communication and imitation on the basis of the relationship to the mother, is less active where a mother is not present; hence the difficulty and retardation at the time when this second factor should supersede the first one in importance. One or two years later these differences are canceled out again; the

[1] For an illustration, see Report 40.

child is then a full member of a group and speech has become independent of the mother-child relationship.

The differences in speech development described here do not apply to children who enter a residential nursery only after they have learned to speak, that is, it is not a difference in the use but in the development of the function of speech.

Toilet Training

The third important task to be achieved, or at least partially achieved, during the child's second year is training. Here again the residential child is at a disadvantage. It is easier within the routine of a nursery than under the pressure of work in an ordinary household to be clean, orderly, punctual, and hygienic about training; but wherever forcible methods are not used, the results of toilet training are slow to come under residential conditions. In this sphere, imitation—the fact that the child lives in a group of other children of the same age who are all equally dirty—can be discounted as an agent. Toilet training is not learned by imitation. What makes itself felt is the fact that toilet training, if not achieved in babyhood as a pure reflex action, is the result of a restriction which the child imposes on important inner urges under the influence of the mother. If the child is attached to and handled by one person exclusively, as happens at home, this restriction will develop in consequence of his emotional dependence. Whenever the child changes hands, or is cared for by varying nurses, as happens invariably in a nursery, or does not care for the nurses who handle him, the process will be lengthened and made more difficult.

At the time of the mass evacuation we had a clear demonstration of how young children who have been perfectly clean at home lose their bladder and sphincter control when separated from their mothers. It is a known fact in all residential nurseries that a child whose training for cleanliness presents special difficulties can finally be made clean only if taken over completely by one person for a while. It is equally well known that many children in nurseries maintain their good habits only when in contact with certain nurses and will refuse to function when helped by others. These differences in personal contact are far more important for the final result than any other factors—observing regular times, regulation of diet, etc. Toilet training can, of course, be achieved under pressure of fear and punishment even where emotional contact of a positive kind is absent. But no conscientious and understanding educator will ever advocate such methods.

The child's muscular skill and independence, gained in the nursery as described above, plays no part in the development of cleanliness.

Feeding

The position is again completely different where eating is concerned. There is a marked difference between the child's reaction to food under home and residential conditions, but on this point the advantages are on the side of the residential child, or at least they may be so if the institutional setting is favorable. This means that in most residential nurseries the children are "good eaters," i.e., are interested in their food and enjoy it if it is good, and that eating difficulties are on the whole less prevalent than in private homes. Where abnormal reactions occur, they appear rather in the form of greed and overeating than in the form of inhibition, lack of appetite, or refusal of food.

The popular explanation of this well-known fact is that children in their own homes are frequently "spoiled" in this respect; that is, many mothers, at least in middle-class families, are overanxious where feeding is concerned, and in some cases they urge the child to eat and even to overeat. These children then refuse what is offered to them, develop idiosyncrasies, etc. It is taken as proof of the correctness of this explanation that such eating difficulties do not develop in families where mothers are careless, negligent, and not interested in the feeding of the child. It would thus seem that the child eats all the better the less the mother worries about the matter.

This theory, though only superficial and incomplete, is still correct in one main point: namely, that eating difficulties are closely connected with the child's relationship to the mother. When followed up from the first stages of the breast or bottle feeding of the newborn baby, this interrelation of reaction to the mother and reaction to food may be described as follows:

Interest in food begins earlier than interest in people. In the first weeks of life the newborn baby experiences nearly everything that reaches him from the external world as unpleasant. He is still used to the lack of stimuli in the intrauterine existence. Light, noise, change of temperature are all equally unpleasant and even frightening. The first pleasant experience is the intake of milk, that is, of food which satisfies the urge of hunger. With the constant repetition of these pleasant experiences, the child slowly learns to recognize that at least part of the outside world is pleasurable. He forms an attachment to food—milk—and, developing further from this point, to the person who feeds him. As described above, love for food becomes the basis of love for mother.

The emotional attachment of the child to the mother, to the father, and to the other people of his immediate surroundings later on outgrows the stage where material gain —satisfaction of hunger—or gain of pleasure generally are the only important factors. In the course of childhood material love of this kind changes to real love, which takes into account the qualities and individuality of a loved person, and is able to give and even to make sacrifices in exchange for what is received.

But the experiences of the first year, when love for food and love for mother were identical, leave their imprint on the reaction to food throughout life. The child from his side shows every inclination to treat food given by the mother as he treats the mother, which means that all the possible disturbances of the child-mother relationship turn easily into eating disturbances. When we observe cases of "bad eaters," it becomes clear how exactingness toward the mother can turn to greed, obstinacy against the mother to a tightly closed mouth and refusal of food, and anger with the mother to playing with or wasting of food. These, of course, are not the only known reasons for eating difficulties in childhood, but they are the most primitive and most common ones.

Wherever the mother in her own behavior perpetuates the feeding circumstances of the first year (i.e., wherever she insists on giving the food actively, on urging the child to eat it for her sake, where she is angry, disappointed or offended when the food remains uneaten, as if it were a personal affront to her), she strengthens the child's infantile attitudes to eating and makes it impossible for him to outgrow them. The inclinations of mother and child then work in the same direction, and the child continues as in babyhood to treat the food as he treats the mother and the mother as he treats the food.

Whenever the mother adapts her behavior to the growing abilities of the child, when she recedes into the background as the giver of the food and only provides food in a more distant and unemotional manner, the child will enter into a next stage of reaction to food: he will eat, or refuse nourishment, according to whether he is hungry or not, and not according to whether he loves or rejects his mother, or wants to please or anger her. Even though the basic significance of food will remain the same for the individual's unconscious, and may show up in times of emotional strain or mental illness, so far as the child's conscious and normal life is concerned, eating will be free to follow the dictates of hunger, and will be less drawn into the complications of the child's affections; that means the child will become a "good eater."

We can now understand why it is that the conscientious and anxious mothers produce eating difficulties, whereas the negligent mothers have children who eat well.

Under institutional conditions the absence of the mother which is a serious drawback in so many ways, proves in this respect for once an advantage. There are certainly institutional children who eat too much for emotional reasons: they try to substitute the satisfaction of one instinctual urge—hunger—for the satisfaction of another—love. But in an institution feeding is on the whole a matter of eating as such, without the idea of a mother figure interpolated between the child and the food. Food is liked for its own sake, and eating is one of the recognized pleasures of all institutional life.

The pleasure can, of course, be spoiled or lessened if it is surrounded with too much discipline, as, for instance, long waiting, which at this age is an excessive strain; sitting quiet, which is never again so difficult as in the toddler stage; insistence on table manners, i.e., use of the spoon before use of an instrument comes naturally; insistence on eating everything and on "eating up." The pleasure in eating can on the other hand be greatly strengthened if the child is allowed some freedom of movement, some freedom of choice regarding type and quantity of food, and if manners are not considered important in themselves but allowed to develop as a natural result of growing skill. It is for purely practical reasons easier to give the child this freedom in a nursery than in a family.

Since the child in a nursery never eats alone, mealtimes, with the pleasure they bring, can be made to play an important part in the child's development toward taking pleasure in social life and adaptation to it.

Summary

The institutional child in the first two years has advantages in all those spheres of his life which are independent of the emotional side of his nature; he is at a disadvantage wherever the emotional tie to the mother or to the family is the mainspring of development. Comparisons between children under these contrasting conditions serve to show that certain achievements such as speech and toilet training are closely related to the child's emotions, even though this may not be apparent at first glance.

CHAPTER 2

Early Relations Between Residential Infants

We have chosen four different aspects of the infant's life to illustrate the differences in development under home and institutional conditions: muscular control, speech development, toilet training, and feeding. The differences in each case were quantitative: muscular control and good eating habits develop more quickly and easily in institutions, speech and toilet training are delayed when the mother's influence is missing. Still, all children will eventually walk and talk, be trained for cleanliness, and become more or less independent eaters. Development is helped or hindered by the outside setting; early acquired disturbances may leave their traces for all later life, but essentially the lines of development will remain the same.

This is not so where the child's emotional life is concerned. Here, change of condition, i.e., lack of the family setting, produces serious qualitative changes. The basic emotional needs of the institutional child are, of course, the same as those of the child who lives at home. But these needs meet with a very different fate. One important instinctual need, that for early attachment to the mother, remains, as we know, more or less unsatisfied; consequently it may become blunted, which means that the child after a while ceases to search for a mother substitute and fails to develop all the more highly organized forms of love which should be modeled on this first pattern. Or the dissatisfaction may have the opposite effect: the dissatisfied and disappointed child may overstress his desire to find a mother, and remain continually on the lookout for new mother figures whose affection he might gain. These are the infants who change their allegiances all the time, are always ready to attach themselves to the latest newcomer, and are at the same time exacting, demanding, apparently passionate, but always disappointed in whatever new attachment they form.

On the other hand, another form of emotional contact, that with other children, is precociously stimulated and developed. Under normal family conditions contact with other children develops only after the child-mother relationship has been firmly established. Brothers and sisters are taken into account for ulterior motives: for instance, as playmates and helpmates. But apart from these relations with them, love and hate toward them are usually not developed directly, but by way of the common relationship with the parents. So far as they are rivals for the parents' love, they arouse jealousy and hate; so far as they are under the parents' protection and therefore "belong," they are tolerated, and even loved. Under institutional conditions the matter is completely different. At the time when the infant lacks opportunities to develop attachment to a stable mother figure, he is overwhelmed with opportunities to make contact with playmates of the same age. Whereas the grownups in his life come and go in a manner which inevitably bewilders the child, these playmates are more or less constant and important figures in his world.

Matters in this way are completely reversed. These institutional children do not start out to meet a world of contemporaries, secure in the feeling that they are firmly attached to one "mother person" to whom they can revert. They live in an "age group," that is, in a dangerous world, peopled by individuals who are as unsocial and as unrestrained as they are themselves. In a family they would, at the age of 18 months, be the "little ones" whom the elder brothers and sisters are ready to protect and consider. In a crowd of other toddlers they have to learn unduly early to defend themselves and their property, to stand up for their own rights, and even to consider the rights of others. This means that they have to become social at an age when it is normal to be asocial. Under pressure of these circumstances they develop a surprising range of reactions: love, hate, jealousy, rivalry, competition, protectiveness, pity, generosity, sympathy, and even understanding.

In the following pages we illustrate this point with incidents that took place in the daily life of our own residential children between 1, 2, and 3 years old. The examples range from instances where playmates are treated as if they were dolls or lifeless objects, to occasions where the relations between the children seem hardly different from those between adults.

OTHER CHILDREN TREATED LIKE TOYS OR LIFELESS OBJECTS: INDIFFERENCE TOWARD THEIR FEELINGS

Little or no illustration is needed for the fact that normally infants have little conception of other infants' feelings, and take notice of their presence only when that can be made use of for the purposes of play. The other child then serves the purpose of a doll or teddy bear, with the one disadvantage that this living toy is not so accommodating as the lifeless ones. This behavior is not restricted to very early stages of development, but occurs quite frequently around the second year, especially at times when the infant copies a motherly adult in his imaginative play.

1. Rose (20 months) looked on with interest when several children had their noses wiped. Suddenly she picked up an old envelope, ran from one child to the other, and wiped their noses with it.

The action was imitative and expressed her fantasy of being the nurse; but no feeling for the children was included in it.

2. Paul (2 years) loved to comb the other children's hair, disregarding the fact that they disliked it. He rushed from one child to another and maltreated their hair with a comb. There was only one child who did not mind, Larry (20 months). Thus, whenever Paul had made a child cry with his combing, he ran back and combed Larry, before he attacked his next unwilling victim. This game continued sometimes for several minutes.

In this instance, as in example 1, all the pleasure lies in the action of combing, and feelings for the other children play no part.

3. Freda (20 months) pushed four children over in succession and tried to sit and rock on them. Each of them cried in turn and had to be rescued from her. When Freda was defeated in her aims, she collected five soft toys, piled them up, and rocked on them.

In this case it is difficult to decide whether the toys were substitutes for the children or the children, in her first attempt, for toys. It is more likely that both, children and toys, were substitutes for some other imaginary partner in Freda's fantasy.

The same type of behavior can constantly be observed where feeding is concerned. Children start to feed each other very early, the pleasure evidently being derived from the fact that they carry out actively what at other times they submit to. This must not be mistaken for a wish to satisfy the other child's appetite, which would be a purely altruistic gesture.

4. Rose (21 months) asked urgently "more, more," when she had finished her first helping. The nurse who was feeding Bert (16 months) next to Rose, left the table to fetch Rose's second helping. Rose immediately picked up the spoon and continued to feed Christopher.

5. Stella (18 months) was sitting next to Agnes (15 months). She took Agnes's spoon and tried to feed her. She heaped up a spoonful of food and put it into her own mouth, then she pushed an empty spoon into Agnes's

mouth. This she repeated several times until finally she emptied the whole contents of Agnes's plate into her own.

In this case it is easy to see that the action which apparently takes the other child into account is in reality purely egoistic. The pleasure of feeding—active repetition of passive experience, imaginative play—is added to the pleasure of eating.

OTHER CHILDREN TREATED MERELY AS A DISTURBANCE: AGGRESSIVE ACTS AGAINST THEM

There are three sets of circumstances which give occasion for aggressive reactions of one infant toward another. One is the indifference and lack of realization that the older child is an equally sensitive human being, which has already been described. The other two comprise instances when the other child is felt to be a hindrance in the way of fulfilling a desire, i.e., when the playmate either claims the love or attention of a grownup whom the infant wants to have exclusively to himself—jealousy (examples 6 and 7) —or when the playmate claims a toy which the child has no intention of surrendering—envy (examples 8, 9, 10).

6. Freda (18 months) and Violet (13 months) were both playing on the floor. Violet asked to sit on the nurse's lap and was taken up. So Freda, too, wanted to sit on the nurse's lap. She hit Violet until she, too, was taken on the lap; at first she was nice to Violet, but soon turned against her and began to hit her hard.

7. Agnes (19 months) sat on the nurse's lap; Edith (16 months) tried to push her off, but was not successful. Edith hit Agnes; Agnes pulled Edith's hair; Edith pulled

Agnes's hair. The nurse moved Agnes to her other side to protect her against Edith, who was the stronger one. Edith, suddenly thwarted, looked at the nurse with fury, hit her, pulled her hair, and then suddenly petted her and gave her a kiss.

8. Agnes (19 months) had a teddy bear in her arms; Paul (2 years) rushed to her, grabbed the teddy, and ran away with it. Agnes screamed and pursued Paul. At first he ran faster than she, then she reached him, got hold of his arm, and ran with him through the nursery, both children screaming. Agnes fell, and as she still clung to Paul's arms, he fell too. On the floor, she grabbed hold of his hair and pulled it. He bit her arm; she pinched his cheek; he hit her and, in doing so, lost the teddy. Agnes took it quickly, got up and ran away, hiding behind the nurse's apron.

9. Rose (22 months) had a wooden horse for pushing, but did not show much interest in it. Sam (20 months) was delighted with it and pushed it across the room. After a while Rose ran up to him silently and took the horse. Sam looked up amazed and began to cry. Rose passed him by with the horse. He got up his courage, walked after her, and grabbed hold of her dress. Rose fell down, but still held the horse. Sam now pulled at one end of the horse, Rose at the other, both screaming. Sam after all captured the horse and pushed off, still crying. Rose ran after him, and, with a quick movement, recaptured the horse. Sam threw himself on the floor in despair, and Rose, who pushed her horse along, happened to trip over him and fell. This restarted the fight, both pulled hard at the horse, both cried, both refused to take another toy. In the end the nurse removed the horse and peace reigned immediately.

10. Terry (2 years, 2 months) loved the big push dog of

the nursery, and all other children somehow accepted the assumption that he had the first right to play with it. When he was away at home for two and a half days, Agnes (19 months) got a chance to play with the dog. When Terry returned, he wanted to resume ownership, but Agnes did not feel inclined to surrender the dog. Terry pulled and shook the dog; Agnes screamed but held tight. Terry threw the dog over, and Agnes went down with it. She clung to it with one hand and grabbed hold of Terry's leg with the other. Terry scratched Agnes. Agnes got up, still holding on to the dog, and pulled Terry's hair. Terry hit her, and Agnes continued steadily to pull his hair, still holding on to the dog with one hand. When Terry again pushed Agnes and the dog over, the nurse rescued her and Agnes only wanted to be comforted and gave up interest in the dog.

Whenever envy and jealousy arise between the children, this results in outbreaks of aggression of considerable force. The methods of aggression vary according to the stage of development reached: biting, hair-pulling, hammering on the head, hitting, pushing over take first place between the age of 15 and 24 months. Throwing things and spitting occur only in certain types of children, and more frequently after than before the third year (examples 11 and 12).

11. Bert (13 months) bit Bill, his twin brother, several times, pulled his hair constantly; hit Babette (11 months). Bert (14 months) knocked with a brick on Bill's head; bit Sophie(14 months). Bill (14 months) bit Bert.

12. Freda (21 months) wanted to precede Edith (22 months) on the slide; tried to push her off. Edith caught

hold of Freda's curl and held it; Freda caught hold of Edith's plait and held it too, both children screaming.

So far as recognition of the consequences of aggressive acts is concerned, we can at that age distinguish three main phases. In the first, the child does not realize what harm his hostile acts may do to the other child. His own feelings—jealousy, envy—prompt him to take aggressive action, but his realization does not go beyond the relief which the outbreak provides for these feelings (examples 13 and 14). In the second phase, the child realizes that his enemy gets hurt or harmed, but he does not mind; he rather enjoys seeing the result he has produced, that is, seeing the other child cry (example 15). The third phase includes the feeling of being sorry for the other child and repentance for the action, either because of identification with the other's feelings—"he feels the hurt as I do"—or because of a common relationship to a mother figure—"he belongs to her and she would not like me to hurt him." The latter feelings are not strong enough to prevent the child from aggressive outbursts, but strong enough to lead to acts of reparation after the outburst has relieved his feelings (example 16).

13. Bert (12 months) hit and scratched his own twin brother, Bill; Bert's face remained peaceful, Bill cried bitterly.
14. Larry (16 months) often took a toy away from another child. When that child cried, he was very surprised, and did not know what he had done.
15. Jessie (20 months) hit Bessie, her twin sister; was proud of it.

16. Dick (2 years, 3 months) was in a phase of special aggressiveness toward other children. The expression on his face left no doubt about his enjoyment of every kind of hurt which he was able to inflict on others. This reaction changed slowly when he grew attached to a particular nurse. Once again he had attacked Ida (22 months) and was found with a tuft of her hair between his fingers. The nurse reproached him for his conduct. He was repentant, went back to Ida, held his clenched fist over her head, opened out his fingers, and carefully returned the tuft of hair to the place where it belonged.

Reactions of this kind can be observed in family as well as residential life. But, as mentioned before, children who live in age groups have more frequent occasion to be jealous—the more so when we try to give them mother substitutes—and they are in an almost continual state of envy which is occasioned by the necessity to share toys; therefore they appear to the casual observer to be more aggressive. It would be more accurate to say that they have more occasion to be aggressive. If to this we add the fact that their victims, of the same age, are at the same time more helpless and, for the same reasons, more aggressive than older brothers and sisters would ever be, we shall be better able to understand why aggressive moods are so much in the foreground in a group of residential infants. It is of special interest to observe how hostilities seldom remain restricted to the two children between whom they started, and how quickly they spread and include others who in the beginning took no part in the outbreak of the quarrel (examples 17 and 18).

17. Paul (22 months) snatched Sophie's teddy bear, whereupon Sophie (19 months) cried. Edith (21 months) rushed to Sophie to hit her, and Sophie pulled Edith's dress; Edith cried and pulled Sophie's hair. Agnes (18 months) joined in the fight and came and pulled Sophie's and Edith's hair, whereupon Edith pushed Agnes until she screamed. Next Larry (19 months) joined in the fight, he went over to Agnes and pushed her over. In the meantime Edith had recovered and hit Larry until he pulled her hair so that she screamed. While all this was going on, Sam (23 months) came by, petted Edith's hair, and made affectionate noises.

18. Sophie (17 months) played peacefully with a doll's cup. Sam (21 months) took it away; Sophie screamed but began to play with another toy after a short time. Edith (19 months) was after the same cup and tried to take it from Sam; they fought until Edith was victorious and ran away with the cup. Sam lay down on the floor screaming, then got up, took the empty posting box and tried to hammer with it on Edith's head. Edith lay down on the floor, kicked and screamed, but held on to the cup. Ivy (19 months) joined in, sat on top of Edith, pulled her hair, tore the cup away from her and ran off with it. Edith recovered after a while and tried to recapture the cup from Ivy. While they fought on the floor, Agnes (16 months) crawled over to them and took the cup away. Edith tried to get it back, but Agnes stood firm. There stood Ivy, her arms hanging limp in resignation, crying; Edith cried, and Sam and Sophie cried because Sam had tripped over Sophie. Only Agnes stood, holding on to a cot with one hand to steady herself, and waved the cup victoriously with the other hand.

OTHER CHILDREN TREATED AS A MENACE: METHODS OF DEFENSE ADOPTED AGAINST THEM

It is a known fact, though perhaps not sufficiently stressed, that the ability to defend oneself develops later than the ability to attack. The same infants who can be aggressive when prompted by their jealous or envious feelings, who bite, hit, and push in the manner described above, suddenly stand helpless, cry, and run for protection when attacked by others. Often they seem amazed or surprised at the aggressive act of another child, though they themselves have committed similar acts only a few minutes earlier. Sensible methods of defense, by act or word, develop slowly and are seldom fully established before the third year. Some of our bigger boys, 4 to 5 years old, though very aggressive, can still do no more than attack others, and burst into tears as soon as they themselves are attacked. On the other hand, some of the following examples show that occasionally very small infants deal successfully with aggressors, and, by their own determination, force them to abandon hostile intentions (examples 19 to 24).

19. Ivy (18 months) had developed the habit of sitting on Edith's head whenever she found her lying on the floor. Edith (18 months) always cried, but never tried to defend herself or to escape.

20. Sam (21 months) was playing peacefully, when suddenly Larry (19 months) took his ball away. Sam looked at his empty hands helplessly and began to cry.

21. Paul (2 years) was very clever in building. He built

towers as high as himself out of very small bricks. While building, he was always afraid lest some other child might push his tower over. This disturbed his concentration; he kept looking nervously in all directions for approaching enemies. When any child dared to come near, Paul rushed at him, and pushed him over with one quick and energetic movement. When, in spite of all precautions, his tower fell over, Paul lay down on the floor in despair and cried for a long time. Then he sucked his two fingers and started to build again, still sobbing. This procedure was repeated innumerable times.

22. Sophie (19 months) slowly ascended the steps of the slide. Larry (20 months) who followed her and wanted to be quicker than Sophie, pushed her. But Sophie turned round, said, "No, no," and pulled his hair.

23. Sam (22 months) was building with two stools; he needed a third, but Agnes (19 months) was sitting on it. Sam walked over to Agnes and looked at her with pleading eyes for about half a minute. Agnes fixed her eyes on Sam, but did not move. So Sam's eyes became sad, he sucked his thumb, and retired slowly.

24. Sophie (19 months) had a rusk in her hand which Larry (19 months) wanted badly. She began to scream as soon as Larry approached her, evidently guessing his evil intentions. When she screamed, Larry withdrew his hand. He began to busy himself with a teddy bear which was lying between them, played with it, and pointed at its eyes, but had his own eyes fixed on the rusk all the time. He tried repeatedly for an opportunity to snatch the rusk; but Sophie did not give him a chance. Finally, he walked away disappointed.

OTHER CHILDREN CONSOLED, COMFORTED, SOOTHED

Although infants are quick to hurt each other, they are equally quick to pity another child, and to make amends to him for what has happened, especially when the aggressive act has not been committed by them but by a third party. In these acts of "pity" they are evidently moved by an identification with the emotions shown by the victim. Examples 27 and 28 seem to prove that there is little difference between comforting another child and comforting oneself. Identification with the victim is further shown in many instances by the adoption of a hostile attitude toward the aggressor. Thus, the infant who consoles or comforts another often combines a friendly act toward the victim with an aggressive one toward the aggressor.

25. Violet (2 years, 4 months) sat in a corner crying. Agnes (19 months) suddenly rushed to the next toy box, took out two toys, gave them quickly to Violet, and ran away again. This was the first occasion of her being "helpful."

26. Sam (22 months) had just stopped crying but still looked unhappy when Rose (22 months) entered the room. She was evidently struck by his expression, watched him critically for a moment, and then ran to him and petted him.

27. Rose (21 months) watched Edith (22 months) petting Sam (22 months), who was crying. She went to Sam and petted him too, then went to Edith and Freda (22 months) and petted them, and finally she stroked

EARLY RELATIONS BETWEEN INFANTS 573

her own hair and cheek and, with a radiant smile, made affectionate noises to herself.

28. The junior toddlers were waiting for their tea in the afternoon. Bill (23 months) and Paul (2 years) sat at the same table. Paul played with a little tin box which Bill wanted to get from him. When he tried to reach it, he caught his finger in it and began to cry. Paul saw that Bill was hurt, immediately lifted his own finger, and put it into Bill's mouth to comfort him.

29. Edith (21 months) had been hurt by Paul (23 months) and cried terribly. When Sam (20 months) saw Edith unhappy, he came to comfort her, Larry (19 months) watched the scene and went to help Sam to comfort Edith.

30. Jeffrey (2 years, 5 months) fell off the push dog and cried bitterly. Bridget (2 years, 8 months) rushed to the dog, hit it, and shook it until it fell over. Then she picked it up again, hit it once more, and then seemed satisfied.

31. Sam (21 months) was playing peacefully (see example 20), when suddenly Larry (19 months) took his ball away. Sam looked at his empty hands helplessly and began to cry. Edith (21 months) had watched this scene; she rushed over to Larry, bit him, took the ball away from him, brought the ball back to Sam, and stroked his hair until he was comforted.

32. Dick (2½ years), who went through a phase of special aggressiveness, wanted to have a toy bus with which Irwin (2¼ years) was playing. He threw himself on Irwin and knocked him down. Irwin fell unluckily and cut his lip on the toy. The nurse comforted him and showed Dick what he had done. Dick was obviously frightened and looked at Irwin with wide eyes. Then he looked round the room, saw Kitty (2½ years) holding a doll, ran to her,

knocked her over, took the doll from her, and gave it to Irwin, saying: "Poor Irwin, poor Irwin, have dolly." The nurse showed him that Kitty was crying now and tried to make him understand that it was nice of him to try to comfort Irwin with the doll, but that he could have found a toy to give him without hurting Kitty. But Dick did not seem to understand. He repeated several times: "Kitty naughty girl," because she did not want to surrender the doll; he was exclusively concerned with Irwin's bleeding lip.

INFANTS HELPING EACH OTHER

The same attitude which leads to the acts of consolation just described, prompts the children to help each other in all the various tasks of everyday life. On the basis of the same needs and wishes, one infant perfectly understands and identifies himself with the difficulties and desires of the other children.

33. Jock (14 months) cried because he has lost his rusk and could not find it again. Sam (21 months) walked over to him, found the rusk on the floor, and gave it to him.

34. Rose (19 months) sat at a table and drank her cocoa. Edith (17 months) climbed up and tried to take the mug from Rose's mouth. Rose looked at her in surprise, then turned the mug and held it for Edith so that she could drink the cocoa.

35. Jessie (2 years) was pushing a doll's pram around the garden. When she came to the corner of the path, she could not turn, pushed hard against the edge of the path, and then began to cry. Bessie, her twin sister, came to the

rescue and pushed the pram around the corner for her. A short while later Bessie was pushing the pram, got stuck at the same corner and cried. This time Jessie came and turned the pram around the corner for her. Each seemed able to do for the other what she could not accomplish for herself.

36. Edith (21 months) had taken off her shoe and sock and tried hard to put them on again. Paul (23 months) watched her from a distance, then rushed over to her, sat down on the floor, and took the sock out of her hand. He tried with surprising patience to put it on Edith's foot, his mouth open, his tongue far out, breathing heavily. Edith watched his face and immediately imitated his expression. For two or three minutes both children were absorbed in their occupation and had an expression of the utmost strain on their faces.

37. Nurse Jean fetched Bridget (2 years) from the shelter dormitory in the morning. Since the dressing room upstairs was already full of children, she only took that one child. When passing other beds, Bridget heard Jeffrey (2 years) cry. She stopped and said: "Jeffrey crying, Jean." The nurse explained that Jeffrey would have to wait a little, and proceeded to take Bridget upstairs. Suddenly on the middle of the staircase, Bridget turned round, said: "I go to Jeffrey," and went back. The nurse waited for her to return, but then followed her to see what had happened. In the meantime Bridget had opened the net of Jeffrey's bed, so that he could get out, and had pushed the stepladder to Bill's bed to let him get out; she was just about to push the steps to Dan's bed. She was holding his hand and saying: "Not fall down."

DIRECT EDUCATIONAL INFLUENCE OF INFANTS ON EACH OTHER

Restriction of Aggression, Greed, Dirty Habits

It is common knowledge that children educate each other and that, in families, the influence of older brothers and sisters makes itself strongly felt as an addition to the educational influence of the parents. Many children who are unwilling to obey their parents are quite ready to obey the commands and prohibitions of older children. Imitation of examples set by older children seems easier, and their rebukes or even punishments, though effective, seem to hurt less. This educational help rendered by older brothers and sisters is one of the reasons why the whole process of upbringing is smoother where the family is large.

But this type of "education" through the agency of older children is very different from the influence which infants in the same age group exert on each other. Whereas older brothers and sisters act as parent substitutes—parent figures on a reduced scale—these contemporaries in an age group are equals in status. One child can influence the other if at that moment he is the stronger one, i.e., because at that moment he is a menace to the other child; the latter will then obey him out of fear. Or one infant can influence the other because at that moment he is further advanced in some achievement—walking, toilet training, etc. The position will be reversed when another achievement plays the greater role in which the second child surpasses the first. That means that the children influence each other on the basis of superior strength or superior achievement. Fear of each other and admiration for each other are the deciding factors in this respect. Observation shows that, owing to these interrelations between the infants, certain results are produced which at first glance are not very different from the results produced by education proper: aggression is checked, wish fulfillment is postponed, and certain "good habits" are acquired under the pressure of these circumstances.

38. Freda (21 months) pulled Sam's hair. Sam (21 months) cried but did not defend himself. Jeffrey (2 years, 4 months) crossed the nursery quickly, hit Freda twice, and then comforted Sam. When Sam stopped crying, Jeffrey once more turned to Freda and looked at her with indignation, whereupon Freda immediately shrank back into a corner. Then Jeffrey walked away, obviously pleased with himself.

In this case it is clear why Jeffrey can exert such influence. He is 7 months older and considerably stronger than Freda. Since he would not hesitate a moment to use his superior strength, he constitutes a very real danger to Freda. She checks her aggression out of fear.

39. Sam (21 months) built with bricks in a corner of the room. Freda (21 months) approached him carefully, with the obvious intention of destroying his building. Sam looked up and said: "No, no." Freda changed her intention: she hesitated for a moment, then picked up a brick and gave it to Sam; slowly she collected all the bricks in the room and handed them to Sam in succession.

In this case the result achieved is due to other causes. Sam and Freda are at the same age; there is no difference in strength between them; Sam is a particularly gentle child who is not feared by anybody. This time Freda does not stop her destructive action out of fear. She is impressed by Sam's unexpected determination to a degree which changes her destructive intention to its opposite. She now helps him instead of harming him.

40. Bessie (19 months) had a comb in her hand; Jessie, her twin sister, a toy with which she played. Bessie wanted the toy but checked her impulse to take it. Suddenly she offered the comb to Jessie; Jessie took it quietly and surrendered the desired toy. There was not a sound from either of them while this exchange took place.

All children in our groups learn very early that to snatch a toy from another child invites trouble, i.e., an outbreak of resentment or unhappiness from the victim. The method adopted most frequently is exchange: they offer something with one hand and take away with the other. Again, as in former instances, this gesture is only apparently altruistic; it signifies restraint of greed or aggression acquired under the pressure of bitter experience. Occurrences of this kind may be observed in our Nursery constantly. For instance:

41. Maggie (2 years) cried because Dinah, her sister (3 years) had snatched a toy from her. Bridget (2 years), who had witnessed the scene, tried to restore order. She snatched away the toy from Dinah and returned it to Maggie. When Dinah now threw herself on the floor and cried, Bridget went to look for a substitute, found an old toilet paper roll, and brought it to Dinah. When Dinah

refused it, she gave it to Maggie, taking the toy at the same time from Maggie to bring it to Dinah. To Bridget's great concern, Maggie now cried as well as Dinah. That was too much for her. First she hit both, then tried to comfort both, and when nothing helped she gave up.

42. Carol (3½ years) tried to snatch a doll from Jessie (2 years). Jessie bit her so that she had to let the doll go. Bessie, Jessie's twin sister, came to the rescue and hit Carol from behind. Jessie suddenly stopped biting and shouted: "No, no, Bessie, not hit."

It is not clear in this case why in Jessie's code, which she tries to impart to Bessie, biting is allowed but hitting forbidden.

43. Bridget (2 years, 4 months) and Dick (3 years) were sitting together at breakfast. They talked to each other happily until Dick began to smear his porridge all over the table. Bridget wrinkled her nose in disgust: "Stop it, Dicky, you dirty boy." Dick: "No, I won't." Bridget, very cross: "Dicky, I don't like it, you naughty." Dick, shouting: "No." Bridget, very angry indeed, disgust in her face: "Dicky, I won't sit with you anymore. I sit with Marion" (the nurse). She picked up her plate and mug and dragged her chair over to the nurse, muttering and grumbling all the time at Dick.

In this instance, Bridget, though younger, assumes educational superiority on the basis of her better manners. She has just completed her toilet training, but has become at the same time very intolerant toward all children who are not quite up to her standards of cleanliness in either lavatory or table manners.

The position between the two children is reversed in the following instance, two months later.

44. Bridget joined the dinner of the bigger children for the first time and did not know how to handle a fork. Her friend Dick watched her at first and then said: "Not like that, Bridget, look at me." Bridget looked at him and copied him carefully right through the meal.

The following two examples demonstrate how consideration of the other child, based on identification with his desires, leads to real acts of sacrifice and generosity. Aggression in these cases is completely checked.

45. Sam (21 months) held a piece of paper in front of his face and played peekaboo. Sophie (20 months) wanted the paper and screamed. So Sam tore the paper in two and gave one part to her. Then both children played peekaboo; they did it in turns and laughed heartily.

46. Jeffrey (2 years, 4 months) returned from a walk with a new book which he had been given as a present. He was delighted with it and showed it to everybody. When Teddy (2 years, 1 month) saw the nice book, he took it away. Jeffrey screamed, ran after him, and recovered it. Teddy immediately began to cry disconsolately until Jeffrey gave him the book again. Teddy stopped crying, but Jeffrey now did not dare take his property away again. So they both sat down and looked at it together. Teddy kept the book all afternoon.

FRIENDSHIP BETWEEN INFANTS

Under ordinary conditions friendships of long duration are believed to be very rare among young children. Lasting attachments are formed to grownups or to older children; playmates of the same age are used for purposes of play only, and friendships fall apart when the momentary reason for them—the play—has ended.

Matters are different under residential conditions. We observe many instances of friendship among infants which last days, weeks, or even months. Playmates are certainly not chosen indiscriminately; in playing together the partner often seems no less important than the game. Partnership of this kind is most outstanding in several pairs of twins who live in our Nursery. It is interesting to note that this natural partnership, which appears in twins, develops in a similar manner, only quantitively less, in many residential infants (see Burlingham, 1952).

47. Reggie (18 to 20 months) and Jeffrey (15 to 17 months) had become great friends. They always played with each other and hardly ever took notice of another child. This friendship had lasted about two months when Reggie went home. Jeffrey missed him very much; he hardly played during the following days and sucked his thumb more than usual.

48. Sophie and Larry (both 19 months) had founded a building society. Whenever one of them started building, the other joined in quickly, and then they built in turns, each putting a brick carefully on the tower and then waiting until the other had put his brick on. They used ten

to twelve bricks and were very happy in their companionship.

49. Sophie (19 months) loved to sit in a certain cupboard. When she wanted company, and when the right child was near her, she called energetically, "More, more," and pointed at the empty space next to her. She usually invited Edith (21 months) or Agnes (18 months). As soon as the invited child sat down beside her, Sophie began to bang her feet on the floor and the other child joined in. If an unwanted child tried to sit in the cupboard, Sophie quickly pushed him away with a loud "No, no."

50. Bessie (22 months) became very submissive to Tom (2 years). For weeks she helped him in all his occupations and joined in all his games. She carried bricks for him when he was building and placed the chairs for him when he was playing train. He was grateful for her services, and returned them occasionally. For instance, when Bessie once tried to climb on a chair and got into a rather awkward position, he suddenly appeared and held the chair for her.

51. Several junior toddlers were playing on the floor. Sophie (15 months) got upset by another child and began to cry bitterly; nothing could comfort her, she just cried and cried. Terry (20 months) came up to her and looked into her face. She took no notice and went on crying. Terry was very puzzled and began to shake his head; he shook it so violently that he sat down on the floor with a big bump. He laughed and Sophie stopped crying for a second, then started again. Terry got up, shook his head and bumped down again with a loud laugh. Sophie smiled and forgot to cry. Terry repeated this performance as many as fourteen times. He was nearly worn out and quite dizzy, both children shaking with laughter. The other children

got interested, but as soon as they came near, he stopped and even pushed one of them away, to start again when he and Sophie were left alone.

INSTANCES OF LOVE PLAY, TENDERNESS, AFFECTION

The following examples show behavior between infants which is hardly different from the expressions of love and affection between adults.

52. The nurse who entered the rest room during the children's afternoon nap found Paul (2 years) and Sophie (19 months) standing at one end of their cots kissing each other. She was amused and laughed. Paul turned around and smiled at her for a moment, then again held Sophie's head between both his hands and kissed her over and over again. Sophie smiled and was obviously pleased.

53. This love scene between Paul and Sophie had its continuation. Sophie's favorite toy was a brown teddy. Paul had learned that he could make her unhappy by taking the teddy away and stop her unhappiness by returning it to her. Five days after the kissing incident he used this knowledge to attract her attention specially. He took the teddy away and Sophie began to cry. He ran to the other end of the nursery and then back to Sophie, returned the teddy to her and was very pleased. He repeated this at least ten times during the afternoon.

54. Ivy (20 months) and Agnes (15 months) were taken out in the pram. They played with each other and kissed and hugged each other most of the time. Ivy was the one who started it over and over again and Agnes responded. Both children laughed with pleasure.

55. Sophie (20 months) stood in a corner of the nursery and looked at Larry (19 months). Larry noticed her and went to her, saying "Ay! ay!" Sophie put her arms around Larry. They stayed like that for quite a while.

56. Tom (20 months) and Stella (17 months) played with each other on the floor. Suddenly Tom pushed Stella over so that she lay on her back, her hands under her head. He climbed on her and rocked. Both children looked perfectly happy. Then Tom got up and walked away and Stella looked at him once more and got up too. When, in the afternoon, Tom entered the nursery, Stella immediately lay down on the floor again and resumed the position of the morning. She looked at Tom in an expectant manner, but got up when he took no notice.

57. Henry (2 years, 7 months) and Ralph (3 years, 4 months) have had a friendship of long standing. One morning Ralph was looking at a "storybook," pointed excitedly to the capital B on the title page and called out: "Look, look, that's Henry and me." The whole morning he looked at books in the nursery and every time when he saw a capital B, he said over and over again: "That's Henry and me."

The form of the letter B suggested to him the picture of two friends embracing each other.[1]

---

[1] After our Monthly Report 26, on which this chapter is based, was sent out, we received two very similar letters from two of the oldest friends of the Hampstead Nursery. These two friends and readers of our Reports expressed concern that our children, in our descriptions, seemed so very naughty, aggressive, and unrestrained. This did not seem to agree with the impressions they had received on their visits to the Nursery, where they had been struck by an atmosphere of peace and serenity in the children and by the quiet educational influence exerted by the grownups. They were worried lest readers who had no occasion for such visits might form a

wrong idea of the state of the children on the one hand, and the lack of proper guidance on the other. One of these letters suggests that, to prevent such misunderstandings, we should more clearly define our views about the role of asocial behavior in small children, its origin, treatment, and final transformation into the opposite, or sublimation, i.e., steering into channels which prove socially useful.

In response we can only say: descriptions of the aggressive reactions of infants and of their battles with each other often take longer than the actual occurrence. Infant's emotions, whether positive or negative, are quick and violent. For purposes of everyday life they are evanescent and therefore often ignored; for purposes of understanding they have to be pinned down for observation.

To return to our series of "social" or "asocial" reactions: the children certainly do not fight all the time, just as they are not comforting to each other, helpful, or affectionate all the time. We only wished to show that both extremes of attitude toward their contemporaries, aggressive fighting as well as affectionate love, are under certain conditions within their range even at that early age.

CHAPTER 3

Introduction of the Mother Relationship Into Nursery Life

It is a fallacy to conclude that the variety of emotions which the young child in a residential nursery develops toward the playmates of his own age group can make up in any way for the emotions which he would normally direct toward his parents. The latter remain undeveloped and unsatisfied, but many observations show that they are latent in the child and ready to leap into action the moment the slightest opportunity for attachment is offered by the outward circumstances. This is all the more noticeable, the less a child has knowledge of, or opportunity to form an emotional attachment to, his own mother.

FORMATION OF ARTIFICIAL FAMILIES

We have repeatedly made the experiment of dividing up some large "age groups" of children into small units of three, four or five under the guidance of one young nurse or teacher who acted as their foster mother where motherly care was concerned. In all these instances the group reactions of the children quickly changed to the emotional reactions of children in a natural family setting. They formed a strong and possessive attachment to their nurse and were at the same time more exacting, but also more willing to make sacrifices for her, than they had been before. Certain steps in development which had been difficult or impossible in the group setting, for instance, toilet training, were under these changed conditions easier to accomplish. The other children of the same "family" were then treated with the mixture of jealousy and toleration which is one of the characteristics of the brother-sister relationship; but this tolerance was not extended outside the family. The children quickly developed an understanding of the other families and respected each other's rights to the possession of a particular adult. The younger children express all these reactions in their behavior, the older children very clearly with the help of speech. They talk about their "own" nurses as if they were precious possessions, compare them with each other, or boast of them as other children do of their mothers, etc. Artificial families are usually arranged so that two nurses substitute for each other on their days off, and children treat this substitute foster mother with a lesser degree of possessiveness, but still as something of their own.

1. Derrick (3¾ years) said on his way home from a walk: "When my Sara is off, it's my Martha, and when my Martha is off, it is my Sara." Arrived in the house, he did not find Sara, so he said at once: "My Sara is all gone,

my Martha now." Derrick is an extremely difficult problem child who hardly lets himself be touched by anybody except "his Sara," or in the second place "his Martha."

2. Bridget (2½ years) belonged to the family of Nurse Jean of whom she was extremely fond. When Jean had been ill for a few days and returned to the nursery, Bridget constantly repeated: "My Jean, my Jean." Lillian (2½ years) once said, "My Jean," too, but Bridget objected and explained, "It's my Jean, it's Lillian's Ruth, and Keith's very own Ilsa."

3. Bridget (2 years, 8 months) and Jeffrey (2½ years) had the following conversations. When Bridget returned from the measles sickroom, where she had been separated from Jean, she was more jealous than ever and did not allow Jeffrey even to mention Nurse Jean's name without saying, "It's my Jean." The first morning Jeffrey took it quietly, just looked at her, and did not answer. In the afternoon he got upset about it, looked at Nurse Jean and began to cry. Jean explained to Bridget that it was quite true, that she was her Jean and that Jeffrey had his Sara, but that Sara was ill at the moment, so Jean had to look after Jeffrey until Sara was well again. Bridget seemed to understand, she played and did not mention the subject again until teatime, when she suddenly turned to Jeffrey and said: "It's my Jean, it's your Sara, Jeffrey, isn't it? All right?" Whereupon Jeffrey said: "All right, my Sara." Next day at lunch when the children were sitting next to each other again, Bridget restarted the subject in a very provocative way: "It's my Jean." Jeffrey hit her with his spoon and said in a furious voice: "Your Jean." Bridget was so pleased with her success that she did not even complain about being hit.

INTRODUCTION OF MOTHER RELATIONSHIP

Acceptance of the family grouping also produces a certain amount of reserve and resentment on the part of the children, which makes itself felt especially when the mother of one family tries to help or take care of members of another. But reactions of this kind are confined to such intimate ministrations as, for instance, undressing, potting, and bathing.

4. When Nurse Ilsa asked Christine (4 years) one night whether she would like to be bathed by her, Christine said: "No, 'cause you don't know how to bathe girls. You can only bathe Bob and Martin."

5. When Nurse Ursula wanted to bathe Kitty one evening, Kitty refused and said: "You like to bath Jessie and Bessie." She repeated this several times and was persistent in her refusal.

As mentioned previously, these family arrangements are restricted to the motherly care of the children and do not extend to their occupations during the day. But some children even insist on being reproached or corrected only by their "own" people.

6. Bridget (2 years, 8 months), when told by another nurse that she had done something wrong and that this was "not nice at all," only gave her a furious look, stamped her foot, and shouted: "My Jean." (It was Jean's day off.)

7. Tony (4 years) was told by a nurse to get off the windowsill on which he was standing. He got most indignant about it. He said: "Don't talk to me like that. Sister Mary does not! You have to say, please come down from the windowsill."

Some children show and express great understanding of the others in this respect.

8. When Derrick (3 years) was cross with Nurse Ilsa and threatened, "I'll put you in the water" (the most popular threat used by the children), Shirley (4 years, 9 months) said: "No, Derrick, you can't do that, 'cause Bob [who is in Ilsa's family] won't have no Ilsa left and he needs one."

9. Shirley (4 years, 10 months) said at night in bed: "I have a very nice mummy. I like her very much. Mrs. B. is a nice mummy and Mrs. G. too. All children have nice mummies, but Hannah [a young nurse] must come to see her Kitty on Sundays and bring her cake. Kitty has no nice mummy, that's why she has her Hannah."

SPECIFIC NATURE AND CONSEQUENCES OF THE MOTHER RELATIONSHIP

Repeated experience proves the importance of the introduction of this substitute mother relationship into the life of a residential nursery. A child who forms this kind of relationship to a grownup not only becomes amenable to educational influence in a very welcome manner, but shows more vivid and varied facial expressions, develops individual qualities, and unfolds his whole personality in a surprising way. On the other hand, it has to be admitted that family arrangements of this kind introduce very many disturbing and complicating elements into nursery life. Children who have shown themselves adaptable and accommodating under group conditions suddenly become insufferably demanding and unreasonable. Their jealousy and, above all, their possessiveness of the beloved grown-up may be boundless. It easily becomes compulsive where the mother relationship is no new experience but where separation from a real mother and a former foster mother has occurred before. The child is all the more clinging, the more he has an inner conviction that separation will repeat itself. Children become disturbed in their play activities when they watch anxiously whether their "own" nurse leaves the room on an errand or for her hour off, or whether she has any intimate dealings with children outside her family. Tony (3½ years), for instance, would not allow Sister Mary to use "his" hand for handling other children. Jim (2 to 3 years) would burst into tears whenever his "own" nurse left the room. Shirley (4 years) would become intensely depressed and disturbed when "her" Marion was absent for some reason, etc. It is true that all these children had had to cope with a series of traumatic separations in their lives.

It is of the greatest interest to watch the difference in behavior shown by the children in these intimate relations with their chosen foster mothers on the one hand and with the group teacher in the nursery on the other. We are in this respect often reminded of the difference in behavior which children who live with their families show in the day nursery. They are sometimes perfectly good and social in the nursery and extremely difficult at home. This is not—as many nursery school teachers seem to think—due to the fact that the mother does not know how to handle the child whereas the teacher does. It is due to the difference in the emotional response to mother and teacher, a difference which we find reflected in the different response to the "family mother" and the group teacher in a residential home.[1] The mother relationship or its substitute awakens emotions in the child which in their turn give rise to passionate demands which clamor for satisfaction. This first and early love reaction to a mother enriches the life of the child by laying the foundations for all future love relationships. Like all love, it entails a wealth of complications, conflicts, disappointments, and frustrations. The child is usually quite unable to express or even consciously to realize the nature and extent of his demand on the mother or mother substitute. It displaces this unconscious wish to all sorts of substitute gratifications, none of which—even if it were capable of fulfillment—will ever satisfy his need.

10. Jim was separated from a very nice and affectionate mother at 17 months and developed well in our Nursery. During his stay he formed two strong attachments to two young nurses who successively took care of him. Although he was otherwise a well-adjusted, active, and companionable child, his behavior became impossible where these attachments were concerned. He was clinging, overpossessive, unwilling to be left for a minute, and continually demanded something without being able to define in any way what it was he wanted. It was no unusual sight to see Jim lie on the floor sobbing and despairing. These reactions ceased when his favorite nurse was absent even for short periods. He was then quiet and impersonal. Love on the

[1] One salient element in this difference is due to the fact that the mother or "family mother," handles the child's body, whereas the teacher in a day nursery, or the group teacher, does not. The activities of feeding, dressing and undressing a child, bathing him, tending to his physical needs, putting him to bed, etc., all evoke a different type of response.

one hand, and intense feelings of frustration on the other, seemed inextricably bound up with each other in his case.

11. Martin, who came to our Nursery at 16 months, formed a similar kind of attachment to his beloved Ilsa from the moment when he entered her group at approximately 2 years. He was an especially healthy and robust child, full of fun, active, and mischievous. In his relations with Ilsa he would turn into a passive and clinging baby at the slightest provocation. This behavior became intensified when he was about 3 years. Whenever he came home to Netherhall Gardens from the nursery class which we run for our children in Wedderburn Road, he apparently thought that he could spend the rest of the day constantly in Ilsa's company. Whenever this was not possible, he flew into violent tempers and lay on the floor crying for long periods of time. On a certain day he was more of a tyrant than ever before, obviously looking for trouble. When Ilsa told him to put on shoes, he wanted boots; when he got cake, he wanted chocolate; when Ilsa wanted to bathe him in the big tub which he usually loves, he asked for the little one. He was exhausted when he was in bed at last, sent her away without "good night" and then cried because she had not said "good night." After such scenes he stammered badly for several hours, sometimes for a whole day.

The next morning he started off in a similar manner. When at breakfast he said he did not like "that sugar" on the cornflakes, and when Ilsa asked what kind of sugar he wanted, he stamped his foot and stuttered: "Bl—black sugar." When he saw her laugh, he suddenly roared with laughter himself, said very sensibly, "There is no black sugar," and was perfectly all right for the rest of the day.

12. In our Monthly Reports, we described similar reactions which Tony, then 3½ years, developed in the beginning of his intimacy with Sister Mary. He would send her out of the room in the evening when she offered to stay with him and call her back in despair as soon as she had left him. He would accuse her of having hurt him in some way or of having neglected his small hurts or ailments. He would wake up in the middle of the night and complain to the night nurse that Sister Mary had not said "good night" to him, in spite of the fact that she had done so, had looked after him, and fulfilled his wishes to the best of her ability. At 4½, when he was going through a difficult time owing to the remarriage of his father, he would suddenly interrupt his play, search for her, and say over and over again: "I want to tell you something. I want to tell you something." When asked what he wanted to tell, he did not know. Sometimes he said: "I want to kiss you," but it was quite clear that the kiss was not his real reason and that the real nature of his demand was not known to him (see especially Reports 22 and 36).

Behavior of this kind is naturally not welcome in the nursery. It acts as a disturbance to the other children and is often criticized sharply by the other members of the staff who cannot help but feel that this particular nurse has "spoiled" this child and that the child would be much better off, i.e., much quieter, without the disturbing complications of this intimate relationship. This is true only in the sense in which we would all be better off, i.e., more sensible, without emotions. In reality it is not the absence of irrational emotional attachments which helps a child to grow up normally but the painful and often disturbing process of learning how to deal with such emotions.

As stated earlier, even the secure and uninterrupted

relationship of a small child to his parents is full of conflicts, disappointments, and unfulfilled longings. The child wants to possess father or mother exclusively and in every sense of the word, which he cannot do. Restrictions of the child's demands are taken as rebuff, the necessary refusal of bodily intimacy creates unhappiness, guilt, and inhibition. Comparison with the parent of the same sex brings home to the child a sense of his own smallness and inefficiency.

The first family setting is the framework within which the instinctual drives and emotions of the child grope toward their first objects. The child can never completely possess these objects, but in this first display of his feelings he learns "to love," to cope with his instinctual drives and thus lay the foundations for his character formation, a process which entails a great deal of discomfort. It is this first parent relationship which the child repeats, sometimes in a lessened, sometimes in an intensified, degree on the parent substitutes, if they are offered to him, in a residential institution.

FURTHER CONSEQUENCES OF THE SUBSTITUTE MOTHER RELATIONSHIP IN THE NURSERY

The introduction of the mother relationship into nursery life, necessary as it seems to us, is not only accompanied by all the disturbing emotional elements described above, but further brings with it in the danger of renewed separation.

Nurses do leave at times or, in the course of their training, change from department to department, and separations of this kind, when an intimate attachment has been formed, are frequently no less painful than the initial separation from the mother. Here the child again displays all the conflicting emotions of sorrow, longing, and resentment which we have described as involved in the separation from the mother. Examples of this kind are countless. Especially recent and striking is the following.

13. Reggie, who had come to our house as a baby of 5 months, went home to his mother when he was 20 months, and has been with us ever since his return to the Nursery 2 months later. While he was with us, he formed two passionate relationships to two young nurses who took care of him at different periods. The second attachment was suddenly broken at 2 years, 8 months when his "own" nurse married. He was completely lost and desperate after her departure, and refused to look at her when she visited him a fortnight later. He turned his head to the other side when she spoke to him, but stared at the door, which had closed behind her, after she had left the room. In the evening in bed he sat up and said: "My very own Mary-Ann! But I don't like her."

The fact that such renewed separations are bound to happen is often used as an argument against family arrangements in the nursery. But argumentation of this kind seems to us erroneous. When choosing between the two evils of broken and interrupted attachments and an existence of emotional barrenness, the latter is the more harmful solution because, as will be shown later, it offers less prospect for normal character development.

SPONTANEOUS ATTACHMENT TO AN ADULT

We have shown how quickly the latent parent-child relationship becomes manifest, for instance, when opportunity is offered through formation of artificial family groups. These inner urges of the child do not always wait for carefully thought-out arrangements. They arise in answer to actions of the grownups: whoever merely takes care of a child for any length of time in a motherly way may easily become the chosen foster mother of this child. But children also choose their foster mothers where no previous action on the part of the adult has provoked the process; it seems at first sight as if they choose at random. Closer investigation of every such occurrence shows that these apparently spontaneous attachments of the children really arise in response to a feeling in the adult person, in many cases a feeling of which the adult was not aware in the beginning, or the reasons for which became apparent only after some searching.

A young nurse, for instance, felt attracted to one of the liveliest little boys in the Nursery. When questioning herself she found that he resembled the favorite brother of her childhood. Another nurse felt attracted to a child whose tragic loss of his parents reminded her of her own tragic separation from her family. Another one felt specially drawn to small girls whose family constellation reminded her of her own position in her family with all its consequences, etc. In all these instances the children responded to this hardly conscious attitude with violent attachments from their own side. It seemed as if the emotion that lay dormant in them had only waited for an answering spark in some adult person to flare up.

It is essential for all people who live and work in close contact with children to realize the existence of these emotional trends in themselves and through realization gain control over them. Although the adult in the nursery serves as object and outlet for the emotions which lie ready in the child, the children should on no account serve as outlets for the uncontrolled and therefore unrestrained emotions of the adults, irrespective of whether these emotions are of a positive or negative kind.

CHAPTER 4

Some Aspects of Instinctual Satisfaction and Frustration in Family and Nursery Life

In the preceding chapters we tried to establish one main fact: that small infants in a residential nursery, though they develop community reactions and enjoy the companionship of children of their own age, search further for objects towards whom they can direct all those emotional interests which they would normally direct toward their parents. We have described how the grownups of the nursery are turned into parent substitutes. It is our next task to discuss how far these emotional relationships satisfy the natural desires of the child and how far they are destined to fail in this respect.

BODILY INTIMACY BETWEEN INFANT AND MOTHER

It is a well-known fact that small infants treat parts of the mother's body as if they were their own. The baby, for instance, first experiences the pleasurable sensation of sucking while feeding at the mother's breast. When he wants the same pleasure between feeding, i.e., at times when the mother's breast is not at his disposal, he substitutes his own finger, or fingers, for the nipple. We assume that in the beginning he does not discriminate between what belongs to his own body and what to the mother's and that the discovery that his own hand is always present whereas the mother's breast periodically disappears probably serves as the first distinction between a body of one's own and an outer world.

The infant plays with the mother in the same ways in which he plays with himself. He pulls her hair, pokes his finger into her eyes, her nose, mouth, and ears or plays with her fingers; similarly he plays on his own face and with his own hands. Pleasure is evidently gained both from his own body and from the mother's. Sometimes, in such a search for pleasure, the two are used in turn.

Some examples of this unity of body between child and motherly person are observed under nursery conditions as well.

1. Lily, from the age of 10 weeks, used to play for a long time with her own hands. This became less frequent after the age of 4 months, when it gave way to play with her rattle or with the frill of her dress. But interest in

hands was revived at 8 months, when Lily began to play with the nurse's hand. The latter once rested quietly in the baby's cot and Lily suddenly touched it, held it, and moved it a little, in turn. She laughed and kicked while doing so and became so excited that after a while the nurse had to remove her hand. She had never before reacted to any other incident in her life with as much happiness and excitement.

2. Rose had always, since babyhood, sucked her thumb before falling asleep. At 21 months she began the following bedtime plays with her favorite nurse. For several days she put her hand in the nurse's mouth and then fell asleep. In a next phase she would try to take the nurse's hand in her mouth. She would open it wide to get in as much of the big hand as possible. Another evening she was sucking her thumb in the usual way. Suddenly she nodded her head, took a corner of her blanket—the same corner which she always used to grasp tightly during thumb sucking—tried to push it into the nurse's mouth, smiled contentedly, and fell asleep.

3. Between the age of 2 and 3 Dick developed an unusual way of finding bodily satisfaction at bedtime, or when he wanted comfort after a temper. He grasped the forefinger of a person of whom he was fond, held it tightly, and tried to push it hard into the inside corner of his eye. His whole body became tense while doing so, and his face showed an expression of extreme pleasure. The fingers he tried to get hold of were those of four nurses with whom he was on specially good terms. He would occasionally use his own finger, but always tried to get hold of one of these others, if possible.

4. Jeffrey, between 2 and 2 years, 3 months, developed

various ways of playing with his favorite nurse. When she dressed him, he would explore her face; he would touch her eyes, in particular, and be delighted. When she bent her head to lace his shoes, he would put the forefinger of each of his hands into her ears and laugh with delight. Though, at this time, he had outgrown his violent thumb sucking, he would resort to it when being dressed before breakfast.

Very frequently then he would lift his thumb and put it into the nurse's mouth. When she gave signs of not liking it, he would take her own thumb and put it into her own mouth. He had at this time just learned the first verse of Baa Baa Black Sheep. He loved to sing it, but instead of clapping his hands as the other children did, he would slap her face in the rhythm of the song. Whenever the doctor used a spatula to look at his throat, he would open his mouth willingly, but would try to make her take the other end of the spatula into her mouth.

This substitution of the mother's body for the small child's is even more frequent where the pleasure of eating is concerned. Mothers often describe proudly how "generous" their small children are, i.e., how willing to give them a bite of something which they are eating or to put a spoonful of food into their mouths when they are fed. They are usually surprised to see this early generosity disappear about the end of the second year and give way to a period of intense selfishness when the child wants to keep all the good things strictly to himself. It seems to us that, looked at more closely, this early generosity does not deserve its name; it has very little in common with the altruistic and self-denying quality which may appear in the same child 2 or 3 years later, as a result of character development. The infant in his first 2 years does not really renounce pleasure to give to his mother; it is more correct to say that he fails to distinguish between himself and his mother. Pleasure given to the mother feels like pleasure given to himself, which means that the apparently altruistic action is, in reality, still egoistic. When the next step in development is made, and the mother definitely becomes part of the outside world, this first semblance of "generosity" naturally disappears.

Innumerable examples like the following may be observed even under institutional conditions.

5. Violet (14½ months) was eating a biscuit. Several times she put it in the mouth of her favorite nurse as if it were her own.

6. Jeffrey, from early babyhood, found eating especially pleasurable. About the age of 2 to 2½ years, when he developed a special attachment to his new "family mother," he expressed his oneness with her not only by wanting to let her suck his finger, but also by sharing his feeding pleasures with her. One day, for instance, he was eating a slice of apple. He held one end in his mouth and tried to push the other end into her mouth. Suddenly he pushed the whole slice into her mouth, looked at her laughingly, said, "All gone," and was obviously pleased—an unheard of occurrence with Jeffrey who could never bear to be parted from his food. But in spite of his obvious greed, he would from then onward always try to feed this nurse with his lunch when she sat at his table. He may seem rather old for this reaction, but this delay is probably due to the fact that he has never lived with his mother and that this attachment to the new "family mother" is the first close and steady relationship in his life.

It is not the purpose of these examples to show what close relationship to mother substitutes the children may form in a nursery, or what possibilities for finding satisfaction are offered to them under those circumstances. Quite the contrary, we take these individual occurrences as proof of the enormous strength of certain natural tendencies in the child, tendencies which under ordinary institutional conditions remain under the surface and betray themselves to the observer only when certain conditions are fulfilled —as, for instance, formation of artificial families, isolation with one nurse in times of illness. Whatever efforts a residential nursery may make to offer "home care" to the infant, the lack in satisfaction given to these primitive desires will remain enormous. We are apt to forget it with those children who are completely under our care, i.e., homeless and motherless. It becomes obvious with all those who are visited by their mothers and go home periodically to visit their families. Every one of our mothers, except those who are completely indifferent and neglectful, will fondle the child, usually far beyond the infant's momentary desire; she will handle him, far beyond the necessities of bodily care. Most of our children share a bed with their mothers—some with the whole family—on their visits home and have done so before they came to us. When they return to the Nursery, for instance, after a Christmas holiday of two or three days and nights, sleeping alone is felt as a great hardship and deprivation. Some mothers certainly treat the child's body with possessiveness. They cannot leave it alone, kiss the child one minute, slap it the next, and continually interfere with the child's movements or his handling of his own body. The child is not supposed to put his finger into his mouth, or nose, or ears, to rub his eyes, to scratch himself, to masturbate, etc. But all the bodily stimulation which the mother interferes with on the one hand is given to the child on the other through this incessant handling by the mother herself. We may assume on the basis of much evidence that the child's feeling of oneness with the mother's body has a parallel in the mother's feeling that the child's body belongs to her.

To make our point quite clear. We are at the present moment not discussing whether this mother-child relationship is helpful or harmful to the infant, or what consequences these early experiences will have for later life. We merely show that these tendencies exist, that they find very full expression and satisfaction under home conditions, and that they are necessarily stunted and left largely unsatisfied in an institution. Nurses, however devoted and affectionate they may be, are taught to keep within the limits of objectivity. If they want to be successful as educators, they cannot work merely on the basis of motherly feelings, but rather must develop and exchange these for a more general interest in the whole process of development of the children under their care.

AUTOEROTIC HABITS IN A RESIDENTIAL INSTITUTION

In Report 12, we traced back the preponderance of autoerotic habits in the nursery to the effect of sudden separation from the mother. What is true for children after the shock of separation is certainly true for those who have been reared in an institution from babyhood. The infant's early desires, as described above, find their satisfaction partly on the mother, partly on his own body. When, as happens invariably in an institution, gratification derived from the substitute mother relationship falls far short of what the child would normally experience, autoerotic gratifications loom larger and fill the empty places in the child's instinctual life. With the small infants thumb sucking, rocking, and head knocking take first place; masturbation, apart from its earliest appearance in babyhood, assumes importance at a slightly later stage.

Thumb Sucking

We do not venture to say that sucking is really more prevalent in residential babies than in those who are brought up in families. Sucking for pleasure may be observed profusely under all conditions, though perhaps it is more striking to the observer where many babies are seen doing it in the same room and at the same time. A survey of sucking made at any one time in our baby rooms shows that no two babies suck alike and that there is any amount of variety according to (*a*) the date when sucking begins; (*b*) the finger or fingers used; (*c*) the stereotyped position or playful activity of the other fingers during sucking; (*d*) the position or activity of the whole body during sucking; (*e*) the frequency and intensity of sucking with the individual baby; (*f*) damage done to the skin of the sucked parts, etc.

But, if there is little difference between family and residential babies during the sucking period itself, there is a conspicuous difference in the date of its termination. Residential infants tend to prolong sucking as a method of comforting themselves through several years of childhood, whereas children under home conditions outgrow this autoerotic habit before the end of the second year.

Rocking

Some of our infants begin to rock automatically whenever they are left alone in a confined space (crib, pram, playpen), or when isolated for reasons of infectious disease. Toys are thrown out or disregarded at such times and the rhythmic movement of the body remains the sole occupation.

7. Freda, as a baby, lacked the usual interest in toys. From the age of 6 to 10 months her only pleasure was a rhythmic movement of her whole body. At 9 months, these movements were accompanied by all sorts of noises. At 10 months the movements of the body ceased and only the rhythmic movements of the mouth remained. There was no gradual development of sitting, crawling, and standing while the rhythmic movements were in action. But at 11 months, after they had disappeared altogether, she learned to sit up, to kneel, to stand up, and to walk round her cot all within a week.

8. Ivy, at 10 months, rocked so continually in her cot in the baby room that she was transferred to the junior toddlers' department long before the usual time, in the hope that greater freedom of movement and more varied occupation would lessen the need for autoerotic gratification. This worked at the time, but a year later automatic rocking combined with masturbation broke out in full force again at a time of prolonged illness with consequent restriction of movement.

9. Tom, between 6 and 8 months, rocked so continually in the baby room that he was transferred to the next age group when he was only 9 months old. His rocking ceased immediately and he became extremely skillful and energe-

tic in movement and muscular control. Rocking returned temporarily a year later at a time of illness with consequent restriction of movement.

About the age of 2 years, he lost contact with his mother who abruptly ceased her visits to him. He became extremely dissatisfied and developed three rather disturbing reactions: violent thumb sucking; overeating; and passionate temporary attachments to strangers and guest workers.

Head Knocking

Head knocking, according to our observations, appears about the age of 1 year, as a sign of frustration and impotent anger. At one period, when we had an especially persistent head-knocker in the junior toddlers' room, it spread through imitation in a group of ten infants. Head knocking is usually accompanied by crying. In some instances one might be led to believe that the child cries as a result of the pain inflicted on himself by knocking or banging his head. But closer observation shows that it is rather the other way round. The child first cries as an outlet for his anger or frustration and then follows up this expression with the more violent one of head knocking.

10. Whenever Sidney (13 months) was thwarted in any way, he threw himself on his stomach, knocked his head violently and repeatedly on the floor, and cried.

11. Bert, at 14 months, knocked his head against the top bar of his cot whenever he was cross. At 15 months, during a period of illness and recovery, he did it constantly in a ferocious way, so that the nurse who took care of him was in constant worry lest he might do himself more serious damage.

12. Bert (13 months) knocked his head accidentally against the leg of a table while crawling round the room. He stopped in surprise, looked at the table leg, and tried to knock his head again, at first very gently, and then harder and harder with great concentration.

At 16 months he restarted head knocking on the second day of an illness (pneumonia), but stopped the habit again after a week.

13. Babette (12 to 16 months)

At 12 months: On the first days when she was put on the floor for crawling, she often let her head drop forward and bang on the floor. This was at that time regarded as a sign of tiredness.

Several days later, she banged her head repeatedly until she got red marks. She was stopped, but it was very difficult to distract her attention.

She banged her head in the bathwater, seemed surprised that it did not feel like the floor, and did not repeat it.

Several days later, she banged her head so incessantly on the floor that she had to be kept off the floor.

At 14 months: She knocked her head violently when she was isolated in the empty sickroom.

At 15 months: When put into her bed for a nap against her wishes, she threw herself against the cot bars and banged her whole body as well as her head repeatedly.

When other children took her toys or attacked her, she always banged her head in despair. Sometimes she would compete with another child for the possession of a toy and then suddenly stop and bang her head instead.

When she showed affection to Bert (17 months) she repeatedly and gently knocked her head against his.

At 16 months: She threw herself on the floor and

banged her head over and over again when not allowed to take another child's toy.

In the garden she threw herself on the grass when thwarted, bent her head toward the earth, but did not touch the grass. A fortnight later, she began on one occasion to bang her head on the grass, but stopped after the first knock, and with head bent, walked on all fours to another place where no grass was growing and there banged her head twice on the ground.

14. Jack (16 months) did not acquire the habit of head knocking, in spite of the example given by several children in his group. But once, when he discovered his own reflected image in a glass door, he first looked behind the door as if to find his double and then, smilingly, bumped heads with his reflection. He did it eight times, with evident pleasure.

15. Rose

At 21 months: She would sometimes kneel down quickly and bang her head violently on the floor without apparent reason.

At 23 months: When told not to do something, she turned round, banged her head quickly three times on a small table, and then returned peacefully.

When forbidden to pull another child's hair, she threw herself on the floor and banged her head violently four to six times.

When asked to return another child's toy, she obeyed reluctantly but without crying; then she turned round as if looking for something, grasped a small chair with both hands, and knocked her head three times violently against it. That done, she peacefully pushed the chair back to its right place and returned with a cheerful face.

Masturbation

We have so far not observed any increase in baby masturbation under our nursery conditions. Where the second phase of masturbation, 2½ to 5 years, is concerned, our observations are still very incomplete. But, apart from certain cases of problem children with excessive and compulsive masturbation, this autoerotic form of the child's expression seems to keep more within ordinary limits than the more infantile habits of rocking and head knocking. The reasons for this difference may be various and require further elucidation.

Summary

Thumb sucking, rocking, and masturbation betray their function as autoerotic gratifications unmistakably; head knocking differs from them in important respects. In the case of the former activities, the child's body becomes the object of his search for pleasurable sensations. In the case of head knocking, the child enacts on his own body his own aggressive and destructive tendencies. He really hurts himself, but, instead of minding, he enjoys or disregards the hurt. Head knocking shares a number of important characteristics with the autoerotic pleasures: both absorb the child's whole interest while they last; both are repetitive; and both have a tendency to increase and intensify while they are enacted; both may at times work themselves up toward a climax.

It is rare for the infantile habits of rocking and head knocking to reach such degrees under family conditions.

They are usually observed in rare individual cases; sometimes in abnormal children; and sometimes under conditions of neglect where children are denied all other outlets. But our rockers and head-knockers were normal, well-developed children in every other respect and certainly were given a reasonable amount of outlets. What is responsible for this increase of autoerotic and "autoaggressive" manifestations is evidently the fact of institutional life itself.

THE SMALL CHILD'S WISH TO BE APPRECIATED AND ADMIRED: INFANTILE EXHIBITIONISM

It is counted as a great educational achievement in the nursery school when young children learn to play with their toys or handle the educational apparatus for its interest and without claiming continual attention, appreciation or praise from a grownup. Many modern educational toys are so constructed that success or failure are either excluded altogether (for instance, in some of the apparatus for learning to distinguish between sounds, colors, textures, weights, etc.) or are demonstrated unmistakably by the material itself (for instance, insets, puzzles, geometric forms). The child in this way is prompted to test his own efforts and to find his own satisfaction in objective achievement.

These educational devices are directed against a powerful natural tendency in the young child, which is firmly rooted in his instinctual and emotional life. The young child, in this primitive stage of his development, likes nothing better than to "show off" and, in his intimate life with his parents, gives free rein to this wish, sometimes greatly to the disturbance of other equally important interests. Mothers always complain that their children will not "play by themselves," that they demand attention in spite of having toys, that they interrupt their play with exclamations like, "Look what I'm doing!" "Look what I've done!" or that, when several children are in competition with each other, their "Look at me!" becomes a sort of battle cry. It sometimes seems as if this insistent claim for admiration outweighs by far the child's interest in the occupation itself.

This tendency to show off or, to call it by other names, to boast, to exhibit, expresses itself in the realm of the child's occupations or achievements, but it neither originates in nor restricts itself to this part of the child's life. In the evening, at the time of undressing and bathing, many small children will get into a high mood as soon as they are naked; they will dance about and play all sorts of tricks with great pleasure and complete abandon. This is all the more apparent, the more they are restricted in this respect during daytime. But children not only enjoy showing their naked bodies; they equally enjoy showing off their dresses, new shoes, a hair ribbon; they show their bigness, their cleverness, their being good; at other times naughtiness, illness, bodily hurts may become the subject of their demonstrations. There is, in short, nothing in the child's life which may not at times be used to claim admiration or at least attention.

Every small boy, at some time in his life, proudly exhibits his genitals in front of his mother. Since this is quickly recognized as forbidden, it first vanishes and then reappears, disguised as a demand for help, for attention to a pain or hurt, etc.

This primitive exhibitionism of the child is met and countered by an equally primitive tendency in the mother, which on its side is firmly rooted in the so-called "mother instinct," which includes the tendency to overestimate the child. To the average mother the child's features and body seem beautiful or at least good-looking, though the child may look plain to an objective observer. The child's advances in bodily development and his achievements in muscular control, though ordinary steps in normal development, are in the parents' eyes surprising accomplishments. Ordinary intellectual progress is magnified and taken as a sign of future brilliance; small talents are praised out of all proportion.

This overestimation of the child, which is the hallmark of the mother-child relationship, is, on the part of the mother, a narcissistic reaction. The child has begun life as part of her body; so far as her feelings are concerned, he remains just that in the first years of his life. He is therefore judged and treated, not objectively as part of the outer world, but with the tolerance and subjective overvaluation which we all extend to our own reactions. Mothers react and judge equally subjectively where the child fails to come up to their expectations: with a deep narcissistic hurt, as if they had discovered a defect or suffered disfigurement on their own bodies.

Because of this state of affairs, the child, under ordinary family conditions, finds in the mother a more or less willing partner for his display of bodily and mental accomplishments, and derives a great deal of satisfaction from this important side of his attachment to the mother. But this happy partnership between child and mother is not destined to last. As the child grows older, the mother's attitude changes, often very abruptly, the child's exhibitionistic advances are rebuffed, and nagging and criticism often take the place of the former admiration, which is then shown to a younger member of the family. Consequently the child himself turns against his own wish to show off, represses it or turns it into the opposite. Overshyness, diffidence, clumsiness, and all sorts of inhibitions may then take the place of former freedom and abandon. However this may be, this early phase of exhibitionistic development leaves its mark in one way or the other for all later life.

It is easy to see that ordinary institutional life offers little scope for the display and satisfaction of these tendencies. The children, as described above, live a community life, not singled out for partnership with one particular grown-up. This does not mean that these children do not try to show off, boast, and exhibit, as all children do. But, through lack of response, through dissatisfaction and frustration, their infantile exhibitionism takes a different course. Instead of becoming the carrier of attachment to one person, it displays itself indiscriminately in front of every stranger; it may turn toward the playmates; or, when the child cannot enforce attention through positive achievements, he may concentrate on achieving the same end with dissocial behavior, illness, and temper tantrums.

Whenever a child forms one of the substitute-mother relationships which we have described, his exhibitionistic tendencies attach themselves firmly to the newly found loved person. Showing off may then become overwhelming in its force and make use of every possible opportunity to express itself.

Indiscriminate Exhibition

16. Visitors to all residential war nurseries, ours not excepted, will notice that single children often run up to them and, in spite of their being complete strangers, show

off their shoes, their dresses or other articles of clothing. This behavior is only shown by children who are emotionally starved and unattached.

17. Paul (2 years) came to us as a completely homeless and unattached child. At first he would claim everybody's attention with his only word "hello" and an empty smile with which he greeted friends and strangers alike. At the age of 3, he would still show off to everybody minute objects (buttons, little sticks, tiny pieces of material) which he picked up wherever he went. He was not really interested in these objects, they only served to engage the object's attention.

18. Bob, another homeless child, who had never lived with his own mother, went through a period of intense exhibitionism and masturbation at the age of 3. He displayed his genitals indiscriminately in front of everybody.

Exhibition with Articles of Clothing

19. Rose (17½ months) got hold of the coat of one of the small babies. She wrapped it round her neck like a scarf. When the nurse who saw her said: "How pretty!" she walked round the room with it and looked very pleased. From then onward, she would wrap around her neck whatever clothes or nappies she could get hold of (even wet nappies, if they were within her reach). She would always look at the nurses questioningly and wait for admiration.

When she was 18½ months old, she received a new silk dress for a special occasion. As soon as she was dressed in it, she lifted the skirt and walked about like that. When an apron was put on top of it, she alternately lifted the apron and the dress.

She kept the habit of lifting her dress after this occasion. Very often she looked at her naval when she had lifted her skirt. It was never quite clear whether she wanted the nurses to admire her dress or to look at her navel.

20. Freda (2 years) upon entering the playroom in the morning would run to whatever nurse was present and say: "Frock, pretty, pretty," holding up her skirt and striving hard to get attention, although she wore the same dress which she had shown off many times before.

21. Whenever Edith (2 years) had a new ribbon in her hair, she would walk about self-consciously fingering it. She showed it to her favorite nurse by pointing to it whenever she met her.

22. Whenever Ivy (2 years) had a certain red and white dress on (which suited her well and had obviously been admired by the grownups), she would keep on lifting up the skirt and saying: "Pretty, pretty." She would behave in similar ways with many articles of dress, or toys, or flowers, but never so markedly as with this particular dress.

23. Teddy (2¼ years) had a special passion for hats. When he could get hold of his blue beret, he would parade for a long time in it, trying it at various angles and always coming to his favorite nurse for admiration.

Exhibitionism within the Substitute-Mother Relationship

24. Bessie (2¼ years) behaved similarly toward her favorite nurse. While she was playing apparently contentedly with her and a group of other children, she sometimes stopped her play suddenly, lifted her dress, and said to the nurse: "Look, me got tummy." At least once daily she

came to the nurse, cuddled up against her, and said in an excited voice: "Look, my shoe, shoe," pointing at her feet, or holding one foot up for inspection. This happened especially when the nurse was busy talking or playing with other children. The display of part of her body was used quite naively to attract attention to herself.

25. Bridget, between the age of 2 and 3, showed off in every conceivable way with shoes, dresses, a new belt, with everything she could do, and with all the real or imaginary presents which she claimed her mother had bought for her. About the age of 2 years, 11 months she especially showed off with hurts. Whenever she met the Superintendent of her nursery, she ran to her and showed a place on her arm or leg, saying: "Look at my hurt." As a rule there was nothing to be seen; sometimes there were remnants of former small scratches.

26. Beryl (3 to 5 years) for nearly 2 years expressed a special attachment to one of the organizers of the nursery by "showing off" to her. She would follow her about on her weekly visits to the Country House, hold on to her hand, and give various other signs of affection. But she never asked for anything material, never asked for sweets or presents; she only claimed appreciation and admiration for her belongings. She usually began with a stereotyped sentence: "Come and see my Sunday frock." She would then lead the organizer along to her closet or drawer, would feverishly pull out her things and display them. The articles she showed were always the same, but this did not in the least detract from her desire to show them or her excitement in doing so. At other times she did not mention her clothes, and minute hurts, usually on the tip of a finger, were displayed instead.

27. Bob, at 4½ years, when he had attached himself passionately to his family mother, used every opportunity to show her that he was a "big boy" or a "big man." When, for instance, he went downstairs with her, he often stopped before the last three or four steps and said: "Now you watch me how I can jump." When warned that the distance was still too great for him, he said: "You don't know what I can do," insisted on jumping, and hurt himself regularly. This did not prevent him from enacting the same scene on the next occasion.

Showing off to Playmates

28. Bob (4 years) was playing with part of the Montessori apparatus all by himself. Shirley (4½ years), at the other end of the room, was looking at the toys displayed on the shelf. Seeing a box in which colored beads were sorted, she said: "Alf did this one day, because he was a big boy, didn't he?" Bob heard this, ran to Shirley, and asked her in a very excited way: "What did Alf do when he was a big boy?" Shirley pointed at the box containing the beads. Bob took the box, saying: "Me big boy too," but he did not begin to play with them. He changed his mind after a minute, put them back on the shelf, and resumed his former work. It was clear that he was not interested in the beads; it was only the desire to be admired by Shirley which had lured him away from his occupation.

29. Between the ages of 3 and 3½ Martin lived out a fantasy of being a "big man." He tried to impress his family mother, as well as his own mother who visited him daily. He insisted on wearing high boots and sometimes

refused to take them off when he went to bed. He showed off to everybody in a big cowboy hat in which he appeared even at the breakfast table. He showed his strength by pushing and carrying objects far too heavy for him. Added to this was the display of a loud, deep voice, quite unsuited to his childish appearance. Anyone who was not impressed by these displays was told all day long: "Me big man."

He found it impossible to give up being big, even where it was quite unsuitable. One day he was overheard in a conversation with Bob (4½ years). Bob said: "When I was small, I was in a pram." Martin torn between the desire to copy Bob and to remain "big," answered: "When I was small, I was a big soldier—and I was in a pram."

Transition from Infantile Exhibitionism to Shyness

30. Anne, at 6½ years, demonstrated clearly how the primitive showing off of young children becomes involved and complicated at a later stage. She was especially graceful in her movements and had for this reason been accepted as a pupil in a dancing class. She liked to display to the nurses what new steps she had learned in her weekly lesson. But as soon as the people whom she had collected for this purpose were ready to watch her, she would hide her face, keep everybody waiting, and say that she really could not do it. When told that there was no need to, and when everybody had turned their attention elsewhere, she immediately began to dance, but sometimes stopped herself again after the first steps with the same excuse.

This wavering between evident shyness and even more evident exhibitionism is of course well known, even in adult life. In Anne's case it still served the purpose of drawing even more attention to herself.

INFANTILE CURIOSITY

It is of equal interest to follow another, closely allied, instinctual tendency of the child's: his curiosity.

One of the benefits modern education has derived from analytic child psychology is a new attitude toward infantile curiosity. Whereas in former times parents and teachers used to frown on the child's attempts to know, to find out, to investigate, and to explore, these activities are now understood to be valuable and legitimate activities in every normal childhood. Under the conditions of orthodox teaching methods children were forced to acquire knowledge in which they had no interest; therefore they remained uncooperative, except when put under pressure. The modern teaching methods of the nursery and infant schools, on the other hand, make a point of being guided by the child's own innate curiosity. The modern nursery school provides toys which take the fact of childish curiosity into account. By playing with them, the child can find out what things are made of, how they fit together, what is inside them, how they can be taken apart and put together again, etc. The modern elementary school (see Hill, 1937) succeeds in finding methods which turn all necessary knowledge, including such complicated matters as history and geography, botany and zoology, chemistry, etc., from formal subjects into food for the insatiable curiosity of the young child. Nursery and elementary schools of this kind can therefore be certain of the full and willing cooperation of their children. It is in this respect not a case of the child having to adapt his wishes to those of the grownup world; these new successes in teaching are due to the adult world having for once adapted its methods to the nature of the child.

The position is less happy where cruder, i.e., less sublimated forms of the child's curiosity are concerned. As previously described with regard to infantile exhibitionism, these instinctual tendencies neither restrict themselves to nor originate in the realm of play and occupation. They reach out indiscriminately toward the whole surrounding world and express themselves no less insistently on all the materials and objects which are in no way meant for the child's use. The infant who is given a Russian doll, or ball, or barrel, is interested to open up and open up until he arrives at the smallest specimen of the series, which is hidden in the deepest inside. But the same urge which prompts the child to accept this toy contentedly may prompt him to open up and take to pieces whatever he can get hold of: a woman's handbag left in an unguarded place, the contents of a sewing basket, or an expensive china doll; older children get to work on alarm clocks, wireless sets or sewing machines with their countless interesting pieces. Such activities are unwelcome and prohibited because they are destructive. In the same manner much of the child's spirit of adventure and discovery is severely restricted by the grownups because it is of potential danger to the child's life.

Childish curiosity is still more disturbing and unwelcome on its earlier level where, as sexual curiosity, it is directed straight toward the body and the intimacies of the parents. The young child gives every evidence of wanting to know everything: how father and mother look when they are naked, or in their bath, or in the lavatory, what they do together when they are in bed; what being married means; where children come from; how they are made; what the differences are between boys and girls.

Modern-minded and enlightened parents who try to satisfy the child's sexual curiosity with bits of information are surprised and distressed at the relentlessness with which the child presses forward from question to question until the answers demanded are far beyond what they had meant to give. When the child is simply refused answers, he will spare no trouble to make his own discoveries. Where questioning into these intimate matters is strictly forbidden, the child's natural curiosity will become either dulled or blunted altogether, including those applications of it which are welcome, or curiosity will displace itself with full force onto harmless matters and produce the well-known compulsive and incessant stream of apparently senseless questioning which has always driven parents to despair.

Where parents, without strict restrictions, just fail to provide satisfying answers, the circumstances of the family setting in themselves will supply endless satisfaction for the child's curiosity. The child will closely observe father and mother in their reactions toward each other; the expressions on their faces, odd bits of conversation, noises heard at night, will serve as the ingredients with the help of which the child builds up his fantasies about the intimacies of the parents. Children can be helped or hindered in the fulfillment of their wishes "to know," but under family conditions they can never be prevented altogether from getting some satisfaction of these desires.

It is recognized that the most "knowing" children are those of the poorest classes where restricted quarters, beds or bedrooms shared, leave no intimacy of the parents undiscovered. Where children have the freedom of the street, their range of discovery and exploring is enormously widened. On higher social levels the children's lives are kept more apart from that of the parents; there is no running around in the streets, and all the conventions and decencies which have to be observed oppose the child's curiosity with full force. In rich families the observation of servants and their intimate lives often takes the place of the observation of the parents in providing knowledge.

Childish Curiosity Under Institutional Conditions

This digression into the various forms in which childish curiosity expresses itself under family conditions is necessary if we want to understand the position in which the child finds himself in a residential home. What is, under residential conditions, the fate of sublimated curiosity which is directed toward toys and learning? What is the fate of the child's pleasures in adventure and discovery? What are the possibilities of satisfying sexual curiosity?

CURIOSITY DIRECTED TOWARD TOYS AND LEARNING

For the average family child the factor of whether he can be admitted to a nursery school or not will determine whether his "curiosity" can be directed into useful channels, for the untaught mother of the poorer classes will probably be unable to procure the proper toys and be helpless in directing the child's activities. Residential nurseries on the other hand, if they understand the need, have excellent opportunities to offer their children nursery school life, toys, and activities. Some of the most thoughtful nursery experts have found that the ordinary residential war nursery, though often handicapped in becoming a real home for the children, can always contain a good nursery school and thus at least satisfy one important desire of the child. It is true that in this respect the residential home does not offer more than every good day nursery school does, but it should at least make a special point of not offering less.

THE CHILD'S PLEASURE IN ADVENTURE AND DISCOVERY

Superintendents of evacuated war nurseries have repeatedly described how young children who have never been outside of London before their evacuation enjoyed the discovery of a completely new country world with all the unaccustomed pleasures provided by plant and animal life. These exceptional circumstances should not lead us to ignore that the institutional child, even though given some outlets for his spirit of adventure which it may have lacked at home, is on the whole segregated, shut off, and excluded from most of the realities of life. He lives in an artificial world, namely, a community where infants are in the majority and where all the activities of the day are centered around the children. He cannot in this way fail to get a distorted picture of life. He cannot acquire knowledge of the various jobs and trades, except those which deal with children; he acquires little idea of money, since he is not taken shopping or sent on errands; he has little conception where the necessities of life come from, since things are handed out when necessary. The children never see the buying or hear the plans for it discussed. There is in many nurseries little opportunity to be alone, or without supervision, or to wander freely, even within the confines of the house. All this works toward establishing ignorance of the world and acts directly against the spirit of adventure.

CURIOSITY DIRECTED TOWARD SEX AND FAMILY MATTERS

There is no other instinctual urge of the child's for which, in institutional life, conditions are further removed from the normal.

The child has ample oportunity to collect knowledge concerning the difference between boys and girls, i.e., to observe the naked bodies of his playmates. Residential nurseries are, with hardly any exceptions, coeducational, and few attempts are made to separate the sexes for purposes of sleeping, undressing, and bathing. The routine of toilet training in many nurseries is so arranged that at least the infants are taken to the lavatory at specified times and in groups. Shame about bodily functions develops later than usual under these conditions. Whatever may be the matter with the body of one child (circumcision, slight malformations, graver deformities) becomes common knowledge. This does not mean that the infants necessarily form correct ideas of either anatomy or the differences between the sexes. Objective observation conflicts with the results of fantasy and imagination. Young children hold their own theories concerning the use of the various parts of the body and the difference between the sexes and its origin. When what they think and what they see does not coincide, their fantasy usually proves stronger than reality.

According to our observations, infants first notice the difference between boys and girls between the ages of 1½ to 2 years. In two cases little girls gave obvious signs of distress when they noticed a boy's genitals at that age. Children often react to these first observations in a negative way: instead of remarking on the difference in the genitals which they have noticed, they stress the fact that some other parts of their bodies are alike. A special interest in each other's navels and breasts is shown by many of our children between the ages of 1½ and 2 years.

31. Babette (15½ months) and Christopher (17 months) were potted next to each other. Several times Babette lifted Chris's vest and touched his tummy. Chris pushed her away angrily each time and pulled down his vest, until she gave up.

A week later, she and Rex (13 months) were both naked on the changing table at bathing time. Babette noticed Rex's breasts. She pointed to them repeatedly and said something in her baby language. She kept looking at the nurse questioningly, "talking" all the time.

A day later, she and Rex were again bathed at the same time. She discovered her own navel and again looked at the nurse and at it alternately for a long time, "talking" with great intensity. For a second she looked searchingly at Rex, but he was already wrapped in his towel and she did not touch him. A second later she had lost interest.

32. Rose discovered her navel at the age of 18 months. She lifted her dress many times a day, pointed at her navel, or touched it. This never happened when she was in her cot or playpen, only when she was running about the room.

33. Rose (19 months) watched Donald (2 months) in his bath. She looked at him with a very serious expression, then lifted her frock and looked at her navel. A moment later she put her hands between her legs, which she had never done at any other time.

34. Annette (22 months) stood next to Sam's cot one

evening when Sam (18 months) was being undressed. She kept her eyes fixed on him during the undressing, bathing, and drying, and walked away only when his nappies were on again. From this day on, she always interrupted her play as soon as she realized that it was his turn to be bathed. She watched the proceedings and several times tried to handle him. He was at this time the only boy in Annette's room.

35. Jessie, at approximately 2 years, began to show great interest in her body, especially her tummy, patting it, showing herself sometimes, pulling up her frock during playtime with a delighted "Look, me tummy!" This was followed by a period when she compared her own body with her sister's, her mother's and the nurse's. Conversation during dressing or bathing often ran as follows: "Me got tummy. Mummy tummy? Bessie tummy? Ilsa tummy?" "Mummy nose, Jessie nose?" "Bessie ears, Ilsa ears, Jessie ears?" This again was followed by a phase when she tried to lift her mother's and other adults' skirt to look for their knickers.

36. Jim (2½ years) examined his body while being undressed, and looked at his navel: "Look, big hole here, very big hole." When looking at his chest: "Me got bubble here, more bubble." He was delighted, then went about the room, asking the other children, "You hole? You bubble?" Then to the nurse: "You bubble? You hole?" He laughed a great deal while doing this and was very excited.

37. Dick (3 years, 8 months), while looking at his chest, suddenly said to the nurse: "Me got two buttons there, you open it?" He then looked at all the other children's "buttons" in the dressing room, tried to touch and pull them, then returned to the nurse and said sensibly: "The buttons not open, what are they for?"

38. Bob (4 years, 3 months) climbed into his bath while the nurse was outside the room, and covered his genitals with his flannel. When she returned, he shouted: "You can't see my tooti now, it's all gone." When asked why, he said: "If you can't see it, perhaps you think I'm Jane."

39. Bobby (7 years) watched the only baby in the Country House with great interest for a while, then turned round and asked: "And who took out all her teeth?" Her toothless gums had evidently impressed him very unfavorably.

This was only one of many remarks made by our older children, which showed that they believed that a girl's body had been damaged in some way.

Such constant opportunity for watching other children stands in sharp contrast with the manner in which institutional infants are cut off from the intimacies of adult life. It depends on chance, i.e., on the location of the staff quarters, how complete their ignorance remains in this respect. Conditions in our two residential nurseries, for instance, are quite different from each other. In the Country House the children pay frequent visits to the nearby staff rooms and often share meals with their nurses in the kitchen. In Netherhall Gardens the staff bedrooms are remote from the children and the babies and small toddlers never see a grownup sleep and hardly ever at a proper meal. With the bigger toddlers special arrangements were made to have members of the staff share their meals, or they would certainly have formed the idea that adults never eat.

The following are some observations from the room of the young toddlers, 14 to 24 months.

40. Every now and then the nurse would change her overall in the room. Whenever she started to undo the buttons, the bigger children came and pointed at the overall. As soon as her dress became visible, the whole group of children gathered around her. They looked at her in amazement, some shouted, some were perfectly silent. As soon as the next overall was safely buttoned over the dress, they went away again.

41. The children suddenly discovered that the nurse had hairpins which could be pulled out. One day they pulled out so many that her hair came undone. While she did it up again, one child shouted: "Look, look!" The others looked at her with large surprised eyes and remained silent. They tried to get at the hairpins again as soon as she had finished.

42. While a nurse was in the garden with the children, something went wrong with her shoe and she took it off to have a look. Sam (22 months) stared at her stocking in bewildered amazement. She immediately put the shoe on again and he calmed down. He went away, saying: "All gone."

Lack of opportunity to watch and to observe such matters is only one element in a generally abnormal situation. Not only that these infants do not get familiar with all the processes of adults' dressing and undressing, getting up and going to bed; they hardly ever see the private property of adults and—except by accident—have no opportunity of investigating it; they hardly ever—except by accident—overhear private conversations. Since parents, if they appear together at all, only do so for short hours of the day, the infants can glean no details which pertain to married life. There is no way of penetrating into the secret where babies come from, since babies arrive in the nursery often enough without the older child ever having seen their mothers. There is certainly no possibility of collecting information about the role of the father, neither in his relationship toward the mother, nor in his usual role of protector and supporter of the family.

In the place of an emotionally charged, sometimes very stormy family atmosphere which stimulates the child's curiosity, the average institution confronts its inhabitants with a set routine. It is interesting to see how small children, in the absence of other food for their curiosity, try to penetrate and investigate the details of such a routine. The conceptions of "on duty" and "off duty," "off hours," the details of medical inspection, become invested with the emotional significance of leaving or homecoming of parents, or other family events. Staff meetings or lecture courses, the subjects of which remain mysterious to the children, are regarded by them with jealous suspiciousness as children regard whatever activities of the parents go on behind closed doors. Inquiring into the relations of members of the staff to each other assumes the importance of prying into the relations between father and mother.

We are used to seeing children build the picture of their world after the pattern of the intimacies of family life which they have been so eager to uncover; it is somehow with grave misgiving that we see them do the same with the set and artificial routine of institutional existence.

43. As in every nursery, the toilet accessories of our children are marked with pictures instead of with names. The objects of these pictures assume great importance for them. When Nick (3¼ years) saw the moon for the first time, he said: "Look, it's little David's moon." For

Nick, the symbol on David's toothbrush and comb did not signify a picture of the real thing; the moon in the sky seemed to him a picture of what was of such importance in the nursery.

44. Susan, at the age of 4, first saw the moon one morning from the nursery window. She asked: "Has she been up there all night?" When the nurse said yes, Susan said with great understanding: "I see, night duty."

45. Susan, in particular, concentrated the greatest amount of attention on all the details of rotation of duties. She could be relied upon at any moment of the day to know where anybody in the big concern was busy, who had gone downstairs with a tray for the kitchen or upstairs on some other errand, which nurse had had her hours off and who was still expecting them, or whose day off it was. She not only was interested in it, she followed it all with a most critical eye so as to detect any possible flaw in these, to her, highly important arrangements.

46. Betty (4 years) was an extremely sensitive child who entered the Nursery in a state of great upset. She had lost her father through death, had been separated from her mother, and vaguely knew about the mother's possible remarriage. She counted the days between her weekly visits home and lapsed into a bad state when all her calculations were thrown out by a sudden illness of her mother. Her inability to solve the riddles of separation, reunion, death, and remarriage became manifest in a compulsive preoccupation with "on" and "off times." She would ask every nurse, and even visitors: "What is your name? Where do you live? Where do you sleep? Are you off on Sunday? Are you off on Saturday? I am off on Sunday!"

47. Susan, who was ill in the sickroom, was visited by the Superintendent of her nursery department and asked

her for a drink. But before the latter had time to do anything, she added, with a triumphant look on her face and in aggressive tones: "In this room you have nothing to decide, you must ask Sister for everything."

48. The following conversation between Bertie (5¼ years) and Ray (5 years) was overheard. Bertie: "You know, Alice is the head of the whole house!" Ray: "Yes, but John is the head of the boiler and greenhouse."

49. A group of children had been moved from Netherhall Gardens to emergency quarters in a staff hostel during the measles infection. When their return to the main nursery was discussed, Anne said: "I don't want to go back to Netherhall. I want to stay in the house where my Ruth [her family mother] lives." When told that after all she could see Ruth more often in the nursery where the latter worked all day, Anne answered: "It isn't where she works that matters, it's where she sleeps."

50. Katrina (8 years) saw the doctor before the student's anatomy lecture with a big book under her arm. She wanted to open the book, found the picture of a cross-section of a human body, and seemed to look at it with interest and understanding. But before the doctor actually went into the staff room, she asked her: "And whom are you going to cut open today?" In her imaginings about the goings-on in the closed staff room, she had turned the theoretical lecture into a horrible operation with one of the students as the doctor's victim.

SUMMARY

Early instinctual wishes have to be taken seriously, not because their fulfillment or refusal causes momentary happiness or unhappiness, but because they are the moving powers which urge the child's development from primitive self-interest and self-indulgence toward an attachment and consequently toward adaptation to the adult world.

To sum up once more:

> *The infant who shares his bodily pleasures* with his mother learns in this way to love an object in the outer world and not merely himself.
>
> Lack of such gratification with consequent increase of *autoerotic activities* diminishes the child's interest in his surroundings; with excessive thumb sucking, rocking, or masturbation the child creates a comforting world of his own into which he may withdraw and thus become unreachable for outside influence.
>
> The child's *abilities*, gifts, and talents develop at least partly in the services of the *wish to be admired*. Appreciation which the child receives may, as shown above, lead to further efforts in the same direction. Rebuff and indifference may have the opposite effect.
>
> *Infantile curiosity*, if at least partially satisfied, drives the child toward imitation of the grownup world and thus puts vast energies at the disposal of the wish to learn and to develop. Refusal of all knowledge or of the opportunity to acquire it may spread to the child's intellectual interests and set up inhibitions of all kinds.

The normal and healthy growth of the human personality depends on the circumstances of the child's first attachments and on the fate of the instinctual forces (sex, aggression, and their derivatives), which find expression in these early and all-important relationships.

CHAPTER 5

The Role of the Father in the Residential Nursery

It is taken for granted by all who are familiar with the conditions of residential nursery life that there is hardly a place for the father in the residential child's real world. Fathers, of course, do appear as visitors, either on occasional Sundays or on leave from the Forces. But whereas visiting mothers behave naturally enough in the nursery, deal with their children in a variety of ways, examine their bodies, cut or curl their hair, rearrange their clothes, bathe, and put them to bed occasionally and, according to their nature, either overwhelm them with sweets or use the short time together for criticism and nagging, fathers are usually inactive, shy, and awkward. They feel uncomfortable in this world of women and children, are at a loss in the face of overtures made to them by their children's playmates, and many of them are obviously glad when visiting time is over. There is nothing in their attitude which might remind the child—even remotely—of the position they would hold under normal family conditions: they are neither the providers of material goods nor the last court of appeal in all matters which concern the child. Although lately some residential nurseries have made attempts to reserve at least some "mothers' rights" for visiting mothers, there are to our knowledge hardly any residential homes which create similar opportunities for fathers.

In this book as well as in the Monthly Reports we have repeatedly shown what serious consequences the separation from the mother has for the child's development. But even though the mother herself is lacking from the residential child's daily life, her functions are taken over by other "motherly" people. The child who is not cared for, handled, fed, bathed, petted, and played with by his own mother is thus handled and taken care of by others whom he learns to accept as mother substitutes. But there is no one who, to the child's knowledge, takes over the functions which his own father, owing to absence, illness or death, cannot fulfill. Impersonal and invisible powers, i.e., the organization, the committee, the governors, a board, provide the material means for the child's upbringing and, by their decisions, determine the child's fate. These powers are beyond the range of the infant's comprehension and play no part in his actual life. There is thus no father substitute who can fill the place which is left empty by the child's own father.

We may well wonder why this conspicuous fact has not attracted more attention or created more concern regarding the normality of the child's upbringing. Where it is a question of older children, especially boys, one often hears the opinion expressed that it is hardly possible for mothers to handle and restrain them without a father's help; with adolescents of both sexes juvenile courts frequently quote in their summing up of a case of delinquency the absence of the father as the determining factor in the child's dissocial development. It is a matter of common knowledge that one cause of the delinquency of adolescents and preadolescents in war and postwar periods is the incompleteness of the family setting owing to the father's absence in the Forces.

But where infants are concerned, the need for the mother and the mother's importance for the child's wellbeing and physical and moral development looms infinitely larger. The evacuated infants, for instance, cried above all for their mothers. Retrograde steps in development (for instance, bed wetting), emotional upheavals, loss of functions and abilities (for instance, of speech) were invariably ascribed to separation from the mother, not the father. Mothers who visit without the father are always welcome; fathers who visit unexpectedly often (perhaps owing to a mother's illness) are frequently rejected and are unable to bring comfort to the child. When an infant in a residential nursery is confronted by sudden danger (painful medical treatment, inoculation, vaccination), he always calls out for his absent mother. We have never under these circumstances heard a child demand the presence of his father, though in air raids they will sometimes cry out for their fathers. These and similar facts are apt to create the impression that the presence of the father is of minor importance in the infant's life.

Even if this should be true so far as superficial appearance is concerned (detailed observation of a young child may reveal a very different picture), it is certainly not true in any deeper sense. The infant's emotional relationship to his father begins later in life than that to his mother, but certainly from the second year onward it is an integral part of his emotional life and a necessary ingredient in the complex forces which work toward the formation of his character and personality.

As described above, the infant's relationship to his mother begins in connection with the satisfaction given to his first needs for nourishment, warmth, and comfort. From this primitive starting point develops the child's love for the mother. The infant normally remains demanding toward his mother, though his wishes change from desire for material comfort to desire for love, affection, admiration, knowledge, exclusive possession, and all the various gratifications which arise during the successive phases of the infant's instinctual development. The child's love for the mother remains undisturbed whenever she is able to grant satisfaction.

When, owing either to circumstances or to her consideration for the child's socialization, she is forced to refuse satisfaction, the child feels anger against her which, due to the frantic violence of infantile feeling, quickly rises to rage, hate, and death wishes. Normally, the infant after the first two years should be able to tolerate restrictions to a certain degree without violent outbursts: in his further development he has to learn to renounce pleasures willingly for the sake of the mother. This interchange of mother's love for instinctual restriction then becomes the basis of conscience and character formation.

The infant's relationship to his father progresses on somewhat different lines. While the acceptance of satisfaction is the main ingredient of the first tie to the mother, the earliest emotions directed toward the father are bound up with feelings of admiration for his superior strength and power. The father in his turn becomes the giver of material advantages and is gradually recognized as the power behind the mother around whom normal family life is centered. But he remains a less familiar figure, removed from the immediacy of the infant's violent reactions by his intermittent presence and absence—a figure that by his "bigness" calls forth in the child the wish to imitate him, to become like him or, in the infant's imagination, to possess his miraculous qualities and exercise them at least in fantasy.

There are two points where disturbances cannot fail to enter into this otherwise satisfying relationship. It is the father's role, even more so than the mother's, to impersonate for the growing infant the restrictive demands inherent in the code of every civilized society. To become a social member of the human community the child has to curb and to transform his sexual and aggressive wishes. What the mother does in this respect in minute-to-minute and day-to-day criticizing, praising, and guiding the father normally reinforces by his very presence. Although he himself is in the eyes of the child the embodiment of every sexual and aggressive power, his influence at the same time acts strongly in the direction of repression and transformation of instinctual wishes. As in the case of denial from the mother, the child's secret anger and rage are raised against the father by his attitude.

The second disturbing element is of at least equal intensity. The father of the normal family, who is the object of the child's love, is at the same time the rival in, at least the boy's, fight for the sole attention and possession of the mother. Although father and infant may be the best friends at certain moments, at others they are certainly enemies and competitors where the mother is concerned. The child bitterly resents his own inferior strength and helplessness in the unequal struggle. This constellation causes hostility and secret revolt against the father, but simultaneously reinforces the young child's wish to imitate and to identify with him and thus to acquire the power to win and possess the mother.

The boy's progress toward adaptation to the adult world thus leads through stormy phases of his emotional relationship to the father figure. The possibilities of abnormal development (dissocial, neurotic, perverted) are various: admiration for the father's strength may develop into fantastic fears of the fate the boy might suffer at his hands if he remains either too aggressive or too self-indulgent (masturbation fears) or too insistent in his wishes toward the mother. Anxieties of this kind may lead to complete giving up of all such desires with consequent passivity, loss of capability, phobias, and inhibitions in all directions. Early and complete revolt against the father, on the other hand, which is not kept in bounds and neutralized by the normal loving side of the relationship, may lead to an estrangement from or break with all the moral demands of which the father was the representative, and thus to the commonest form of dissocial and delinquent development.

Girls, naturally, are spared the conflict of feeling which arises out of the rivalry with the father. They go through a similar phase of admiring love for him which, with them, reaches its climax in the wish to be like the mother and supersede her in the father's affection. The longings and disappointments which arise from this eternally unfulfilled wish fill the child's fantasies, direct her imaginative play, and determine her later self-assurance or lack of confidence in being loved.

Far from being of minor importance, the father, where he is present, is thus one of the main determining influences in the child's life. It is worth investigating what happens in those cases where the father is absent and where no substitute figure exercises a similar influence.

RELATIONSHIP TO DEAD FATHERS

For our resident children it seemed comparatively easy on leaving home to accept the separation from their fathers, and even their fathers' leaving England for services overseas. In striking contrast to this comparative indifference was their complete inability to accept the fact of the father's death where this occurred. All our orphaned children talk about their dead fathers as if they were alive or, when they have grasped the fact of death, try to deny it in the form of fantasies about rebirth or return from heaven. In some cases this happens under the direct influence of mothers who hide the truth from the child to spare him pain; in other cases fantasies of an identical nature are the child's spontaneous production.

1. Susan (4½ years), who lost her father in the raids, said: "My father is deaded, he has gone far away to Scotland; he will come back, much later when I am quite big."

"My father is in the army now. Mummy says he isn't dead anymore. The army is far away."

"My daddy is in the navy now, he cannot come back, there is too much water."

"My daddy is coming next Sunday. Yes, yes, he is coming Sunday. You will see, he will bring me the biggest piece of chocolate you have ever seen."

2. Bertie (5½ years), whose father was killed in the raids, said:

"Why can't all killed daddies come back and be little babies and come to the mummies again?"

"God can make my daddies alive, can't he? Why cannot God put people together again if they have been killed and send them down from heaven? I know why: because He hasn't got the things together, all the stuff. After the war God will have everything again. We have to wait until after the war, then God can put people together again." [1]

3. Peter (4 years) whose father was killed in the raids:

"My daddy is killed, yes, my sister said so. He cannot come. I want him to come. My daddy is big, he can do everything."

"I have seen my daddy in the street. He has a nice uniform. Yes, yes, it was him; mummy says he will come back."

"My daddy is taking me to the Zoo today. He told me last night; he comes every night and sits on my bed and talks to me."

Visits from these dead fathers are, if anything, mentioned more often than the visits of ordinary living fathers, and the insistence on their coming is all the greater. The

[1] For further details of Bertie's development in this respect, see Report 21.

changing fantasies about their activities and the presents which they are going to bring are inevitable defenses against the inner feeling of loss and deprivation.

RELATIONSHIP TO AN ABSENT FATHER

Julia is the example of a child who never lost or changed her longing for her living father during the whole time of her separation from him. For two years, from 3½ to 5½, she was constantly homesick for him and talked about him in the most admiring tones and in almost abnormal terms of endearment. She called him "a lovely boy" and described his cleverness, his bigness, in glowing terms in all her bedtime talks. When after two years she visited her family, her feelings broke out with such violence that she overrode her parents' objections and induced them to allow her to stay at home in spite of difficult circumstances. Her father was a small tradesman, elderly, morose, rather strict and uncompromising with his large family of unruly children. In her case the purely positive, loving, and admiring element in the father relationship was particularly outstanding.

We have shown in earlier reports how this difference between the real aspect of a father and the father image in the child's fantasy was present in the case of Tony, where in fact it dominated the whole picture. As described in Reports 22 and 36, Tony's real closeness to his father ended at the age of 18 months, with the outbreak of the war and the father's enlistment in the army. From then onward it was restricted to quarterly leaves and still later to rare visits home; while Tony was with us, to two to three times yearly for one or two days. Moreover, this father did little to keep up the connection in his absence, i.e., not more than a very occasional postcard or present. Still, during visits the father was affectionate and friendly with the child, especially after the mother's death, and showed interest in his pleasures. But in spite of sympathy with the boy, he understood little of the complexity of the child's feelings, introduced one young woman to him on one leave as his prospective stepmother and then, on his next leave, appeared newly married with another young woman and greeted the child with a demand to "kiss your new mummy."

Out of the meager, and in many ways disappointing reality, Tony fashioned the fantasy of a father to whom he formed the most passionate, loving, and admiring relationship. When he was about 4 years old, his father was seldom absent from his thoughts. All his interests centered around him and he mentioned his name continuously in every conversation. When he picked blackberries, flowers, leaves, he wanted to keep them all safe for his father. When a child fell down and cried, he would say (referring to an accident of his father's): "My daddy did not cry when he fell out of the army lorry, did he?" When he saw a child run, he would say automatically: "My daddy can run much faster." When he disliked having his hair washed, he asked: "Does my daddy cry when his hair is washed?" When bathed he would say: "My daddy can dive in the water." He would eat greens though he disliked them, so as to "get strong like my daddy." The big toe was for him "the daddy toe"; every army lorry on the road meant for him the lorry of his father's army unit. Whatever deeds of omnipotence the other children ascribed to God, Tony ascribed to his father.

We also reported that this overintense loving relationship to the father was at the time intermixed with hostile reactions, complaints of the father hurting him, and insistence that Tony did not like him anymore. Although we are well acquainted with all children's ambivalent relations to their parents, there is reason to assume that in Tony's case this was increased by his mother's death. So far as the father was left as the sole parent after this tragic event, he was overvalued; so far as he was also an object of jealousy as the mother's possessor, he was blamed for her death, which his alleged power had not prevented and which in the child's fantasy his male aggression might have brought about.

HISTORY OF A FANTASY FATHER

Another father whose image was constantly alive in his son's mind was Bob's (from 2 years, 8 months to 4 years, 10 months).[2] According to Bob, his father's feet were bigger than anyone else's; he could run "faster than the puffer trains" and "fly like a bird." He "owned a big big car with lots of wheels on it." He had "golden hair and lovely pink eyes" (when another child praised her mother's blue eyes); he had "much longer plaits" than Betty who had the longest in the Nursery. Although Bob's admiration for his father was to all appearances identical with Tony's, there was one striking difference between the circumstances of the two boys where their fathers were concerned. Whereas Tony's father was, though idealized, a real and living person, Bob's father was nonexistent and thus purely a product of the child's imagination.

Bob was born illegitimately and had never known his

[2] The observations about Bob have been carried out and collected by Dr. Ilse Hellman.

father. His mother had boarded him out soon after birth and up to his entry into our Nursery he had lived in various homes and seen his mother rarely. From then onward she visited him regularly and he grew very loving toward her. Simultaneously he chose a substitute mother in the Nursery and attached himself passionately to her.

He first mentioned his "daddy" at 2 years and 8 months, when he cried for him in moments of despair. This was taken to refer to the elderly foster father of his last billet. These foster parents visited Bob twice and on both occasions he sat on the man's lap and cried when he left. This "father" was not referred to again after the first 2 months. Bob's full interest turned toward his mother, who at this period worked in the neighborhood of the Nursery and visited him daily.

The next mention of a father occurred at 3 and 2 months when he announced: "My mummy and daddy are coming on Sunday," and related that he had been on walks with both of them. This was believed to refer to a possible man friend of the mother's and was disbelieved only when his fantasy developed. He told everybody that his daddy had visited him in the Nursery, which was certainly not true, and had brought him a toy car, which was in fact the possession of another child. Bob began to be very sensitive whenever he felt himself disbelieved. He asserted over and over again that his daddy was real and he would sometimes stop in the middle of a game and shout: "Yes, I do have a daddy!" though no one had at the time disputed it.

For at least 3 months he gave no further information about his father, merely reasserting repeatedly that he existed. At 3 years, 5 months his father image took on a new and definite shape. Bob at this point went through a naughty and destructive phase and found it extremely difficult to stand denials, to curb his greed, and to overcome his excessive and exhibitionistic masturbation. For the sake of his substitute mother he tried to cope with all these difficulties, but failed over and over again, and had many outbreaks of temper and despair. His father image at this time combined forces with Bob's forbidden wishes. Whenever he did wrong, he explained: "My daddy told me to," or "My daddy likes it." One of the incidents consisted of Bob's inciting other children to throw all their best soft toys into the garden lavatory. He was extremely upset about it afterward and admitted: "I did it. But my daddy told me to."

When he was 3½ an incident brought unexpected and welcome confirmation for his fantasy. His mother brought a man to visit in the nursery, and introduced him to Bob as an uncle. Bob made the widest use of this opportunity. He insisted on calling the man daddy, held his hand, sat on his lap, and generally behaved toward this stranger as if he had found an old and long-lost friend. The man had to sit on Bob's bed in the evening until he fell asleep. He never reappeared, but Bob continued to use him as an important piece of evidence to strengthen the claim for his father's existence: "Yes, and I do have a daddy for real. You remember, he had a mackintosh and came to Wedderburn Road and he sat on my bed."

At 3 years, 10 months Bob invented a new figure, modeled after a 9-year-old boy whom his mother knew and referred to as "big Bobby." "Big Bobby" quickly developed into an "ideal Bob," who could do everything and possessed everything that Bob wished for himself, for instance, a car and a bicycle, Bob at this time made a stand against his own fears and passivity. He began to boast, wanted to pull and push things far beyond his strength, and always jumped down more steps than he could manage successfully. "Big Bobby" accordingly could jump high, "right up into the sky." Bob at this time made definite efforts "to be good." Big Bobby was accordingly "always good and when he was naughty the other day, he fell over afterward and broke his leg all to bits." In sharp contrast to the role of his earlier fantasy father, Big Bobby did not side with Bob's forbidden wishes. Bob would say, crying: "Big Bobby does not like it when me naughty."

At the age of 4 his father fantasy once more gave evidence of violently aggressive images within him. Talking about his "family," he explained: "I have got a new daddy. The uncle killed my daddy and my new daddy came and killed my uncle." His father, he declared at this time, was dead. He had "fallen out of an airplane. He was a bomb and he fell down and he went all to pieces." This was at a time when Bob began to use swearwords and, instead of being affectionate toward his substitute mother, talked to her in an aggressive way.

A short time later the father fantasy and the fantasy of Big Bobby finally fused together. The development of Bob's conscience, made under the influence of his substitute mother, was reflected in the fact that his father afterward never did anything that could be considered wrong. He became altogether strong, big, and beautiful and, in the course of the next months (4½), took over the function of setting right whatever seemed to Bob wrong with the world. When Bob saw a house which had been destroyed by bombs, he said: "My daddy has lots of bombs which don't break houses." When watching the canary's cage being cleaned of the droppings, he said: "My daddy does not like his birds to do big job all the time; he puts calcium in their water." When the Nursery canary died, he said: "My daddy has lots of dicky birds which never die."

The fantasy image of Bob's father followed and reflected in this manner the course of the boy's development: from careless destructivenes to a horror of destruction—"harmless bombs"; from putting toys into the lavatory to an objection to even birds doing "big job"; and from fantasies about killing to the wish for a world where nobody has to die. When Bob was 3 years old, his "father" was simply the image of a person whom he could love and admire, and show off proudly to other people. At 3½ years Bob used his father image to represent his own instinctual wishes; at 4 years his father, very much like Tony's father, became the embodiment of everything that was big, beautiful, strong, and good. At 4½ the fantasy father definitely took over the role of the boy's conscience which had developed in the meantime.

CHAPTER 6

The Growth of the Child's Personality under Nursery Conditions

IMITATION IN THE NURSERY

Imitation of Adults

With the young child emotional attachment to a grownup invariably results in developing resemblances to that person. Infants who live with their parents copy them almost automatically in countless ways: they reproduce their facial expressions and their gestures, they naturally use the same words, develop the same tastes, and are decisively influenced by whatever fads or abnormalities may be present in the parents: they copy their abilities and occupations whenever possible. So long as the parents are the only emotionally significant people in the child's world, imitation is restricted to the family circle. When the growing child learns to love, fear, and admire people outside the family, the urge to copy reaches out toward these figures. The daily behavior and the imaginative play of children gives ample evidence of the existence of these tendencies.

1. Whereas nearly all our children take great pleasure in their meals, Anne (5-6), whose mother worked in the house and who usually shared her meals, developed any number of food fads in imitation of her. If her mother did not eat vegetables, she would leave them on her plate untasted; if her mother disliked potatoes, Anne, who loved them at other times, would refuse to eat them, etc.

The residential child without parents, who has made attachments in the Nursery, does the same with the people and the behavior patterns in which his feelings have become involved. Rose, for instance, at 18 months, said, "Oh dear, oh dear" as her favorite words and would screw up her face and nod her head in a certain way. Both peculiarities belong to the nurse who had had sole charge of this delicate child from the age of 2½ months.

Many children of all ages copy the habits of their "family mothers" with regard to handling other children or their dolls. They use the same expressions for purposes of praise or criticism; they imitate the routine activities of washing, scrubbing tables, putting away clothes; they use the same means to comfort a smaller child or to solve disputes. The result of such imitation is at times surprising and seems incongruous in its high degree of professional efficiency. An aggressive and unruly boy of 3½, for instance, who desires to sit on a certain chair, will not tear it away from his occupant, but grasp a footstool which he silently offers in exchange. He imitates a method which he has seen in use innumerable times. Boys will act as sick nurse to others or comfort crying children, not because they have feminine leanings and prefer such activities to the exclusion of more manly ones but because the sick nurse or the night nurse is their chosen "family mother."

2. Claude (4¼) refused to go to bed one evening and demanded to be on shelter duty with his family mother. She agreed and took his wish quite seriously. He copied all her actions, and did whatever a nurse on evening duty in the shelter dormitory has to perform. He tidied slippers, brought pots, and comforted crying children. While the nurse sat with one of a pair of twins (2 years) who cried, he sat on the stepladder and comforted the other twin with exactly the same words and attitudes for at least 10 minutes.

Such imitation, of course, includes behavior which is not used in direct contact with the children but which the children, following the curiosity about grownup life, pick up with special interest and pleasure. They are, in fact, part of the child's imaginative play of being "grownup" himself.

3. When several children were playing in a bedroom, Harold (3¾) had placed two chairs beside the radiator and sat on one with his feet on the other. When somebody came into the room, he explained: "I'm off, I'm in the staff room, reading."

4. Susan (4½) had left her teddy bear and all its clothes

strewn all over the floor. When asked to clear away, she answered: "I'm sorry. I'm off."

The children naturally imitate what they consider the grownups' ways of enjoying themselves. Here the, to them, mysterious meetings play the greatest part. Copying the staff meetings, head of department meetings, students' meetings, etc., the bigger children have begun children's meetings from which all the smaller ones are rigidly excluded.

5. When Anne (5¾) was unable to fall asleep one evening, she called the night nurse to her shelter bed. When the nurse had climbed the stepladder to see what she wanted, Anne settled herself comfortably on her pillow and said quite seriously: "And now, let us have a little meeting."

These latter forms of copying may seem funny in the telling, but they are certainly not meant to be funny by the child.

Imitation of Contrasting Behavior Patterns

Children who are attached to their own visiting mother, on the one hand, and to their "family mother" in the Nursery, on the other, often have considerable difficulties in combining, not only their affections, but the imitations which result from them. Their mothers' methods of dealing with them are in some cases diametrically opposed to the means used in the Nursery. When this happens children will sometimes develop both types of behavior which they use alternately.

6. Susan (4 years) for instance wavered between her attachment to a very severe real mother and a friendly and understanding "family mother" in the Nursery. Consequently she wavered in the treatment of her doll. After the mother's visit she would treat the doll very strictly, nag and scold it, and punish it for invented misdeeds. When two or three days had passed by without her seeing her mother, Susan would revert to the methods of the Nursery, speak nicely to the doll, encourage and comfort it, until the same cycle began again with the mother's next visit. In a similar manner her speech and the expressions she used would alternate between what she had heard in the Nursery and the abrupt, half-menacing tones of her mother.

Other Models for Imitation in the Nursery

Apart from the "family mothers" the doctor is the most imitated person in the Nursery. This too leads to a pattern of behavior which seems completely out of place at this early stage. To an outsider the children's attitude in this respect might suggest unusual precocity or abnormal hypochondriacal leanings. But the explanation lies simply in the emotional relationship to the doctor, which is a mixture of the affection felt for her as a person; the admiration for her medical tools; the belief in her power over all matters of health and sickness; and fear of the pain which she has to inflict when preventive measures like injections or small surgical actions become necessary. Imitation of the doctor may express itself in "doctor play" or in the children's behavior, i.e., display of medical knowledge in daily life.

7. Bridget (2 years, 3 months) saw a dog eat something

off the street. She stopped and called across the road: "Not eat it, doggie! Get diahee."

8. Martin (3 years) visited an aunt who gave medicine to her baby. When an hour later the baby was given a piece of cake, Martin shouted excitedly: "Not baby cake, baby diarrhea, got medicine."

9. Janet (4 years), like all the other children, is familiar with the doctor's stethoscope. When she saw the doctor go upstairs with it, she asked: "Somebody coughing up there?"

10. Anne (6 years) said excitedly: "You must take Paul's temperature. He never screams, but he is screaming terribly now, so he must be ill."

Summary

In all the instances quoted the processes of imitation which are at work in the child are the usual ones. The children copy and take over the modes of behavior which they can watch in their loved grownups in the Nursery, just as they would copy their parents and their modes of behavior if they lived at home. If the results of such imitation are unusual or abnormal at times, this is merely due to the unusual and abnormal circumstances under which residential infants are living.

FAMILY BEHAVIOR PATTERNS IN THE NURSERY

Apart from the types of behavior described above, which are directly traceable to nursery influence, our resident children develop, surprisingly enough, attitudes which in normal life are traced back to stimulation by example from the parents.

Infants, between 15 and 24 months, play with each other either in affectionate or in crudely bodily ways which, if it happened in the family, would be taken as evidence of their having witnessed affectionate or sexual behavior between their parents (see ch. 2). They do so, even though they have never had the normal opportunities of watching their parents or sharing a bedroom with adult people.[1]

Boys, between 3 and 5 years, develop the various masculine attributes which are commonly thought to be due to imitation of a father figure. Where their relationship to their "family mothers" in the Nursery is concerned, they change at that age from passive dependence and demandingness to manly and protective attitudes. They make offers of marriage, just as boys of that age do to their mothers.

11. Bob Smith (3 years, 11 months) kissed his family mother good night, saying: "Good night, Ilsa Smith." Or they offer marriage in the name of their fathers. Tony (4½ years), shortly after his mother's death said to his favorite nurse: "Couldn't you be my mummy? Would it not be nice if you would be my mummy and my daddy, my daddy?"

They begin to look down on mere females.

12. Bob (4½ years) asked a young nurse why she was a girl. When she explained that the difference between boys and girls was a natural thing and that people were born that way, he looked at her full of pity, took her face between his hands, and kissed her.

[1] See also *Writings*, Vol. IV, ch. 7.

Instead of demanding protection, they offer comfort. When Tony (4½ years) heard that his favorite nurse had no father and mother, he turned to her and said protectively: "But I am something for you, aren't I?"

This change of attitude happens spontaneously, as a step of development. It may be accompanied, as in the case of Bob and Tony, by fantasies concerning a father; but it is in itself not directly due to a father's influence. Many of these boys have never met their fathers, have never lived in intimate contact with a man, or have been separated from their fathers in their earliest babyhood.

Girls, from approximately 2 years onward, develop marked motherly attributes in relation to their playmates, to younger children, and to dolls, even though they may not have experienced a mother's care from early babyhood, nor have had the occasion to watch their mothers with a younger baby. In their case, of course, it is more difficult to separate the pattern of behavior offered by their real mothers from that shown by the nurses.

Imaginative play in the residential nursery is thus not as different from imaginative play in the day nursery or in the family as one might expect. The children stage all the usual family games with changing distribution of roles ("You be daddy," "You be mummy," "You be baby") and compete, as usual, for the role of father.

As shown in the examples of the last chapter dealing with the role of the father, the children make the widest use of every detail of real family life which they can get hold of. Whenever they visit their parents or receive visits, their reactions in imitative behavior and imaginative play are so strong that one is often led to believe that the most exciting incidents must have happened during those visits.

In reality, the most insignificant occurrences or actions on the part of their parents are sufficient to give powerful stimulation to tendencies which lie ready within them. The emotions of the family setting and the patterns of behavior which belong to them are latent in the children and become manifest on every possible occasion. (See Tony's father stirring the cornflakes; Bob and the man with the mackintosh.)

Children who have no parents participate in the experiences of playmates. The minority of our children who go home on visits bring back impressions of family life to the Nursery which are quickly taken up and used by those who lack similar opportunities. One child with a living or visiting father can thus spread the conception of the father figure with consequent play and behavior through a whole group of fatherless infants.

Whenever infants leave their families to enter a nursery, they have to go through a long and painful period of adaptation. There is nothing in their psychological makeup to prepare them for community life. Whenever, on the other hand, children return to their families or are admitted into new families, they reassume or acquire the emotions and the behavior appropriate to family relationships in an extremely short time.

DEVELOPMENT THROUGH IDENTIFICATION: CHARACTER FORMATION

Every serious type of education tries to produce a state of mind in the child in which he adapts to the standards of the adult world, not because he is continually urged to do so, but because they have become his own.

Infants, for instance, can be trained to become clean in a number of ways: through establishing automatic reflex actions, holding out after meals, etc.; through fear of punishment for "accidents"; or through consistent praise for good results on the pot or lavatory. But no child will remain reliably clean for any length of time, and through changing outward circumstances, until he has made the wish for cleanliness his own and feels the same dislike, or even disgust, for dirty habits which rule the grownup world round him.

Children may be induced to share their sweets with others. In one of our nursery groups they regularly offer the Superintendent a percentage of whatever sweets they receive as presents with the words "for your children"; the Superintendent's "children" are of course their own friends and playmates, but the expression shows that the gift is made out of consideration for their common "mother." This does not mean that they have acquired generosity or dealt with their selfishness or their greed. They are not "altruistic" or "generous" in the real sense of the word until the moment when they themselves, without any pressure put upon them, cannot bear the disappointment or the longing glances of other childen without sharing with them. In dealing with aggressive tendencies, education works toward the point when hurting another ceases to be pleasurable and the opposite feeling, pity, is aroused instead.

In dealing with the infantile sexual impulses, most parents will not rest content until the child exchanges his own naive enjoyment in their gratification for whatever evaluation or condemnation of them are prevalent in his immediate surroundings.

Such a complete change of heart is effected only in slow stages. In the beginning of life the child is ruled merely by his own desires. He next learns to renounce gratifications for the sake of the parents. Derrick (3½ years), said about his family mother: "If Sara loves me, she can't love me wet." In the next phase he begins to share the parents' valuations. Bridget (2 years, 3 months), when placed on the lavatory after an accident during the last stage of her toilet training, said with sudden relief: "No more weewee on the floor. Mummy does not like it, Jean [her family mother] does not like it, Bridget does not like it."

The educational task is completed in each particular respect when the child stands firm in his newly acquired attitudes, without further need to invoke the images of the people for whose sake this reversal of all inner values has been undertaken. He has then established within himself a moral center—conscience, superego—which contains the values, commands, and prohibitions which were originally introduced into his life by the parents, and which now regulate his further actions more or less independently from within. The firmness and strength, in some cases the inexorability, of these new moral powers in the child depend largely on the strength and depth, and the general fate, of the attachments which give rise to them.

It is at this point that the institutional child is at his gravest disadvantage. An infant in a residential nursery may acquire the rough and ready methods of social adaptation which are induced by the atmosphere of the toddler's room; methods of attack and defense, of giving in and sharing, "swapping," etc.; he may further acquire conventions and behavior patterns in obedience to the nursery routine and in imitation of his elders. But neither of these processes, though adding to the growth of the child's personality, will lead to the embodiment of moral values which is described above. Identification of this latter kind takes place under one condition only: as the result and residue of emotional attachment to people who are the real and living personifications of the demands which every civilized society upholds for the restriction and transformation of primitive instinctual tendencies. Where love objects of this kind are missing, the infant is deprived of an all-important opportunity to identity himself with these demands.

Our parentless nursery children, as shown above, do their utmost to invent their own father and mother figures and live in close emotional contact with them in their imagination. But these products of their fantasy, necessary as they are to the child's emotional needs, do not exercise the same parental functions. They are called into life by the infant's longing for the missing love object, and as such satisfy his wishes. They are the personification of inner forces, moving in the child, and as such give evidence of successive stages of development. But they are reflections of the child's conscience, where this is being formed under another person's influence, not the originators of this conscience, as real parents are.

The logical people to play this role in the residential child's life are the adults of the nursery. Success or failure of education in the residential nursery will therefore depend on the strength of the child's attachments to them. If these relationships are deep and lasting, the residential child will take the usual course of development, form a normal superego, and become an independent moral and social being. If the grownups of the nursery remain remote and impersonal figures, or if, as happens in some nurseries, they change so often that no permanent attachment is effected at all, institutional education will fail in this important respect. The children, through the force of inner circumstances, will then show defects in their character development, their adaptation to society may remain on a superficial level, and their future be exposed to the danger of all kinds of dissocial development.

CHAPTER 7

Conclusions

The continuance or discontinuance of residential nurseries after the war will probably be decided by social and economic needs and not on the basis of psychological requirements. In spite of this it may be helpful to have the psychological circumstances of a residential nursery outlined in one's mind. There are realms in the infant's life where the residential nursery can be helpful by creating, very much on the lines of the nursery school, excellent conditions for development, as health, hygiene, development of skills, early social responses. There are, as described above, other realms, where it is important for residential nurseries to recognize their limitations, as in emotional life, character development; they will then face, and more effectively fight, the consequences of such limitations.

Readers who are familiar with the concepts of psychoanalytic psychology will realize the special interest which has driven the authors to begin this investigation. Psychoanalysis has, from its beginnings, drawn attention to the overwhelming importance of the first five years of life. During this period primitive instinctual forces are openly at work in the child (infantile sexuality with its ramifications and derivatives; primitive aggression). In the first attachments to the parents, the so-called oedipus complex, the child brings these forces into play, and through identification with the parents' wishes, superego formation turns against them and defeats its own former aims. Infantile instinctual life thus becomes for the greater part repressed and unconscious, i.e., forgotten. Its manifestations vanish from the surface and the growing child begins a new life on the basis of its repressions and defenses.

Since we are used to seeing these developments happen under the influence of the oedipus complex, i.e., the relationship to the parental figures, it is of great interest to us to investigate what happens when the whole family constellation is completely absent; how the child reacts to the lack of emotional response; how he substitutes for it by fantasy activity; and how the inner forces which control, transform, or repress the instincts will contrive to work under these circumstances.

Residential upbringing, where it is inevitable, offers opportunities for detailed and unbroken observation of child development. If these opportunities were made use of widely, much valuable material about the emotional and educational response at these early ages might be collected and applied to the upbringing of other children who are lucky enough to live under more normal circumstances.

Bibliography

AICHHORN, A. (1925), *Wayward Youth*. New York: Viking Press, 1935.

BENNETT, I. & HELLMAN, I. (1951), Psychoanalytic Material Related to Observations in Early Development. *The Psychoanalytic Study of the Child*, 6:307-324.

BURLINGHAM, D. (1952), *Twins: A Study of Three Pairs of Identical Twins*. New York: International Universities Press.

―――― & BARRON, A. T. (1963), A Study of Identical Twins: Their Analytic Material Compared with Existing Observation Data of Their Early Childhood. *The Psychoanalytic Study of the Child*, 18:367-423.

DAVIS, C. M. (1928), Self-Selection of Diet by Newly Weaned Infants: An Experimental Study. *Amer. J. Dis. Child*, 36:651-679.

FREUD, ANNA (1946a), The Psychoanalytic Study of Infantile Feeding Disturbances. *The Writings of Anna Freud*, 2:39-59.

―――― (1946b), Problèmes d'adaption posés par l'éducation des enfants qui ont souffert de la guerre. *Psyché* (Paris), 1:181-188.

―――― (1947), The Establishment of Feeding Habits. *The Writings of Anna Freud*, 4:442-457.

―――― (1951), Observations on Child Development. *The Writings of Anna Freud*, 4:143-162.

——— (1956), Psychoanalytic Knowledge Applied to the Rearing of Children. *The Writings of Anna Freud,* 5:265-280.

HELLMAN, I. (1962), Hampstead Nursery Follow-up Studies: I. Sudden Separation. *The Psychoanalytic Study of the Child,* 17:159-174.

HILL, J. C. (1937), *The New Approach: 1. An Introduction to Geography. 2. An Introduction to Science. 3. An Introduction to History.* London: Oxford University Press.

KENNEDY, H. E. (1950), Cover Memories in Formation. *The Psychoanalytic Study of the Child,* 5:275-284.

Index

Abreaction, 318
Accident, 135-136
Adaptation, social, 479
Admissions, applications for, 12-14, 28, 81, 104-107, 117-119, 217-218, 223-224, 375-383; reasons for, 5-7, 68-71
Adolescence, 637
Adult
  forming special attachment to children, 597-598
  see also Air raid, Staff
Aggression, 275, 475, 518, 634, 664
  among children, 221, 312, 359, 564-569, 572, 584-585; see also Children, fighting
  of children, 23, 161-163, 187
  directed against self, 611-612
  and education, 161-163, 477, 659
  inhibition of, 166, 169, 203
  restriction of, 576-580
  and submission, 355-365
  transformation, 477-479, 639
  see also Behavior
Agoraphobia, 170
Aichhorn, A., 543, 665
Air raid
  adult's reaction to, 25-26
  children's reaction to, 7-9, 11-12, 27-28, 160-163, 278-282, 330-335, 385-391, 403, 414-417, 469-472; see also Air raid anxiety, Anxiety attack
  children: talking about, 93, 330-335; not talking, 194-195
  effect on daily routine, 407-417
  incidence of, xx, xxiii, 24-25, 43, 69, 270-271, 276-277, 284-285, 295, 311-312, 326-327, 329, 336, 339-340, 346, 349, 352, 367-368, 374-375, 385, 393, 397, 406-407, 418-419, 437, 452-454, 458, 461-464, 466-468, 481-482, 495-496
  and increased applications, 375-376
  renewed, 311-323
  viewed as punishment, 279
  warnings, 270-271, 276-277, 416-417
Air raid anxiety, 7-9, 112, 280
  child's dependent on adult's, see Mother, anxious
  lack of, 27, 164-166
  persistence after evacuation, 425-428
  provoked by surroundings and undergoing changes, 390-391

Air raid anxiety—*Continued*
  types of, 163-172, 277
  see also Anxiety, Fear, Mother, Noise
Ambivalence, 365-366, 645
  of mother, 226-230, 232-233
American Foster parents, xvii, xx, xxiv-xxv, 14, 74, 122, 136, 151, 215-216, 218, 272-273, 305, 329, 338, 407, 505, 508, 531-532, 544, 646
Anal phase, 521; *see also* Toilet training
Animals, 287, 427, 445, 654-655
  death of, 357
Anxiety
  and aggression, 166
  and air raids, *see* Air raid anxiety
  ascribed to animal, 427
  changing content of, 98-99
  defenses against, 319-321
  and emotional relationship to adult, 321-322; *see also* Mother, anxious
  fantastic, 428
  and father relationship, 190
  lack of, in presence of unexploded bomb, 45-47
  neurotic, 319
  phase-specific, 169
  and physical illness, 261-262
  and toilet training, 490-491
  see also Fear
Anxiety attack (state), 12, 279-280, 390
  following air raid, 313-323, 333-335
Apathy, 39
Asthma, 33
Attachment
  changing constantly, 37-38, 82, 205, 560, 608
  dependent on physical care, xxi, 592
  leads to unselfishness, 244-245
  to mother, not dependent on her personal qualities, 178-179
  to nursery, 138-139
  to parents' gifts, 113-114, 140, 203
  to real and substitute mother, 222
  to sick nurse, 242-246
  to substitute mother, 220-221, 242-246, 297, 356-366, 438-451, 587-598, 603, 615; *see also* Jealousy
  see also Clothes, Toy
Autoerotic behavior, 202-203, 475, 552, 605-612, 634; *see also* Masturbation

Babies' Center, xxiv, 67, 79, 89-90, 119-121, 197, 534
Babies' Rest Center, *see* Babies' Center, Children's Rest Center
Baby Department, 94-98, 134, 248, 436
  effect of air raids on, 410-411
  illness in, 119-121
Barron, A. T., 540, 665
Bedtime difficulties, 243; *see also* Sleep
Bedtime ritual, 371-372
Bed wetting, 112, 201-202, 205, 220, 243-245, 280, 296, 368, 401, 449-450, 637
Behavior
  aggressive, 357, 401-405, 433
  antisocial, 475
  compulsive, 177
  expressing child's understanding of events, 198-199
  outlet in, 198-199
  phobic, 207
  return of infantile modes, 200-211; *see also* Regression
  stereotyped, 354-355
Behavior problems, 98, 194, 199, 353-366, 472-473
Bennett, I., 540, 666
Billets
  social problems, 173-174
  unsuccessful, 6, 19-20, 82, 85, 112-116, 146-147, 202, 205-207, 226, 231

INDEX 669

Billets—*Continued*
see also Evacuation, Foster parents
Birth fantasies, 334-335
Bladder and bowel control
attainment, see Toilet training
loss of, 401-402, 449, 554
Body, care of, xxi
Bomb, unexploded in nursery garden, 43-47, 63, 165
Boy
development of, 186-187, 636-637, 645-649, 656-657
relation to father, 636-637, 639-640; see also Tony
Breast feeding, 182, 248, 386, 514-515, 544-545, 555, 600; see also Mother, nursing
Bronchitis, 6, 14, 33-34, 70-71, 73, 109, 310
Burlingham, D., 464, 468, 540, 581, 666

Character development (formation), 274-275, 350, 483, 494, 544, 595-596, 602-603, 638, 658-662
Chicken pox, 311, 399, 452, 457, 461
Child, Children
acceptance of substitute objects, 183-185
affection and tenderness for each other, 583-585
afraid of being returned home, 456
aggression of, see Aggression
antisocial, 543
avoiding contact with other children, 355-358
bombed out, 5-6, 12, 144-145
bomb-shocked, 73-74, 127
comforting: adult, 657; other children, 331, 572-574, 652; self, 320-321
convinced of return of dead parents, 288-293, 641-643

copying staff meetings, 92-93, 653
craving for immediate substitute satisfaction, 440-441
differences in reaction to substitute mother and teacher, 591-592
early disappointments, 187-188
educational ideas of, affected by experience in nursery, 348-349
fatherless, 30-31, 61-66; see also Death, Father
feeding adults, 603-604
fights among, 221, 312; see also Toy
finding new baby at home, 373
first, 545
forgetting parent, 51, 190-191
free to select food, 523-525
friendship with other children, 362-366, 369, 581-583
generosity of, 428-429, 441-442, 451, 580, 602-603, 659
handling of difficult, 472-473
helpfulness of, 91-93, 433-434, 500-501, 574-575
home visits of, see Visiting
hospitalized, 6-7, 56-57, 249, 344
identical psychological situation of orphaned and evacuated, 52-53
indifferent to: feelings of others, 562-564; mother's visit, 228
lack of fear when confident in adults, 312-313; see also Mother, anxious
losing possessions, 300
love play among, 583-585
maintaining relationship to parents and staff, 214-215
neglected, 544
object relations of, see Attachment
reaction to changes in staff, 444-445
re-enacting parents' quarrels, 199
relationship to each other, xix; see also Child, treating

Child, Children—*Continued*
  sharing possessions, 363, 659
  showing off, 619-620
  transferring past feelings to present events, 318-319
  treasuring parent's presents, 113-114, 140, 203
  treating: others like lifeless object, 562-564; others as menace, 570-571; own possessions better than group-owned, 273
  undernourished, 70-71, 73, 153
  understanding of war events, 23, 157-160, 277-283, 416-417, 458
  see also Development, Infant, Mother relationship, Residential children
Child psychology, psychoanalytic, 537-538
Children's Rest Center, xxiii-xxiv, 3-5, 11-12, 24, 69, 168; *see also* Babies' Center
Christmas, 136
  home visit, 191-192
Clinging, 40, 82, 183, 242, 245, 355, 370, 443, 591
  compulsive, 38
  to memory, 51, 448
  to toy, 197
Clothes
  attachment to, 85-86
  exhibitionism with, 616-618
  fads connected with, 441
Clothes Report, 272-273
Compulsive mechanisms, 38, 177, 207
Conscience, 167-169, 363-364, 366, 638, 649, 660-662
Conscientious objectors, 256
Coughing, nervous, 33-34, 112, 261
Country House, xxiv, 55, 79-81, 99, 105, 107, 113, 120, 132-135, 156, 160, 224-225, 249-250, 256-260, 271, 284, 295-296, 300, 306, 310, 312, 324, 326-330, 332, 336-338, 340-341, 346-348, 351-352, 367-368, 374-375, 384-385, 392, 394, 396, 406, 414, 437, 443-445, 448, 451-453, 457, 461, 463, 465, 469, 472, 481-482, 495-496, 504, 512, 519, 527, 536, 539, 628-629
  admits Netherhall children, 417-435
  American pilot crashes nearby, 466-468
  bombing of, 276-277, 279-281, 284-285, 311
  opening of, 87-94
  parents' bus to, 111-112, 342-343
  quarantined, 121, 136, 139, 212-214, 228-229
  shoe repair shop, 344
  used for vacation of London children, 239-240, 247-248
  as whooping cough station, 261-262, 271, 273
  workshop, 285-286, 341
Coupe (gardener), 259, 431-432
Crime, 256
Criminal, 543
Croup, 120
Cruelty, of children, 287, 476; *see also* Aggression
Curiosity, 365, 475-476, 621, 652
  infantile, 621-634
  under institutional conditions, 624-634
  sexual, 357-362, 365, 622-623, 626-634, 656

Dann, G., 55
Dann, S., 55
Davis, C. M., 524-525, 665
Day care, 591-592
Daydream, 200
Day nursery, 350, 657
  and working mother, 253-254
Death
  acceptance of, 291-294
  and air raid anxiety, 171-172
  child's understanding of, 156-159, 286-287

INDEX

Death—*Continued*
  children's attitudes to, 286-294
  of father, 30-31, 52, 61-66, 70, 74, 84, 101-102, 156, 171-172, 195-197, 256, 288-294, 313, 318, 322, 332-335, 352, 354, 358, 364, 393, 434, 506, 636
  of mother, 240, 256-257, 297-298, 303, 368, 645
  natural, interpreted as violently inflicted, 292-293
  of parents, 52-53, 143-144, 211, 309, 540
  preoccupation with, 360, 365
  wishes, 188-189, 287-288, 638
Defense, 664
  against aggression, 570-571
  against anxiety, 319-321
  against loss, 643
Delinquency, 637, 640
Denial, 165-166, 320
  of death, 64-65, 100-102, 196-197
  of discomfort, 281
Depression, 192
Destruction, child's reaction to, 160-163
Development
  in absence of father, 636-638
  accelerated after introduction of family groups, 221-222; see also Attachment
  arrest, 397
  of boy, see Boy
  of concentration camp children, xix
  difference between boys and girls, 636-637
  failures, 544
  of girl, see Girl
  instinctual, 274-275
  of institutional and family children, compared, xviii, 350, 543-664
  intellectual, 366
  physical, 275
  regression in, 397-405
  retarded, 219-220

sexual, 365-366
  of social relationships, 366
  and stable mother relationship, 219-222
  transitional stages, 477
  see also Emotional development
Diphtheria, 213, 266
Disgust, 488-492, 659
Displacement, 492, 623
Doctor game, 654
Dream, 64-65; see also Nightmare

Eating, 520-522, 554-559
  conflict about, 199
  disturbances, 528-529, 555-557
  pleasure in, 564
  see also Feeding, Food
Eczema, 83-84, 109, 240
Education
  and aggression, 161-163, 477, 659
  and curiosity, 621-622
  and eating, 520-522
  and fear, 166-169
  and nursery routine, 274-275
  and object relations, 130-133, 222
  see also Upbringing
Ego regression, 398
Emotion, lack of, 205-206
Emotional development, xviii-xxi, 186-187, 546
  influenced by other children, 559-584
  and mother substitute, 594-595; see also Attachment
  regression in, 397-398
Envy, 564-568, 570
Epilepsy, 465
Evacuation, 6, 28, 49, 71-72
  and loss of bladder and sphincter control, 554; see also Bed wetting
  mother's reaction to, 145-147, 234-236, 253
  objections to, 53
  and preparation for, 208-211
  previous, 145-147
  reaction to, 172-174

Evacuation—*Continued*
  of unattended children, 176-179
  see also Billets, Country House, Separation
Exhibitionism, 475-476, 478, 612-620, 634
  indiscriminate, 615-616
  infantile, 612-615, 622
  and substitute mother, 617-619
  transformation, 620
Experiment by fate, xix

Family
  and child's curiosity, 623-624, 626-634
  creation of artificial, 219-222, 356, 586-598
  dissolution, xviii, 7, 472; *see also* Death; Mother, working
  wartime difficulties of, 393-395
  see also Development
Family romance, 174
Fantasy
  about absent: father, 304; mother, 355; parents, 66
  about air raid precautions, 331-332
  of being nurse, 562
  concerning father, 289-299, 657
  expressed in stories, 359-366
  infantile sexual theories, 626-627
  of lost family life, 51
  of nonexistent father, 645-649
  outlet in, 199-200
  of return of dead father, 641-643
  about substitute mother, 450
  of wish fulfillment, 447
  see also Birth fantasy
Father
  ambivalence to, 370-371
  child's preoccupation with absent, 301-302, 304-305
  fantasies about, *see* Fantasy
  hospitalized, 135, 300
  hostility against, 298-299
  identification with, 186
  memory of, 435
  mentally ill, 104-105
  real and fantasied, 643-644
  relationship to: 59-60, 182, 185, 187, 190, 245-246, 556, 638; absent, 643-645; dead, 641-643; development of, 638-639; fantasied, 643-649
  remarriage, 369-373, 594
  resentment of, 298
  rivalry with, 639-641
  role of, in residential nursery, 635-649
  separation from, 643-645
  visiting, 37, 297-298, 300, 302-304, 635, 637, 658
  see also Death
Fear
  of animals, 357, 365, 414
  at bedtime, 357
  of big man, 47
  of crying, 355
  of death, 281
  of father, 640
  of impulses, 166
  infantile, 167-169
  of injection, 267-269
  of instincts, 479
  of noise, 385-391, 426
  of other children, 577-578
  of punishment, 167-169
  and real danger, 164-166, 316-317
  for safety of parents, 428
  no shame about, 322-323
  of sirens, 387-389, 413-416
  see also Anxiety, Air raid anxiety, Noise
Feeding, 231, 482-483, 602
  common institutional practices, 516-518, 558
  difficulties (disturbances), 224, 248, 386, 518
  failures, 515
  method, in nursery, 512-518, 520-526
  modification of child's attitude to, 522-526
  schedules, 514-518
  see also Eating, Food

INDEX 673

Femininity, 366
Fire watch, 94, 271
Food
  basis of love for mother, 556
  craving for sweets, 440
  fads, 651
  methods of serving in institution, 516-518, 558
  as parent substitute, 203
  production, 258-260, 271-272, 277, 344-345
  rationing, 16-17, 29, 80, 136, 148-150, 153-154, 172, 296
  refusal, 137-138, 274, 490, 515-517, 555
  restrictions, 203
  self selection by child, 523-525
  served cafeteria style, 274, 423, 525-526
  specimen menu, 150
Food Reports, 16-18, 35, 48-49, 88, 107-108, 148-152, 296
Foster mother, 226, 250, 296, 587, 597
  problem of, 174-175
Frankl, L., 484
Freud, A., 125, 442, 529, 665-666

Games
  aggressive and sexual, 359
  "fairy dance," 362
  re-enacting getting lost, 354-355
  sexual, 365-366
  see also Doctor game, Play, War games
Garden Department, 421-422
Gilchrist, W., xxiv
Girl
  development of, 186-187, 636-637, 657-658
  relation to father, 640-641
God, 282-283, 290
Goldberger, A., 432, 449-451, 509-510
Greed, 203, 363, 478, 490, 555-556, 603
  restriction of, 522-523, 576-580

Grief, 198, 291
  in small child, 183-185
  see also Mourning, Separation
Guilt, 189
  following air raid warning, 416-417
  and separation, 189-190

Hampstead Nursery
  daily routine and air raids, 407-417
  description of setting and organization, xxiv-xxv, 67-71, 74-81, 90-94, 105-107, 239-240, 247-248, 407-417, 419-423
  educational attempts in, 479-480
  finances, xxiii-xxv, 9, 215-216, 218-219, 224, 240, 248, 295, 338
  hospital department, 77; see also Health Report
  household and maintenance departments, 421
  introduction of family groups, 219-222, 356, 586-598
  kitchen department, 89, 421-422, 537
  maintaining contact with parent, 72, 76, 78, 111, 211, 474-475
  not run on institutional lines, xxv
  planning for postwar resettlement, 306-309, 454-456, 459-460, 505-510, 530-532
  toddler department, 77-78; see also Toddler
  see also Baby Department, Country House, Netherhall Gardens, Residential Nursery, Training scheme, Wedderburn Road
Handicraft teaching, 285-286
Head banging (knocking), 397, 412, 606, 608-612
Health
  safeguarding physical and psychological, 71-72, 76-77, 127-131
Health Reports, 14-16, 33-35, 39, 42-43, 56-58, 132-136, 152-156, 212-213, 218, 225, 240,

Health Reports—*Continued*
  248-250, 260-264, 273, 277, 285, 296, 310-311, 324-325, 327-328, 330, 337, 339-340, 342, 344, 346, 349, 351, 367, 374, 384, 392, 396, 406, 418, 436, 452, 457, 461, 463, 466, 472, 481, 496-504, 512, 519, 528
Hellman, I., 84, 138, 313-316, 333-335, 353, 399-404, 482-494, 540, 645, 665-666
Herzberg, M., 5
Hill, J. C., 621, 666
Hitler, A., 63, 168, 281-283, 332, 416, 428
Homesickness, 177-178, 189, 204, 643
Humor, 321
Hyndman, F., 55
Hypochondriasis, 654

Idealization
  of dead father, 292
  of nonexistent father, 645-649
Identification, 664
  with aggressor, 572
  with desires of others, 574-575
  and development, 658-662
  with father, 304-305, 640
  hysterical, 34
  with moral demands, 661-662
  with other children, 580
Illegitimate children, 104-105, 233, 237, 308, 382-383, 474
Illness, *see* Physical illness, Mother
Imitation, 546, 550, 552-553, 562, 576, 580, 608, 634, 639-640
  of adults, 650-653, 661
  of contrasting behavior, 653-654
  of substitute mother, 651-653
Immunization, 325, 327
Impatience, 522-523
Impetigo, 56, 133, 155, 240
Inanimate object, 287
Infant
  common feeding situation of, 514-515
  5-12-month-old develops better in family than nursery, 545-547
  immunization of, 325, 327
  institutional vs. family, xviii, 350, 474-475, 544-545; *see also* Development, Residential children
  lack of distinction between his and mother's body, 600-605, 634
  need to be mothered, 125-131
  overfed, 96-98
  physical stimulation of, 604-605
  undernourished, 94-96
Infectious diseases, 6-7, 57, 120-121, 132-134, 154-156, 607
Influenza, 15, 21, 119-120, 134, 154, 225, 310, 351, 367, 374, 452
Inhibition, 322, 478, 634, 640
  of activity, 353-366
  see also Aggression
Injection, 263, 266-269, 654
Instinctual drives
  and development, 514-518, 538, 595, 633-634, 638, 664
  and education, 475-480
  regression of, 397
  restriction, 639
  satisfaction and frustration in family and nursery life, 598-634
  and toilet training, 489-494
  transformation, 275, 477-479
Isolation room, 57, 121, 133, 261, 263

Jealousy, 222, 242, 356, 371, 403, 428-433, 441, 445-446, 448, 502, 560-561, 564, 566-568, 570, 587, 590-591
  following introduction of family groups, 221
  of foster siblings, 175-176, 193
  lack of, 303-304
  shaking earlier attachments, 431-433

Kennedy, H. E., 540, 666
Kut [Rosenfeld], S., 353-365

Language, see Speech
Laughter
  hysterical, 207
  uncontrollable, 85
Learning and curiosity, 624-625
Love object, overestimation of new, 441-443
Loyalty conflict, 61, 139, 439, 445-448

Marriott, T., 125-126
Masochism, 268-269
Masturbation, 203, 397, 475, 552, 605-607, 611, 616, 634, 640, 647
Maturation, xviii
Measles, 6, 19, 71, 133, 249-250, 263, 266, 273, 311, 324-325, 327, 330, 337, 339-340, 481, 509
  epidemic, 496, 498-508
Medical Report, see Health Reports
Medical treatment in nursery, see Health Reports, Pediatrician
Memory
  of absent parent, 51, 183, 191-193; see also Father
  clinging to, see Clinging
  comforting, 186
  of events, 93-94, 98, 172, 199, 244, 278-279, 301, 330, 434-435
  expressed in abnormal behavior, 100
  of past, 184
Milk Kitchen, 77, 123, 538
Mood, uncontrollable, 501-503
Mother
  ambivalence of, 226-233
  anxious (imparting fear to child), 8-9, 12, 73-74, 112, 161, 169-171, 279-280, 385-391, 545, 557
  attitude to toilet training, 483-485

bombed out, 467-468
confinement of, 47-48, 70, 81, 144, 238, 324, 348, 384, 401-402
conscious and unconscious wishes for child, 226-230, 234-236
correspondence with, 509-510, 528
difficulties of, in wartime, 250-257
disappointed in child's home visit, 192-193
and emotional development, xix-xx
employed by Hampstead Nursery, 22, 108, 135, 143, 271, 295, 507
equating naughtiness with crying, 352-353
expecting new child, 379-382; see also Mother, confinement
"forgetting of," 51
"getting rid of child," 250
gradual weaning from, 400-401
hospitalized, 21, 31-33, 39, 58-59, 62, 85, 113-116, 141, 198-199, 205, 214, 257, 289-291, 297, 332-333, 354-355, 469
identification with, 186-187
included in life of nursery, 128-129; see also Hampstead Nursery, Visiting
lack of fear in, 170
living on army allowance, 254-255
maintaining contact with child, 228-229
negative reaction to baby, 233-234
of newborn babies, 252-253
not informing children about death of father, 291, 641
nursing, 55, 70, 94, 108-109, 117, 248, 295, 324, 338, 374, 392, 396, 474
overestimation of child, 613-614
physically ill, 48, 113, 238, 379-382

Mother—*Continued*
positive reaction to baby, 230-232
possessiveness of, 174, 230-231
reaction to separating from child,
  see Separation
residential, 535-536
transferring difficulties to Hampstead Nursery, 108-111
unfit, 308-309
unmarried, 382-383
untaught, understanding of child, 112-116
working, 7, 49-50, 69-70, 82, 85, 88, 108, 224, 254, 352-353, 376-379, 393-395, 537, 651
see also Death, Evacuation, Visiting
Mother relationship
breakdown in, 202
consequences of introducing substitute, 590-596
development of, 128-131, 179-193
disturbances in, 38-39
early, 546-547, 638
and emotional development, 560
and feeding, 555-557
introduced into nursery life, 219-222, 356, 586-598
and physical intimacy, 600-605
and speech development, 550-553
of toddler, 186-190
Motility
development, xviii, 547-549, 559
restriction, 412-417, 607-608
Mourning, 34, 51, 66, 84, 130, 183;
  see also Grief, Separation
Muggeridge, E. G., xxiv
Mumps, 121, 225, 263, 273, 277

Narcissism, of mother, 614
Need satisfaction (fulfillment), 179-181
Netherhall Gardens, 28, 54-55, 67, 74-78, 87-94, 105, 134-136, 140, 155, 212-213, 219, 230, 238-240, 247, 249, 259-263, 276, 284, 295-296, 306, 310, 324, 326-327, 333, 337, 407-408, 444, 448, 453-454, 466, 472, 495, 505, 511, 534-535, 540, 593, 629, 633
children evacuated to Country House, 417-428
Neurosis, 478, 640
Night fears, 365
Nightmares, 403-404
Noise, 320, 331, 334, 385
fear of, 385-391, 426
reactions to, 278, 469-472
Nonsense talk, 361
Nurse
rarely sees healthy child, 264-265
role of, 275
see also Simon, M.
Nursery school, xxi, 125-126, 350, 538, 591-592, 621, 624-625, 663

Object, flight from and search for, 38-39
Object relations
interrupted, 200-201
pleasure in, 552
positive, 441-443
possessive, 591
see also Attachment, Child, Development, Emotional development
Obstinacy, 494-556
Oedipus complex, 664
Oral phase, 521-522

Pain, 266-269, 320
Panic, 322
Parent
cooperating with nursery, 9-10
disappointed by home visit, 137-138
evaluation of nurseries, 255
illness of, 143, 257
loss of, 61-66, 472, 597; *see also* Death
occupation of, 143
overvaluation of, 60

INDEX

Parent—Continued
　relation to Hampstead Nursery, 108-116; see also Hampstead Nursery
　and war distress of, 255-256
　see also Death, Father, Mother
Parent Sundays, 455-456, 467; see also Visiting
Passivity, 640, 648, 656
Pediatrician, 15-16, 57, 121, 156, 225, 602, 633
　children's relations with, 15-16, 34, 265-266, 268-269
　imitation of, 654-655
　rarely sees healthy child, 264-265
　see also Stross, J.
Personality
　deviations in absence of families, xix
　impoverished, 477
Perversion, 640
Phobia, 170, 640
Physical illness, 5-6, 545, 607-608
　and psychological development, 265-266
　reaction to, 57-58, 497-498, 500-503
　unaffected by visiting rules, 155
　see also Health Reports, Pediatrician, Mother, and sub specific illnesses
Pity, 287, 476-477, 567, 572, 656, 659
Play, 581
　change in, 363
　and fantasy, 358
　function, 621-622
　imaginative, 563-564, 651-652, 657-658
　outlet in, 196-198
　of separation, 51
　see also Games
Pneumonia, 34, 56-57, 70-71, 120, 134, 154, 261, 310, 325, 327-328, 444
Punishment, 269, 279

Rage, 267, 289, 639

Reaction formation, 480
Reality reversal, 293-294
Regression, 200-211, 480, 552
　in behavior, 412-413
　and development, 637
　following disappointment, 370
　as disturbing factor in development, 397-405
　in eating habits, 412-413
　and separation, 209, 448-449
Religion, 283, 290
Repression, 322, 476-477, 479, 494, 521, 664
　of emotions, 246
　of negative feelings, 191
Residential children
　age on admission, 534-535
　admitted as infants, 473-475
　assigned to specific workers, 219-222, 356, 586-598
　compared to family-reared, xviii-xxi, 350, 474-475, 543-664
　developing family behavior patterns, 655-658
　early relations between, xix, 559-585
　family situation of, 143-144
　lack of: opportunity to watch adults, 629-634; provision for emotional needs, 127-131
　length of stay, 532-534
　no substitute for father, 636
　1-2-year-old, compared to family-reared, 547-553; see also Infant, institutionalized
　overeating, 557-558
　permanently homeless, 308-309
　personality development of, 650-662; see also Development
　see also Children, Hampstead Nursery
Residential Nursery
　case for and against, xix-xx, 543-664
　disbanding, 307-309
　effect dependent on age of child, 544-558
　effect on young child, 349-350

Residential Nursery—*Continued*
 limitations, 350, 663-664
 and wartime education, 71-74, 77, 626-629
 see also Hampstead Nursery
Reversal, 521
Ringworm, 342, 344, 346
Robertson, James, 4, 46-47, 459-460, 462
Rocking, 203, 397, 475, 606-608, 611-612, 634
Rosenfeld, S., *see* Kut, S.

Scarlet fever, 121, 133-134, 154-155, 198, 212, 228, 241, 296, 396, 441, 466
Schwarz, H., 4
Separation
 child's reaction, xix-xxi, 19-22, 35-36, 40, 83, 112, 156, 177-179, 189-190, 208-211, 403-405
 effect of, in early stages of development, 179-185
 expectation of repetition, 438-439
 from father, 641
 improving child's anxiety, 280
 from mother, 6, 19-20, 34-35, 50-53, 130, 280, 364-365, 554, 596, 608, 636-637
 mother's reaction to, 49-50, 226-236, 253
 from parents, 72, 75-76
 preparation for, 38-41, 208-211, 245, 398-405
 problems, 81-86, 140-141
 repeated, 10, 19-20, 58-59, 206-207, 241, 296-297, 591
 shocks: 127-128, 140-141, 297, 605; despite preparation for, 398-405
 in slow stages, 209-210, 398
 from substitute mother, 443-445, 448-449, 592-593, 595-596
 sudden, 36-40, 398
 traumatic, 591
 viewed as punishment, 189-190

Sexuality, 275, 634
 and education, 659
 infantile, 187, 664
Sexual differences, 357-362, 365, 626-627
Sexual wishes, transformation, 639-640
Shelter bronchitis, *see* Bronchitis
Shelter sleeping, 7-8, 14, 25, 75, 127, 145, 152, 156, 170, 211, 262, 270-271, 276, 311, 325, 331-333, 386, 407-417, 444, 496, 540, 652
Shoe repair, 497
Sibling
 birth of, 332-335, 400, 403-405
 influence on each other, 576
 relations developing via relations to parents, 560-561
 rivalry, 182, 191, 434, 445
 and speech development, 550
Simon, M., 55, 242-243, 297-305, 313, 347, 368-372, 496-503, 594
Sister Mary, *see* Simon, M.
Sleep
 disturbances, 85, 93, 152, 181, 207, 274, 371-372
 fear of going to, 167-168
 undisturbed by air attack, 25, 43
 see also Shelter sleeping, Tube sleeping
Smallpox, 384
Soap rationing, 213
Social work, 512, 519-520
Soiling, 202, 220, 401-402, 445
Speech
 and behavior discrepancies, 99
 development, xviii, 222, 275, 400, 549-553, 559
 loss of, 402, 404, 551-552, 637
 outlet in, 194-195
 as outlet into conscious thought, 100-101
 stereotyped, 354
 see also Air raids, Verbalization
Spender, S., 334

INDEX

Staff
 accommodations, 28-29, 55, 420-421
 curiosity about, 631-633
 description of, 4-5
 meetings, 22-23, 125, 653
 reduction, 218
 working without pay, 218-219
Stammering, 593
Stomach love, 129-130
Stross, J., 4; *see also* Pediatrician
Sublimation, 585, 622
Sucking, *see* Thumb sucking
Superego, 660-661, 664
Swearing, 357, 360, 648
Symptoms
 hysterical and compulsive, 207
 neurotic, 202, 473
 formation and separation, 21-22

Teacher
 rarely sees ill child, 264-265
 role of, 275
Temper tantrum, 34, 82-83, 98-99, 113, 199, 203-204, 412, 593
Thought formation, 275
Thumb sucking, 23, 34, 199, 202, 204, 274, 401, 404, 440-441, 475, 552, 601-602, 606, 608, 611-612, 634
Tic, development of compulsive, 20-21
Toddler
 common feeding situation of, 515-518
 effect of air raids on, 411-414
 feeding each other, 563-564
 influence on each other, 560-585
 pleasure in movement, 547-549
 see also Child
Toilet training, xviii, 23, 78, 187, 200-201, 386, 400, 408, 518, 521, 553-554, 559, 579, 587, 626, 659
 compared to feeding method, 521-522
 completion, 493-494
 in nursery, 482-494

Tonsillectomy, 346
Toys, 548, 612, 621, 654
 attachment to, 83
 other children treated like, 562-564
 as comforter, 113
 curiosity toward, 624-625
 fighting over, 564-569, 573-574, 578-579
 function of, 622
 repairing of, 285-286, 341
 sharing, 568
 used as parent substitute, 197-198
Training scheme, 122-125, 273-275, 328, 444-445, 537-539
Transference
 of affection to toy, 140-141
 of feelings for family to other people, 222
Traumatic experience, 404
 repetition of, 318-319
 see also Separation
Traumatic neurosis, 160
Tuberculosis, 99, 113-116, 141, 205, 214, 241, 257, 297
Tube sleeping, 6, 13, 40, 70, 73, 105, 178, 386; *see also* Shelter sleeping
Twins, 134, 230-231, 464, 468, 489, 566-567, 578-579, 581-582

Upbringing, 472-480, 664
 modern, 477-479
 principles of normal, 475-479
 repressive methods, 476-477
 without father, 636-637
 see also Education

Vaccination, 213, 261-262, 264, 266, 384, 637
VE Day, 504-505
Verbalization
 and disturbing events, 93, 99-101, 330-335, 371
 lack of, 194-195

Vermin, 155
Violence, 292, 333
Visiting
  by child, at home, 137-138, 191-192, 207, 229, 353, 371, 373, 551, 604, 657-658
  by mother, in nursery, 137-139, 209, 227-232, 252, 393-394, 419, 636-637, 646-647, 653
  by parents, 10, 29, 43, 50, 59-61, 76, 111-112, 139-140, 203, 213-214, 296-297, 299, 369, 371, 421-422; *see also* Parent Sunday
  see also Father, Hampstead Nursery
Vomiting, 93-94, 96, 120, 249, 386

War
  children's thoughts about, 23, 277-283, 416-417, 458
  events, 144-147, 539-540; *see also* Air raids
  games, 23, 27, 65, 163-164, 196-198, 316, 427

impact on medicine, xviii
neurosis, *see* Traumatic neurosis
orphans, artificial, 211
traumatic effect on children, 14
Weaning, 180
Wedderburn Road, xxiii-xxiv, 28, 55, 67-69, 74-78, 87-94, 106-107, 109, 111, 159, 194, 262, 285, 325, 327, 333, 408, 437, 448, 505, 511, 527, 530, 534, 539-540, 592, 647
Weight gain, 15, 95-96, 153, 246, 386, 544
Weiss, J., 4
Whooping cough, 71, 118-119, 133, 250, 261-262, 266, 272-273, 277, 285, 406, 412, 414, 418, 436, 466, 472
Wish
  to be admired, 612-620, 634
  to kill, 287, 355
  transformation of instinctual, 639
  see also Death, Fantasy
Withdrawal, emotional, 204-207, 241, 297, 404
Wutsch, S., 4, 92

List of Some Individual Children

While innumerable children's names are mentioned, some children are described in detail and their development followed over a long period of time. These are listed below.

Anne, 313-323, 332-335, 434-435, 651, 653, 655
Bertie, 30-31, 61-66, 93, 172, 196-200, 214, 257, 280, 289-291, 633, 642
Billie, 5, 19-22, 35, 38, 40, 47, 51, 58-59, 112, 135, 138, 141, 153, 177, 189
Bobbie, 11-12, 46, 153, 168, 194, 645, 656-658
Bobby M., 399-405
Evelyn, 85-86, 98-99, 206-207, 334
Georgie, 99-100, 113, 140-141, 195, 199, 209, 214, 280, 283
Janet, 25, 27, 45, 93-94, 98, 153, 159-160, 195, 278-279, 281, 283, 294, 501
Katrina, 140, 281-283, 312-313, 434-435, 501, 633
Tony, 113-116, 205-207, 214, 240-246, 257, 296-305, 313, 368-373, 594, 643-645, 657-658